WRIGHT IN HOLLYWOOD

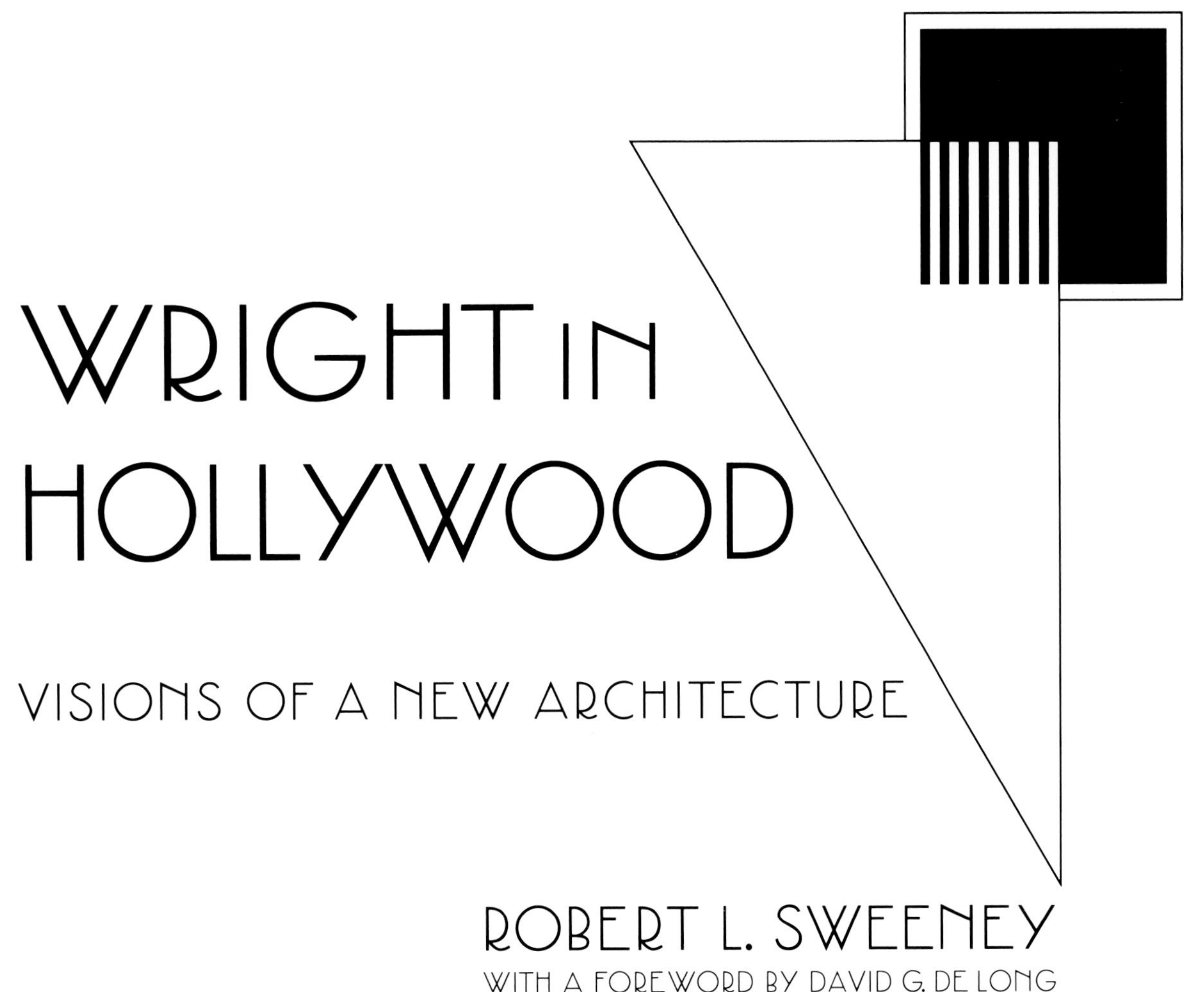

WRIGHT IN HOLLYWOOD

VISIONS OF A NEW ARCHITECTURE

ROBERT L. SWEENEY
WITH A FOREWORD BY DAVID G. DE LONG

THE ARCHITECTURAL HISTORY FOUNDATION
NEW YORK, NEW YORK

THE MIT PRESS CAMBRIDGE, MASSACHUSETTS, AND LONDON, ENGLAND

Sweeney, Robert L. (Robert Lawrence), 1945–
Wright in Hollywood: visions of a new architecture / by Robert L. Sweeney; with a foreword by David G. De Long.
p. cm.
Includes bibliographical references and index.
ISBN 0-262-19337-X
1. Wright, Frank Lloyd, 1867–1959—Criticism and interpretation.
2. Modular coordination (Architecture) 3. Concrete construction.
4. Concrete blocks. I. Title.
NA737.W7S94 1993
720′.92—dc20 93-25104 CIP

This book was edited by David G. De Long, Chairman of the Graduate Program in Historic Preservation, University of Pennsylvania.
Robert L. Sweeney is President, Friends of the Schindler House Los Angeles. His comprehensive annotated bibliography on Wright was published in 1978.

Designed by Charlotte Staub
Published with the assistance of The Andy Warhol Foundation for the Visual Arts
This book was made possible thanks to a Revolving Fund established with the help of The Ahmanson Foundation, The Equitable Life Assurance Company, The Graham Foundation for Advanced Studies in the Fine Arts, Mrs. Agnes Gund, The Henry Luce Foundation, Paul Mayen, Mrs. Barnett Newman, The Nate B. and Frances Spingold Foundation, and Dave and Reba Williams.

In memory of Fred Koeper

CONTENTS

PREFACE AND ACKNOWLEDGMENTS

Frank Lloyd Wright's textile block system has never entered the mainstream of architectural discourse. Several reasons come to mind: the concept of designing and building with concrete block emerged almost of necessity from a period of personal turmoil and professional eclipse in the architect's career; the finest projects were not built; and the imagery of the buildings designed before 1928 could only have appeared old-fashioned to a generation imbued with the iconography of the International Style.

Still, the buildings have a potency unrivaled in twentieth-century architecture. My interest in penetrating these designs led, in 1983, to a suggestion for an article on the southern California houses in response to Jonathan Lipman's invitation to contribute to a special issue of *Oppositions* for which he was serving as guest editor and which was to have been devoted to Frank Lloyd Wright. After my proposal was accepted, I drew Charles Calvo, who had special interest in the decorative block patterns, into the project; we published a preliminary article in the Japanese magazine *SD* (Space Design) before it became clear that the *Oppositions* issue would never materialize.

We had the good fortune to have Edgar Kaufmann, jr., as advisor; he reviewed our preliminary manuscript and suggested a point of view that I adopted when undertaking the book on my own. Mr. Kaufmann observed a tendency by historians to dismiss Wright's work after 1910; he called it "the theme of Wright's senile decay." To him, the opposite was true, but he saw a need less for polemical analysis than for basic information. There is wisdom here: we are only beginning to understand the complexity of the architect. Mr. Kaufmann agreed over lunch in June 1988 to serve as editor for the book; the first draft reached him a few days before his death on July 31, 1989. It was at this point that David De Long graciously consented to become involved in the project.

The research revealed early on that Wright's interest in concrete block construction was far more extensive than has commonly been assumed. I also realized that the technological evolution could be summarized in just three projects: the Millard house of February 1923, in which the concept of double wall or "shell" construction was introduced; the Community Playhouse for Aline Barnsdall of August 1923, in which metal reinforcing rods were to be inserted between the blocks for the first time; and San Marcos in the Desert of April 1928, in which Wright achieved his goal of mono-material construction, synthesizing structure and form.

Though clearly Wright began with structure, form and space interested him more than technology of assembly. It was to display the scope of Wright's vision for concrete block construction and the formal evolution that occurred that I decided to feature all of the projects he envisioned between approximately 1922 and 1932 in a collection of the "brief, in-depth studies" that Mr. Kaufmann favored. The great disappointment of the research is the virtual absence of clarifying information about the Doheny Ranch project that surely sustained Wright's interest in the early phase of exploration. All of the other significant projects are amply documented, and the evidence reveals that the intellect of Wright's idea far surpassed the reality of execution. With the exception of the Millard house, Wright never had an opportunity to build quite as he intended; the other houses that were constructed are compromises. The quality of his vision remains on paper.

Without three people, Bruce Brooks Pfeiffer, Kathryn Smith, and Eric Lloyd Wright, and one event, the new accessibility of Frank Lloyd Wright's archives, the book could not have been completed with any degree of thoroughness. Bruce Pfeiffer, Director of Archives at the Wright Foundation in Scottsdale, and his associates, Oscar Muñoz, Indira Berndtson, and Greg Williams, consistently gave me access to the original material I needed. Kathryn Smith shared invaluable tidbits of information from her own conscientious research; her contributions are noted throughout the book. Eric Wright opened his father's archive early on, providing photographs and construction documents for the California houses; later, he gave me copies of correspondence from which so much of the story emerges. The opening of the Frank Lloyd Wright Archive at the Getty Center for the History of Art and the Humanities, Los Angeles, eased the burden of research enormously. The staff there, Nicholas Olsberg, Gene Waddell, Stephen Nonack, Pamela Kratochvil, Joyce Robinson, and Brent Sverdloff, reflected the energy exerted in creating the new resource.

Eugene Streich, Jim Johnson, Richard Joncas, Thomas S. Hines, and my mother, Elizabeth B. Sweeney, read various drafts of the manuscript and offered comments; all are thanked. Nicole Daniels never refused my requests to visit the Millard house, always a great privilege; Eric Parlee answered questions about his grandfather's role in the construction of the house; and Gary Paul McCowan provided the useful drawing clarifying the block system used in the house. Jeffrey Chusid shared his considerable insight into the Freeman house. Warren McArthur, Jr., helped me sort out the relationship between his uncle, Albert McArthur, and Frank Lloyd Wright in the design of the Arizona Biltmore Hotel. Edward Jacobson allowed the reproduction of Wright's drawings of the hotel now in his possession. Nettie Weston Cunningham recalled life at Ocatilla in 1929. Dr. and Mrs. Dwight Holden graciously opened the Jones house to me on short notice; Florence Lloyd Jones Barnett provided the air view of her parents' house. Robert T. Gelber of Gibson, Dunn & Crutcher retrieved an extraordinary collection of correspondence from his firm's archive detailing William E. Nelson's litigation of the early 1930s; Attilio Gerodetti, Jr., graciously provided early photographs of Nel-Stone buildings.

Others who helped include Ford Peatross of the Division of Prints and Photographs, Library of Congress, Washington, D.C.; and Christopher Vernon. Isrrael Fuentes, Jr., my man Friday at the Schindler House, helped with technical production of the manuscript.

R. Craig Miller's invitation to attend a symposium on Wright at the Denver Art Museum in December 1990, and the assistance of the Centre Canadien d'Architecture in making the trip viable, paid an extra dividend. I took the opportunity to pursue House on the Mesa, to answer questions about the "clients" and the "site" that inspired it.

Karen Banks and Jo Ellen Ackerman of the Architectural History Foundation were a pleasure to work with, Eve Sinaiko offered numerous helpful suggestions during the editing process, and Scott Frances shot the extraordinary nighttime photographs. Finally, I thank David De Long for his wisdom and gentle guidance after Edgar Kaufmann's death, and, of course, Victoria Newhouse, both for her interest in this book and for her substantial contribution to the field of architectural history in general.

Robert L. Sweeney

FOREWORD

DAVID G. DE LONG

Between 1922 and 1932 Frank Lloyd Wright conceived bold visions for a new architecture. It was an architecture new in scale, new in form, and new in means, and it seemed partly inspired by Hollywood, where he sought to establish practice. Apparently determined to pursue the course of change that his Japanese commissions had initiated, he settled there in 1923 after some six years of work in Tokyo. His earlier commission for Hollyhock House (1917–21) must have stimulated his choice, and for a few months he shunned his native Midwest while awaiting the challenge of new clients and unexplored landscapes.

The visions that gradually unfolded over the next decade were by no means limited to Hollywood or even to California, but rather emanated from the Hollywood experience and addressed broad issues without geographic limitation. In the end little was built and the difficulties Wright encountered were many, but the designs he initiated led to some of his greatest achievements in later years.

That Wright possessed a remarkable ability to reinvent himself has long been recognized. His change of direction in the 1920s was in fact one of several such turns that shaped his career; in each instance he was able to retain allegiance to earlier principles while arriving at markedly different conclusions. Such self-imposed periods of upheaval may reflect ties to Unitarian and Transcendentalist thinking, from which a similar charge of self-evaluation and renewal can be extracted. Indeed, the very concept of change seemed fundamental to Wright's approach; as he was to write in 1939:

> Architecture . . . proceeds, persists, creates according to the nature of man and his circumstances as they both change. . . . The law of organic change is the only thing that mankind can know as beneficent or as actual! We can only know that all things are in process of flowing in some continuous state of becoming.[1]

As early as 1914, Wright had indicated impatience with the formulaic ease of his earlier work. Critical of those who too easily and without question emulated this work, he declared a personal need for self-evaluation:

> For every thousand men nature enables to stand adversity, she, perhaps, makes one man capable of surviving success. . . . Reaction is essential to progress. . . . Some time ago this work reached the stage where it sorely needed honest enemies if it was to survive.
>
> The manner of any work (and all work of any quality has its manner) may be for the time being a strength, but finally it is a weakness.[2]

By 1922 Wright had already initiated changes of a somewhat pictorial sort, evoking echoes of pre-Columbian architecture, for example, in the A.D. German Warehouse (1915). Both the Imperial Hotel (1913–22) and Hollyhock House elicited further explorations that proved to be transitional, leading to achievements of significant change. In comparison with these later designs Wright's work before 1910 appears conservative in nature; it is perhaps for this very reason that his earlier work has been more readily appreciated by critics and historians alike. Yet it is only after 1910, and particularly after 1922, that his genius is fully revealed.

Certain obvious influences on Wright's work in the 1920s have not gone unnoticed, and include, in addition to pre-Columbian motifs mentioned above, references to other exotic vocabularies. It is easy to speculate that pre-Columbian and American Indian themes were one means by which Wright led himself toward a reexamination of the roots of American architecture. In partial acknowledgment of this approach he characterized some of his work in the 1920s as "California Romanza."[3] Yet there was more to this than the appropriation of decorative motives, as the architect suggested in recounting his impression of pre-Columbian architecture:

> [These are] mighty, primitive abstractions of man's nature—ancient arts of the Mayan, the Inca, the Toltec. Those great American abstractions were all

> earth-architectures: gigantic masses of masonry raised up on great stone-paved terrain, all planned as one mountain, one vast plateau lying there or made into the great mountain ranges themselves; those vast areas of paved earth walled by stone construction. These were human creations, cosmic as sun, moon, and stars! . . . A grandeur arose in the scale of total building never since excelled, seldom equalled.[4]

Except for its specific historic references this passage could almost be a description of the unbuilt Doheny Ranch project (1923), in which Wright conceived an entire development as a cohesive architectural landscape, with buildings and roadways joined together so persuasively that they enlarged the grandeur of their natural setting. Such manipulation of large-scale elements distinguishes Wright's work in the 1920s, with building-sized components so effectively connected as to herald the vision of the city as a single, integrated structure. He sensed before anyone a potential of the automobile to contribute positively toward the creation of a structured environment, as Doheny and later projects of the 1920s make clear, and the architectural components he envisioned were so fully a part of their setting that the landscape itself seemed reconstructed.

Reflecting on his impression of the Badlands of South Dakota, Wright also perceived the landscape itself in architectural terms and again suggested elements of cosmic importance, attaching symbolic meaning to earth-scaled compositions:

> Endless trabeations surmounted by or rising into pyramid (obelisk) and temple, ethereal in color and exquisitely chiseled in endless detail, they began to reach to infinity spreading into the sky on every side, an endless supernatural world more spiritual than earth but created out of it.[5]

Again Wright's descriptive words recall parallel aspects of his own work, as his unbuilt project for San Marcos in the Desert (begun in 1928). By implication, he suggests an intention for that project far greater than specified in the client's requirements for a resort, for through the medium of architecture humankind was to be reunited with the animating forces of the universe itself.

Wright used simpler words to describe his impression of Japan upon arriving for the second time in 1913, but his sweeping view of the landscape as unified architecture remained consistent:

> Imagine, if you can, sloping foothills and mountain sides all antique sculpture, carved century after century, with curving terraces. The cultivated fields

> rising tier on tier to still higher terraced vegetable fields, green-dotted. And extending far above the topmost dotted fields, see the very mountain tops themselves corrugated with regular rows of young pine trees pushing diagonally over them. Reforestation, the Imperial Government's share in the pattern, everywhere visible.[6]

A similar spirit of structured landscape informs the A.M. Johnson Compound and Shrine (begun in late 1923 or early 1924). In the perspectives, an interconnected complex of buildings rises from terraces that link desert with mountains, and in the foreground diagonal lines depict life-giving channels of water flowing from a central source within the complex itself. None of this is to imply that Wright drew from exotic sources in a conventional manner, but rather that his perception of broad principles governing history found resonance in his own work.

In a preliminary perspective of the Johnson Desert Compound, Wright sketched the forceful lines of his composition over an aerial photograph of the site, revealing not only his command of large-scale composition, but more dramatically his ability to reinforce and amplify the nature of the terrain itself. For other designs of the period perspectives are similarly constructed, with vanishing points extended far beyond the horizon so that an almost global scale is suggested. In such large-scale compositions of earlier years as the Wolf Lake Amusement Park (unbuilt, 1895), vanishing lines are more conventionally contained within the frame, and unity is sustained by symmetrical composition. Beginning in the 1920s, Wright demonstrated how monumental unity could be achieved at even greater scale and without reliance on predictable patterns of orthogonal geometry. In his unbuilt project for Lake Tahoe (1923) conventions are further relaxed, for related to the lodge that bridges to an off-shore island are floating villas that would have described shifting, constantly changing axes. It was a singular achievement.

Wright's exploitation of angled geometries imparts special character to his work in this period. The diagonal extensions of the Johnson Compound had been anticipated in the Doheny Ranch and were fully developed in later designs of the 1920s, so that new spatial configurations were achieved. These were without immediate precedent and opened vistas that Wright continued to explore until his death in 1959.

When recalling his favorite designs, Wright tended to single out those unbuilt projects of the 1920s:

> The best [designs] had life only on paper. The most interesting and vital

> stories might belong to these children of imagination were they ever to encounter the field. Say, the Lake Tahoe Project, the Doheny Ranch Project, San Marcos in the Desert, St. Mark's Tower and others.[7]

Robert L. Sweeney amplifies as many elements of those stories under examination as can be documented at this time, and he clarifies their chronological sequence so that new meanings can be deduced. Thus the Millard, Freeman, Storer, and Ennis houses should probably be considered less as individual structures than as elements that might have been part of the Doheny Ranch project, which Wright was designing at the same time. When viewed as separate entities these houses have confounded some historians who tend to view their individual eccentricities as bizarre rather than part of a larger vision. Yet taken individually they also have much to impart, for they continue the explorations initiated in Hollyhock House and show Wright to be reexamining his earlier work at every possible level, as if he were questioning his own formulation of the world's first, truly modern architecture. For example, these California houses are more massive than his pre-1910 work; they tend to have more firmly differentiated spaces, and they explore richer applications of ornament. If he can be seen as having initiated modernism, he can also be seen as the first adherent to question its immutability, even if only briefly.

Upon examination, the individual houses of the early 1920s reflect additional sources of inspiration. The channeled joints and walled gardens of the Doheny houses, for example, recall countless Italian houses of the sort Wright must have studied while living in Florence in 1910. Affirming his interest, he wrote during his stay there:

> The true basis for any serious study of the art of architecture is in those indigenous structures, the more humble buildings everywhere, which are to architecture what folklore is to literature or folk songs are to music, and with which architects were seldom concerned. . . .
>
> No really Italian building seems ill at ease in Italy. All are happily content with what ornament and color they carry, as naturally as the rocks and trees and garden slopes which are one with them. Wherever the cypress rises, like the touch of a magician's wand, it resolves all into a composition harmonious and complete.[8]

Essential to Wright's visions of the 1920s were the means by which they could be achieved. Never, it seems, did he design without reference to realities of materials and structure. Rarely was he unduly limited by these realities, however, for he worked consistently to stretch the limits of conventional construction.

Wright's attitudes toward materials can be traced to the Arts and Crafts movement, an influence he acknowledged in early writings. At the same time he questioned that movement, urging broader acceptance of machine production. His 1901 talk, "The Art and Craft of the Machine," is best known in this regard,[9] but earlier writings addressed similar themes. Speaking of the potential of the machine, he wrote that it was "a marvelous simplifier; the emancipator of the creative mind, and in time the regenerator of the creative conscience."[10] Later, he praised the machine as "the real tool, whether we like it or not, that we must use to give shape to our ideals. . . . [11] Among the materials made possible by the machine and deserving architectural exploration he included "this plastic covering material, cement. . . . "[12] Yet it was a material that lacked inherent structure: "Aesthetically it has neither song nor story. . . . It is a mixture that has little quality in itself."[13]

Wright identified pattern cast in concrete as one means of elevating an otherwise humble material: "This element of pattern, however it may mechanically be made to occur, is therefore the salvation of concrete in the mechanical processes of this mechanical age."[14] In another context he wrote of the need to conceive construction with a "frame . . . knit together vertically, as well as horizontally."[15] With further study, it gradually becomes clear that the concrete blocks he developed to achieve his visions of the 1920s were no mere adjunct of artistic creation, but a fundamental system that lay at their very foundation.

Sweeney's examination reveals the evolution of Wright's system of concrete block construction and illustrates how essential that system was in the conception of building complexes that followed. The technical problems he encountered were far more numerous than Wright ever admitted, as is now made clear, and the buildings that were erected were not without fault. Yet his perseverance underscores the determination with which he sought the larger, unrealized visions that might have transformed our urban landscapes.

Ultimately Wright focused on other building systems, but his visions of grandly scaled architecture that could serve to reconstruct the landscape remained undiminished, leading to such achievements as Fallingwater (1935–37) and the Marin County Civic Center (1957–59ff). Our understanding of these achievements, and of Wright's genius, would be incomplete without this book, for it was in the 1920s, and through the medium of concrete block, that such mighty accomplishments began.

CHAPTER
ONE

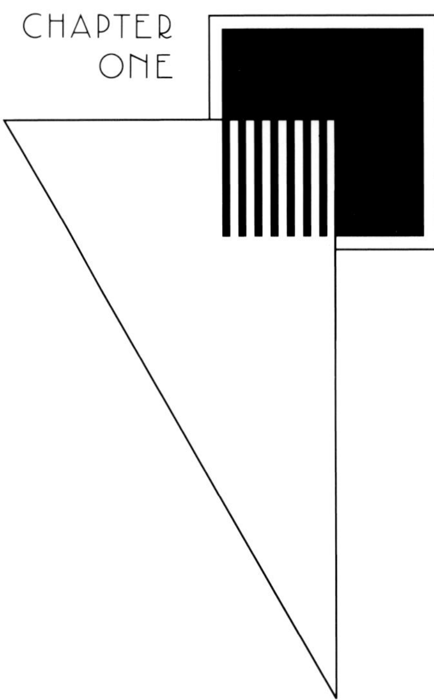

VISIONS OF A NEW ARCHITECTURE

> His work grows quietly out of itself. He is the master of each material, and the modern machine is at the base of his form giving.
> —R. M. Schindler[1]

Perhaps the most remarkable of Frank Lloyd Wright's talents was his ability to renew himself repeatedly throughout his career. His habit was to follow an instinct—to pursue an idea not previously borne out in his work—then to look back. In the early 1920s his interest focused on a new system of standardized concrete-block construction based on the notion of twentieth-century machine technology. The experiment was firmly rooted in the larger concept of architectural simplification, a goal Wright established at the outset of his career and of which he never lost sight; it also grew coherently from recent work, being a logical next step for him to take.

Wright pursued the concept with a sense of mission for a decade, between approximately 1922 and 1932, producing at least thirty projects, of which five were built; he also planned to use the system in several additional projects. The most familiar statements of his intentions appear in his autobiography, begun in 1927 and published in 1932:

> Always the desire to get some system of building construction as a basis for architecture was my objective—my hope. . . .
>
> What form?
>
> Well, let the form come. Form would come in time if a sensible, feasible system of building-construction would only come first.
>
> The concrete block? The cheapest (and ugliest) thing in the building world. It lived mostly in the architectural gutter as an imitation of "rock face" stone.

> Why not see what could be done with that gutter-rat? Steel wedded to it cast inside the joints and the block itself brought into some broad, practical scheme of general treatment then why would it not be fit for a phase of modern architecture? It might be permanent, noble, beautiful. It would be cheap. . . .
>
> All that imagination needed to make such a scheme feasible was a plastic medium where steel would enter into inert mass as a tensile strength. Concrete was the inert mass and would take compression. Concrete is a plastic material—susceptible to the impress of imagination. I saw a kind of weaving coming out of it. Why not weave a kind of building? Then I saw the "shell." Shells with steel inlaid in them. Or steel for warp and masonry units for "woof" in the weaving. . . . Floors, ceilings, walls all the same—all to be hollow.
>
> I had used the block in some such textured way in the Midway Garden upper walls. If I could eliminate the mortar joint I could make the whole fabric mechanical. I could do away with skilled labor. I believed I could and began on "La Miniatura." . . .
>
> I drew my son Lloyd into this effort.[2]

These paragraphs offer a perspective on the textile block system that has gone essentially unchallenged by critics for more than half a century. They suggest a sort of miraculous inspiration—that nothing of the sort had been tried before—and imply well-ordered development. They introduce the important concept of steel-reinforced, mortarless assembly and raise the intriguing idea of mono-material concrete-block construction. Finally, they identify the Millard house, La Miniatura, as the point of departure.

In fact, Wright was creating a minor myth. He wrote with hindsight, from the perspective of several years' thought and the experience of constructing four houses based on the concept. He ignored closely related external developments, which were substantial; and he glossed over a laborious process of exploration. A spirit of invention and experimentation, a reality of trial and error, pervade the textile block system. The name itself needs to be used cautiously; it refers, obviously, to the "warp" and "woof" of metal reinforcing rods. It is a sobriquet that Wright seems not to have used before 1927, and it does not accurately describe the earliest projects.

Wright began in February 1923 with a system of interlocking blocks that were laid on a conventional mortar bed. There was no immediate provision for structural gymnastics. The blocks were without metal reinforcement, were used primarily in wall construction, and were freely combined with standard structural members. The forms of the buildings frequently derived from earlier designs intended for other types of construction; Wright simply translated them into concrete block, albeit with strikingly different results. The buildings relied heavily on ornament cast onto the faces of the blocks for effect. Wright's finest moment in this period was a project for an entire community of patterned concrete-block houses to be built in southern California; nowhere in his work is the excitement of pioneering effort, of sheer creative energy, displayed with greater force.

The steel Wright spoke of was added a few months later, producing the system most familiar today. This was a technological improvement that brought with it the possibility of greater plasticity; however, its full potential was not immediately exploited. Blocks continued to serve structurally only in vertical planes, and the buildings were supported by concealed structural skeletons. Still, throughout this early formative period, there are clues suggesting bolder structural applications to come. Wright was working toward a mono-material building system. He first mentioned this idea in 1926; three years later he demonstrated the synthesis of structure and form he was seeking in drawings for a resort hotel for the Arizona desert. Every formal and technical consideration was accommodated with reinforced-concrete block in a design as near perfection as Wright ever came.

As the structural system matured—a process coinciding with the evolution of the minimalist International Style in Europe—the buildings became increasingly architectonic: forms were simplified, and the initial fascination with ornament all but disappeared.

As Wright acknowledged in his autobiography, he drew his son Lloyd into the effort in the beginning, relying on him for technical advice and for presentation drawings and landscaping. Lloyd also supervised construction of three houses in Los Angeles, largely in his father's absence. Their correspondence and the construction photographs Lloyd preserved reveal the challenge of translating the concept into reality and the compromises that were made. Wright called on Lloyd again in the period of renewed activity later in the decade; Lloyd shared his experience in casting blocks and offered suggestions for revisions; he also completed several more presentation drawings.

According to the architect, the idea of building with concrete block formed gradually in his mind after he came home from Japan, where he had lived and worked intermittently since 1916. If we take him at his word, this would have been after August 1922, when he returned for the last time.[3] Wright was at a crossroads: work on the Imperial Hotel in Tokyo had come to an end; he had been unable to obtain additional large commissions in Japan; and the stability of the Barnsdall Olive Hill project, which had continued in Los Angeles during his absence, was rapidly diminishing. Immediately on his return, Wright traveled to Taliesin in Wisconsin, explaining that he had been ill in Japan and needed a rest.[4] He was at this time fifty-five years old.

Wright left clues that his creative and emotional energies were spent as well. He recalled in his autobiography:

> Experience with the "Imperial" had made all probable experience to come — tame. When I first came back, I really took little interest in such prospects as would present themselves for solution from time to time.
>
> No appetite for less than another Imperial Hotel, I suppose. Or, perhaps, satiated, exhausted by such incessant demands upon my resources as that experience represented.[5]

Wright remained in the Midwest for five months, inactive and searching for direction. In a letter written to Louis Sullivan in November, he confided that he was "extremely hard up — and not a job in sight in the world. My selling campaigns have failed." By the time he left, he was, in his words, "in a smothered rage that knocked my sentiments into a heap in which I could find no good order."[6]

Certainly much of Wright's mood was conditioned by his unstable relationship with Miriam Noel, his companion since 1915.[7] However, he also was stung by harsh criticism of the Imperial Hotel, which he had been counting on heavily to strengthen his position. An article published in *The Architect and Engineer* in November 1922 described the building as "a monstrous thing of supposedly antique influence, but really prehistoric in plan, design, structure, decoration and state of decay." The author commented that the structure, although not entirely complete, contained "numerous large cracks in masonry walls and stone embellishments, which are in part, due to inadequate foundations and seismic disturbances." He concluded that "the errors are so numerous and flagrant that it may be said this structure should never have been built."[8]

The article was written by Louis Christian Mullgardt, an architect who had worked on several projects in Chicago for Henry Ives Cobb and had gone on to design portions of the 1915 Panama-Pacific International

Exposition and the M. H. de Young Museum in San Francisco but who, nonetheless, was of comparatively insignificant stature.[9]

Wright's feelings of vulnerability at the time are confirmed by his response to Mullgardt's venom, which he easily could have ignored; as Thomas S. Hines has correctly observed, "Like [that of] most artists of his stature, Wright's genius was tough and fragile at the same time."[10] This time, in an article, Wright assumed the posture of an artist whose high achievement had been gravely misunderstood, creating an analogy with a play by the late-nineteenth-century Russian novelist Leonid Andreyev, *He Who Gets Slapped:* "A small world of pathos and tragedy," in which the central character, Intellect, in the person of a nobleman, is "the victim of the betrayal that Life on earth becomes to the daring, confiding, aspiring soul." He contrasted his own accomplishments with "the passing show . . . picturesque even if ridiculous. The strings that move the puppets are so evident, the puppets themselves so helpless, the play so vain."[11]

Wright sent his comments to his colleague in Chicago, Howard Van Doren Shaw. Shaw responded reassuringly: "Your work is bound to live; I cannot say the same of his, and certainly nothing else will keep his name alive. What is the use of spreading a manifestly personal and commercial attack?"[12] Wright also sent his article to the *Japan Advertiser,* an English-language newspaper published in Tokyo, where it appeared with a note that the editor had "eliminated . . . several paragraphs of personal remarks. . . . While diverting reading they are hardly essential to the conduct of the debate."[13]

Wright's response to Mullgardt was written in January 1923, while he was still in the Midwest. For Wright, creative rejuvenation frequently coincided with new environments in which to work. This time his sights turned to southern California, where he had visited many times but had never lived. Wright was in Los Angeles by February 1923, when he reported to Sullivan that he had "pitched in here to locate," and invited his mentor to "come out later—to see this ice-cream, cake and soda-water corner of the world."[14]

Little is known of the circumstances that caused Wright to return to the area with such determination, though his practice was to respond to major new opportunity. There is some evidence that he was attracted by vast tracts of land that were then being subdivided and offered for sale, and that could not have escaped his notice; an article appearing in a local newspaper shortly after his arrival announced that he planned to develop the foothill properties between Hollywood and the sea.[15]

1. Sketch for an announcement, early 1923. FLLW FDN, 2201.001

Writing again to Sullivan in March, Wright indicated that he had rented a house for a studio and was at work.[16] The modest house, built the year before, was located in Sherman (now West Hollywood), at 1284 Harper Avenue. Wright had maintained an office in Los Angeles since 1920 in the Homer Laughlin Building, a space used primarily by Lloyd and R. M. Schindler, during work on Olive Hill. An announcement of his departure from there made clear that the move to Harper Avenue was to be temporary, during construction of a permanent studio in Beverly Hills (Fig. 1). The house undoubtedly was chosen for its location; in any event, it was here that the nascent concrete-block system first took form.[17] Joining Wright and Lloyd were Kameki Tsuchiura, a Japanese apprentice who had worked with Wright on the Imperial Hotel, and, briefly, Schindler, whose own radical concrete house was six blocks away.

Shortly after his arrival in Los Angeles, Wright prepared a rambling, iconoclastic statement offering some insight into the work he was about to undertake. He carefully established a continuity of theory and practice, extending back to his 1901 Hull House lecture, in which he advocated "patient study of the Machine at work as the first duty of the modern artist." He went on to declare that "the old structural necessity in Architecture is dead," that there would be "a process of simplification—a rejection of the old meaningless forms. . . . We will have a clean line, a flat surface, a simply defined mass—to begin with." He explained that "Form, in this new plastic sense, is now infinitely more fertile and elastic." There were, in his view, "boundless new expressions in Architecture, as free, compared with post and lintel, as a winged bird compared to a tortoise." [18]

Wright mentioned concrete block only by implication, stating, "This is the beginning of a constructive effort to produce a type that would fully utilize standardization and the repetition of appropriate units." There was also an oblique reference to ornament—so important in the early block buildings—in his comment that "the notion that the legitimate use of the Machine precludes ornamentation is a mistake. The contrary is the case. . . . Little by little, the use of significant virile pattern will creep in to differentiate, explain and quality [*sic*], . . . the materials and structural enclosures." [19]

If the direction Wright was taking seems clear, it is also clear that he undertook the concrete-block experiments with only vague and quickly conceived notions of application. He did not have an immediate formal response, though form interested him more than technology of assembly. He left several tentative studies in which he seems to have been exploring the massing and ornamental aspects of the buildings, but offered little or no clue to their structural system. As Bruce Brooks Pfeiffer has observed, however, the drawings do suggest an evolution from patterned blocks, applied nonstructurally as trim to conventional buildings, to a complete reinforced-concrete block construction system.[20]

Evidence supporting this thesis appears in a "Study for Block House, Textile Block Construction, Los Angeles 1920–1921," which is identified as such and dated solely by Wright's handwritten captions on two drawings. The drawings hint at nothing more than plaster walls articulated with bands of repeated pattern (Fig. 2). Stylistically, this work derives from Sullivan's Wainwright Tomb; it also is a composite of Wright's own work of the period, notably the theater, designed for reinforced-concrete construction, and Residences A and B, built of hollow tile and plaster, on Olive Hill. Also, the date must be viewed with skepticism. Wright frequently annotated his drawings with hindsight, indicating greater precocity than was the case, and no supporting evidence has turned up to suggest that the concrete-block experiments began before early 1923.

2. Study for Block House (project), perspective and partial plan. FLLW FDN, 2103.001

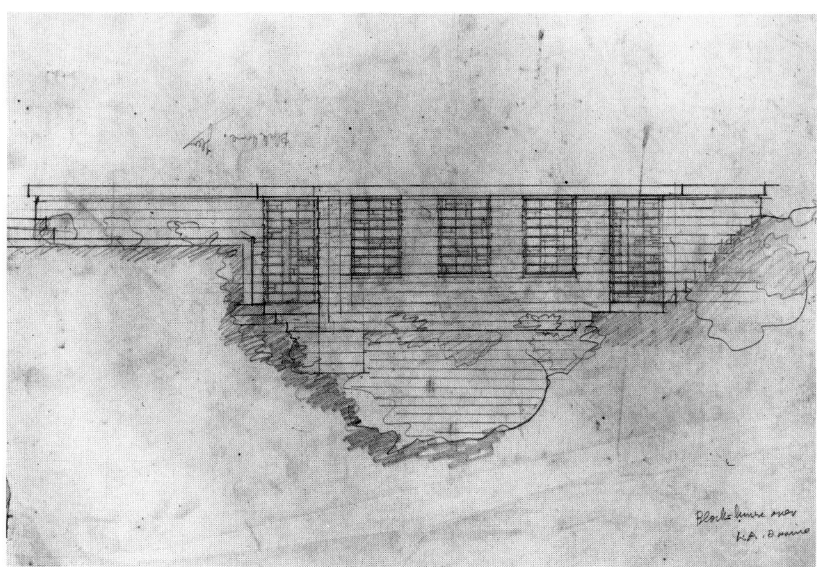

3. Block House over L.A. Ravine (project), elevation. FLLW FDN, 2106.001

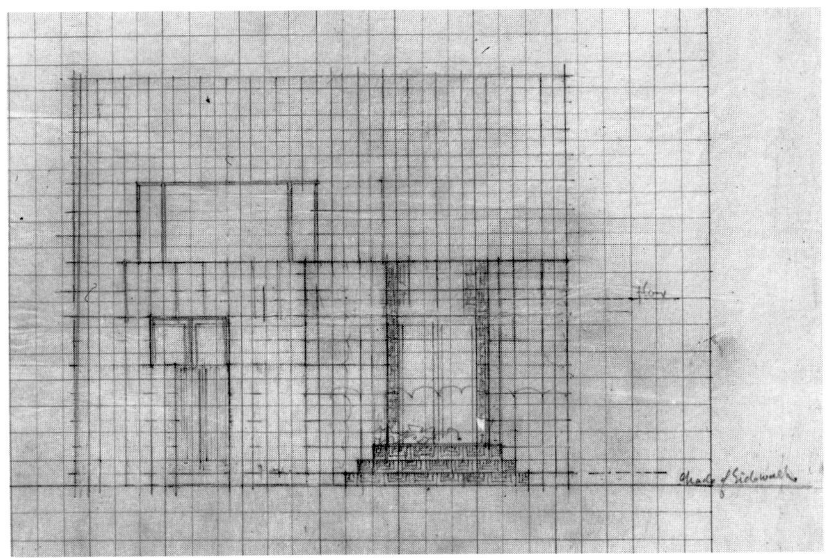

4. Block House, 2-story (project), elevation. FLLW FDN, 2108.003

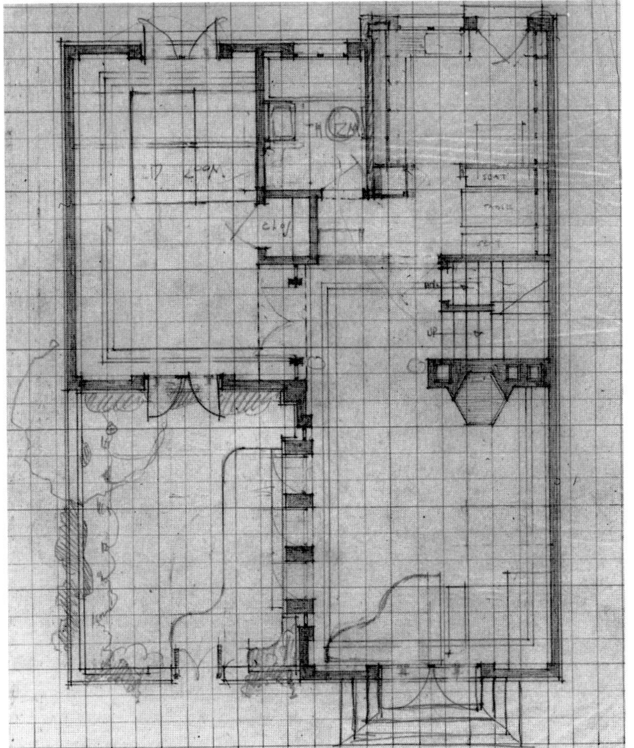

5. Block House, 2-story (project), first-floor plan. FLLW FDN, 2108.001

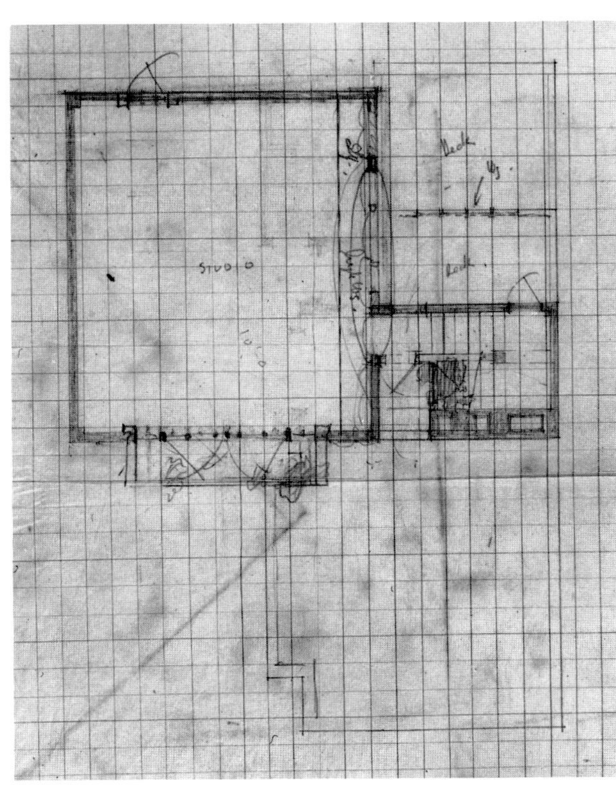

6. Block House, 2-story (project), second-floor plan. FLLW FDN, 2108.004

Two other designs are remarkable for their comparative simplicity. The less developed of these is that labeled "Block House over L.A. Ravine." The only information about it comes from a single elevation drawing, which shows a one-story rectangular building with a slab roof (Fig. 3). A drawing called "Block House, 2-story" (Fig. 4) suggests a step in the development toward the cubic form of the Millard house, a natural outgrowth of building with blocks. The plans are for a two-story, one-bedroom house in which the largest space is a studio on the second floor (Figs. 5, 6). Although the location of the intended site is unknown, the unbroken side walls of the house and the walled front patio suggest a conventional city lot with neighbors on both sides. There were many lots of this description available in the flatlands of Beverly Hills, south of Sunset Boulevard, in the early 1920s. This information and the large studio space on the second floor of the house lead one to wonder if this is a design for the studio Wright announced that he was going to build for himself at Beverly.

DOHENY RANCH, BEVERLY HILLS

The project on which Wright based his hopes in southern California, the one that probably caused him to recall in his autobiography that he "was getting interested again," was surely a visionary scheme for land development at the base of the Santa Monica Mountains, above Beverly Hills.[21] Numerous concrete-block houses were to be terraced on hillsides, in harmony with each other and the site. They were to be linked by roadways, tunnels, and bridges of the same construction, with the contours of the ground and native vegetation left undisturbed. No two houses were alike, and collectively they revealed the almost infinite variety of formal expression possible with the blocks. It is not an overstatement to conclude that most of Wright's initial vocabulary of design for concrete block was resolved in this proposal.

Although there is little conclusive information, the project seems to have been developed over a period of several months. A map of the site, preserved in Wright's archive, provides the earliest date, February 1923. There also is one drawing with the annotation "Los Angeles, March 20, 1923," though, curiously, Wright reported to Sullivan a week later that there was "nothing big here yet—but maybe soon."[22] Wright was still working on the scheme in October, when he mentioned it to his friend William T. Evjue, publisher of the Madison *Capital Times.*[23]

Two presentation drawings support this time span: they effectively summarize the stylistic evolution displayed in other buildings in this early phase of exploration. They also are a compelling display of the strength of Wright's vision, suggesting the immediacy of response for which he is famous. The drawings are unrelated, apparently representing different schemes for separate locations, although both views overlook the ocean in the distance. One drawing for development of a hillside is shown from below; a road ascends through a composition of buildings carefully calculated to emphasize movement toward the pinnacle (Fig. 7). The other site is in a canyon; Wright modified the perspective accordingly, to indicate access from the rim above and a path leading down (Fig. 8).

The buildings in the hillside scheme rise directly from the ground in rectangular masses, with patterned blocks capping bases of concrete—Wright was not yet thinking even of the appearance of mono-material, concrete-block construction—and relate compositionally to the Millard house, designed in February 1923; one is tempted to see its ancestor at the top of the hill. The crestline view depicts a series of podia, forming terraces from which the buildings rise—one of several references to classical architecture that creep into the early concrete-block designs. The forms, however, recall those of the Barnsdall Olive Hill house: battered walls are created with blocks offset vertically and horizontally as they are built up; they terminate in parapets defining the terraces. Roofs are flat or continue to rise in successive stages to a pinnacle in a ziggurat configuration. Wright used these forms in 1924 in houses for Charles Ennis and A. M. Johnson.

If this sequence for the drawings is accepted, it becomes possible to draw conclusions about the structural system intended for each scheme, based on the technical evolution that occurred in the same period. The earlier proposal, coinciding with the Millard house, would have been constructed of double-shell blocks laid on a mortar bed without metal reinforcement. The canyon scheme presumably would have been built with the reinforced blocks. Concrete block is the only exposed building material, and though there is every reason to suppose that a structural skeleton lay beneath, there is a definite shift toward Wright's emerging goal of mono-material construction.

The degree to which plans were developed for individual structures represented in the two perspective drawings is unknown. Plans and elevations for three houses, identified A, B, and C, are all that remain in Wright's archive; inexplicably, these do not appear in the presentation

7. Doheny Ranch (project), Beverly Hills, California, perspective, hillside scheme, 1923. FLLW FDN, 2104.005

8. Doheny Ranch (project), aerial perspective, crestline scheme. FLLW FDN, 2104.008

drawings. They are on two or three levels, but the vertical orientation of the plans is mitigated in elevation by extended wings projecting laterally from the central masses. In all cases, the houses are meant to be seen from below.

House A offers convincing evidence that Wright was groping for formal expression when he began experimenting with the blocks; it also illustrates his habit of adapting familiar forms to various building programs. The scheme derives from a house he had planned for himself in Italy in 1910; that house is for a flat site (Fig. 9). In addition to modifying the method of construction, Wright made adjustments for building on a hillside, adding a foundation and extending the vertical mass down to ground level (Fig. 10). Although the translation of the design into concrete block

9. Frank Lloyd Wright house (project), Fiesole, Italy, perspective, 1910. FLLW FDN, 1005.003

10. Doheny Ranch, House A (project), perspective and partial plan. FLLW FDN, 2104.004

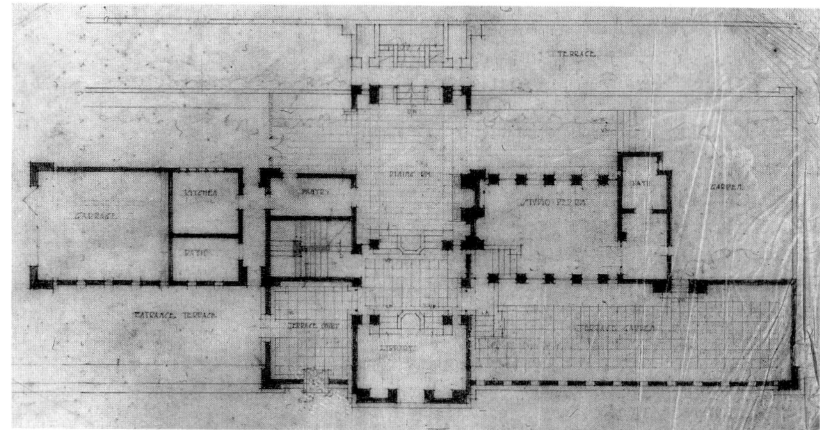

11. Doheny Ranch, House A (project), main-floor plan. FLLW FDN, 2104.024

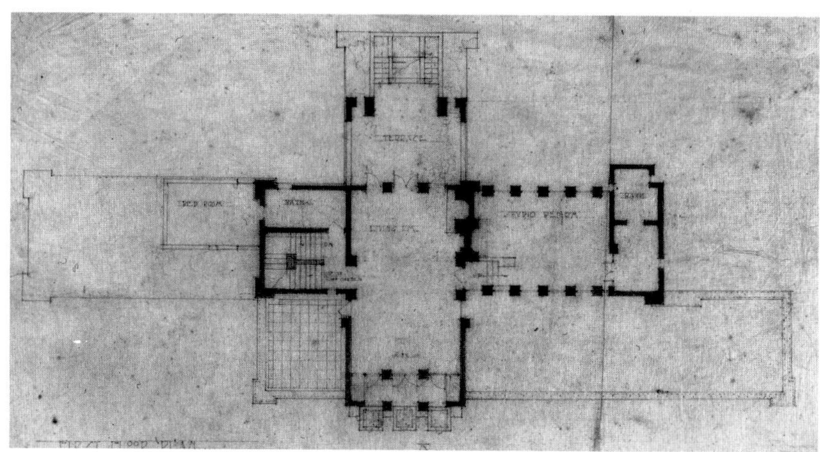

12. Doheny Ranch, House A (project), first-floor plan. FLLW FDN, 2104.023

is smooth, it is not a specific response to the method of construction. The use of the blocks is also tentative. The patterned blocks at the corners of the building are reminiscent of quoins, and the pattern itself—concentric rectangles in relief, with color added for emphasis—had been used in the Imperial Hotel, where it was carved in oya-stone piers. The house is approached from the left in the plan and is entered on the lower level (Fig. 11). The central rectangular volume contains a library and dining room below, living room above. Projecting wings include the garage, kitchen, and two bedrooms, one above the other (Fig. 12).

Houses B and C are more convincing demonstrations of the new plasticity Wright was seeking with concrete block, and both seem related to designs in the hillside perspective. The principal feature of house B is a square volume defined by concentric rows of gently offset blocks, which

13. Doheny Ranch, House B (project), perspective. FLLW FDN, 2104.007

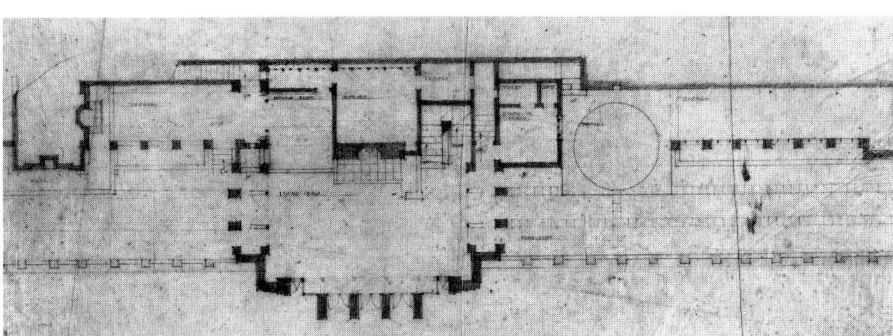

14. Doheny Ranch, House B (project), main-floor plan. FLLW FDN, 2104.019

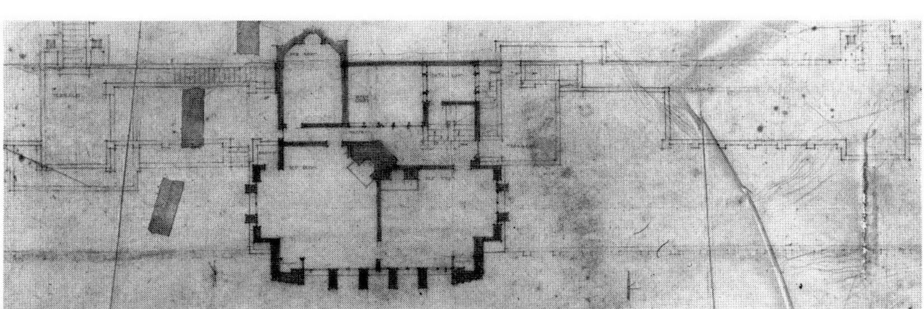

15. Doheny Ranch, House B (project), first-floor plan. FLLW FDN, 2104.017

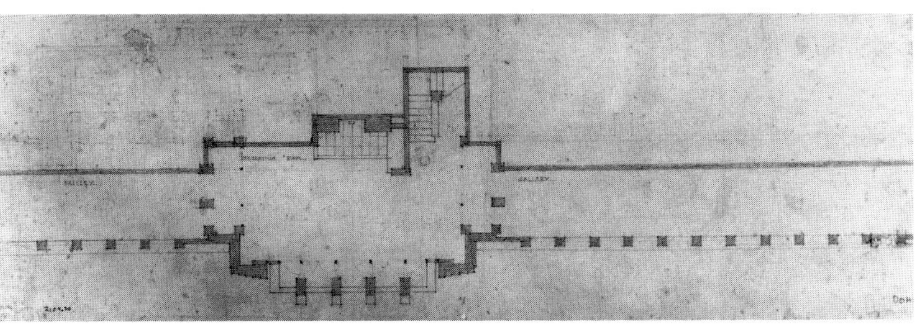

16. Doheny Ranch, House B (project), lower-level plan. FLLW FDN, 2104.020

17. Doheny Ranch, House C (project), perspective and partial plan. FLLW FDN, 2104.006

frame four rectangular piers (Fig. 13). It is approached by an elevated roadway rising from a ravine; this great lateral extension again belies the basic squareness of the plan. A shorter wing, containing a loggia, projects in the opposite direction. The house is three stories high. Entry is at the middle level, which contains the living room, dining room, and kitchen (Fig. 14). Four bedrooms are above, and a recreation room occupies the ground floor below (Figs. 15, 16).

House C is the most adventurous of the Doheny group in terms of concrete-block composition (Fig. 17); it is based in part on nonrectangular angles that would have required special blocks for construction, a technical development Wright did not explore thoroughly until 1929. Its plan is similar to Wright's 1898 River Forest Golf Club, after he remodeled it in 1901. It could hardly be more different in elevation, however, with its great vertical extension and sequence of projecting and receding planes. In spite of the experimental geometry, the plan is symmetrical on the center axis, with the living room and flanking bedrooms on the upper entry level, dining room and two more bedrooms below (Figs. 18, 19).

The client always identified with the Doheny Ranch project is Edward Laurence Doheny (1856–1935), who had struck oil near Los Angeles in

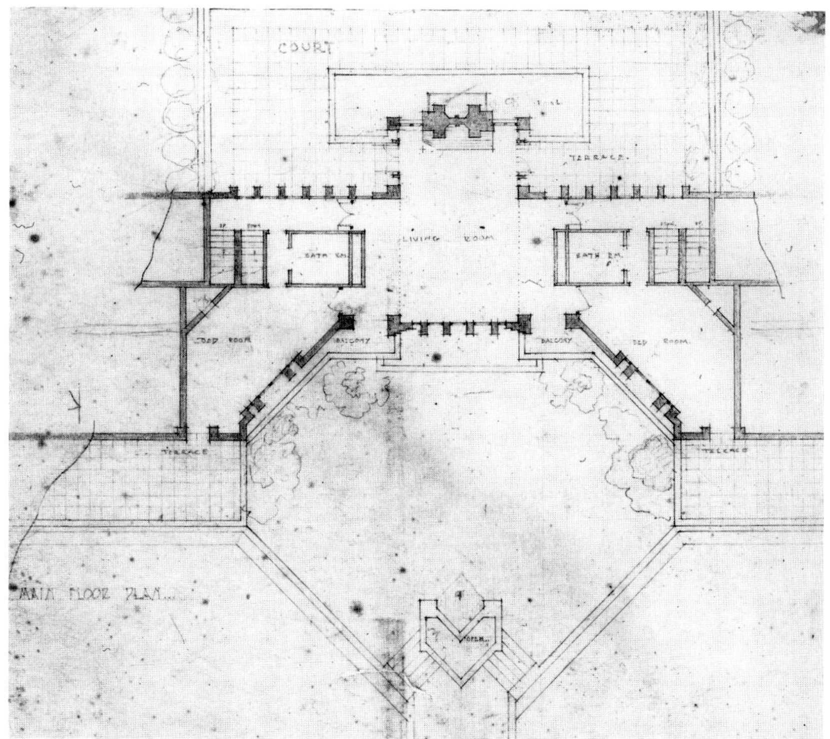

18. Doheny Ranch, House C (project), main-floor plan. FLLW FDN, 2104.012

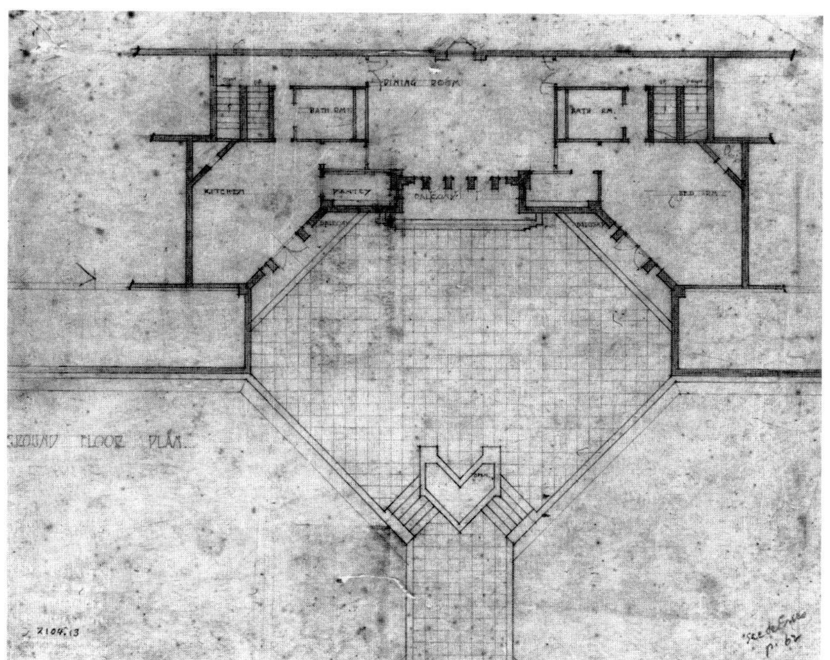

19. Doheny Ranch, House C (project), ground-floor plan. FLLW FDN, 2104.013

20. Doheny Ranch, February 19, 1932. Air Photo Archives, University of California, Los Angeles, Department of Geography. Courtesy of Spence Photo

1892; within a few years he had established the southern California oil industry. His reputation was badly tarnished by his involvement in the Teapot Dome scandal of 1922–24, though he was later exonerated of anything more than bad judgment. He owned the site, 411 acres comprising nine separate parcels, assembled in 1912–13 and developed as a working ranch and weekend retreat for his family.[24] It was described many years later by Lucille V. Miller, Carrie Estelle Doheny's longtime secretary, as a series of small canyons enclosed on three sides by hills and opening to the south to a panoramic view of the city (Fig. 20). It was "a place of enchantment, remote from the world, where dusty trails meandered under giant peppers and eucalypti, a windmill turned lazily in the breeze, and tree-ripened oranges could be had for the picking."[25]

In the end nothing came of the proposal, and the remaining evidence shows no more than a tenuous link with Doheny. Wright was strangely confused about the name of the client, referring to him as Edward H. Doheny, and about the location of the site, placing it in the San Gabriel Mountains, east of Los Angeles. The project may have been a joint dream of Wright's and John B. Van Winkle's, a real-estate promoter, that Doheny did not share. Much later, Lloyd reminded his father of the association with Van Winkle, describing it as "a mutual adventure of yours that did not develop."[26]

The Doheny Ranch project is the consummate statement of Wright's intentions for concrete block in this early phase of exploration, yet, curiously, the architect himself never trumpeted its importance and it remains among the most elusive of his major works. Was the scheme prepared entirely on speculation, as the evidence suggests? Did Wright seek it out after he arrived in southern California, or even invent it? Were the superb drawings made for promotional purposes, as a display of vision, with no real thought of execution; and is it, therefore, no accident that a site plan has not been found? Finally, how does one reconcile such extraordinary accomplishment with the searching statements of February 1923?

CHAPTER TWO

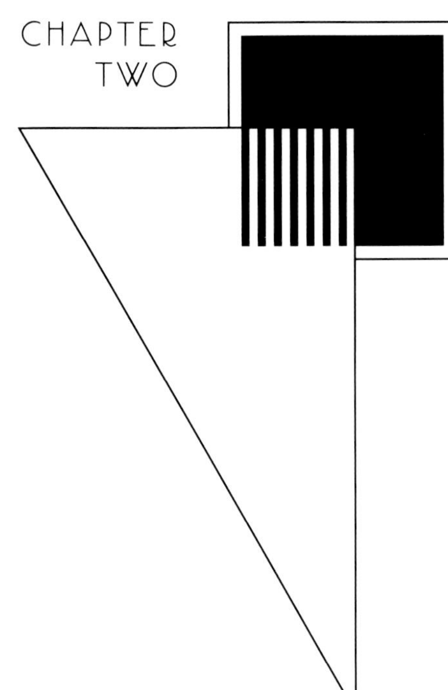

THE BLOCK SYSTEM EMERGES

The earliest indication of the block system itself appears in rough sketches on drawings for two houses in the Harper Avenue studio in early 1923. One of the houses was for Aline Barnsdall, who already was contemplating abandoning Olive Hill; the other was the famous La Miniatura for Alice Millard. The sketches depict two blocks formed to interlock with a hollow space between; expanded metal is indicated for assembly. Nowhere in the finished drawings for these houses is the system worked out in any greater detail, leaving unanswered questions about Wright's intentions and suggesting that much remained to be resolved.

Only recently, with the opening of walls during restoration of the Millard house, has it become possible to interpret these sketches and the method of assembly in detail and to confirm that Wright began with a concept that was very different indeed from the well-publicized system that followed. There are two basic blocks, each fifteen and one-half inches square, which are assembled in pairs: patterned, used primarily for exterior walls, and plain, used only on the interior (Fig. 21). The blocks are designed to interlock; the patterned blocks have flanged edges that embrace the plain blocks with semicircular cavities (Fig. 22). The points of greatest significance in view of the system that emerged a few months later are that the blocks for the Millard and Barnsdall houses have no metal reinforcing rods, and are laid with expanded metal on a conventional bed of mortar.

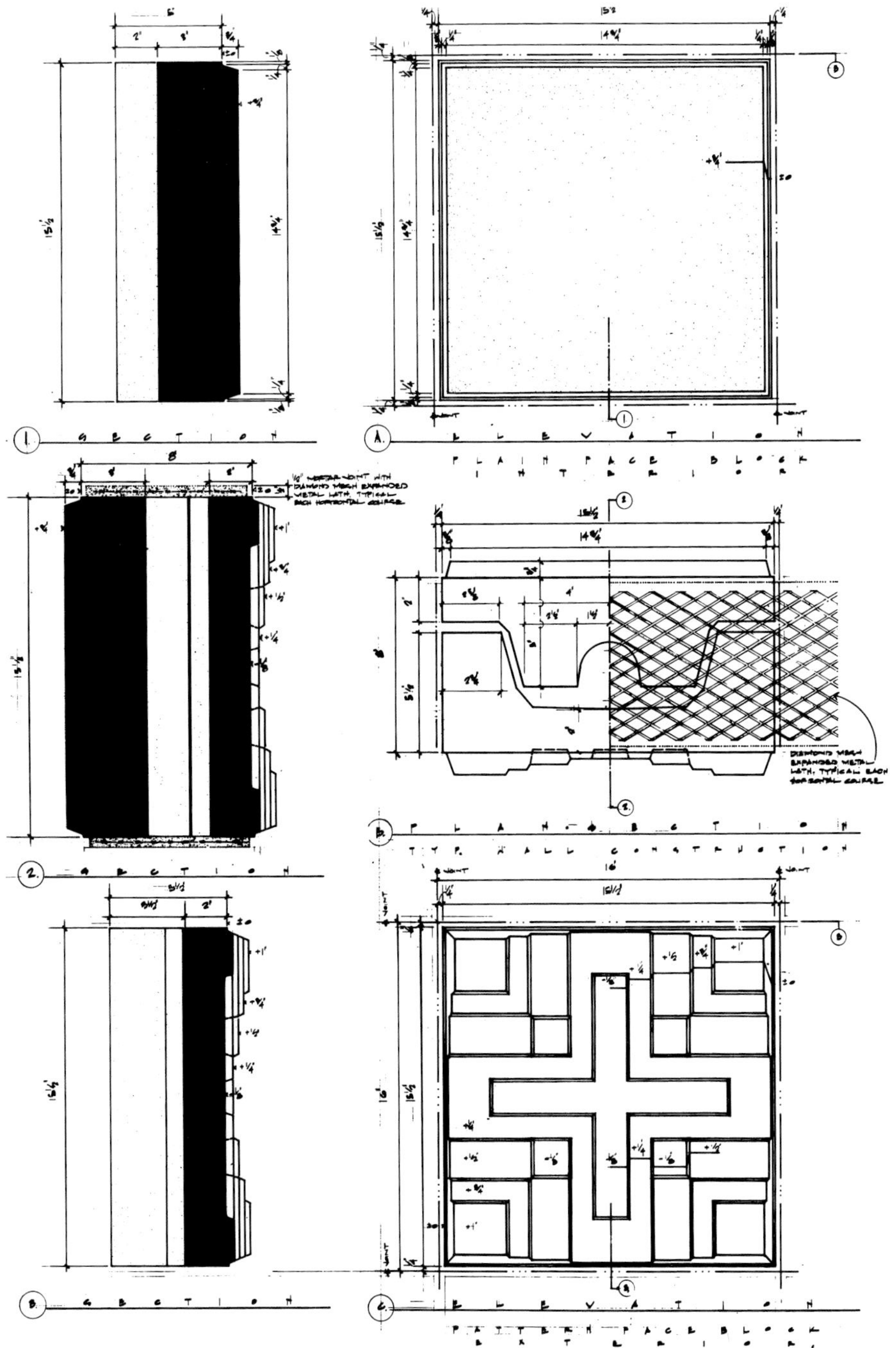

21. Alice Millard house, La Miniatura, Pasadena, California, concrete-block assembly details, 1923. Courtesy of Gary Paul McCowan

22. Alice Millard house, La Miniatura, typical concrete-block wall assembly, revealed during restoration. Courtesy of Gary Paul McCowan

BARNSDALL HOUSE, BEVERLY HILLS

The Barnsdall house was a surprise when it was published by Kathryn Smith in 1979; it does not appear in any earlier list of Wright's buildings.[1] Wright referred to it in his March 3, 1923, letter to Sullivan: "Miss Barnsdall (of Olive Hill has given me a new home to build for her at Beverly — in a beautiful twelve acre mountain side."[2] Two articles in *Holly Leaves,* a local newspaper, both confirm and confuse the facts. On April 20 it was reported that Wright was "now creating another home for her on a 23 acre tract in Beverly Hills."[3] Then, on May 18, the paper stated that "Miss Aline Barnsdall . . . has bought 24 acres . . . adjoining the Douglas Fairbanks estate."[4]

The site was located by Kathryn Smith in 1991, though its overall size remains unclear.[5] There was, in 1923, an undeveloped twelve-acre parcel adjoining Pickfair, the Pickford-Fairbanks estate, on the north, but there is no indication in the Los Angeles County Archives that it was ever owned by Aline Barnsdall. Other, larger sites were nearby but, again, there seems to be no link with Barnsdall. For the record, in contemplating building even on the more modest twelve-acre site, Barnsdall and her architect were upstaging Douglas Fairbanks and Mary Pickford by six acres. In any case, the area was hilly and offered dramatic views of the Los Angeles basin; Wright's conceptual sketch indicates an extended approach through groves of eucalyptus trees.

The Barnsdall house is a grand composition, far larger than anything proposed for Doheny Ranch (Fig. 23). It was designed to extend approximately two hundred feet on two main levels, with shorter perpendicular wings reaching back into the hillside at each end (Figs. 24, 25). A large courtyard enclosed by the house on three sides opens to a grove of eucalyptus trees on the hillside to the rear. In front are several terraces overlooking the view below.

The house is of less interest for its size, however, than as a reinterpretation in concrete block of Hollyhock House, built for Barnsdall between 1920 and 1921 (Fig. 26). Both houses have battered upper walls resting on monumental bases, and both are related to Wright's 1918 Yamamura house in Japan. The Yamamura house was not built until after 1922, but it may be the earliest design in which Wright used sloping upper walls or parapets; they cap flat, projecting roofs (Fig. 27).[6] The house is an asymmetrical, linear composition in response to the irregularity of its sloping site. Hollyhock House is formal and ceremonial, with major and minor axes; it combines the linearity of the Yamamura house with a suggestion of the freestanding pavilions of the new Beverly Hills house. A belt course divides the upper and lower masses, and all windows and doors begin below this line. As in the Yamamura house, there is no exterior suggestion of the penetration of space behind the upper battered walls.

The new Beverly Hills house is a looser composition; individual pavilions are symmetrical, but they are grouped informally, recalling to some degree the south elevation of Hollyhock House. Instead of a continuous roof line or belt course, the division between upper and lower walls occurs at different levels in the building; and voids penetrate the upper walls. Wright also changed the ratio between the upper and lower masses, the battered walls becoming proportionally taller.

Although the general forms of this house do not depend on concrete block, there are refinements in the detailing, surpassing the heavy-handed Hollyhock House, that can be attributed to the new method of construction. Wright used offset courses to animate wall surfaces and explored a new window design, created with stepped blocks, that was developed in the Ennis house. The most extraordinary feature of the building is the living room, a double-height space overlooked by a balcony and surmounted by a dome twenty-five feet high at its oculus (Fig. 28). The dome rises from the line of the belt course and is apparently of concrete-block

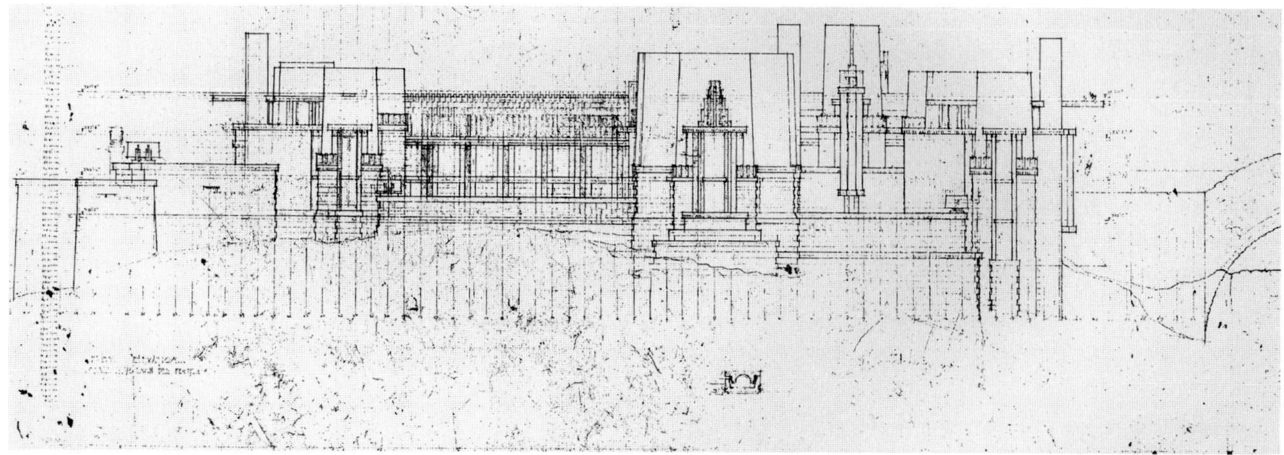

23. Aline Barnsdall house (project), Beverly Hills, California, elevation, 1923. Collection of the City of Los Angeles Departments of Recreation and Parks and Cultural Affairs

MAIN FLOOR PLAN
SCALE 1/8 INCH PER FOOT

RESIDENCE FOR MISS ALINE BARNSDALL BEVERLY HILLS CALIFORNIA

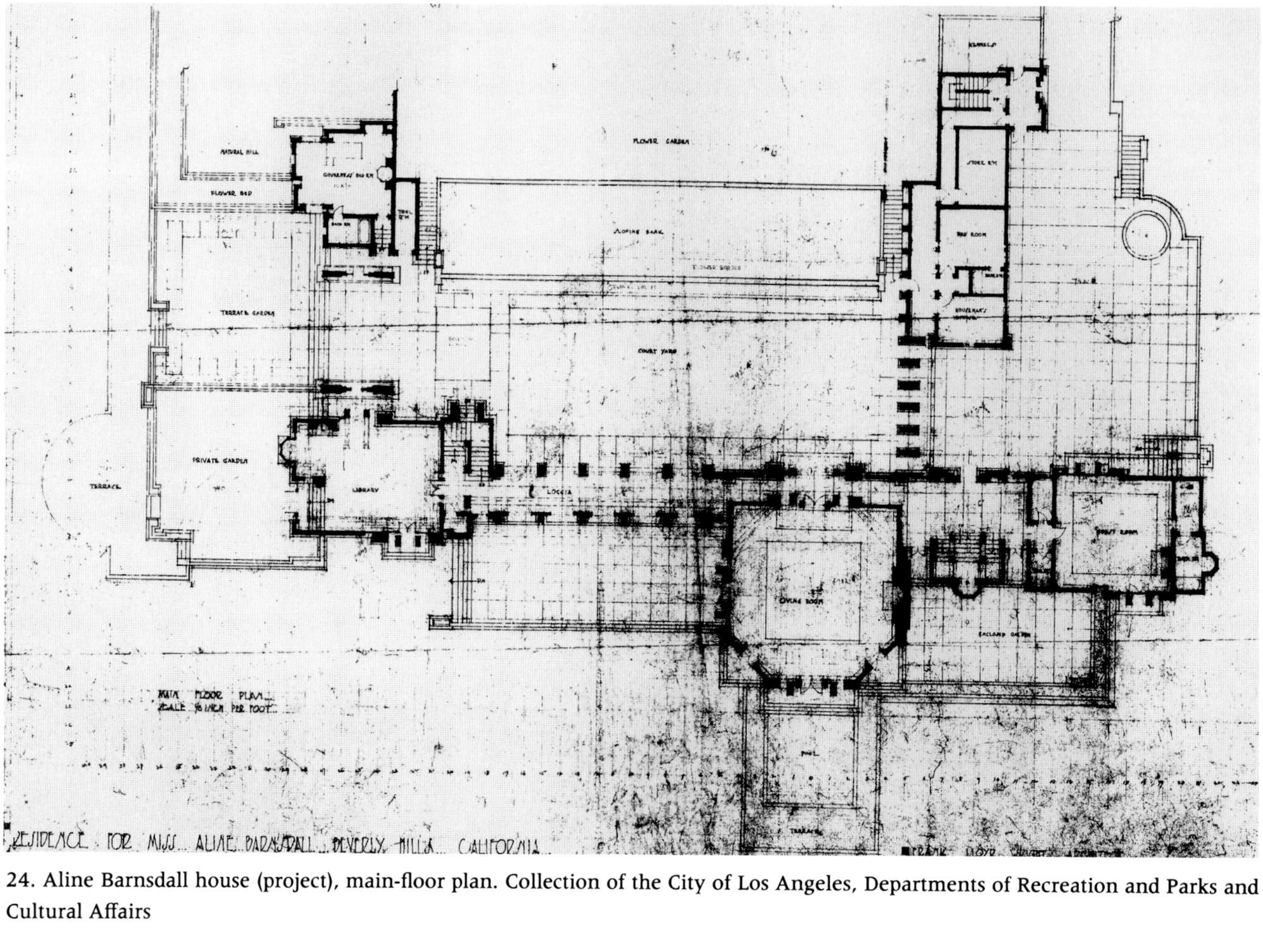

24. Aline Barnsdall house (project), main-floor plan. Collection of the City of Los Angeles, Departments of Recreation and Parks and Cultural Affairs

construction, a technically possible but seismically defenseless idea. Entering the space could only have been a religious experience; the soaring quality of the room, reminiscent of the Pantheon, has caused it to be mistaken for a private chapel Wright designed somewhat later for A. M. Johnson.[7]

Like most of Wright's designs for Aline Barnsdall, the house was never built. Blueprints of the original drawings passed to the City of Los Angeles when Hollyhock House was deeded over in 1927. Curiously, after that the project seems to have been forgotten, even by Wright.

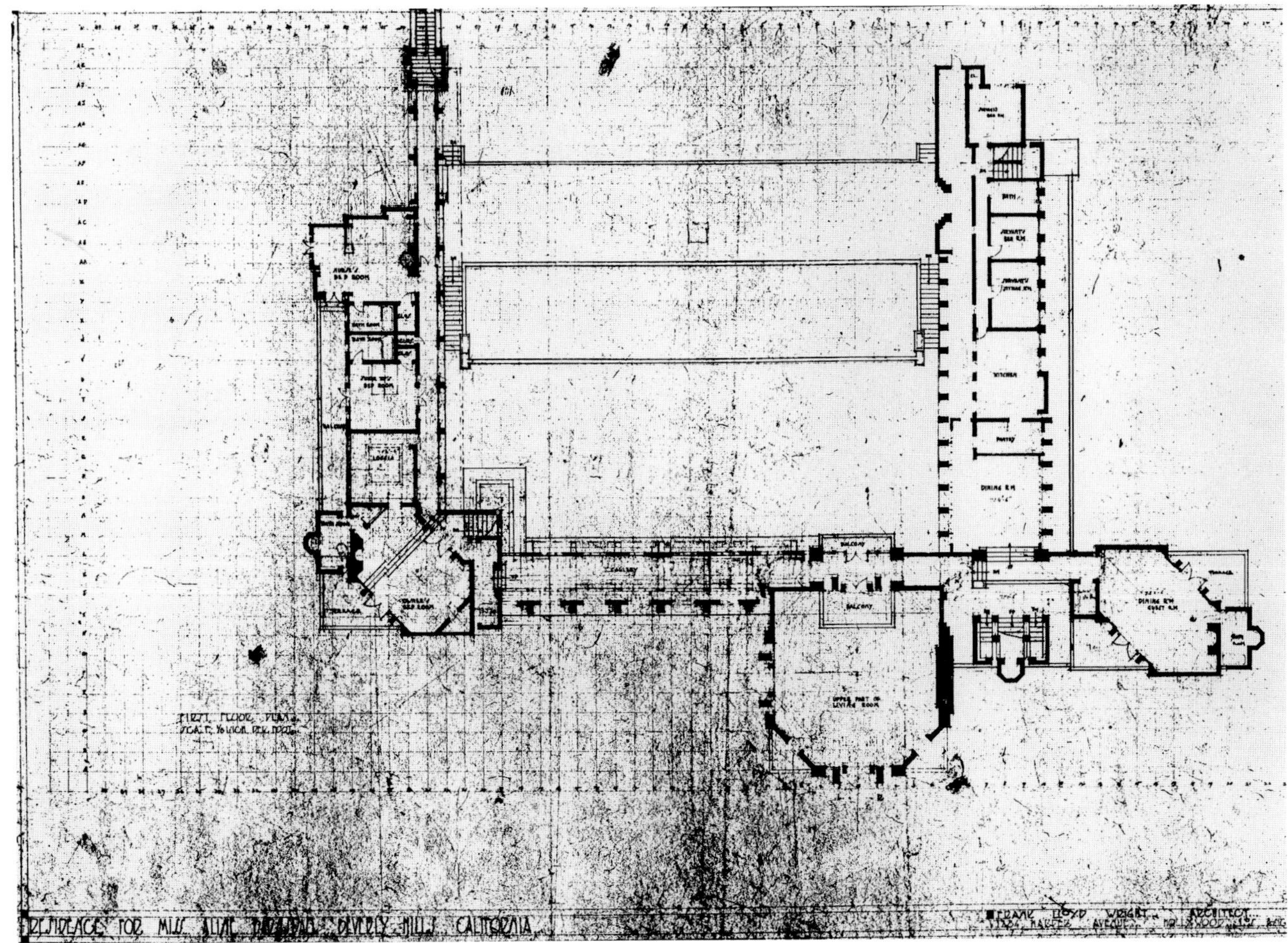

25. Aline Barnsdall house (project), first-floor plan. Collection of the City of Los Angeles, Departments of Recreation and Parks and Cultural Affairs

26. Aline Barnsdall house, Hollyhock House, Olive Hill, Los Angeles, California, west elevation, ca. 1919. FLLW FDN, 1705.005

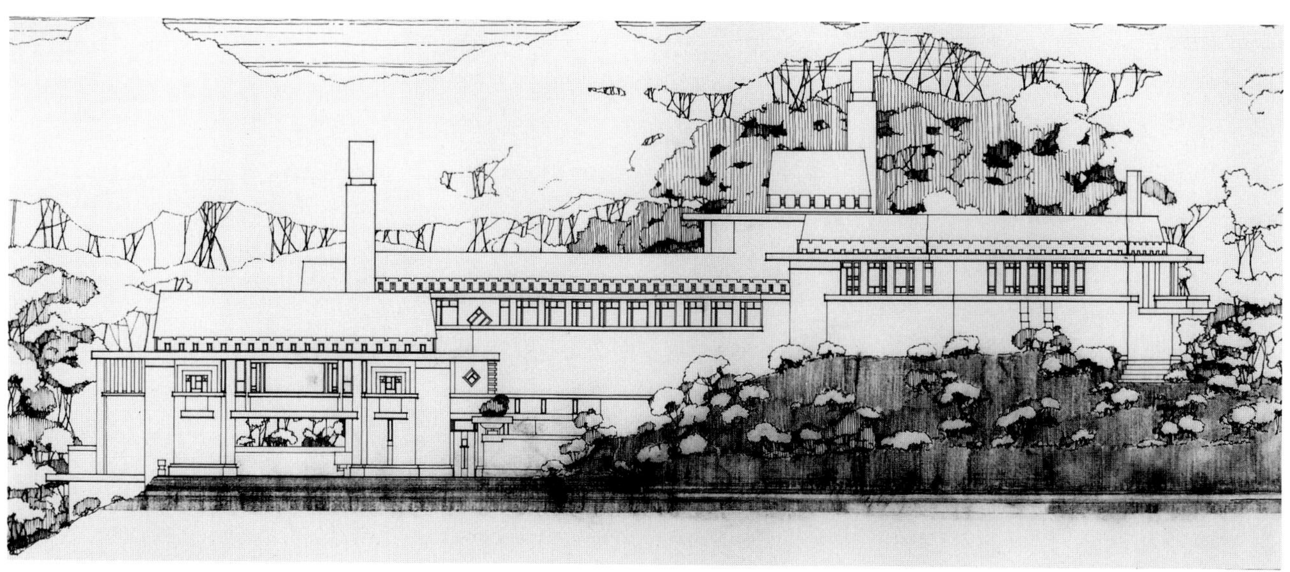

27. Tazaemon Yamamura house, Ashiya, Japan, 1918. Courtesy of Masami Tanigawa

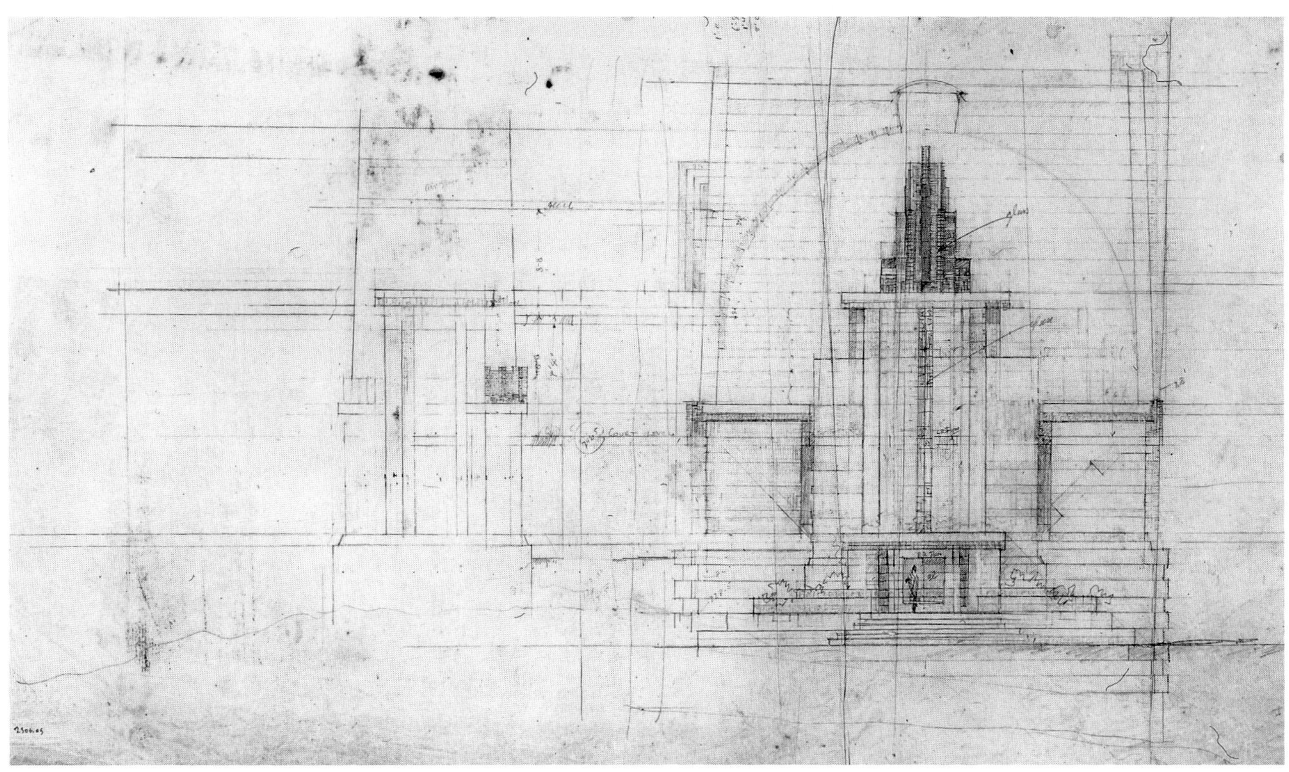

28. Aline Barnsdall house (project), Beverly Hills, California, section, 1923. FLLW FDN, 2009.015

Millard house, La Miniatura, Pasadena

The first of Wright's designs for concrete block to be constructed was a new house for Alice Millard in Pasadena. Its importance to Wright at the time—revealed in his autobiography—is out of proportion to his larger vision for the application of concrete block, but it was a necessary expedient to demonstrate his theories. That Wright was anxious to build is clear from his contemporary comments to Sullivan; the degree of urgency he felt is shown in correspondence from Alice Millard. She later reminded him that she had not contemplated building, but that he had been so eager to try out his "novel system of construction" that he had come to her, offering to design a new house without charging the standard architect's fee, while reserving an interest in the building in the form of a lien. He and

Millard signed a contract stipulating that he would be compensated in the event the house were sold speculatively for profit.[8]

In this project Millard (1873–1938) agreed to be Wright's client for a second time; in 1906, she and her husband had built a house in Highland Park, north of Chicago. George Millard (1846–1918) had a distinguished reputation as a collector and seller of books and for years was manager of the rare-book department at McClurg's (predecessor of Brentano's bookstore) in Chicago.[9] Around 1913 the Millards moved to South Pasadena, where they established a rare-book business in their house on Huntington Drive.[10] After her husband's death, Alice Millard carried on and expanded the business to include European antique furniture and decorative arts, which she purchased on annual trips abroad. La Miniatura was the first of several buildings she asked Wright to design as appropriate settings for the objects she had for sale.

Millard's site was in the Prospect Park tract, which was subdivided and improved in 1906. The tract was adjacent to an area distinguished by numerous examples of the work of Charles and Henry Greene and would, itself, become a microcosm of works by noted architects, including Roland Coate, Myron Hunt, Reginald Johnson, and Wallace Neff. One of the developers was John C. Bentz, a prominent dealer in Oriental antiques in Pasadena, from whom Millard purchased her lot, and whose own house, designed by Greene and Greene in 1906, still stands, diagonally across Prospect Crescent from La Miniatura. The Greene brothers also contributed the design for the Prospect Park tract entrance portals on Orange Grove Boulevard.

The feature that caught Wright's eye was a ravine; he claimed to have spotted it from the nearby lot first chosen.[11] As originally laid out, the lot was an attenuated, five-sided parcel whose narrow ends fronted on Lester (now Rosemont) Avenue on the west and Prospect Boulevard on the east (Fig. 29, Lot 10). It was divided approximately in half in 1910, and Millard initially purchased only the western portion, whose dimensions were roughly 210 by 110 feet. When she added a sixteen-by-thirty-eight-foot corner of the lot to the north to gain access to the street, making it possible to place the garage at the east end of the lot, she was initiating a pattern of patchwork acquisition of surrounding property that she continued until shortly before her death.

Wright adopted the same general forms for the Millard house that he was proposing at approximately the same time for the Doheny Ranch development. The basic plan and elevation were worked out together in a

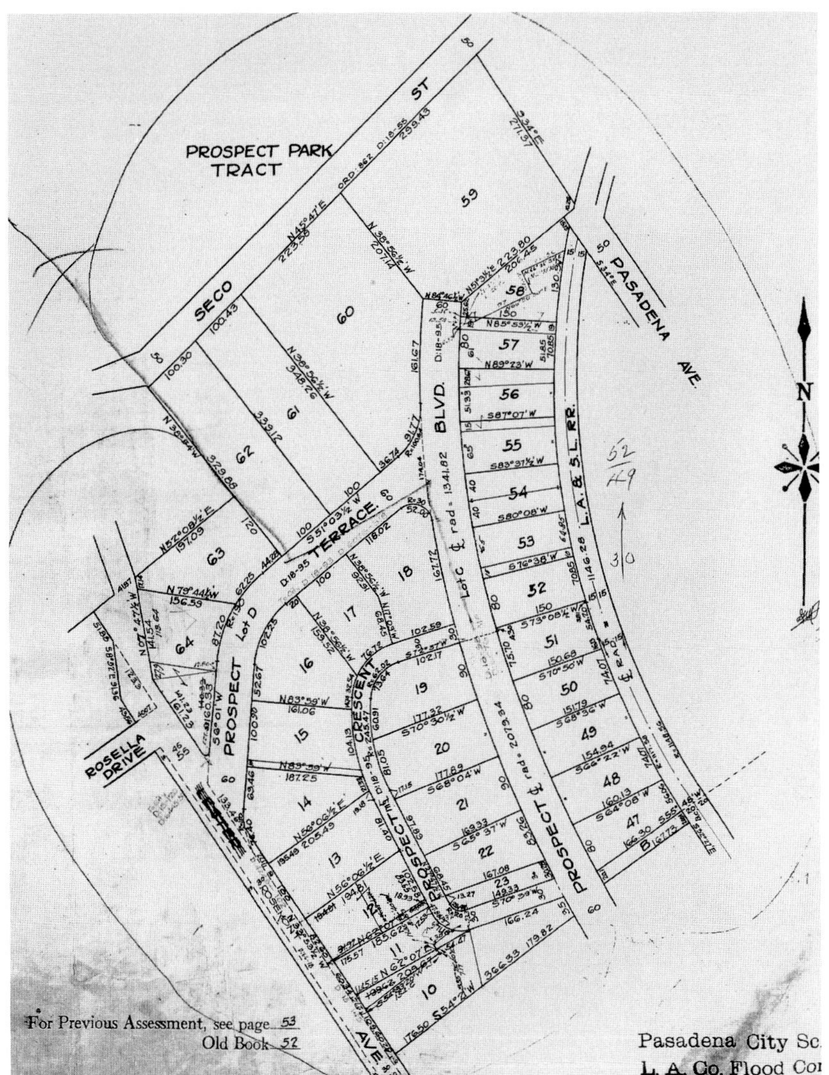

29. Alice Millard house, La Miniatura, site plan. Los Angeles County Assessor, Book 52 (1924–39), p. 49

conceptual sketch showing rectangular masses of patterned concrete block resting on bases of plaster or concrete, flat roofs, and a suggestion of the nature of the block system (Fig. 30). The design process was well under way by late February 1923, when Millard's friend Olive Percival recorded in her diary, "She has decided upon the Venetian Palace plan."[12] The historicist allusion may have been her own, but it does suggest that Wright was knowingly designing for a client with strong European affinities, who had requested "an old world atmosphere."[13] Percival, of course, was re-

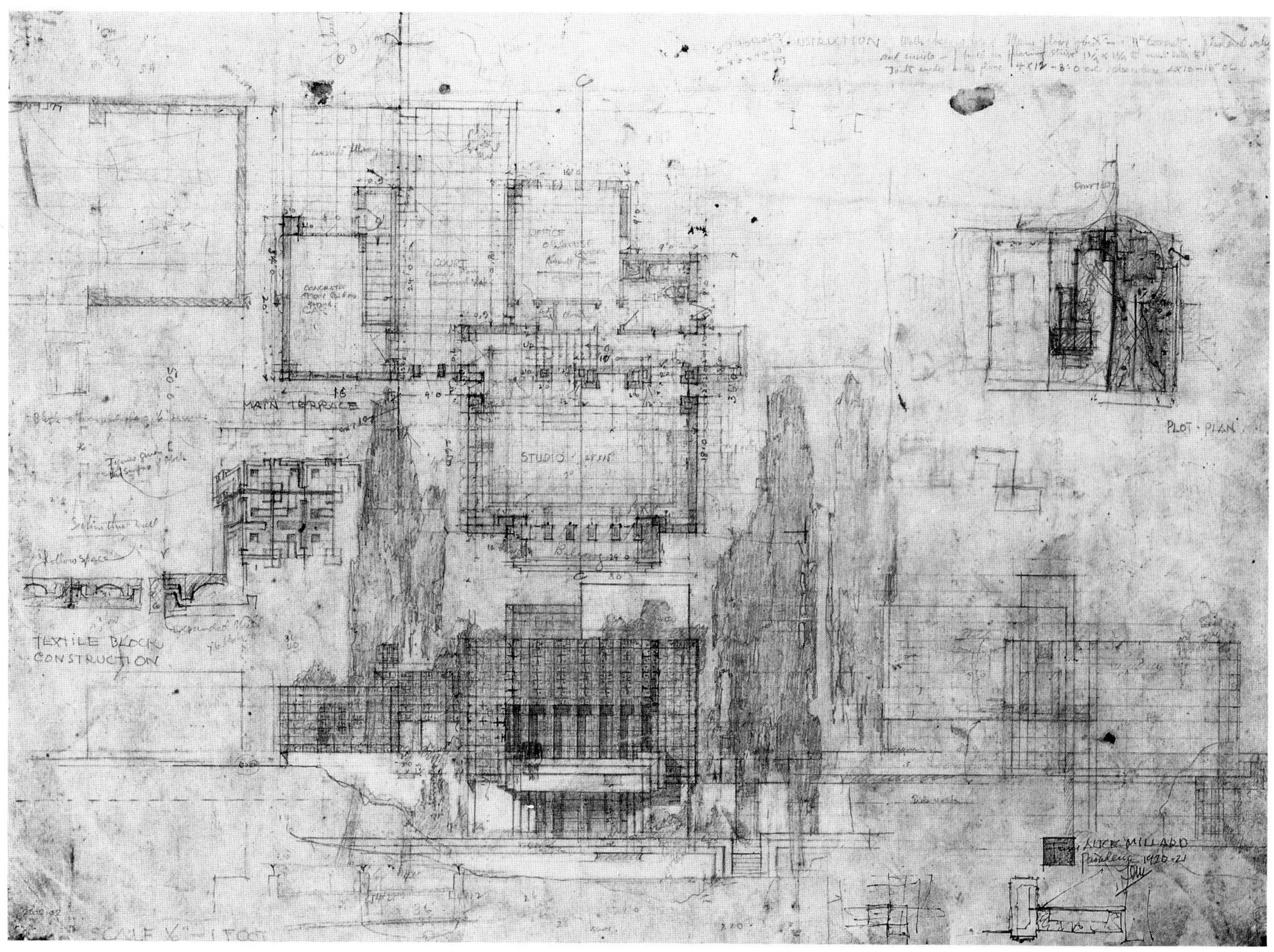

30. Alice Millard house, La Miniatura, plan, elevation, plot plan, and block details. FLLW FDN, 2302.002

ferring to the plan in which the principal floor was raised one level above ground, corresponding to the *piano nobile* of an Italian palace, and to the west or garden elevation, with its projecting balcony overlooking a pool.

The house is organized vertically; circulation spirals around a central chimney-mass. Entry is at the middle level, under a bridge connecting the main building and the garage (Fig. 31). The living room opens directly to the right—too directly, in Millard's opinion. She complained later about the absence of a separate vestibule.[14] The dining room is below, and leads to the terrace and pool (Fig. 32). Three bedrooms are stacked facing Prospect Crescent. Interior balconies overlook the living room and Millard's third-story bedroom (Figs. 33, 34).

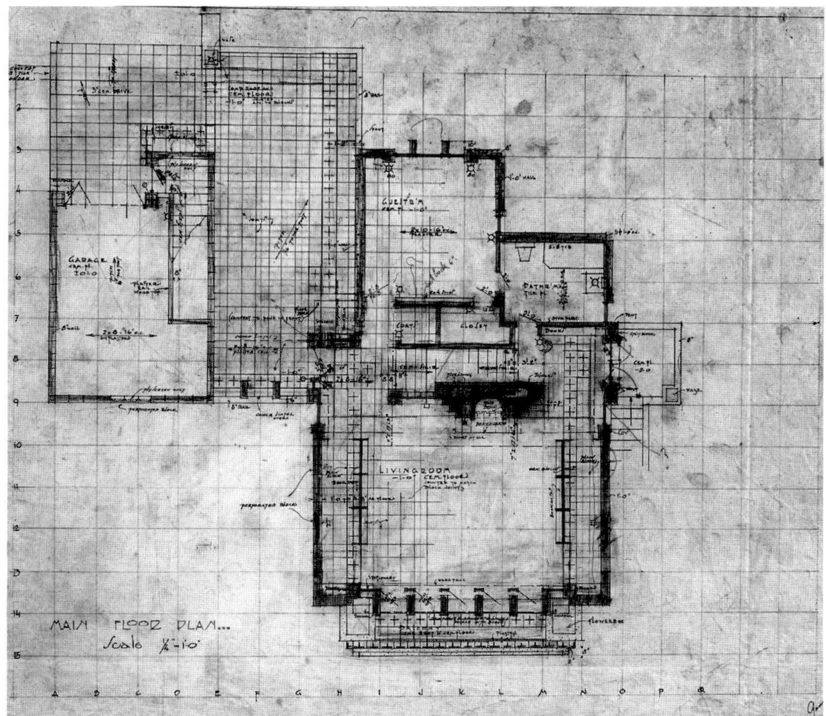

31. Alice Millard house, La Miniatura, middle-level plan. FLLW FDN, 2302.011

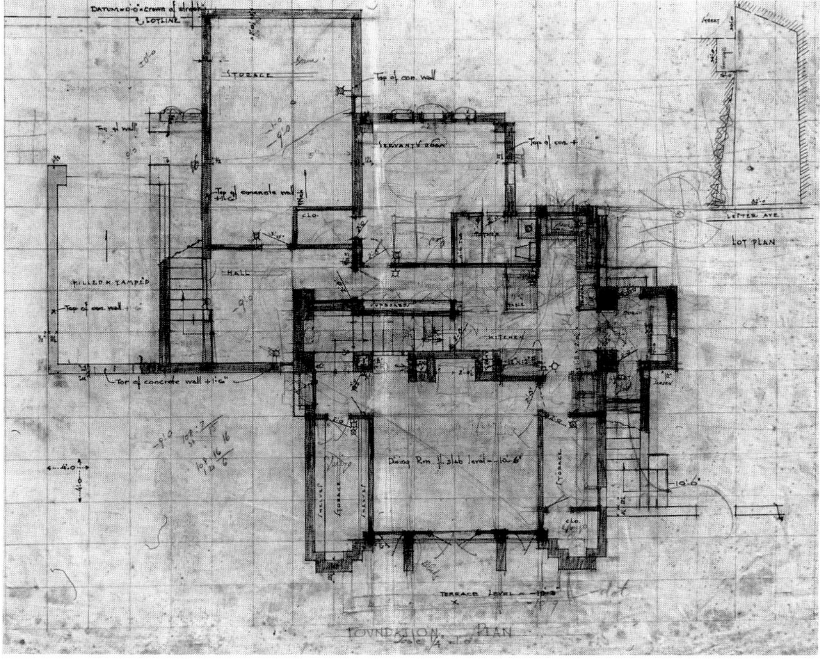

32. Alice Millard house, La Miniatura, foundation and lot plans. FLLW FDN, 2302.015

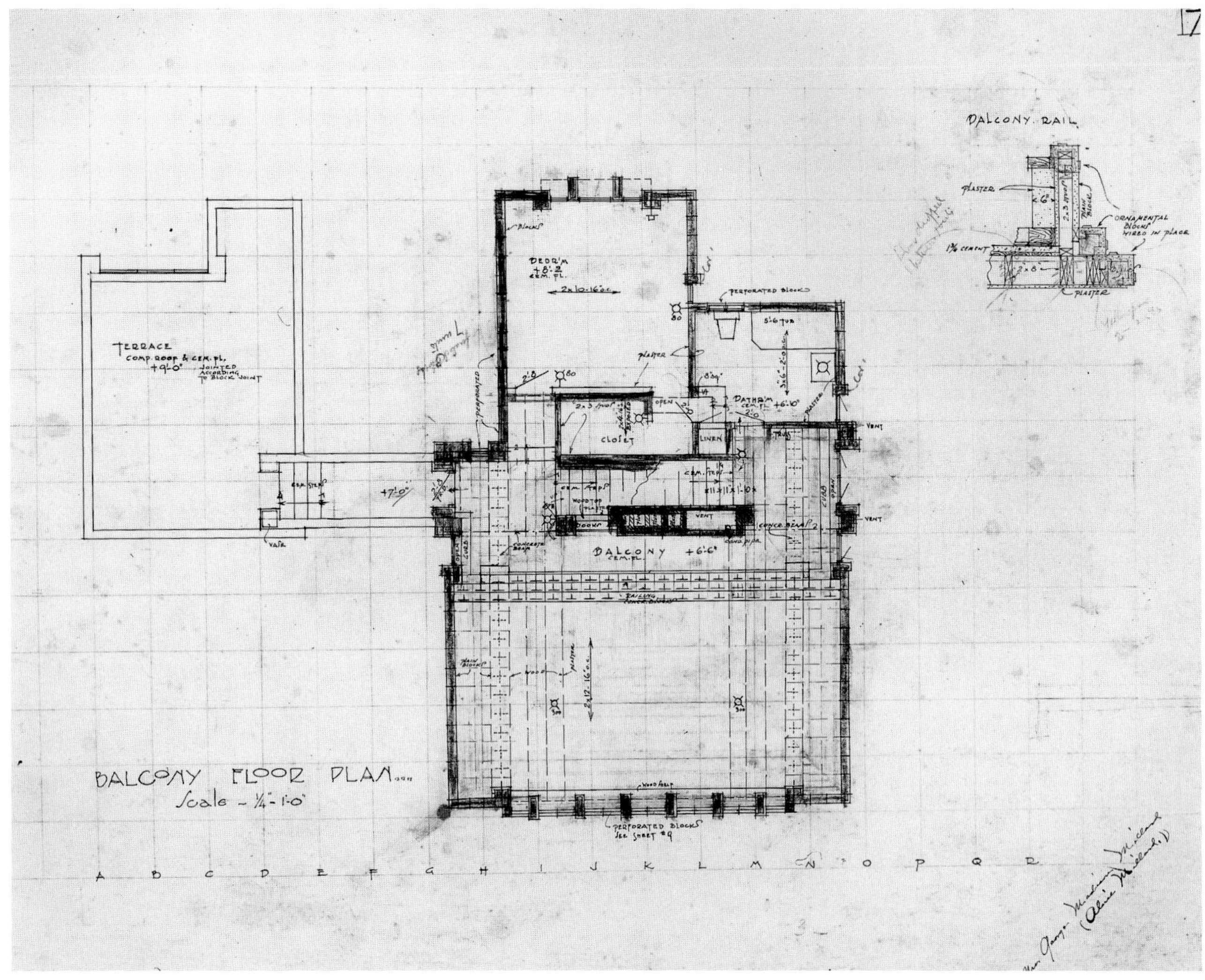

33. Alice Millard house, La Miniatura, balcony-floor plan. FLLW FDN, 2302.012

The working drawings were completed by Lloyd Wright.[15] They reveal a hybrid of concrete block and standard structural components, but are remarkably inconclusive about specific details of the block system itself. Concrete block is indicated primarily for load-bearing perimeter walls. Interior partitions are wooden studs and plaster; floors are concrete scored to match the block joints, or wood; and ceilings are exposed-frame redwood or plaster (Fig. 35). A skeletal concrete frame carries some of the loads. When the blocks are used horizontally, as trim on the balconies, they are wired to the

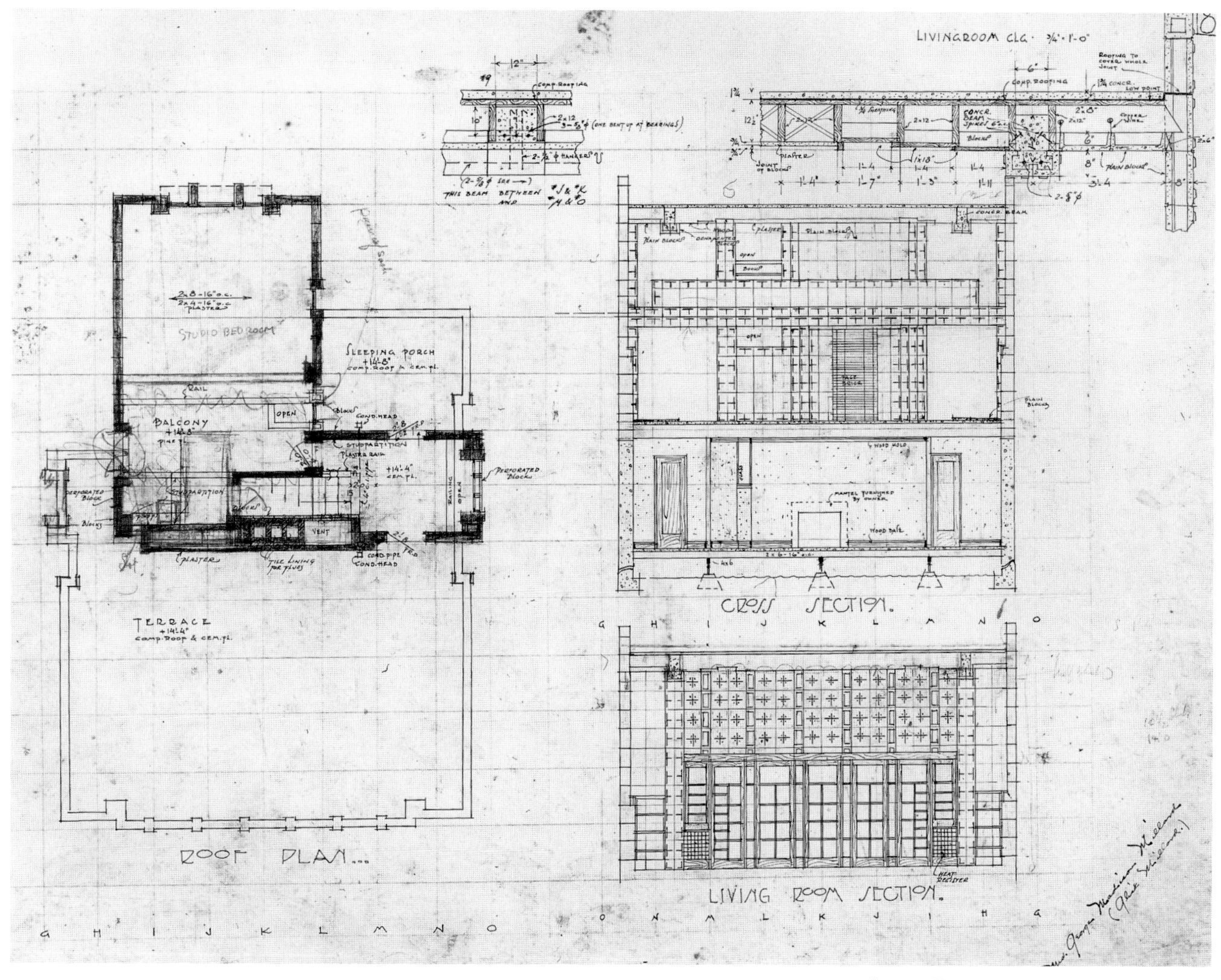

34. Alice Millard house, La Miniatura, roof plan, cross section, living-room section, and beam and living-room ceiling sections. FLLW FDN, 2302.013

substructure (see Fig. 33, detail). The pierced-block screen in the upper west wall of the living room is supported by a concrete beam.

The plans were approved on March 15, 1923. At the same time, Millard signed a contract with A. C. Parlee, a Pasadena building contractor, who agreed to build the house for $9,810. Work was to be completed by October 1.[16] A permit for the foundation had been issued a few days earlier, and excavation soon got under way, though the building permit was not issued until July 10.[17]

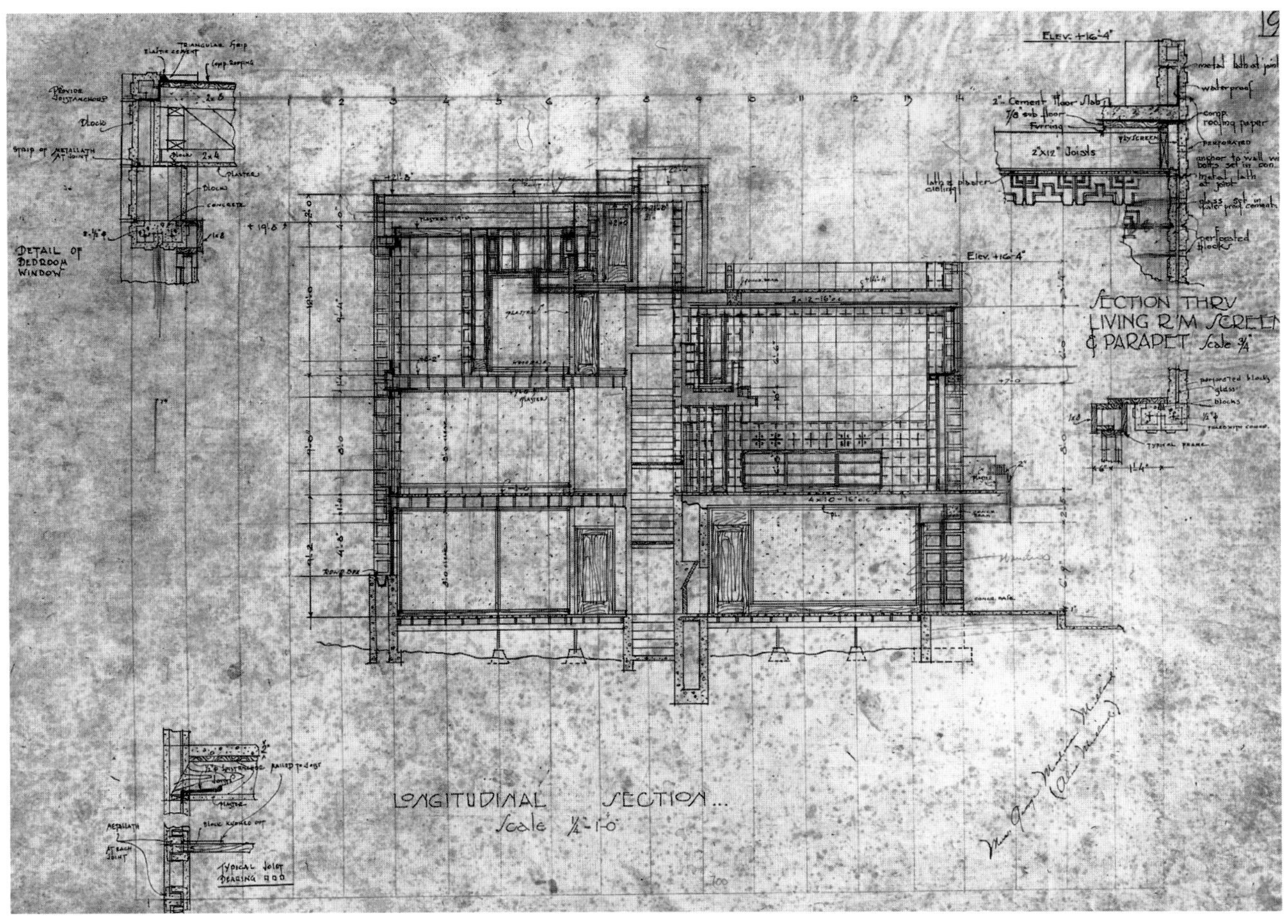

35. Alice Millard house, La Miniatura, longitudinal section, detail of bedroom window, typical joist bearing, and section through living-room screen and parapet. FLLW FDN, 2302.014

Wright devoted several pages of his autobiography to the construction of La Miniatura:

> That house represented about as much studious labor over a drawing board and attention to getting construction started as the Cathedral of St. John the Divine in New York City, certainly more trouble to me than any the architect had with the Woolworth Building.[18]

Although photographs taken by Kameki Tsuchiura in May or June 1923 suggest that work was proceeding with some dispatch — the garden elevation is recognizable, and perimeter walls are up — by no account was construction a smooth process (Figs. 36, 37). Millard summarized the situation in a 1928 letter to Wright, recalling, "Your conduct and mine in the construction of 'La Miniatura' is incomprehensible even to ourselves."[19]

36. Alice Millard house, La Miniatura. Courtesy of Kameki Tsuchiura

37. Alice Millard house, La Miniatura. Courtesy of Kameki Tsuchiura

There can be no doubt that the experimental nature of the block system was the greatest contributing factor. The drawings would have invited, even required, interpretation by the contractor. Also, the concept was deceptively simple. Nowhere in the working drawings do we learn of blocks needed to accommodate special conditions: perforated patterned blocks used as screens to admit light; half blocks, quarter blocks, solid corner blocks; and an eight-by-sixteen-inch rectangular unit that is stacked in single vertical rows to frame windows and doors on the back and front elevations and to form piers at the entrance.

Also, there were problems resulting from the process used to manufacture the blocks. Surviving information is incomplete; we have only Wright's recollections, in which he specifically mentioned the studies and details required to get the flasks and boxes made in which to fabricate the blocks, and experiments to get the right mixture of sand, gravel, and cement, which were varied so that they would not all be the same color.[20] The flasks and boxes to which he referred—the molds—were wood, constructed at the site by a carpenter.[21] One of these molds survives in a worn and weathered condition; even in this state it is evident that it was never a precision object (Fig. 38). In addition, wood by nature expands

38. Alice Millard house, La Miniatura, block mold. Courtesy of Charles Calvo

with moisture; the result was that the blocks produced from these molds were uneven, lacking even tolerances that could be compensated easily by a bed of mortar. In many cases they were assembled with shims so that the joints between them would be true.

Wright, with some justification, ascribed the difficulties of construction to the contractor.

> I drove over daily to carry on, but no builder. . . . Finding him I got promises. Finally Mrs. Millard's builder came to me for more money, explaining that if he got it he could forge ahead. I gave him some more money myself—he didn't forge ahead. . . .[22]

In August, while work was under way in Pasadena, Wright employed Parlee to complete the remodeling of Residence B on Olive Hill. Three months later, on November 7, even though work on the Millard house was badly behind schedule, Parlee's name was indicated as contractor on building permits for the Community Playhouse for Aline Barnsdall and for the Storer house. It was shortly after this that Parlee fell completely from grace. On December 13, Wright paid him $1,515.48 for work on Olive Hill, then instructed his bank to refuse payment.[23]

Wright's reasons cannot be explained with certainty. It is tempting to speculate, however, that his motive was related less to work on Olive Hill than to events in Pasadena. Parlee had received $8,961.50 for his work on the Millard house, yet the building was less than half finished.[24] Parlee finally resigned from the project on January 1, 1924. Millard thereupon proceeded to complete the building herself at an additional cost of $8,636.45.[25]

An informative postscript to the construction process and to the state of development of the block system in early 1923 comes from a lawsuit Parlee filed against Millard in June 1924, three months after the house was finished. Claiming that numerous changes had been made to the original plans, and that therefore his contract with Millard was practically abandoned, Parlee sought $12,029.43 additional compensation for work performed.[26] Wright responded through his attorney, Herbert L. Hahn, filing a counterclaim against Parlee to recover the cost of work completed by Alice Millard. He also agreed to assign all claims in his favor against Parlee arising from construction of the house to Millard.[27]

The case was heard in May 1925. The primary issue was Parlee's assertion that the original plans called for single- rather than double-block wall construction, which he claimed as an extra. It was shown that the claim was an afterthought wholly unsupported by the evidence, with Millard and Lloyd testifying that at no time had any other system of construction been contemplated. The concept and the advantages of the dead air space had been explained by Wright at the time the drawings were prepared and were fully understood by all. The only significant modification in the system was the size of the blocks. Wright had begun with units based on a twenty-four-inch module. Possibly to reduce the weight, he scaled them down to a sixteen-inch module, though their form was not changed.[28] This reduction meant that three units rather than two would be required for each four-foot module.

More important, and revealing of the embryonic stage of Wright's thinking, is the manner in which the details of construction were communicated. The defense conceded that the plans for the house were "somewhat indefinite as to the hollow wall feature," and testimony revealed that many of the specifications were communicated verbally.[29] Wright confirmed this when he wired his attorney: "Much of this not recorded and such specifications as were prepared are missing However blueprints and contract are specific enough to show him up." [30]

The proceedings of the trial described Millard's defense as "clear and convincing, . . . unshaken by cross examination." Unable to substantiate his claims, Parlee lost his case. The court determined "that there remains a balance due to defendant, ALICE MILLARD, in the sum of Five Hundred ($500.00) Dollars." [31] Wright recalled that the judge fined Parlee "for his effrontery." [32]

Alice Millard weathered the ordeals of construction and litigation with conviction. Wright remembered her "fighting for the best of everything for everyone. Be it said she knew it when she saw it. Got it if she could." [33] His assessment was confirmed a half-century later by Lucille Miller: "She adored luxury, but it was a <u>refinement</u> of luxury elevated to an art. . . . She <u>would</u> have quality. . . . She seemed to be <u>all</u> intellect, all soul, all mind. . . . She believed in <u>IDEALS</u>." [34]

An ideal was realized in the Millard house. Though technically primitive, in view of improvements in the block system that were on the horizon, formally it is the most perfect of the block houses built on the West Coast. Its quality stems not so much from unique brilliance of design as from the fact that it is the only house constructed without significant changes to Wright's original concept. Only the elimination of a screen of pierced blocks capping the three-story window on the east elevation and the extension of the window closer to the top of the building had a measurable effect. The result is weaker and lacks continuity with the garden facade.

Actually, much of the success of the house results from its siting; like the two Taliesins and Fallingwater, La Miniatura cannot be imagined in any other location. As in these examples, Wright manipulated the relation of the building to nature for greatest effect. He used the metaphorical association of ravine and water to wed the house to its site, adding a pool to a gully that otherwise would have been dry; Louis Kahn might have explained that the water "wanted" to be there. The house does not rise from the water but next to it, establishing tension between the natural forces that created the ravine and the intrusions of man and, parenthetically, reinforcing the analogy to a Venetian palace.

Wright placed the house at the extreme eastern or Prospect Crescent edge of the property, ignoring the conventional setback line on Lester Avenue and creating the perspective that has made the building so famous. It could be approached from either side: directly by automobile from Prospect Crescent, or on foot from Lester (Figs. 39, 40). It was meant to be seen from Lester; the route to the building leads down several steps to a path alongside the pool, then up to the dining-room terrace. Two eucalyptus trees frame the composition. Reaching the house was not an end, but an opportunity for reciprocal views of the landscape; the finest view is from the roof terrace over the living room. House and site are integrated into an instinctively hermitic composition, acknowledging but not observing the neighborhood.

At close range, the details and organization of the patterned blocks become more apparent. The blocks are cast with a cruciform design symmetrical on both axes; when the blocks are assembled, a new interwoven pattern results. The design offers great flexibility in application; it can be bisected vertically and horizontally to accommodate corners, and can be divided into quarters to form a three-corner block. The applications of the blocks—combinations of plain and patterned surfaces and variations in coursing—are legible, revealing the structure to some degree in all of the block buildings. The use of blocks as a load-bearing perimeter shell in the Millard house is expressed by the very absence of special emphasis: the exterior blocks are all patterned, are laid in unbroken courses conforming to the shape of the building, and cap a base of stuccoed concrete. Those blocks that do serve a supporting function, the eight-by-sixteen-inch rectangular units, are distinguished both by shape and ornament.

The quality of space produced by the blocks is most apparent in the

39. Alice Millard house, La Miniatura. Reproduced from Henry-Russell Hitchcock, *Frank Lloyd Wright* (Paris: Cahiers d'Art, 1928), n.p.

living room. The parts do not all come together perfectly, especially where the block walls meet the redwood ceiling, but the general effect is quiet and reassuringly solid without the predictable heaviness or sense of rawness that concrete usually suggests. Patterned blocks are combined with plain, and a screen of pierced blocks animates the west wall; the reciprocal effect at night, with light inside, is one of the great thrills of twentieth-century architecture (Plate 1). The room becomes more meaningful with the realization that groupings of plain and patterned blocks are not arbitrary but express the structure: patterned blocks form piers for the concrete beams to rest on and face the concrete beams that support the mezzanine balcony and the pierced-block screen (Fig. 41; Plate 2).

40. Alice Millard house, La Miniatura. Reproduced from Henry-Russell Hitchcock, *Frank Lloyd Wright* (Paris: Cahiers d'Art, 1928), n.p.

Millard's bedroom at the top of the stairs, with its high ceiling and balcony, is a similar, though smaller, space, with a subtle adjustment confirming the relationship of house and site. Instead of the broad bank of doors overlooking the pool to the west, there is a tall, slender window framing the ravine at its narrow end.

Although there is nothing specifically "old-world" about the spaces in this house, the "old-world atmosphere" that Wright "said it would have" prevails.[35] A contemporary visitor, Alexander Inglis, commented in the Pasadena *Star News:*

> There is situated in Pasadena, at 645 Prospect Crescent, a house endowed with unusual architectural beauty & an unique old-world atmosphere. It is a

41. Alice Millard house, La Miniatura, living-room, looking east. FLLW FDN, 2302.005

> secluded place, where peace and reverence dwell and the anxieties of the world seem to be left behind when the outer door closes on the visitor. It is like going out of the world for a time to enter here, so subdued is the filtering sunlight, so quiet is the house. Somewhere, in old European castles, perhaps, has this serene quietude been before experienced.[36]

The *Los Angeles Times* critic Arthur Millier was more succinct; he praised La Miniatura as "a completely modern house in which fine old things can quite naturally be themselves."[37]

Frank Lloyd Wright canonized the Millard house in his autobiography. A short time later, it was included in the 1932 "Modern Architecture" exhibition at the Museum of Modern Art in New York, along with the work of the contemporaneous European modernists, although it shared little of their ideology.

CHAPTER THREE

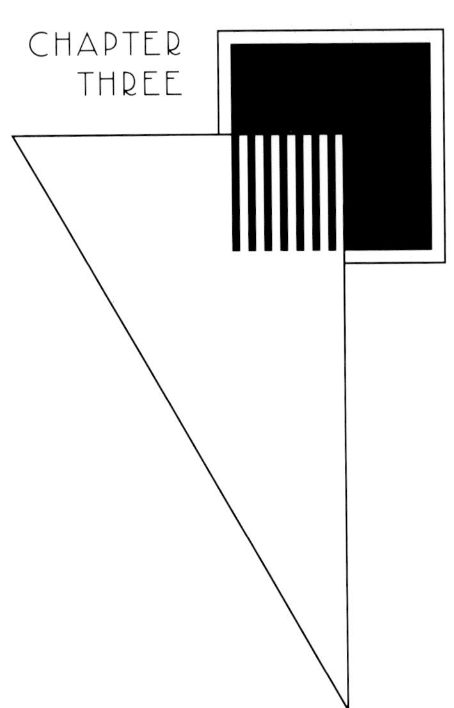

IMPROVEMENTS AND CHANGES IN BLOCK TECHNIQUE

Several months after the Millard house was begun, Wright modified the method of concrete-block assembly and, accordingly, the shape of the individual block units, noting in his autobiography that "improvements and changes were made in block technique."[1] His new concept was based on a system of mortarless construction in which the blocks are held together by a network of internal joints filled with grout and steel reinforcing rods. Wright explained later that by eliminating the mortar joint he could do away with skilled labor; and the addition of steel significantly increased the structural and formal capabilities of the concrete block. Concrete functions in compression; with steel reinforcement it gains tensile strength. This permitted—in fact, encouraged—previously untried applications of the blocks.

At approximately the same time he was rethinking his block system, Wright began the process of securing a patent on his inventions, retaining a Los Angeles patent attorney, W. R. Litzenberg, to complete the application. One patent-application drawing survives; although the information it provides is incomplete, it does reveal the evolution that had occurred. The interlocking blocks used in the Millard house are contrasted with the new blocks, which are cast with semicircular channels around their perimeters; when they are assembled, continuous vertical and horizontal cavities or channels result (Fig. 42). During construction a grid of reinforcing rods is woven between the blocks and the channels are filled with grout.

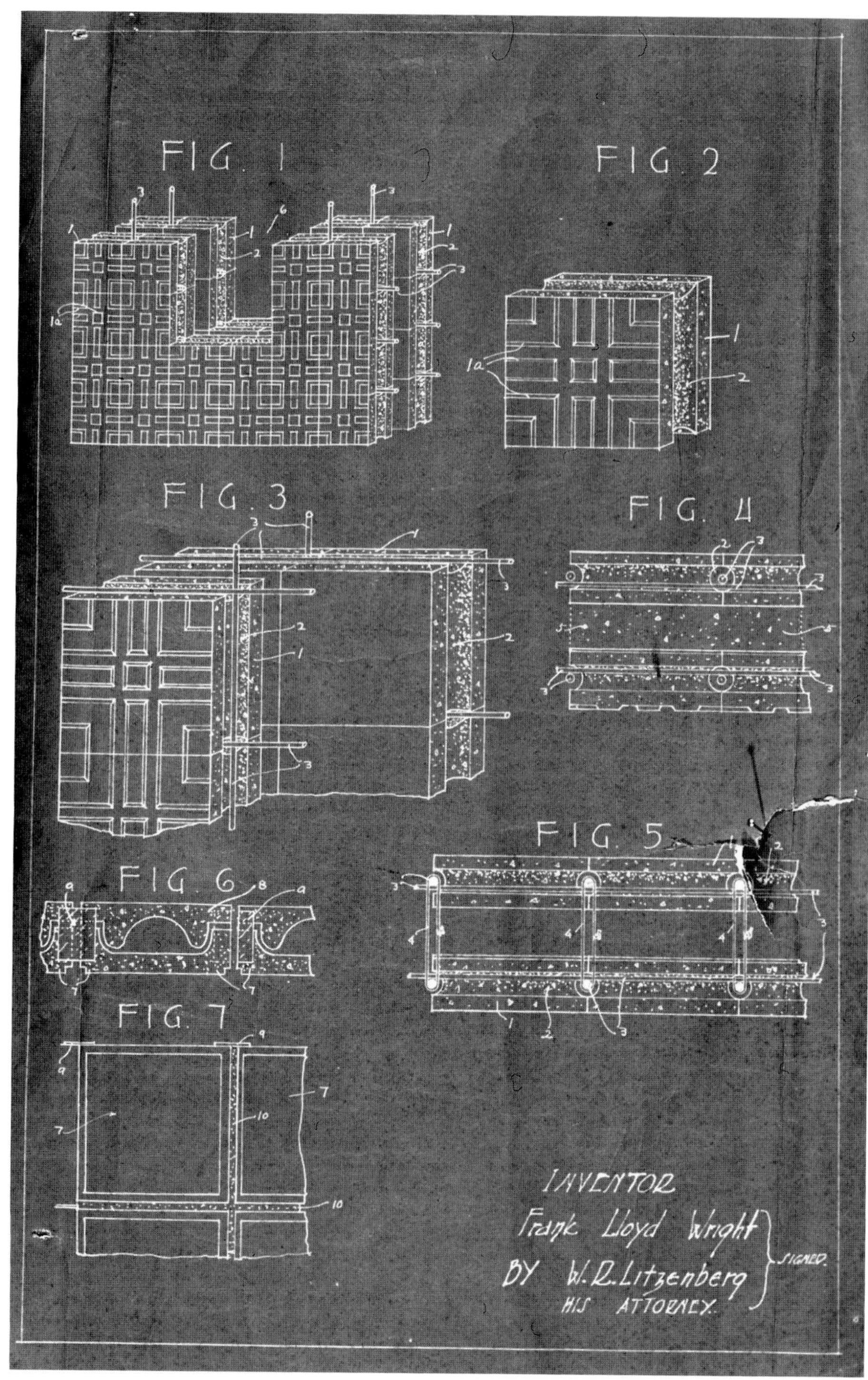

42. Patent drawing, 1923. FLLW FDN, 2111.002

As before, the blocks are erected in double layers to provide identical faces for the exterior and interior of the building, with a cavity left between the layers. The walls are tied together with a loop of wire placed around the reinforcing rods at the corners of the blocks.

Wright first worked out these innovations in drawings for the Community Playhouse for Aline Barnsdall, which are dated August 1923, and in roughly contemporary drawings for the Storer house. He used the same system in the Freeman and Ennis houses that followed.

Community Playhouse, Little Dipper, Los Angeles

The Community Playhouse, known as the "Little Dipper," was the final building Wright designed for the peripatetic oil heiress. It was intended as a private school for her daughter Betty and was to be open to other children, who would pay tuition.[2] In program and name it recalls the Coonley Playhouse Wright had designed twelve years earlier for a rich couple in Riverside, Illinois, who had wanted to give their only child a progressive education in an artistic setting. Central to both schemes is a stage for the presentation of students' plays; hence the name "playhouse." The plans also include kitchens, indicating the working nature of the educational concepts the building was to embody.

The site was on the western down slope of Olive Hill, approximately on axis with Hollyhock House; it overlooked the city below and the Santa Monica Mountains to the north. Access was from a private driveway above; another road below led to Residence B.

The plan of the Little Dipper is based on the intersection of an irregular square and circle; it is symmetrical on two axes, though it incorporates a nonconforming wing to disturb the balance (Fig. 43). The enclosed schoolroom, the square, is oriented on its diagonals; the stage, in one corner, is on axis with the circular outdoor seating area. The cross-axial space is defined in plan and section by a hexagonal "overhead lantern," built of open trusses separated by windows, which extends the length of the building (Fig. 44). The elongated entry and service wing projects diagonally from one side of the square, giving the building its nickname. Wright rotated the building on its site forty-five degrees to the west, and presented it in elevation from above, favoring neither of the prevailing axes (Fig. 45).

It seems impossible to fault the Little Dipper for the resolution of its

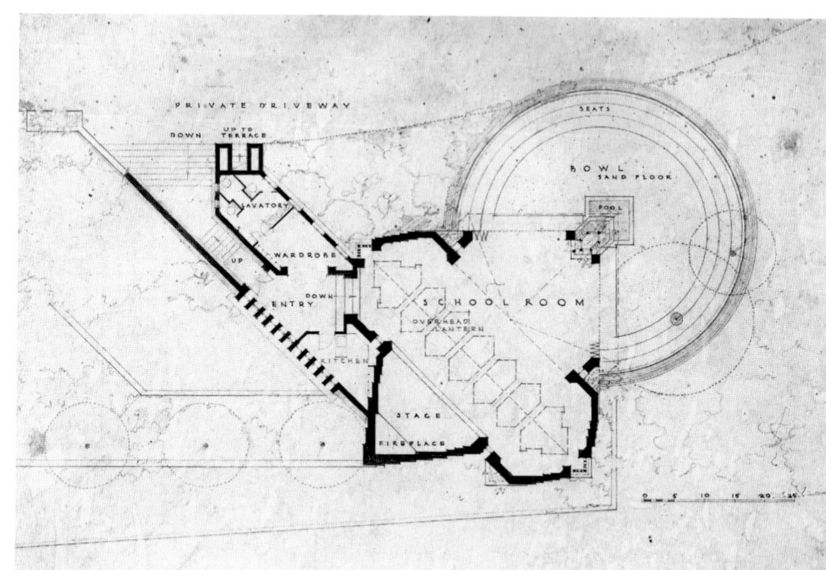

43. Community Playhouse, the Little Dipper (project), Olive Hill, Los Angeles, California, plan, 1923. FLLW FDN, 2301.007

forms. It is an exceedingly complicated building, echoing the fascination with interlocking diagonal geometry Wright expressed in the Doheny Ranch house C and, parenthetically, in furniture for Hollyhock House; but the forms are here expressed with greater confidence and ease.

There is, however, an underlying contradiction in the Community Playhouse. It is a building whose complex forms belie a comparatively simple structural technology. Improvements in the block system aside, the concept is still that of a load-bearing perimeter shell of concrete block embracing conventional wooden floor and ceiling structures (see Fig. 44). The most visible exploitation of the infrastructure of reinforcing rods and grout is the introduction of offset blocks, which would not have been feasible with a conventional mortar bed. By offsetting the blocks 1¾ inches every two courses, vertically and horizontally, Wright achieved a surface plasticity lacking in the Millard house (Fig. 46).

The sense of richness created with the offset blocks derives from experimentation with multiple block patterns. There are four different patterns, one of the patterns having a second incarnation when the block is adjusted to a sixty-degree angle — in combination with plain blocks; there is also a special patterned "column" block. Although each block pattern serves a specific function in articulating a feature of the building, there are numerous special conditions to be accommodated. Block A, the plain block, has three versions: the standard block shape and two variations with enlarged

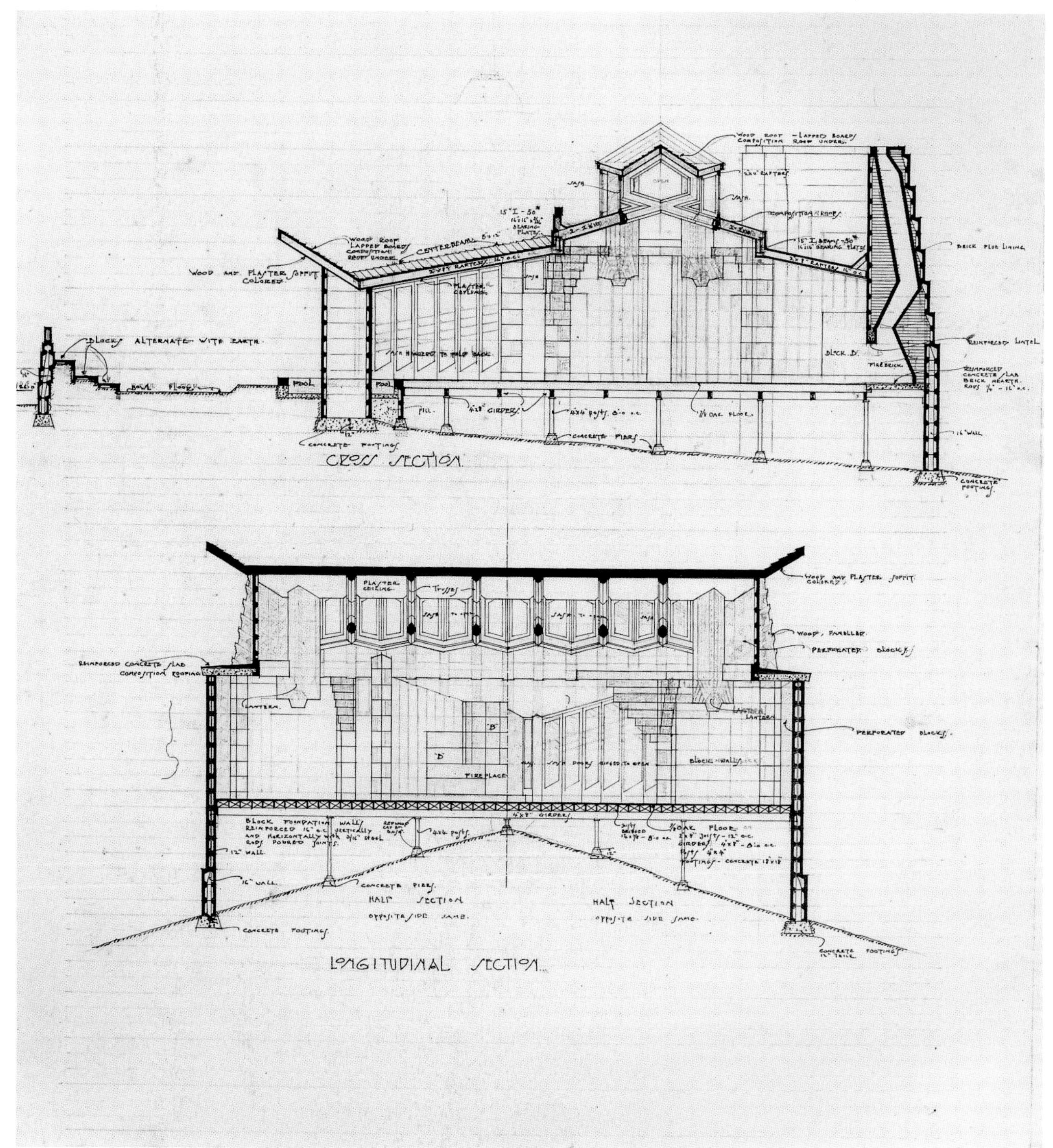

44. Community Playhouse, the Little Dipper (project), cross section and longitudinal section. FLLW FDN, 2301.011

45. Community Playhouse, the Little Dipper (project), aerial perspective. FLLW FDN, 2301.002

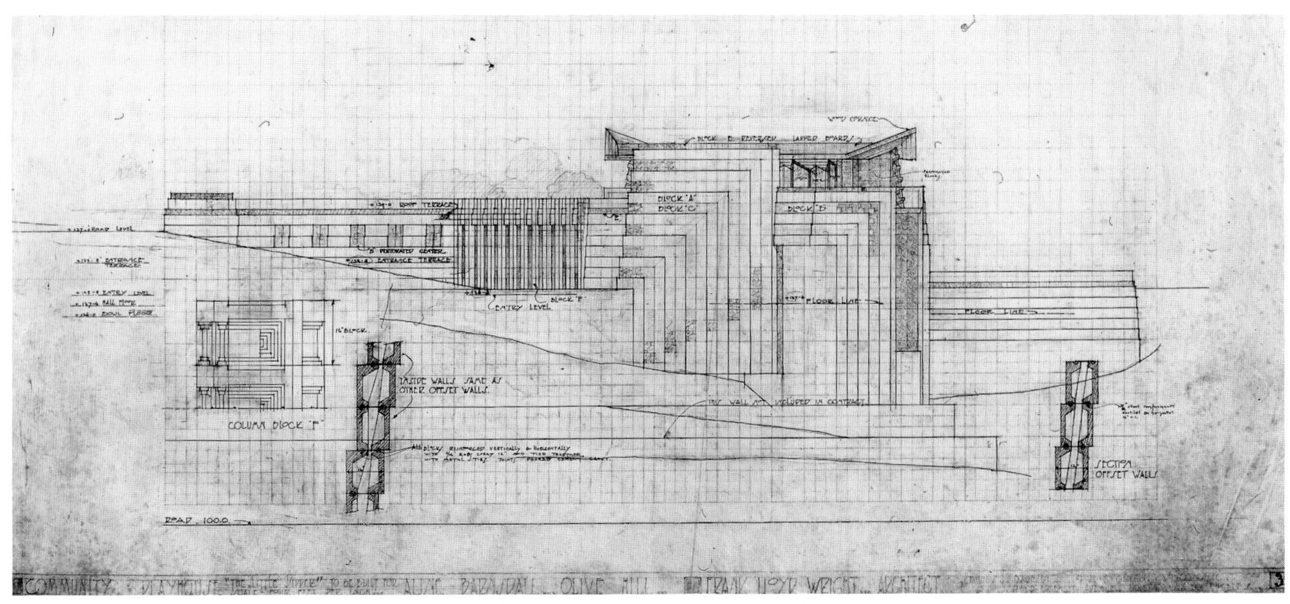

46. Community Playhouse, the Little Dipper (project), northwest elevation, offset wall sections, and block detail. FLLW FDN, 2301.009

returns for offsets (Fig. 47). Block B, an asymmetrical square pattern closely resembling that used later in the Ennis house, is used horizontally and vertically in the prow of the building and in the service wing, where it is grouped in multiples of four and perforated to admit light. This block has six versions (Fig. 48). Block C, the chimney block, has a complex pattern of squares and shapes derived from the 30/60 triangle, but comes only in one standard shape (Fig. 49). It is used in alternating courses with plain blocks. Block D has a square pattern with perforations and is used to admit light at the two ends of the room. It comes in the standard shape or with a mitered corner and also is adjusted to a sixty-degree angle (Fig. 50). Block E, the coping block, is eight inches square, has an asymmetrical rectangular pattern, and is used only in horizontal rows. There are variations for horizontal and vertical corners, and also the pattern can be reversed (Fig. 51). Finally, the two-part "column" block, Block F, requires left- and right-hand variations in the pattern for assembly (Fig. 52). All told, at least thirty different variants of the six blocks are required.

The drawings for the Community Playhouse are of unprecedented clarity. Instead of the "somewhat indefinite" lines indicating hollow block walls in the drawings for the Millard house, the playhouse walls are drawn in section as individual paired block units (see Figs. 44, 46). Blocks for special conditions—offsets, corners, coping, and "columns"—are carefully depicted and dimensioned in detail drawings. In contrast with the plans for the Millard house, here there is no vagueness. Between February and August 1923, the system reached the point of resolution familiar today.

Historically, the enigma of the Little Dipper has been rooted in the extent to which it was completed. Wright stated in his autobiography that it was "destroyed, half way."[3] Henry-Russell Hitchcock, the most prolific of Wright's critics, wrote in 1942 that it had been demolished in 1924.[4] Neither account is entirely accurate. A building permit was issued on November 7, 1923, with A. C. Parlee listed as contractor.[5] According to a complaint filed by Parlee, work was suspended two weeks later, on November 22, after the foundations had been laid, 7,508 blocks had been cast, and 226 blocks had been set. The reason given for stopping work was that the City of Los Angeles had required that the plans for the building be changed; that Barnsdall would not agree to the extra expense entailed by these changes; and that she had refused to honor her contract and pay for work completed up to that time. Barnsdall responded, denying the allegations. The case was dismissed in 1925.[6]

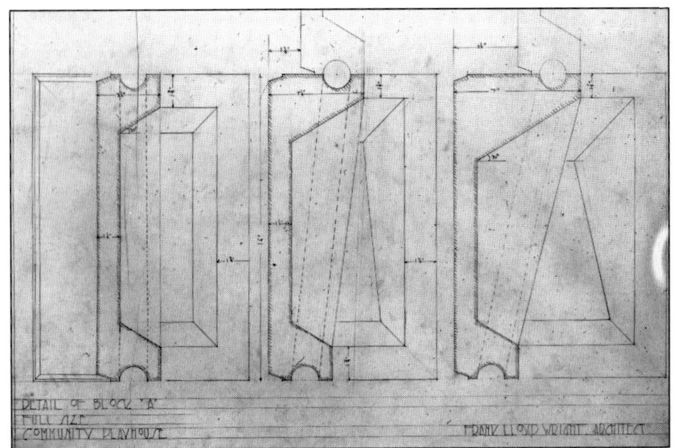

47. Community Playhouse, the Little Dipper (project), Block A details. FLLW FDN, 2301.014

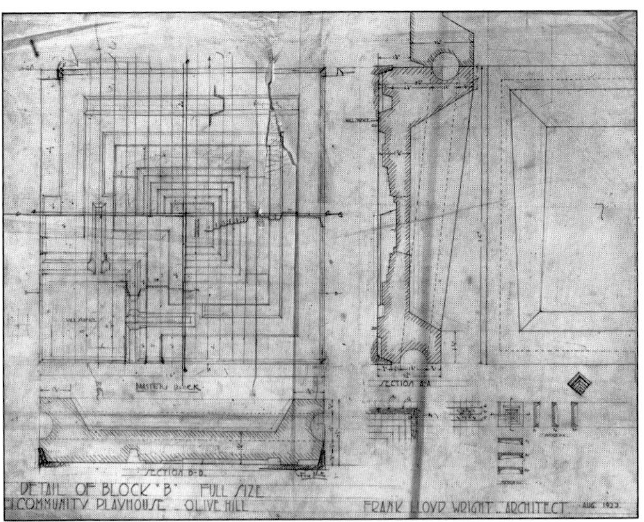

48. Community Playhouse, the Little Dipper (project), Block B details. FLLW FDN, 2301.019

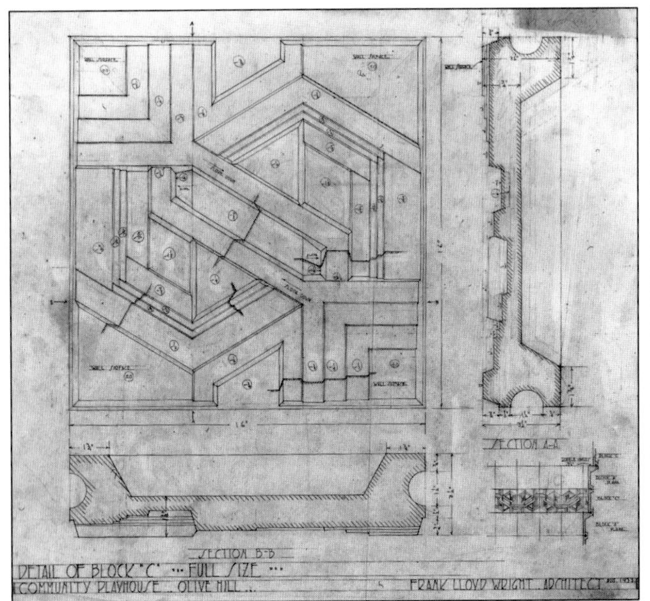

49. Community Playhouse, the Little Dipper (project), Block C details. FLLW FDN, 2301.015

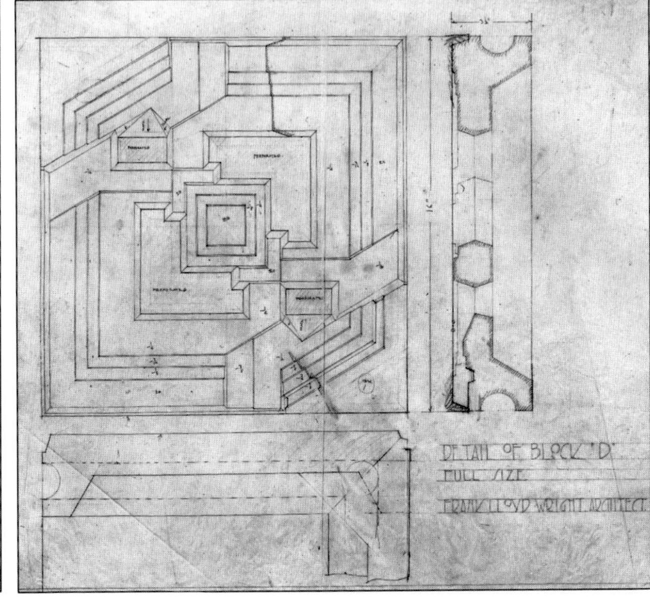

50. Community Playhouse, the Little Dipper (project), Block D details. FLLW FDN, 2301.018

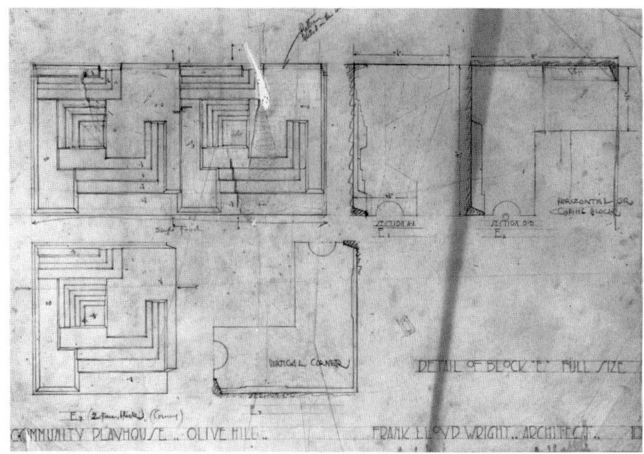

51. Community Playhouse, the Little Dipper (project), Block E details. FLLW FDN, 2301.020

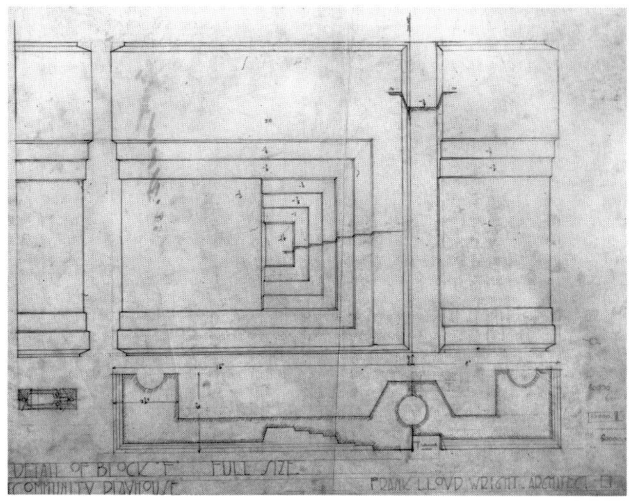

52. Community Playhouse, the Little Dipper (project), Block F details. FLLW FDN, 2301.016

At some point in the negotiations, Wright responded with a new proposal to transform the Little Dipper into a memorial to Theodore Barnsdall, Aline Barnsdall's father. The scheme was predicated on completion of the playhouse, with a new terrace and pergola extending to the north (Fig. 53). Concrete block was indicated for retaining walls, floors, and supports for the roof trellis over the pergola (Fig. 54). The memorial would have been a handsome addition to the Little Dipper, significantly increasing its presence on the hill.

Barnsdall's failure to pursue either project may have stemmed less from bureaucratic interference than from revised plans for Olive Hill. There had been speculation that she intended to deed part of the property to the city for an art center and park. In December 1923 she announced plans to donate ten acres, including Hollyhock House. The proposed gift was declined the following March.[7] It was after this that she turned to R. M. Schindler, who "by the way . . . was ready," Wright noted acidly, to turn the incomplete Little Dipper into a garden seating area, pergola, and pond.[8] Schindler used Wright's system of reinforced-concrete block construction to complete the project (Fig. 55). Its ruinous state led city employees to partially demolish the structure after the 1994 earthquake.

Barnsdall's disenchantment with Olive Hill coincided with Wright's own disillusionment with southern California. He had tried hard to build a practice here, but to no end. Lloyd recalled in September 1970 that

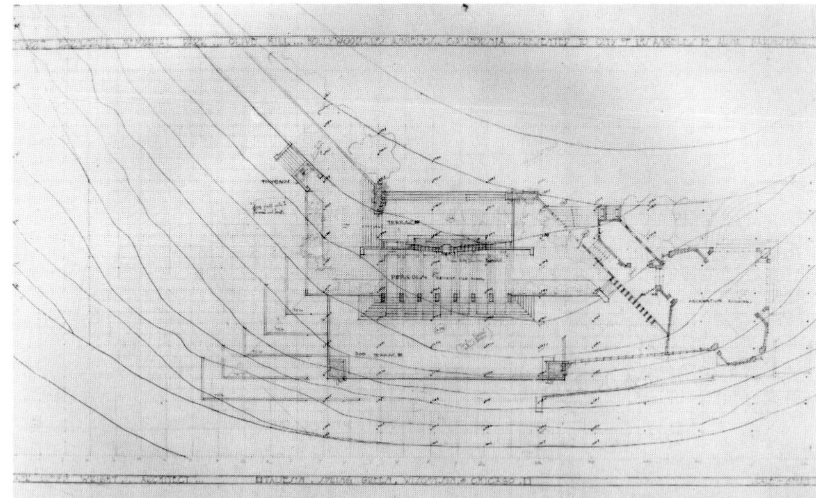

53. Theodore Barnsdall Memorial (project), Olive Hill, Los Angeles, California, plan, 1923. Collection of the City of Los Angeles, Departments of Recreation and Parks and Cultural Affairs

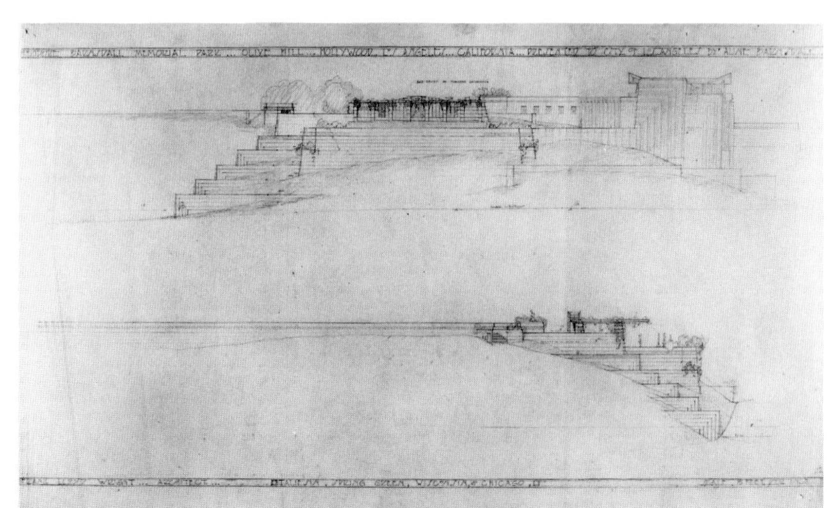

54. Theodore Barnsdall Memorial (project), elevation. Collection of the City of Los Angeles, Departments of Recreation and Parks and Cultural Affairs

> F. L. W. was trying very hard to get started on the West Coast, and he had all kinds of projects going out here, but somehow he could not get the people to play ball with him. He spent considerable time with the Chandlers and General Sherman, trying to interest them in his architectural schemes—they were very amused and entertained by F. L. W., but were unreceptive.[9]

Wright had been prescient in his April letter to Sullivan:

> I long for the substantial background of old Chicago—This is all "to be"—

55. R. M. Schindler, garden seating area, Olive Hill, Los Angeles, California, ca. 1924. Collection of the author, gift of Mrs. Richard Neutra

> The region has been cruelly "exploited"—and is so still. I don't know if they want anything in the way of the "third dimension" yet. We'll see—[10]

The event that should have changed his fortunes was the survival of the Imperial Hotel in the midst of the earthquake and fire that occurred in Tokyo on September 1, 1923. Although the hotel was reported "Burned to Ground" by the *Los Angeles Examiner* on September 3, and "In Path of Fire" by the *Los Angeles Times* the next day, Wright refused to believe the stories and castigated the editors for their audacity.[11] A friend of Lloyd's, Merle Armitage, described

> a daily trip to every newspaper in town. . . . Approaching city editors, Wright would shake his stick at them; with fire in his eyes, he would shout, "I'm going to sue you. This is blasphemy. The Imperial Hotel is not damaged and you are going to pay *me* damages for what you are doing to my reputation."[12]

Finally, a direct wire secured by the *Times* publisher, Harry Chandler, confirmed that the building was standing.[13] Wright recognized the potential for favorable publicity from this circumstance, but confided to Sullivan, "Upon my word I don't know how to go about it. . . . It is surprising how little is accomplished without continuous follow up publicity."[14]

In fact, even before word of the hotel's survival reached Wright, he proposed to rebuild Tokyo with reinforced-concrete block:

> Tokio should be reconstructed upon a more permanent and rational plan,—her wires underground, her streets widened and shaded, the principal residence and business areas restricted to two or three stories.
>
> The first story and if three stories, the second should be hollow or double walls made of reinforced concrete blocks—interlaced by ¼" steel rods every 16", vertically and horizontally. These walls should extend to the window sills of the top story or be used as a railing for balconies or for the top story windows. Upon these walls, resting well within them the continuous concrete floor slabs should be placed at proper levels, the horizontal reinforcing bars interlocking with the vertical bars of the walls.
>
> Within the outer walls and resting on the upper floor-slab should be set and securely doweled the lightest possible scientific timber framing of walls and roof of top story, wired laterally together with telegraph or other rustless wire.
>
> The roof should be plastered and covered with light copper tiles, the outside and inside of the upper story walls covered with plaster or other plastic fireproof material, the ceilings covered with a combination of wood and sheet copper ornamented in infinite variety. . . .
>
> The foundations should be flexible, that is, concrete piles poured into holes made in the mud or ground and a reinforced linear slab built on the mud as on a cushion. The softer the ground upon which they rested, the safer the buildings would be, if the proper proportions were observed in the construction. Concrete blocks with steel interlaced two ways and joints poured are advocated because a really flexible wall is thus secured less liable to damage from pressure or tension and one that would show no cracks. The light continuous floor-slabs for all floor areas below the roof—would insure practical safety from devastation by fire.

These comments are part of a larger essay, "Why the Skyscraper?" dated September 8, 1923, and published a short time later as *Experimenting with Human Lives*.[15] They are important here as Wright's earliest known statement about his concrete-block system and as evidence that within months of undertaking the experiment, he was thinking of universal applications.

Wright went back to Wisconsin in October 1923, announcing plans to return to Los Angeles in a few weeks.[16] Significantly, however, when he was interviewed on his return to the Midwest he mentioned only grand projects: Doheny Ranch and a resort development at Lake Tahoe, which, he said, was to cost millions.[17] Individual houses were of little consequence. Wright was in Los Angeles again briefly in late 1923, but by February 1924 there seemed little doubt that his office was to be in Chicago. Uncharacteristically, he had succumbed quickly. Reminiscing in his autobiography, the architect confirmed his contempt for the area: "I was looking around me in Los Angeles—disgusted. [It was] the desert of shallow effects." [18]

The final three concrete-block houses built in Los Angeles were constructed mainly in Wright's absence, between 1924 and 1926; although he visited the sites from time to time, he remained largely in the Midwest, at Taliesin. Responsibility for supervision was turned over to Lloyd, who had to make construction decisions and resolve complications and emergencies on his own or after delayed correspondence with his father. Although the three houses were built nearly simultaneously, the Storer house was first in sequence.

Storer house, Los Angeles

The Storer house may have been built on speculation, and there is slim evidence that Wright was a participant in the venture. Dr. John Storer is usually identified as the client; however, the building permit and some of Wright's drawings indicate that the house was designed for the Superior Building Company. Confusingly, Wright's address at 1645 North Vermont (Residence A, Olive Hill) is given on the permit.[19] Storer (1868–1933), a homeopathic physician who had practiced in Chicago, had moved to southern California around 1917. Failing the California medical licensing examination in 1919, he turned to real-estate development.[20] To this end the Superior Building Company was incorporated on September 6, 1921.[21] Presumably Storer was the principal in this company, as its address at 1920 Morgan (now Grammercy) Place corresponds with his before he moved into the block house.

The Storer house is another hybrid. It is a translation into concrete-block construction of Wright's second 1922 project for Charles P. Lowes (?–1963), for whom Schindler built a very different house the following year. The Lowes site was in Eagle Rock, near Pasadena. In

56. Charles P. Lowes house (project), Eagle Rock, California, perspective, 1922. FLLW FDN, 2202.004

Wright's design, the house rises from a paved platform that extends toward the street in front as an entrance terrace with a large rectangular pool and to the rear as a patio (Fig. 56). The main volume of the house contains the dining room on the ground floor, the living room above. Two bedrooms, positioned midway between the two principal floors, are in the one-story wing to the right. The kitchen and garage are to the left (Figs. 57, 58).

Wright seems to have first adapted the scheme to concrete-block construction for the original client.[22] He expressed the same interest in offset blocks that he had shown in the design for the Community Playhouse, a refinement giving the composition greater plasticity than either the prototype or the finished version (Fig. 59). One drawing bears the notes "Storer original" and "unit system" in Wright's hand, though the site and plan are still essentially those of the Lowes house, and the building as drawn could not have been constructed on Storer's lot (Fig. 60).

Storer's site was in the Cielo Vista Terrace tract, which was subdivided in

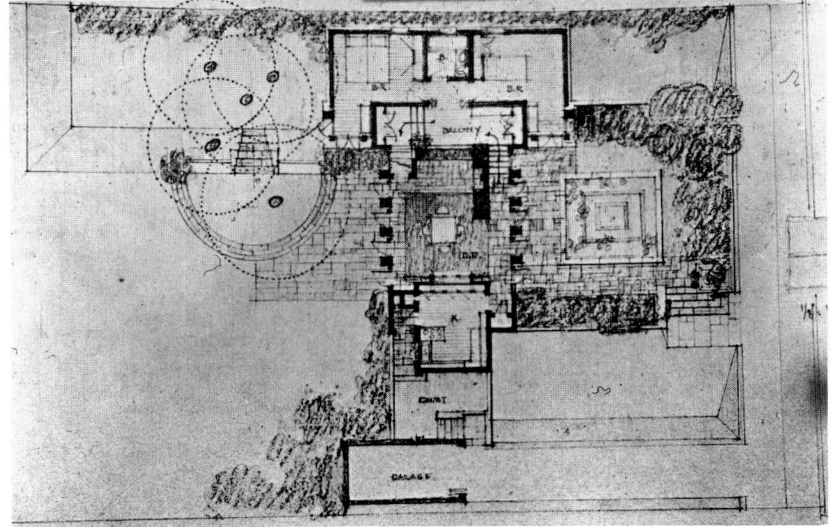

57. Lowes house (project), lower-level plan. FLLW FDN, 2202.002

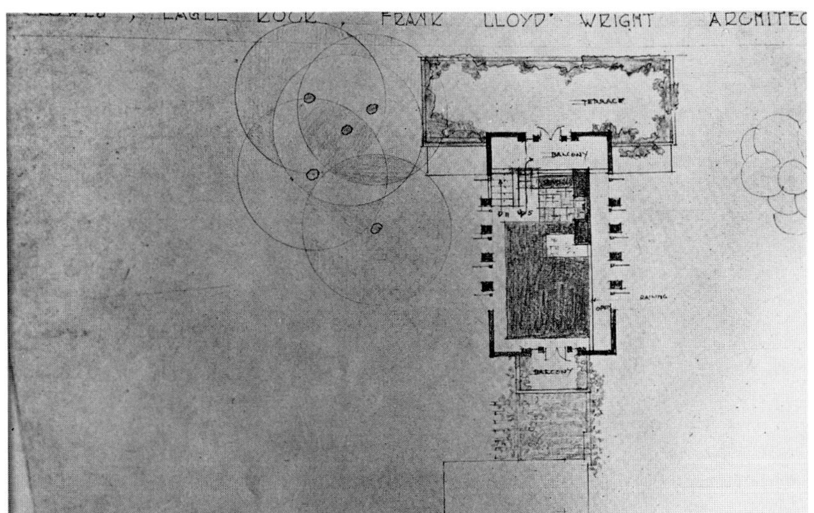

58. Lowes house (project), upper-level plan. FLLW FDN, 2202.003

early 1922 as part of the westward expansion of Hollywood. The tract was in the foothills and offered ocean, mountain, and city views; the streets were laid out by Aurele Vermeulen, a landscape architect who later reviewed Wright's drawings for San Marcos in the Desert.[23] Storer purchased an irregular five-sided parcel that rose steeply up to the rear and was itself overlooked by building sites above (Fig. 61, Lot 3). Wright oriented the house with the southern boundary (truncating a corner of the garage) and extended the front terrace to the easement line.

When the house was redrawn for Storer, several adjustments were made

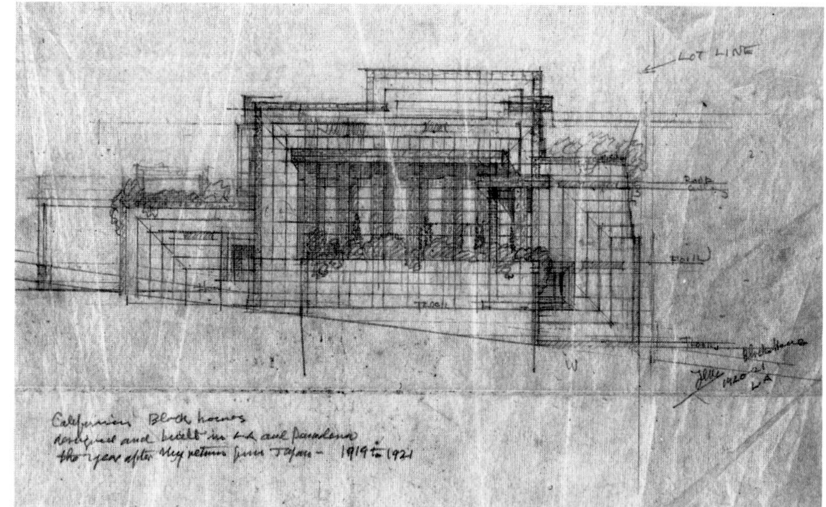

59. Lowes house (project), 1923? FLLW FDN, 2304.001

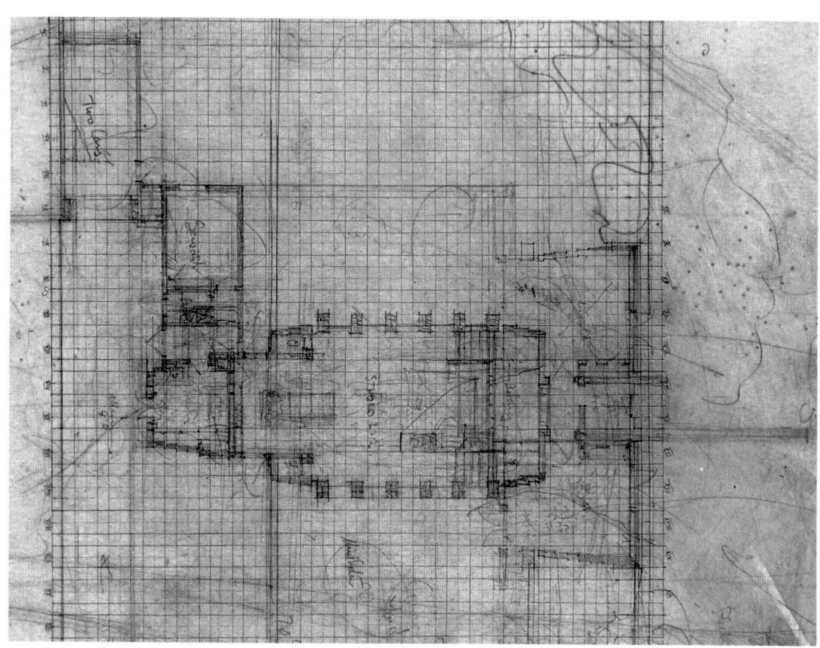

60. Lowes house (project), lower-level plan, 1923? FLLW FDN, 2202.001

for the new site and client. Most significantly, the plan was rotated 180 degrees. Back became front (Fig. 62). Other changes included a new wing behind the kitchen, containing a servant's room and bath; a repositioned garage; and the addition of a second story to the bedroom wing, the two floors being dropped a few steps below the two main floors (Fig. 63). The living room remained on the uppermost level, as before, and opened to terraces at the east and west ends (Fig. 64). The finished elevations closely

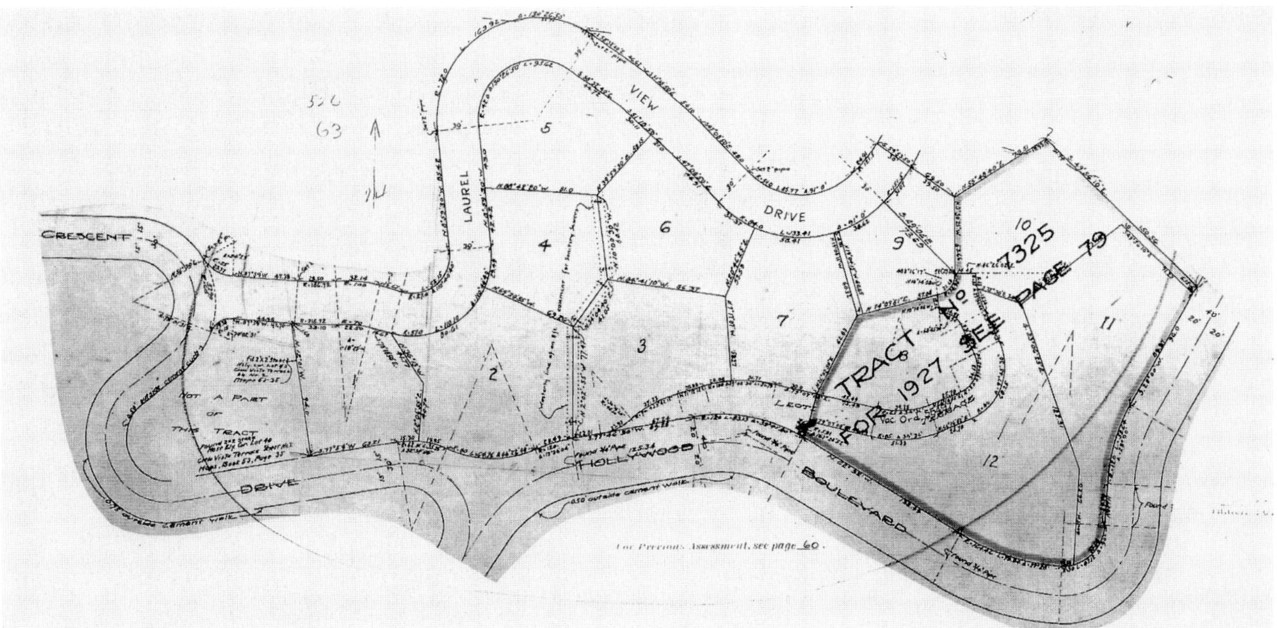

61. Dr. John Storer house, Los Angeles, California, site plan, 1923. Los Angeles County Assessor, Book 526 (1920–27), p. 63

recall the original Lowes project. The blocks were laid without offsets, and the projecting awnings, so necessary to the composition and present in the Lowes project but seemingly erased in the preliminary block scheme, are again indicated (Fig. 65).

The expression of structure is especially straightforward in the Storer house. Parallel rows of hollow concrete-block piers on the front and rear elevations and paired piers on the end elevations support wooden beams and joists in the central volume of the building (Fig. 66). The structural nature of the piers at the south end of the building is expressed by narrow vertical windows separating them from the curtain walls. The beams in the bedroom wing are set into the concrete-block walls on which they rest (Fig. 67). The intellectual economy of the structure extends to the number of block shapes needed for construction: the design was worked out with eleven different basic units.

Unlike those for the Millard house, specifications for the concrete blocks for the Storer, Freeman, and Ennis houses survive, although they seem to have been followed with varying degrees of exactitude. They call for the blocks to be made from sand or decomposed granite. A formula of four parts aggregate to one part portland cement was to be combined with water in a mechanical mixer and blended until it would stand up when squeezed by hand. The mixture was to be used within a half hour. Blocks were to be formed under pressure in machine-made metal molds, which

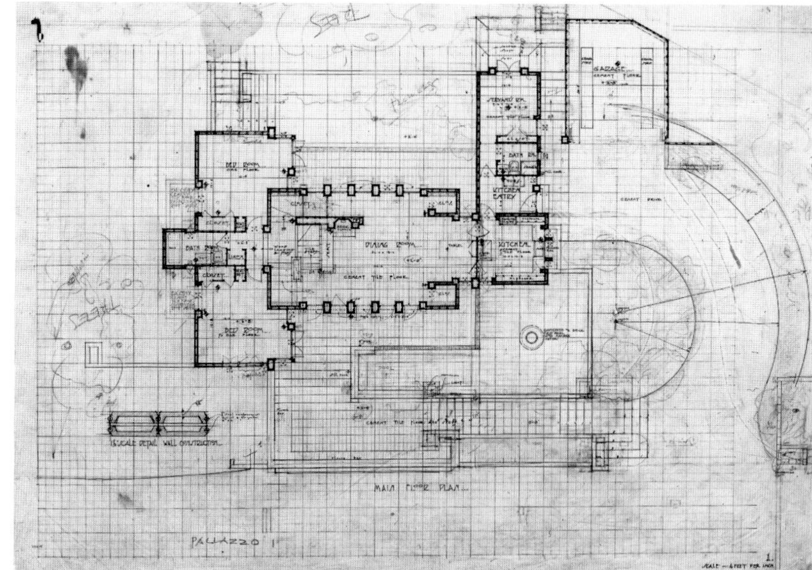

62. Storer house, main-floor plan, with a detail of wall construction. FLLW FDN, 2304.008

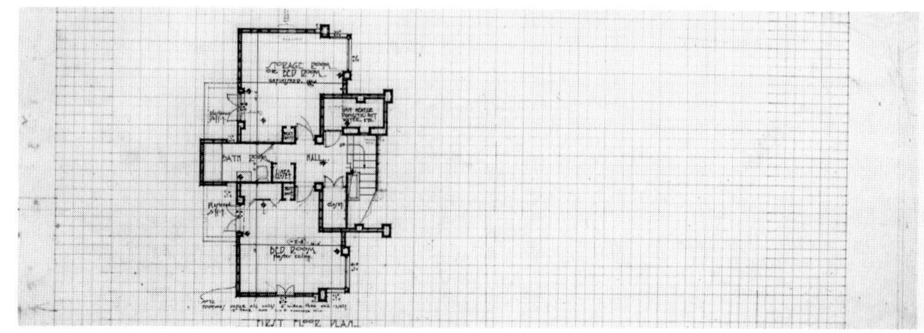

63. Storer house, first-floor plan. FLLW FDN, 2304.009

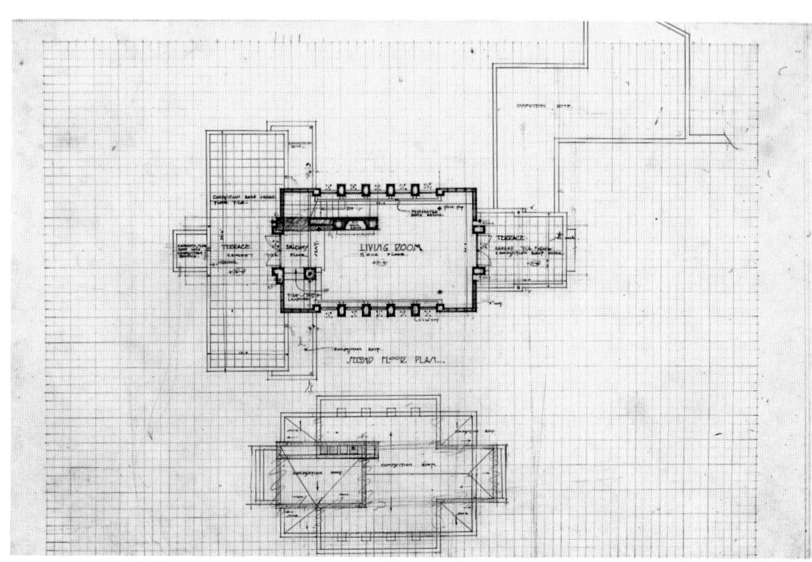

64. Storer house, second-floor plan and roof plan. FLLW FDN, 2304.010

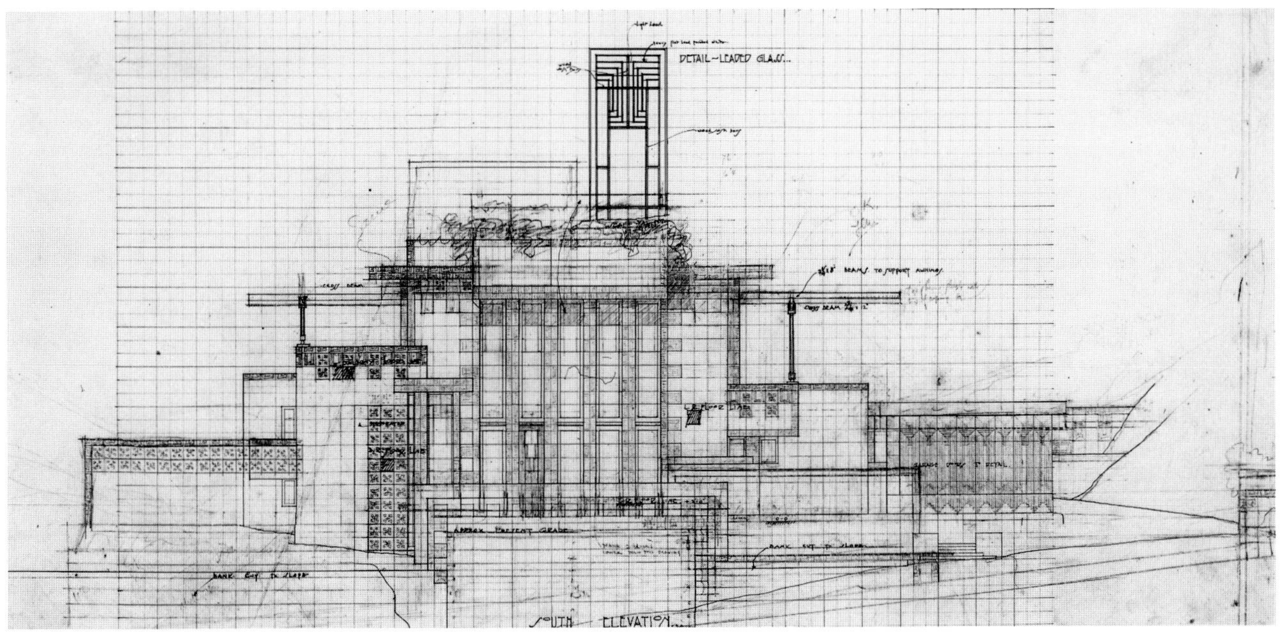

65. Storer house, south elevation. Various details have been erased and redrawn: the roof profile has been modified to correspond to actual construction; and a roof terrace proposed in 1935 has been added. FLLW FDN, 2304.011

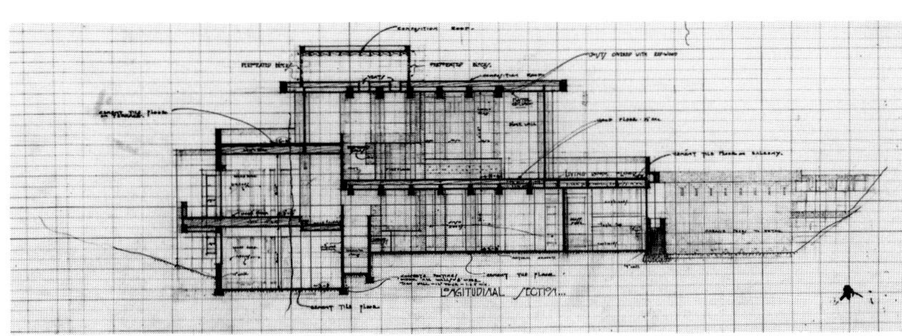

66. Storer house, longitudinal section. FLLW FDN, 2304.014

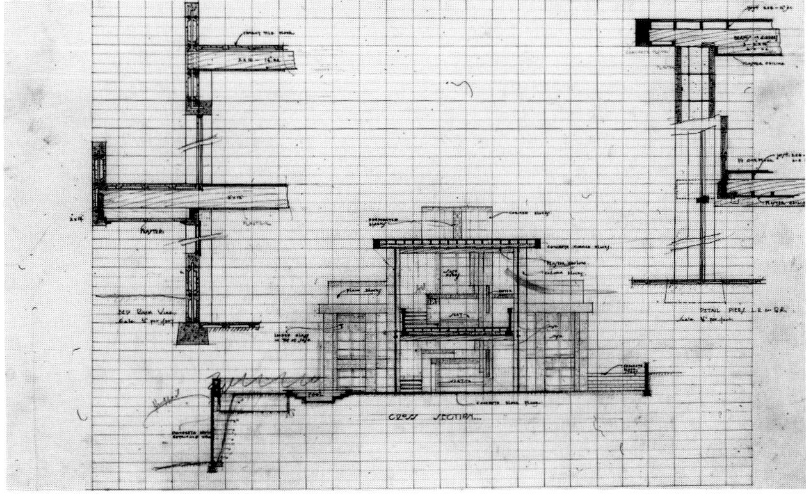

67. Storer house, cross section and details. FLLW FDN, 2304.015

would produce the higher level of precision that the new system of mortarless construction demanded. They were to be removed from the molds immediately, placed over wood saddles, and not allowed to dry within a period of ten days.[24]

Construction of the Storer house was begun inauspiciously by Parlee in late 1923. On December 15, approximately five weeks after the building permit was issued, Storer sued Parlee to regain possession of the equipment used to fabricate the concrete blocks.[25] At this point, the role of contractor fell to Lloyd, who was to encounter numerous pragmatic and aesthetic obstacles and ultimately the wrath of Storer.

As in the Millard house, construction appears to have proceeded efficiently at first; a photograph dated February 17, 1924, shows the walls and piers up to the second-story level and large supplies of blocks ready for assembly (Fig. 68). However, the record reveals that money was an ongoing problem. In April Wright indicated that it was "impossible . . . to assist him [Storer] until after May first and doubtful then." An undated letter from Lloyd then states, "Storer stops all work, pending assistance from you." And on September 15 Wright reported to Lloyd that "John writes me for $3,000 to finish. I can not understand the thing at all." Finally, on October 10, Wright instructed Lloyd to "tell Storer to draw on me for two thousand." [26]

As the house neared completion, Lloyd expressed concern about the result. His father responded on September 15 that "color would help the Storer house—the awnings especially should go on at once. Color if judiciously applied to the piers would help a lot. I think what you say is

68. Storer house, construction photograph, February 17, 1924. Courtesy of Eric Lloyd Wright

69. Storer house. Courtesy of Kameki Tsuchiura

probably true as to its lacking joy. We'll see however before we finish."[27] On October 25 Lloyd sought his father's comments on the awnings, then in place (Fig. 69).[28] Apparently designed by Lloyd, they were much bolder than Wright had indicated in his own drawing, and they were supported by pipes instead of the elaborate copper-sheathed spires first indicated. A completion notice for the house was filed on October 27, 1924.[29]

Unlike Alice Millard and some of the other clients who commissioned concrete-block buildings, Storer has left no record of what he thought of his house as a work of architecture. Although he moved in, the house was placed on the market shortly after completion and was sold in 1927.[30] The first documented impression we find of the house, other than that provided by the Wrights, came in 1931 from Pauline Schindler, by then separated from her husband and renting it:

> the room in which i sit writing is a form so superb that i am constantly conscious of an immense obligation to mr. wright. when my small son,—eight years old,—was feeling very tender toward me one day he said, "muv, i love you as much. . . . as i love this room." such superlative joy does it give us both. like a drama of sophocles, a violin sonata of haendel.[31]

A less ethereal response came from Henry-Russell Hitchcock, who observed that the house "seems to lack privacy," in comparison with the Millard house.[32] He probably was referring to the transparency of the central pavilion, visible from the house on the lot above and from the street below. In fact, the Storer house offers marked contrasts between its public and private spaces; the effect is part temple and part grotto. The living room, with its fifteen-foot ceiling, is the spatial climax; its rows of piers, alternating with voids of glass, and its elevated position, providing an expansive view of the city below, strongly reinforce the temple analogy (Plates 3, 4). The bedrooms, on the other hand, are closed, cavelike spaces; one is partially buried in the hillside.

Further observations about the house can be drawn from comparing the plan as designed to changes made during construction. In plan the house was built basically as Wright intended. Yet the circulation pattern is one of its weakest points. The house is rather beautifully approached from the street by three terraces, providing changes in level and orientation and an increasing sense of enclosure. At the point of entry, however, the clarity of the route diminishes. Five glass doors open from the dining room to the terrace, offering a minor intellectual challenge. Wright's drawing calls for the second door from the left to be of wood. Without this necessary clue, it is somewhat difficult to determine which is the principal entrance. The door at the extreme left, or western end, is the first encountered and is the obvious choice, although entering at this point creates problems. The house as first designed for Charles P. Lowes had its entrance directly into the dining room; the fireplace mass and stairs were to the right, at the long end of the room. When Wright reoriented the plan for Storer, the point of entry was changed to the opposite side and end of the room; and the stairs were brought from behind the fireplace, where they were on axis with the length of the room, to the front. Entering the Storer house through the westernmost door, one confronts two sets of stairs positioned ambiguously to the left; the dining room is to the right. The space lacks architectural focus and offers the newcomer a series of mixed clues — too many choices — upon entering.

With the fireplace mass as a pivot for circulation, the stairs serve the two-story bedroom wing and lead through the living room up to the west terrace. Ideally, the path should end here, but it does not. It continues past the doors to a processional dead end: a blank wall lies straight ahead; to the right is a gratuitous view of the narrow space between the chimney and the north wall of the living room.

Another significant problem results from the reconfiguration of the roof. Like the Lowes project, the Storer house was designed with a flat roof that extends beyond the four sides of the building, terminating the upward thrust of the piers and forming cantilevered lintels. The design was modified to include a sort of monitor roof without clerestories, extending the length of the living room and projecting over the east and west doors leading to the second-floor terraces. Presumably the roof was added to gain needed head room over the west door; aesthetically, its presence seriously compromises the clarity of the original concept. Also, the projecting edges of the roof are trimmed with blocks, a purely decorative application that Wright did not repeat in similar circumstances at the Freeman house.

Further evidence of Wright's wish to use the blocks in an overhead span appears inside the house. The working drawings specify blocks laid as tiles on the floors of the dining room, service wing, and terraces, but there are no ceilings. During construction, a concrete slab with exposed blocks on its underside was added to the east end of the dining room; presumably, the blocks served as formwork for the slab. The blocks do not function structurally, of course, but this is still the first demonstration, however tentative, of Wright's mono-material vision: "Floors, ceilings, walls all the same."

Improvements And Changes In Block Technique

Four different block patterns are used in the Storer house; the house is the only one built that employs more than one design. The patterns are applied systematically throughout the building, the geometry of each serving a specific purpose. The most common patterned block is a corner unit eight by sixteen inches on a side and decorated with a concave pattern of concentric half squares that read as a whole when two faces of the block are seen. Variations are a coping block with three faces, and a three-corner block (Fig. 70). Its reciprocal is a sixteen-inch convex pattern, returning at

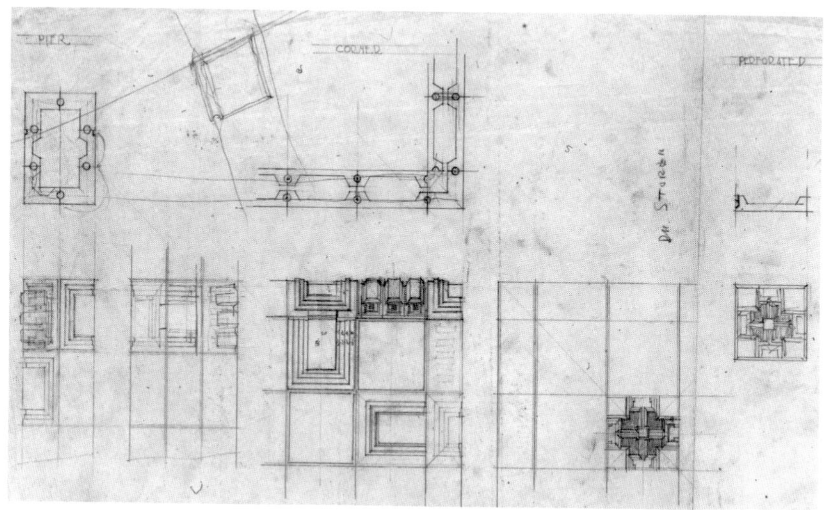

70. Storer house, pier and corner-block assembly and block patterns. FLLW FDN, 2304.004

one end only. Another corner block is decorated with three projecting rectangles; these blocks are used for piers and the living room chimney breast. The last patterned block is a perforated cruciform, used for screens and in the parapets, often with lights behind.

Composing with multiple block patterns did not produce consistent results, particularly in the interior of the Storer house. It lacks the systematic resolution of block pattern with purpose seen on the exterior, and the patterns occasionally collide visually when they are juxtaposed. This is especially true in the walls projecting from the fireplaces, which admittedly were modified during construction (Fig. 71).

The finished house, though not without strong merit, was a compromise, the result of a client with insufficient capital, an absentee architect,

71. Storer house, dining room, looking west, ca. 1924. Courtesy of Eric Lloyd Wright

and an inexperienced construction supervisor. Though self-deprecation was not characteristic of Wright, he expressed his sentiments openly to Lloyd:

> I've just come from the Storer House. It's a tradgedy [*sic*], from my standpoint, but I can see how hard you've worked to pull it out—and approve many things you did. I have been thinking things over and I guess in the heat and shame of the failure and loss I've been thinking more of myself than of you, more heedless than I ought to be. You've got to stay here and the thing ought to be fixed up for you as well as may be. I took that stand with the Dr—who broke out bitterly against you. I did what I could to show him where he came in and I came in—as well as for our share of the blame.[33]

In 1935 the fifth owners of the Storer house, Charles H. and Helen K. Druffel, encountered a problem not uncommon to owners of hillside view lots: neighbors objected to trees blocking their vista. On June 7 the owners of three lots directly above the Storer house filed suit, charging that the Druffels had allowed eucalyptus trees growing on their property and on the boundary line between the properties to grow to such a height that views and light were obstructed and that the plaintiffs' property consequently had depreciated in value.[34]

Three days after the litigation was initiated, Helen Druffel approached Wright, explaining that when they had bought the house it was entirely surrounded by eucalyptus trees, but that by the time escrow closed all the trees had been topped and the house "towering above" took away from the beauty of her own place. Now, more than a year later, the people were insisting that the trees be topped again. Druffel inquired if it would be all right to build a roof garden on top of her house, planting a four-foot hedge of eugenias along the roof edge, so that the other house would not show so prominently.[35]

Wright responded with a plan for minimal changes that took their cues from the lines of the existing structure. He suggested enclosing the roof with a parapet the height of the existing chimney. The chimney would be raised six block courses and enlarged to the north, to accommodate an access stair. A cantilevered awning would extend from the chimney wall. Wright made the revisions on an existing elevation drawing, erasing or drawing through unwanted lines and indicating new construction (see Fig. 65).

The roof-garden scheme was never carried out. Even though Wright did not encourage the change, it would have enhanced the house. The parapet strengthens the front elevation, partly by obscuring the roof profile. The new design also brings the circulation through the building to a satisfying conclusion. The roof is reached from the living room by an extension of the existing stair that winds around the fireplace. The path continues past the doors to the west terrace to a new stair, constructed in the space between the fireplace and the north wall; a dead end is replaced with opportunity for further exploration.

FREEMAN HOUSE, LOS ANGELES

Samuel (1889–1981) and Harriet (1890–1986) Freeman were the youngest and least affluent of Wright's southern California clients. He was a jewelry salesman; she was interested in modern dance and pursued progressive social causes. They may have learned of Wright and his work on Olive Hill through her sister, Leah Lovell; late in life, Harriet Freeman recalled that "after seeing Wright's buildings there, I couldn't imagine choosing another architect."[36] Though soon angry with Wright, the Freemans remained in their house until their deaths, some sixty years later.

Their building site was in the Hollywood hills, above the intersection of Highland and Franklin avenues. It was small and sloped steeply to the south; the boundaries were approximately seventy by seventy-five feet, but also included a narrow, wedge-shaped appendage (Fig. 72, Lot 3). Its selling point was the view: all of Hollywood lay below.

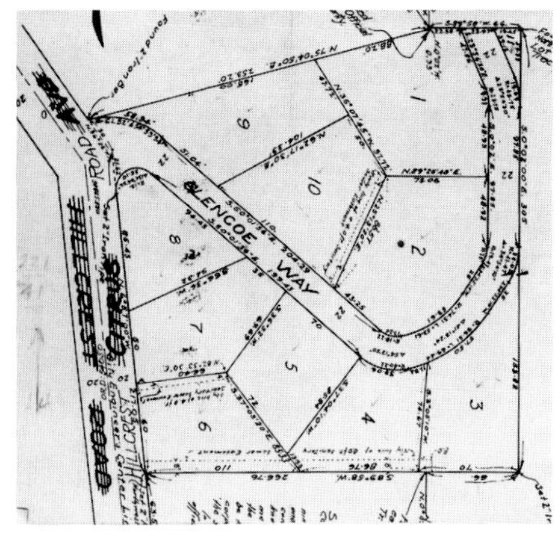

72. Samuel and Harriet Freeman house, Los Angeles, California, site plan, 1924. Los Angeles County Assessor, Book 221 (1920–27), p. 41

Wright responded by turning the house away from the street and opening it to the view: the front elevation is essentially a blank wall; the back is almost entirely glazed. As he had done before, Wright began with a composition of offset blocks which was later simplified (Fig. 73). The plan is on two levels, with the living room and kitchen above and two bedrooms and a bath below. Wright placed the house on the extreme northern boundary of the site, taking advantage of the extra wedge-shaped property for the garage.

No project was reworked as thoroughly during the design process as the tiny Freeman house. Two sets of working drawings were finished one month apart, in January and February 1924. Comparison of these drawings reveals that the changes were less formal than technical, suggesting that they resulted not from aesthetic indecision, but from structural necessity. Both schemes rely partially on the principle of the cantilever: wooden roof and floor structures are slipped like shelves into a perimeter

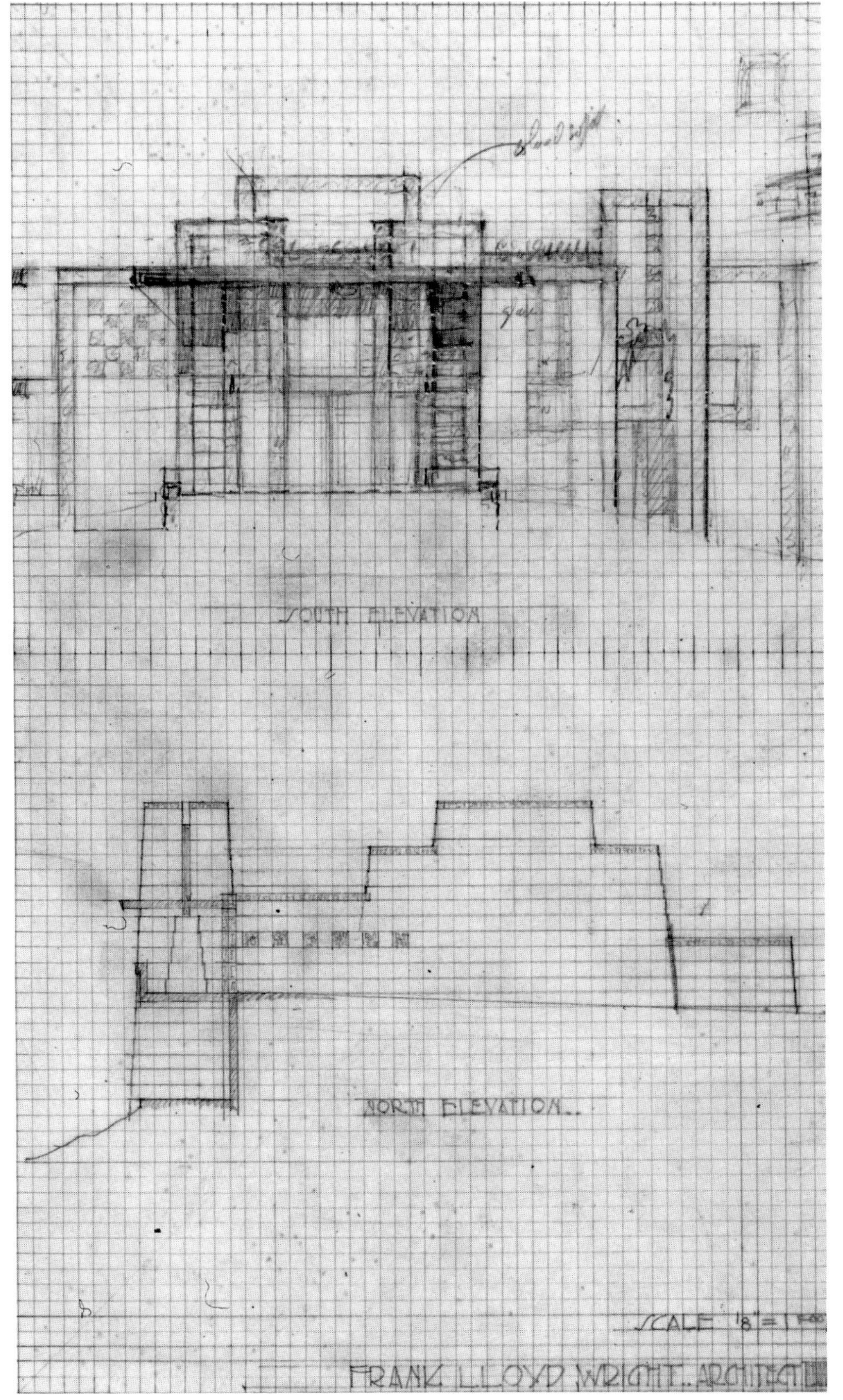

73. Freeman house, elevations. FLLW FDN, 2402.005

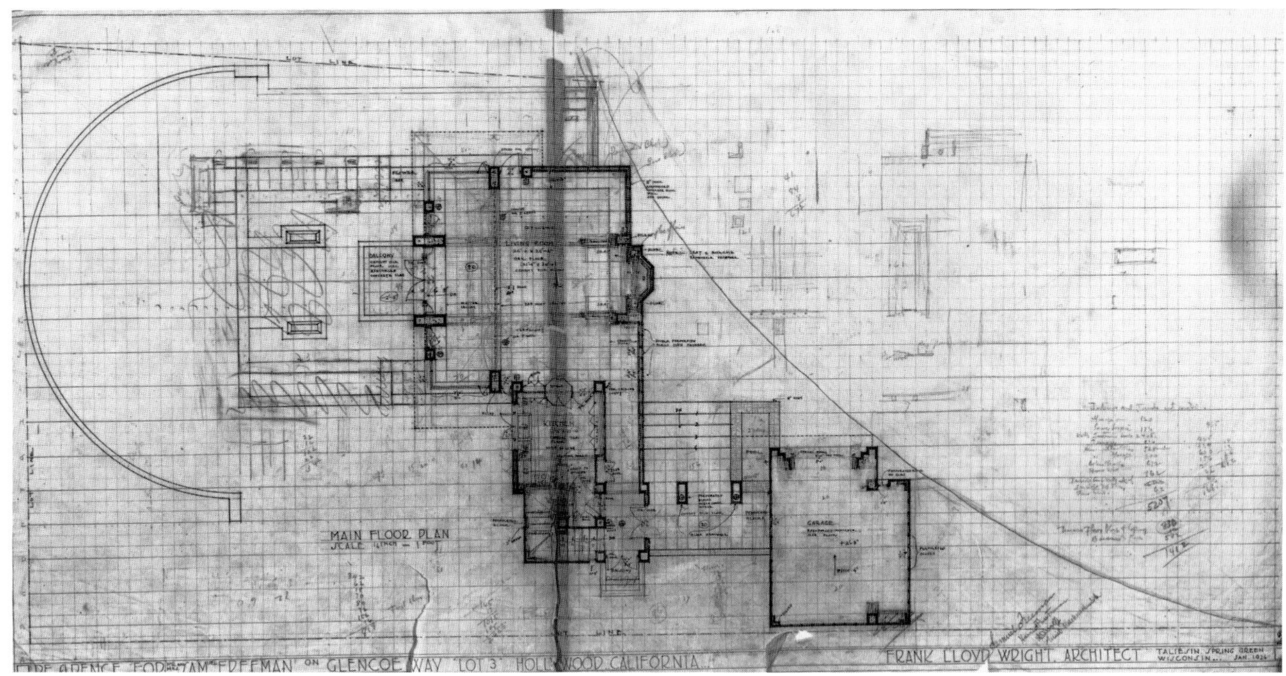

74. Freeman house, main-floor plan, January 1924. FLLW FDN, 2402.015

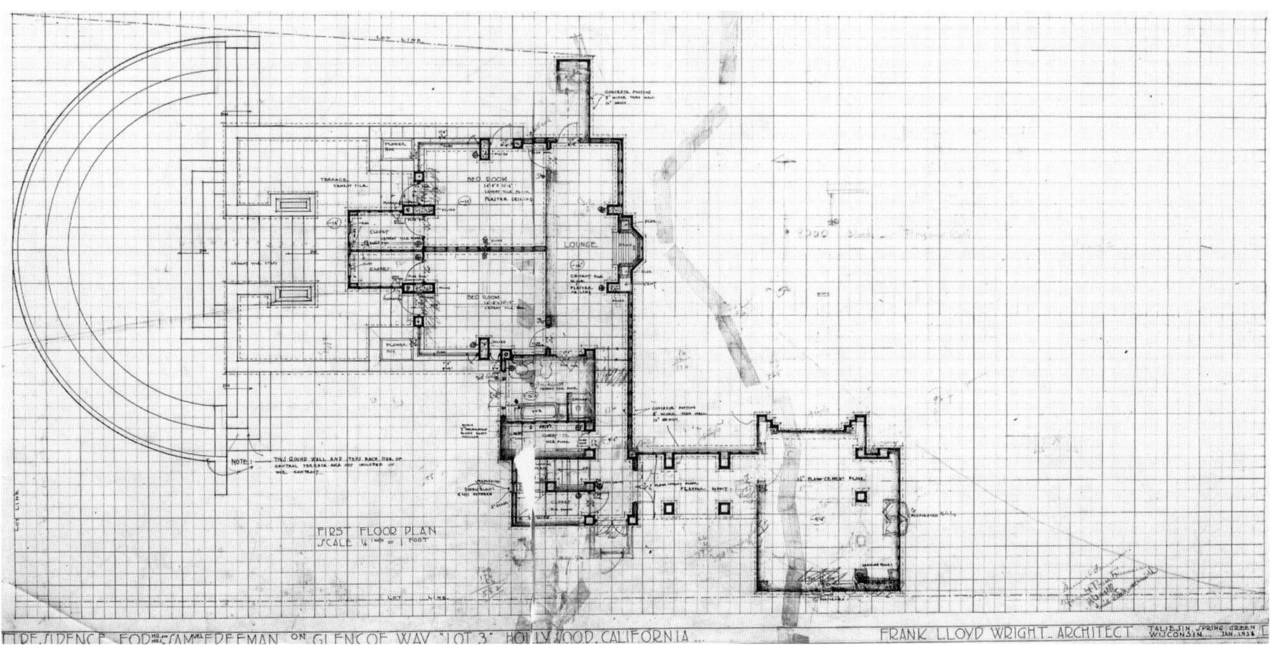

75. Freeman house, first-floor plan, January 1924. FLLW FDN, 2402.014

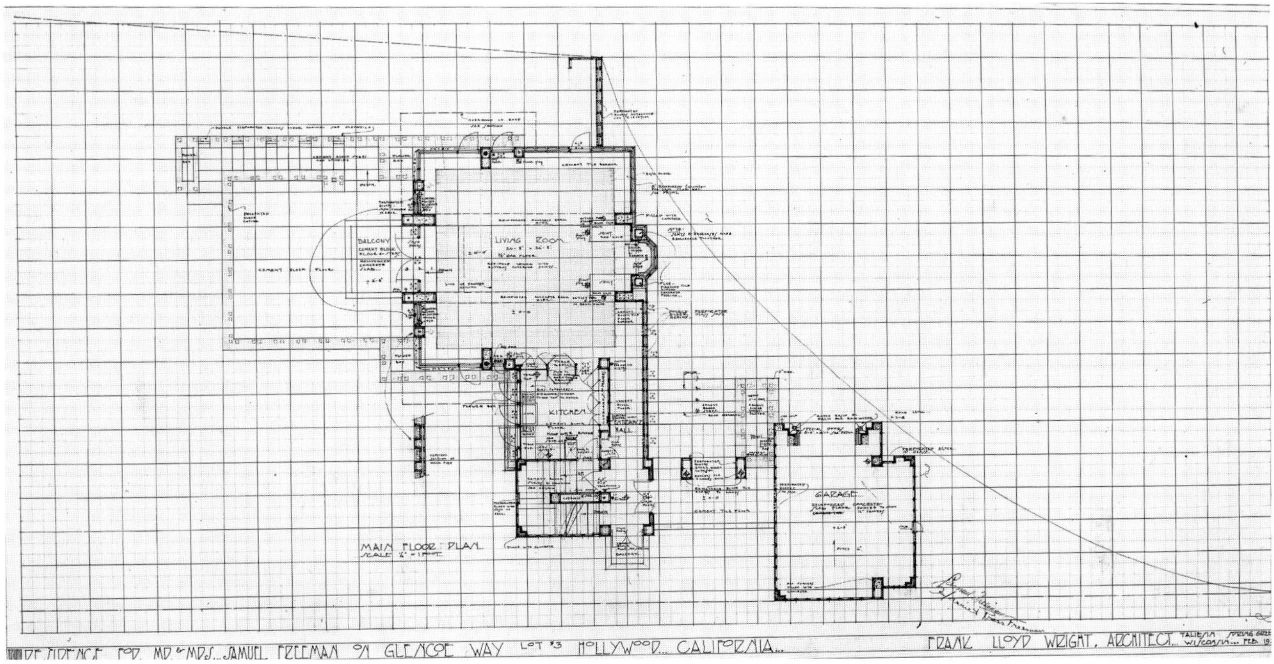

76. Freeman house, main-floor plan, February 1924. FLLW FDN, 2402.026

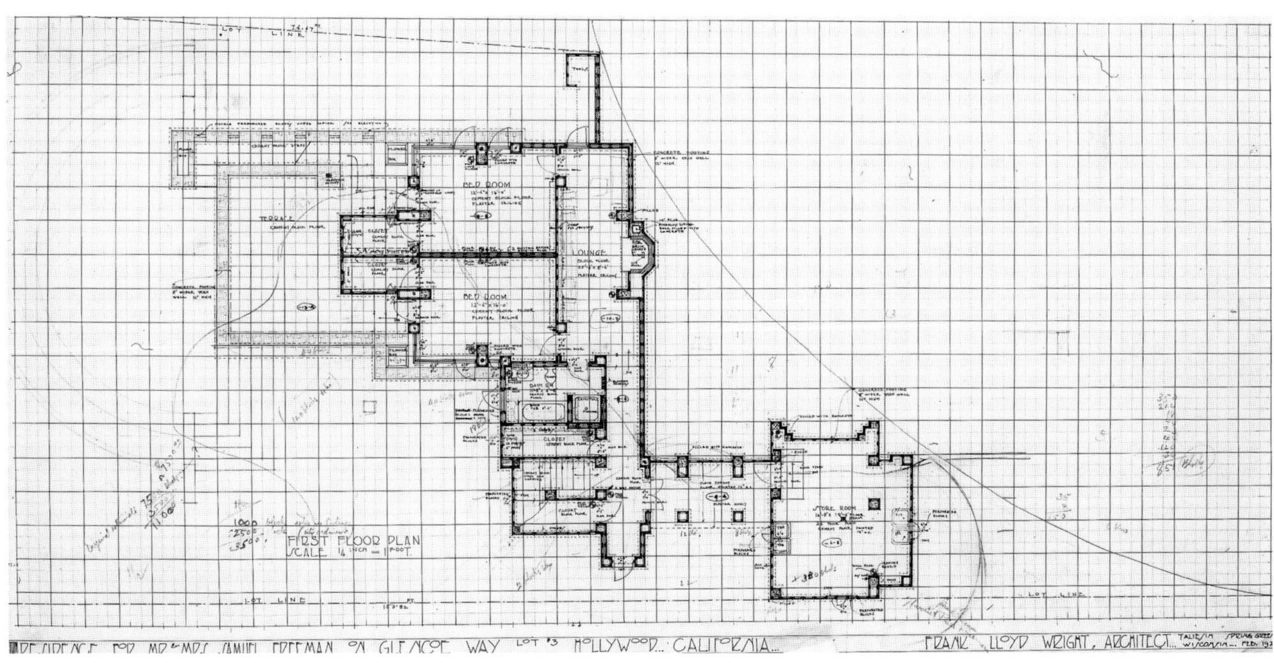

77. Freeman house, first-floor plan, February 1924. FLLW FDN, 2402.025

network of concrete-filled block piers. The effect is enhanced by a pair of two-story mitered corner windows that begin at the soffit and continue past the projecting edges of the upper floor, dematerializing traditional notions of support. Solid walls are formed with concrete block between the piers.

In the first scheme, the downward thrust resulting from building on so steep a site is acknowledged by a doubling up of the piers on the north-south axis. The east-west piers are linked by an I beam that serves to stabilize the building in a direction perpendicular to the natural forces (Figs. 74, 75). It is easy to speculate that this structure could not have withstood the lateral forces created by the steep hillside site, and that Wright quickly realized that additional north-south reinforcement was necessary.

With this in mind, the architect completed a second set of working drawings the following month, February 1924. The east-west I beam was replaced by a pair of reinforced-concrete beams spanning the living room north to south (Figs. 76, 77). These beams tie the seismically vulnerable south side of the building to the more substantial northern side. Apparently at this point an east-west concrete beam on the line of the original I beam was also introduced, although invisibly, and concrete reinforcement was added to the cantilevered corners of the living room, adjacent to the two-story windows.[37] The forms of the house were modified accordingly.

The house was built from this second set of plans. On January 26, Wright and Samuel Freeman signed a contract stipulating that the house would cost $9,100.[38] Three days later, the Freemans signed another agreement with H. J. D. Wolff, a contractor who had worked on Olive Hill, that the house would be finished in six months, or on August 1, 1924.[39] Nothing more is known of Wolff except that he had no role in building the house; on February 26 the Freemans and Wright signed a third agreement, appointing Lloyd as contractor. The final agreement contains a clause reminiscent of Wright's contract with Alice Millard: if the cost of the Freeman house exceeded $10,000, Wright agreed "to furnish whatever sum may be necessary to complete the work according to Plans and Specifications and to become a partner with MR. & MRS. SAMUEL FREEMAN to the extent of such payments as he — FRANK LLOYD WRIGHT — may be called upon to make and be reimbursed when . . . the property may be sold as an investment."[40]

The building permit was issued on April 8, and construction photographs indicate that work began much as it had at the Storer house

78. Freeman house. Courtesy of Eric Lloyd Wright

(Fig. 78).[41] Storer had had a mechanical mixer at the site, but a more labor-intensive procedure was followed at the Freeman house. Byron Vandegrift, who made many of the blocks, recalled the process in 1983:

> I was the only one making the block. I used to have to carry the cement and sand from where they'd dump it on the street [and] then mix it by hand. [Lloyd] had a big iron table out there. . . . We had an aluminum form . . . it was about this thick and sixteen inches square and you'd put the top right on it after you had leveled it off. . . . They had a small sledge hammer . . . and we put a two-by-four block on this sixteen-inch-square thing and pounded it down and it was enough to hold the block together and [then] you took the form out right away. I'd make over a hundred, some days. As soon as I pounded it in we'd lay them down . . . and water them. . . . He had me experiment and showed me how much stronger the blocks got if you watered them a couple of times a day for three weeks.[42]

The molds that Vandegrift used were discovered in the garage of the Freeman house after Harriet Freeman's death. The basic mold is a four-sided, cast-aluminum flask, 17⅞ by 17⅞ by 4⅞ inches, with machined faces. It has a tin liner plate for the bottom, and a cast-aluminum die, again

79. Freeman house, metal block mold. Courtesy of the University of Southern California

with a machined face, for the top (Fig. 79). The flask is hinged at three corners for disassembly and is secured by a latch at the fourth corner. A semicircular, convex rib creates the void or channel on the perimeter of the block. The liner plate is shaped to form the coffer on the back side of the block. The top die is plain or patterned as required.

Construction continued for thirteen months. By September indications of trouble began to surface: on September 15, Wright discussed errors in the initial land survey in a letter to Lloyd. Then, on October 10, Wright instructed Lloyd to tell Freeman to draw on him "for enough to keep going." On November 19, Lloyd told his father that Freeman could not meet the payroll, that he was "held responsible to labor commission . . . car taken in." Similar problems continued into January, when

Lloyd reported "Work at a standstill . . . Freeman absolutely unable to meet any obligations."[43] The Freemans had in fact accumulated a backlog of unpaid invoices for materials and labor that resulted not only in the stoppage of work but also in a series of liens; between January 12 and April 14, 1925, sixteen liens, totaling $3,388.56, were filed against the property.[44] Wright helped out somewhat; he telegraphed Lloyd on January 8 that he had "settled Freeman bills."[45] There is no documentation to reveal the extent of his total financial contribution to the project, or whether he or Freeman took care of the remaining debts. A notice of completion for the house was filed on March 23, 1925; the total cost was $21,888.17, about two and one-half times the architect's estimate.[46]

Like the Storer house, the Freeman house, as built, is a compromise; Wright's designs frequently did not improve when he reworked his initial concept. He first responded with a scheme that acknowledged and subtly reinforced the near axiality of the site with Highland Avenue. The main volume of the house was a square, bisected on the upper level by an implied line extending from the fireplace in the center of the north wall of the living room through the pair of glass doors at the opposite side of the room and on to the street below. On the lower level a wall separated the two bedrooms, the line of the wall continuing out through a perhaps overly grand stairway, leading to a semicircular garden below (see Figs. 74, 75).

The structural realities Wright seemingly faced, and his resolution of them, had the adverse effect of diminishing the subtlety of the original spatial concept, particularly in the living room. As the room was first designed, the southernmost third, beginning at the point of the I beam, was given definition by changes in ceiling height and floor material: the ceiling was dropped and the floor surface changed from wood to stone. The effect was to mitigate the regularity of the space by creating a cross axis with the dominant north-south axis, and forcefully to contrast the ephemeral, glazed portion of the room with the solid, womblike northern end. When the paired concrete beams were introduced, the room was again divided into thirds, but assertively on the main axis (see Fig. 76). While the first impression is that of a successful integration of the space with the vista below, the effect is in fact contrived. The beams are overbearing, their message too obvious. The southern third of the room is again defined by a lowered ceiling, but with distinctly diminished impact in contrast with the original concept.

The house offers several other intellectual dilemmas — minor by comparison, but worth noting. The entrance hall, reached through a small loggia connecting the house and the garage, extends twenty feet toward the living room. Perforated blocks line the space: one expects them to contain lights, but they do not. At night the corridor is uncomfortably dark. The corresponding ground-floor corridor is similarly without light. Perhaps most difficult to understand is the "lounge," a long, narrow room at the end of the corridor onto which both bedrooms open. There is a second fireplace here, directly under the one in the living room, but it seems gratuitous. The space is dark and uninviting; the only natural light source is a glazed door at the far end.

While the Freeman house is not without problems, it also is enormously provocative. The Freemans were modern people, and among the early block buildings their house comes closest to embracing the tenets of modernism. The sense of the cantilever; the thin, projecting roof slab; and the two-story, mitered corner windows — for many the most memorable feature, indeed the real glory of the Freeman house — combine to produce an architecture that anticipates the future, rather than recalling the past (Figs. 80, 81; Plates 5, 6).

The Freeman house also has the most adventurous block pattern. The house was designed for construction with only a single patterned block, combined, as always, with plain blocks. In the first scheme, the pattern has a square motif reminiscent of one of the blocks for the Storer house. This was transformed in the February drawings into an asymmetrical pattern of disparate geometric shapes, dominated by a square and chevron. There are both left- and right-hand versions, and in application the blocks are occasionally turned upside down. At least one critic has seen this second pattern as an abstraction of the eucalyptus tree; if, however, there is an organic interpretation, Wright never said so.[47]

There is less relationship between the combinations of plain and patterned block and structural function in the Freeman house than in the buildings that preceded it. On the exterior, patterned blocks are used in single courses as trim on all horizontal and most vertical edges. Piers are formed of alternating courses of patterned and plain blocks. Perforated patterned blocks are used to admit light in the entry and in the living room, where they appear in the clerestory and as screens in the south wall. Patterned blocks are used sparingly inside, perhaps with greatest effect around the fireplace.

□ □ □

In no case did Wright attempt to fully furnish one of his California block houses. He did design bookcases for Millard's living room and similar,

80. Freeman house. Courtesy of Kameki Tsuchiura

81. Freeman house, living room, looking southwest. FLLW FDN, 2402.011

82. Freeman house, living room, looking north. Courtesy of the University of Southern California

though not identical, metal lighting fixtures for the Storer and Freeman houses. For the Freemans he also designed a pair of highly architectonic pewlike benches to flank the living-room fireplace (Fig. 82), a pair of bookcases backing the benches, and an octagonal dining-room table. The table was placed in an opening in the wall separating the living room and kitchen, to be accessible from either side. This wall itself, designed as an elaborate construction of cabinets and screens, was greatly simplified when the house was built.

Although it is generally beyond the scope of this book to comment on later changes made to the buildings by other designers, it does seem important to mention R. M. Schindler's work at the Freeman house. The Freemans turned to Schindler for modifications early on. They found in him a kindred spirit who knew and admired Wright's work and had the ability and willingness to design on an extremely limited budget. Schindler began modestly, but as his friendship with the Freemans grew and their resources increased, he returned again and again, until his death thirty years later, leaving an indelible stamp on the building.

The most significant changes occurred in 1928 and 1932. In 1928 the wall between the west bedroom and the lounge was removed to create a larger space, and both bedrooms were furnished. Also, the benches flanking the living-room fireplace were discarded and replaced with a pull-out sofabed and wall unit. Then, in 1932, the open loggia connecting the house with the storeroom under the garage was enclosed, and the storeroom itself converted into an apartment.[48]

Surprisingly, Schindler's modifications and additions display little of his well-known affinity for Wright's work. The remodeling projects produced much of the awkwardness of the plan as it is perceived today. And though much of the furniture is built in, it ignores the grid of the concrete blocks. Other pieces, fascinating geometric constructions in themselves, are too emphatic for the spaces they occupy. The effect is more of collision than resolution. It is difficult now, however, to imagine the house without Schindler's furniture and fruitless to speculate what Wright might have done, given the opportunity.

Ennis house, Los Angeles

The final concrete-block house in southern California was built for Charles W. and Mabel Ennis. It was the largest and most elaborately conceived design Wright managed to carry out. For the first time he was able to build with the offset blocks he had proposed repeatedly; there is extensive, if nonstructural, use of blocks in overhead spans; and new compositional forms are introduced. Though badly flawed in execution, the house is the most complete summary of Wright's theories of concrete-block design and construction as they had developed by 1924. "You see," he wrote to the Ennises, "the final result is going to stand on that hill a hundred years or more. Long after we are all gone it will be pointed out as the Ennis House and pilgrimages will be made to it by lovers of the beautiful—from everywhere."[49]

In the early 1940s the architect was invited to work on the house again by a new owner, John Nesbitt. Wright then proposed changes to the interiors to bring them more in line with his original intentions, and he designed furniture for the house for the first time. That work, however, was never undertaken.

Charles and Mabel Ennis were owners of a men's clothing store in Los Angeles. In spite of the prominence of their house and their apparent affluence, little is known about the Ennises.[50] The primary information about them derives from city directories, death records, and two brief obituaries for Charles Ennis in local newspapers. He was born in Indiana in 1858, she in Ohio in 1863. They lived first in Indianapolis and, after a brief stay in Pittsburgh, moved to Los Angeles around 1901. The following year the Los Angeles city directory listed the new firm of Smith & Ennis Men's and Youths' Clothing. This was a short-lived partnership; two years later, Ennis had his own store. In 1923, with the entry of Mabel Ennis's brother as vice president, the firm was renamed Ennis and Gill Clothing. Charles was president; his wife, secretary and treasurer. Shortly after, the Ennises retired.

According to his obituary, Ennis devoted the remaining five years of his life to horticulture, presumably taking advantage of the vacant lot next to his house, which he also owned. He died in December 1928, and his funeral was conducted in the house. Mabel Ennis continued living in the house until it was sold in 1936.[51]

Although the Ennises moved several times between 1901 and 1924, their two former residences still standing are small and undistinguished. There is nothing in them to suggest that the couple would become patrons of modern architecture, hire so unconventional a designer, and build so experimental a house. Artistic and social ambition came late in life. To Wright they must have seemed a godsend. In contrast with the other, comparatively impecunious clients who built block houses in southern California, the Ennises presented an opportunity to carry out a design of great elaboration.

The Ennises' site suggested a major statement as well, though its presence was more a result of position than of size. It was a steep mound at the base of the Santa Monica Mountains, elevated well above—and easily visible from—the city below; it also could be seen from Olive Hill. The site was not enormous. It was approximately one-half acre, created by combining two adjoining lots, and therefore, arguably, was out of scale for the area. It was defined on three sides by Glendower Avenue (Fig. 83, Lots 22, 23).

Wright's scheme is for two buildings, the main house and a chauffeur's apartment and garage, separated by a paved courtyard. The whole rises from a podium surrounded by massive retaining walls, which provide a suitably monumental base but also exaggerate the apparent size of the

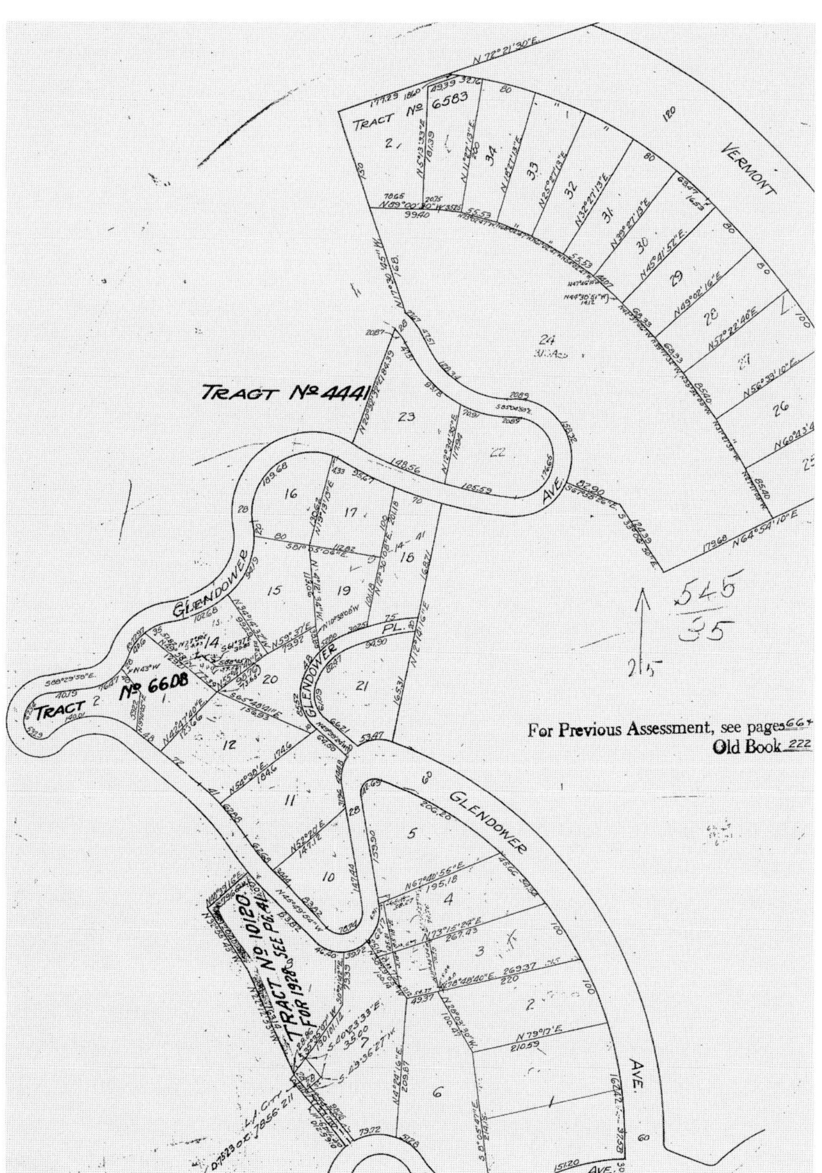

83. Charles W. and Mabel Ennis house, Los Angeles, California, site plan, 1924. Los Angeles County Assessor, Book 545 (1924–30), p. 35

84. Ennis house, perspective. FLLW FDN, 2401.003

building. Still, the enclosed space is by no means small, extending 248 feet across the site (Fig. 84).

Unlike the compact, vertically oriented compositions of the Millard, Storer, and Freeman houses, the Ennis house has an attenuated plan in which the principal rooms are all on the second level. The unifying element is a one-hundred-foot-long loggia on the north side of the house, linking the main rooms and setting them open to the city view. The center of gravity in the Ennis plan is the dining room, the largest space in the house. The living room and Mabel's bedroom, extending to the east, complete the central mass. Charles's bedroom is at the end of the loggia, standing free of the main structure. Service areas and a guest room are placed west of the dining room (Fig. 85).

The forms of the Ennis house have a direct connection with those of the new Barnsdall house in Beverly Hills, designed several months earlier, but there are also important advances. Both houses are laid out as a series of pavilions reflecting special functions indicated on the plan, and both depend on battered walls for effect. The massing in the Barnsdall house,

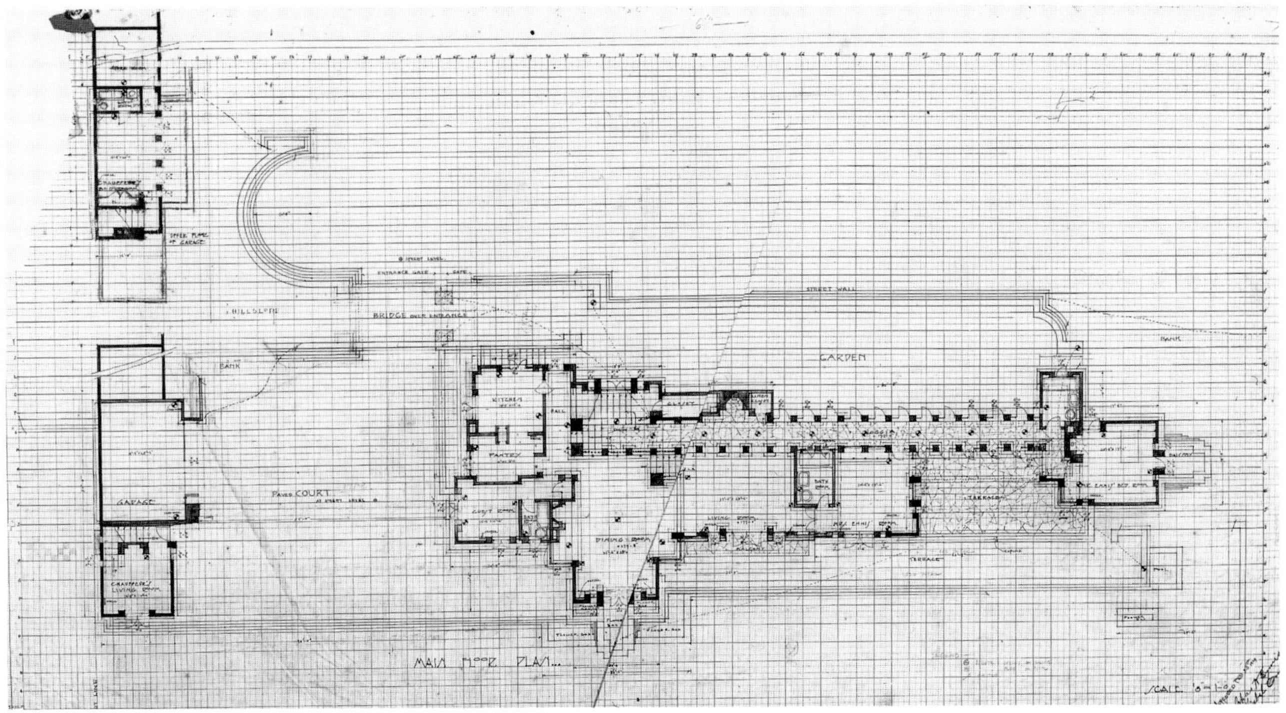

85. Ennis house, main-floor plan. FLLW FDN, 2401.009

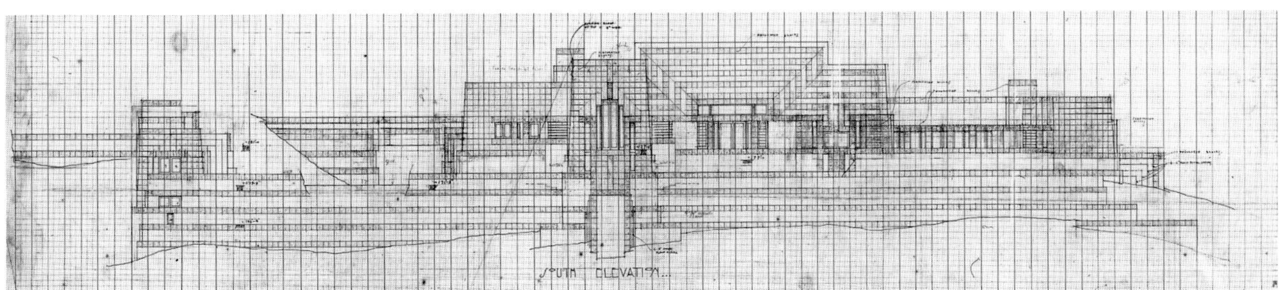

86. Ennis house, south elevation. FLLW FDN, 2401.011

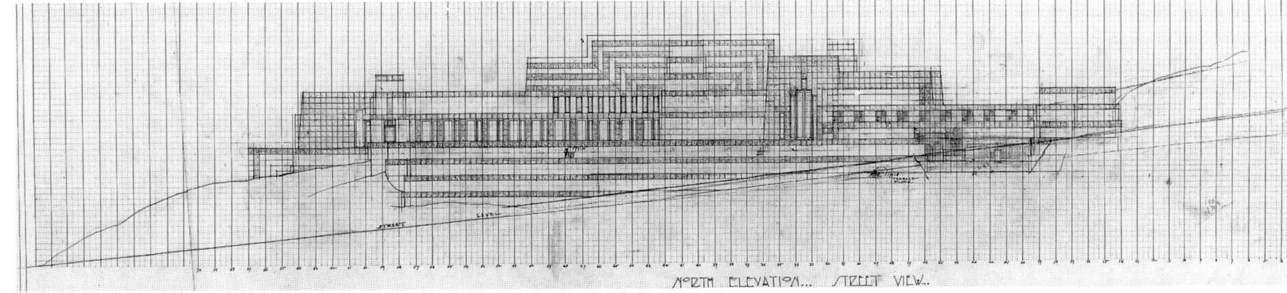

87. Ennis house, north elevation, street view. FLLW FDN, 2401.012

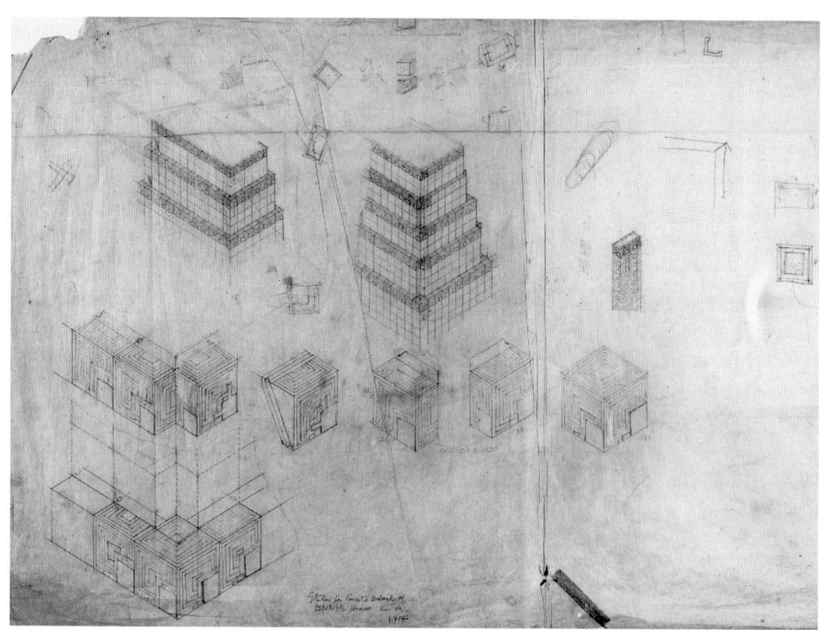

88. Ennis house, block details. FLLW FDN, 2401.004

however, is consistent; upper battered walls are separated from the base by a belt course of projecting blocks. The Ennis house combines three distinct forms: the stratification of the Barnsdall house; a simplification in which battered walls rise unbroken from the base of the building; and newly introduced telescoping masses (Figs. 86, 87). Combinations of plain and patterned block units are used to define the individual volumes and to weave the composition together; there is a new sense that the blocks themselves determine the forms. The block pattern is an asymmetrical composition of squares, which could have been rotated and grouped to create larger patterns, but this was not done. Wright seems to have considered carefully the effect of the partial patterns that would result when less than a full block face was exposed (Fig. 88).

The Ennis house, a formal and spatial composition requiring numerous detail drawings for clarification, reduces structurally to little more than an elaborate post-and-beam system, combined with load-bearing concrete-block walls. The house is not supported by the podium, but rises directly from the ground below, as the working drawings reveal. The plan of the superstructure is quite legible in the foundation: lengths of wall rest on continuous poured-concrete underpinnings; fragments of walls and piers are expressed independently (Fig. 89). Perimeter walls rise directly from footings on the ground. Horizontal spans are supported by concrete beams

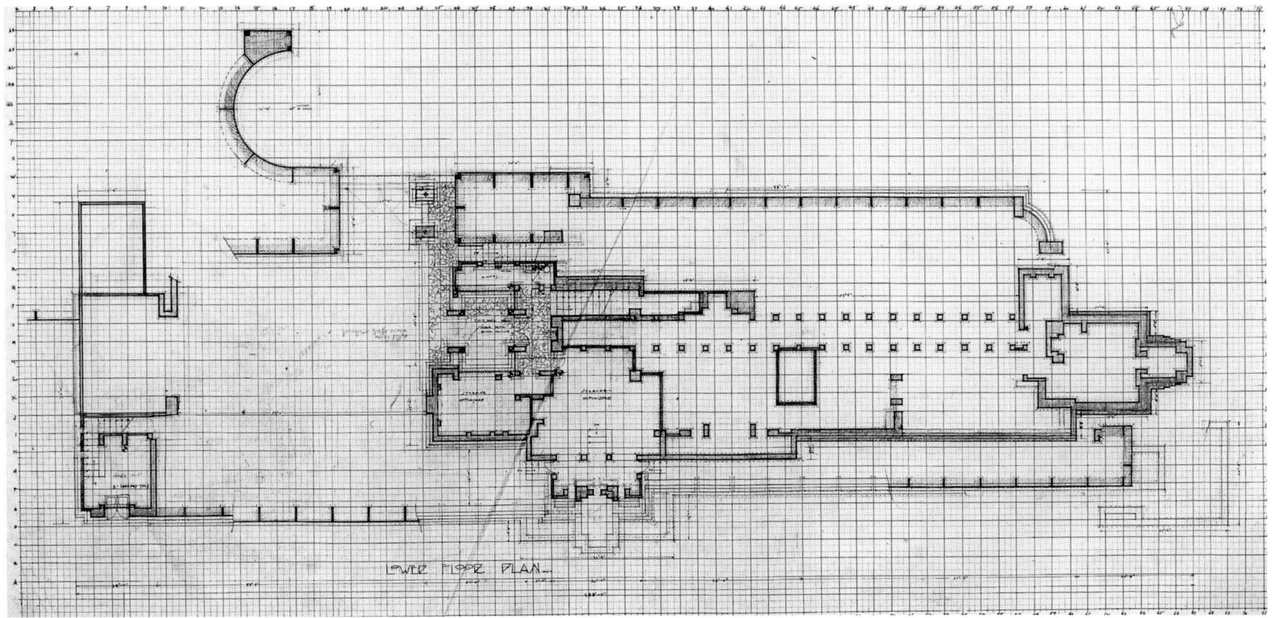

89. Ennis house, lower-floor plan. FLLW FDN, 2401.008

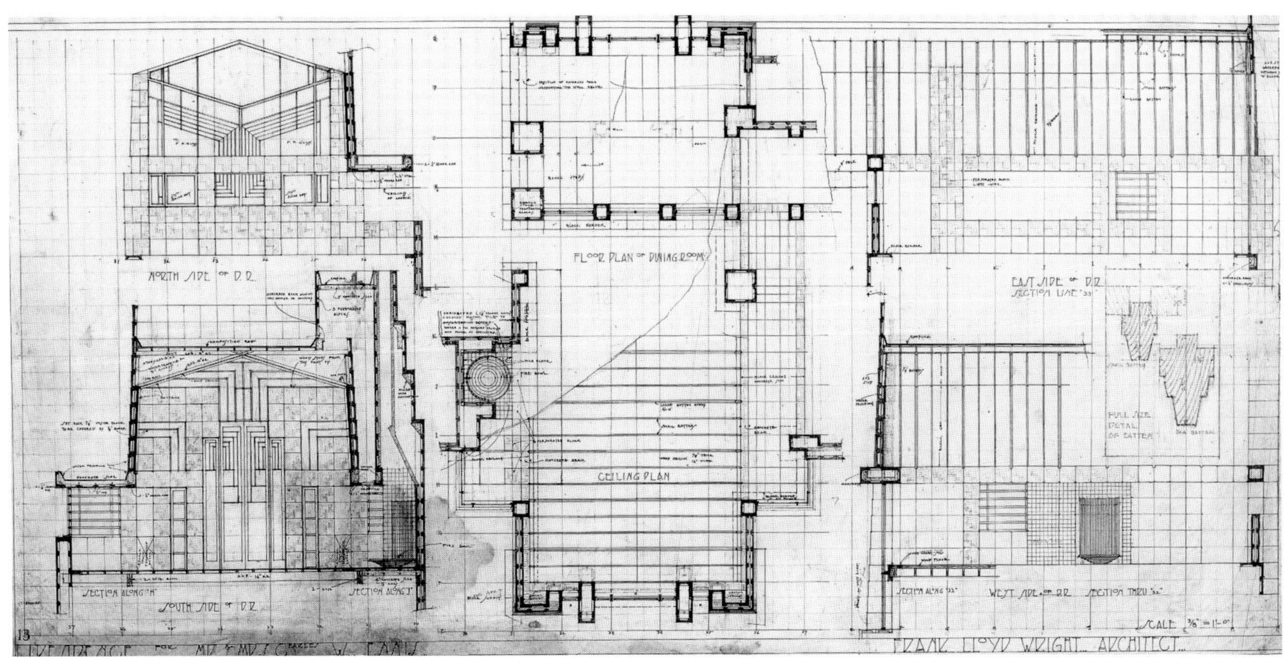

90. Ennis house, dining-room sections, elevations, ceiling plan, and details. FLLW FDN, 2401.020

and lintels; the point is made most dramatically in the dining room, where the battered upper walls rest on concrete beams. There is extensive use of the blocks in ceilings—in the entry, loggia, and dining room—but the application is entirely dependent on concrete slabs, to which the blocks are wired (Fig. 90).

The plans for the house were approved by the clients on February 25, 1924. At the same time, the Ennises signed a contract with Lloyd for supervision of the construction and landscaping. Blasting and excavation began the first week in March, and soon a miniature factory was set up to manufacture the blocks (Fig. 91). The molds seem to have been passed from house to house as needed, although Charles Ennis ordered several additional units.[52]

Separate building permits for the house and chauffeur's apartment and garage were issued on May 1.[53] The construction sequence is revealed in a series of photographs from Lloyd Wright's archive. The retaining walls are structurally independent and were built first; behind them is an elaborate system of reinforcement to resist lateral forces. Perpendicular crib walls are spaced at eight-foot intervals (Fig. 92). Twelve-inch-square concrete beams anchor the walls to the hillside; these were constructed after the retaining walls were in place (Fig. 93). Additional support was provided for the motor court: parallel rows of concrete footings in line with the crib walls were poured directly on the ground. Finally, the entire cavity between the retaining walls and the natural grade was filled with soil or sand (Fig. 94).

91. Ennis house. Courtesy of Eric Lloyd Wright

92. Ennis house. Courtesy of Eric Lloyd Wright

93. Ennis house. Courtesy of Eric Lloyd Wright

94. Ennis house. Courtesy of Eric Lloyd Wright

95. Ennis house. Courtesy of Eric Lloyd Wright

96. Ennis house. Courtesy of Eric Lloyd Wright

After the retaining walls were up, the chauffeur's quarters were built, then the main house, beginning with Charles Ennis's bedroom, at the east end. The photographs illustrate the remarkable way in which the retaining walls grew almost morphologically into the chauffeur's apartment; there is no line of separation (Fig. 95). The only clue that the walls conceal habitable space is a row of small windows inserted into them. As the structure progressed, it assumed something of the potency of a ruin under excavation (Fig. 96).

In June, four months into the construction process, Ennis hired a chemical engineer to analyze the "Pre-cast Block, Reinforced Concrete System" as it was being used in his house. The engineer's report sheds additional light on the block-fabrication process. The blocks were made from decomposed granite blasted from the site during excavation for the building. The aggregate was passed over a screen of quarter-inch mesh. The finer particles that fell through the screen were used for the blocks. A mixture of one part cement and four parts sand was combined in a Blystone Mixer with enough water to give it the consistency of foundry sand. The rest of the procedure paralleled that used at the Freeman house: after the top die was in place, it was stamped with a heavy weight to create a dense block that could be removed from the flask immediately and transferred on the tin liner to a rack (Fig. 97). It was kept moist as it cured with frequent spraying. The total time for molding standard blocks was about two and one-half minutes.[54]

Work continued through the summer, and on August 19 Lloyd telegraphed his father, "Ennis delighted Work progressing rapidly, effectively."[55] The message was a palliative; a truer assessment of the situation comes from Wright's subsequent letter to his clients:

> The time is approaching when things always look darkest, in the building of a building. . . . The work is slower than I anticipated, the City has interfered in points unnecessary wholly, arbitarily [*sic*] adding some to costs. . . . Our contour survey was wrong and so more wall actually necessary than our drawings indicated.[56]

Things could only have looked darkest on September 15, when Lloyd appealed to his father for help; the south retaining walls of the house were bulging and cracking and the lower blocks popping (Fig. 98). Lloyd suggested several remedial measures; Wright responded on September 26 that he believed the "cracks nor bulge of no great significance."[57]

The patience and confidence of the Ennises were being tested and by

97. Ennis house. Courtesy of Eric Lloyd Wright

early October—seven months after work had begun—they were exerting rapidly increasing control over the construction of the house. Lloyd telegraphed his father on October 8: "E proceeds with forman [*sic*] and crew in effort to save fees Holding you responsible for indefinite action." Finally, on December 10, the Ennises and Lloyd terminated their contract.[58]

It seems clear at this point that the Ennises were building a house they were unable or unwilling to understand. Lloyd wired his father in Febru-

98. Ennis house, FLLW FDN, 2401.003

ary 1925 that they were modifying the heads of several windows, substituting "lintels" for stepped-up openings and ignoring the planned interweaving of blocks; he also noted that they were making the ceilings flat rather than pitched and several courses lower than specified. Wright responded, asking Mabel Ennis to "kindly be guided by intelligence and grace rather than by unenlightened expedients destroying the virtue of all we suffered for."[59]

Lloyd responded again to changes that had taken place in a letter written three weeks later, on February 25, to Charles Ennis:

> With your builder, you have revised or entirely destroyed the architect's plans for the building, as accepted by you, and you were fully aware of the fact that you were doing so. The errors thus made have seriously marred what is a magnificent building.

He included a list of seventeen specific modifications that had been made since his resignation in December, commenting that "under the circumstances, it was obviously ridiculous and pointless for me to continue."[60]

Writing in 1937 to a later owner of the house, Lloyd asserted that "Mrs. Ennis took over the job and ran it for herself from the foundations up hoping, no doubt, to save money with the usual unsatisfactory results of such a pinch penny policy."[61] Lloyd was upset about numerous changes that had occurred during construction; however, he exaggerated Mabel Ennis's influence in the early stages. The plan of the house conforms closely to the original design, and the exterior walls, constructed under Lloyd's supervision, are generally faithful up to the windowsills. The most significant change to the lower walls was the addition of several block courses to the base, made necessary by the inaccurate survey, as Wright had explained in his September 4, 1924, letter. The result was an unfortunate increase in the bulk of the house. One unexplained change to the plan was the repositioning of the front door. The entry was designed with a loggia, which served as a transition space between the motor court and the house; at the time of construction, the door was moved twelve feet west to open directly off the court, and the loggia became an entrance hall (see Fig. 89).

It was above the windowsills that the forms and spaces of the house were most greatly altered, in no case to the betterment of the result. Various changes in massing and in the coursing of plain, patterned, and perforated blocks diminished the harmony of the building and increased its visual weight. Inside the house, in addition to the revised ceilings, a glass screen, planned to separate the dining room from the loggia, was not built; and the low wall separating the dining and living rooms was reduced further by one block course; these omissions alter the spatial flow (see Fig. 90). Elaborate iron grillwork, executed by Julius Dietzmann, a local iron craftsman, was added to several spaces in the building; the fireplace hood in the dining room also came from Dietzmann's studio.[62] Other changes included the substitution of white marble for shale paving in the entry and loggia and the introduction of chandeliers.

Two more changes should be noted. The leaded-glass windows in the house are beautiful, but they are not the designs indicated on the working drawings. Wright originally suggested a simple rectangular design, coordinated with the block pattern (Fig. 99). The windows that were installed are too delicate in scale, recalling Wright's much earlier work, and are graphically unrelated to the building (Fig. 100). They were executed by the Judson Studios in Pasadena, but the cartoons have not been located and the designer remains unidentified.[63] The second change was in the bathrooms. Wright had intended that the walls, floors, and ceilings be constructed of plain-face blocks with half-inch gold mosaic tile set in the joints. The Ennises chose instead to cover the walls and floors with tile and to plaster the ceilings; marble basins are supported on wrought-iron legs.

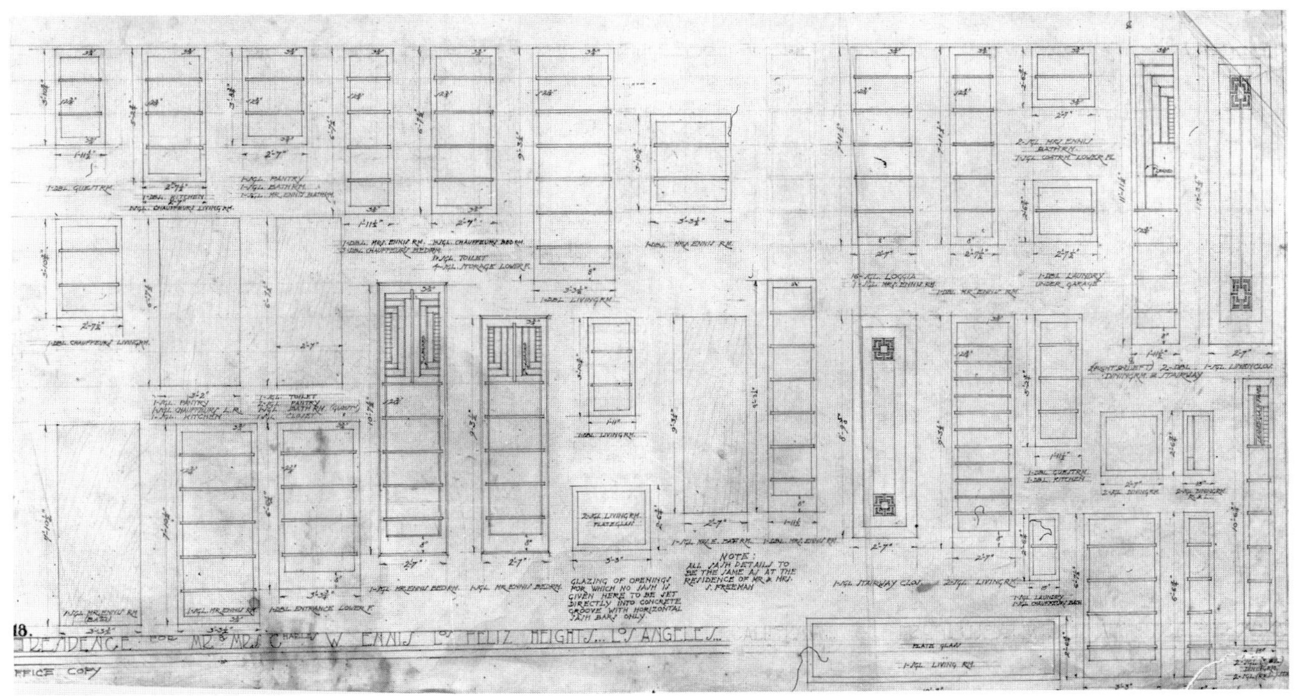

99. Ennis house, window and door details. FLLW FDN, 2401.025

100. Ennis house, window detail. FLLW FDN, 2401.019

The chauffeur's apartment and garage were completed in December 1924; the house itself in August 1925, although interior work continued until September 1926.[64] With the exception of some drawings for wall lamps, which were not produced, there is no evidence that Wright designed furniture for the house. A photograph published in the *Los Angeles Times* in November 1926 reveals the original furnishings, which were not what the architect or his son would have chosen; the caption notes that "Mr. and Mrs. Ennis designed many of the fixtures for their home and largely superintended the building" (Fig. 101).[65] One looks in vain for mention of the Wrights.

Hitchcock's reaction to the Ennis house was that "the monumentality

101. Ennis house, living room, ca. 1926. *Los Angeles Times* photo

102. Ennis house, north elevation, looking east, ca. 1926. *Los Angeles Times* photo

suits the site, but is rather undomestic."[66] He was correct, and the architect agreed. The house is too big, "way out of concrete block size . . . out of bounds," Wright acknowledged three decades after it was completed.[67] The problem has less to do with overall size than with scale; Wright was capable of designing very large houses that read as a collection of small parts and thus maintain their intimacy. The Ennis house is an assemblage of outsized forms that collectively are of Brobdingnagian proportion. The devices he used to give plasticity to the composition and to reduce its mass—offset blocks, alternating rows of plain and patterned blocks, and telescoping forms—do not effectively lessen its monumentality (Fig. 102).

There are spatial problems as well. Entry is abrupt; there is no transition from the paved court to the interior, Wright's planned sequence having been destroyed when the loggia was enclosed. There also is a loss of clarity at this point; with the door at the far end of the loggia, as designed, one entered a narrow space that forced movement toward the stairway to the main floor. The entrance hall, as built, is ambiguous; the stairway is not visible, and one has the strange sense of entering a grand house through the basement, and not knowing which direction to turn. The sense of arrival is compromised at the top of the stairs by the elimination of the planned screen separating the dining room from the loggia. The spatial sequence should have led to the living room first; as it is, one sees the dining-room floor at an awkward angle.

The Ennis house, as designed, has the most abstract spaces of any block house. The two houses of comparable scale, a contemporary project for A. M. Johnson and the earlier Barnsdall house, both retain metaphors of domesticity: the living room is the dominant space, with a fireplace as its focus, and there is clear separation of public and private areas. In the Ennis house, the living room is subordinate to the dining room both in size and prominence of position; the dining room is elevated a few steps to overlook the living room and has the higher ceiling. Its size, imposing fireplace, and great window overlooking Los Angeles below make it a room to be lived up to. Meals here should be served with ceremony. By no means intimate, it remains, however, a space of greater containment and focus than the living room; if the architectural forces in the dining room are centripetal, those in the living room are the opposite. The most noticeable feature there is the location of the fireplace, which is not actually in the room, but visible from it across the loggia, a very unusual statement from Wright (Plate 7). The fireplace is balanced off axis on the opposite wall by a pair of glass doors opening to the southern view; but again the focus is external to the room.

There is unorthodoxy as well in the relationship of these two vast spaces — which suggest entertaining on a grand scale — and two adjacent bedrooms. The guest room is nestled between the dining room and the pantry, a location that ordinarily would be turned over to a servant. Mabel Ennis's bedroom opens directly from the living room; the two rooms are expressed as one mass in elevation.

The scale and form of the Ennis house defy ordinary perceptions of residential design; yet it is precisely these qualities that give it such commanding presence. Much of the experience of the building comes from its plan and calculated relation to the site. The house rises massively above the city of Los Angeles, but the winding roads of the Hollywood hills make it only indirectly accessible. The first view is from below. The sense of climax is heightened by a prolonged approach, in which the house weaves in and out of view and is seen from different angles along the way. The house finally serves as a pivot, the road curving around it to the motor court. A monumental gate emphasizes the transition of entering; a low wall around the court begins the sense of containment. From this outdoor room the visitor has a return view of the city below and the path he has followed.

The rite of passage continues inside; a door off the motor court opens to the entrance hall on the ground floor. Here the space is suddenly dark and confining, a Wrightian device in preparation for the burst of energy that follows. The path leads up a flight of stairs and concludes at the heart of the building, the dining room in front of the fireplace. Surely no space in twentieth-century architecture is so suggestive of pagan ritual. The Ennises seem to have understood the religious iconography of their house, turning to Mayan sources for decorative inspiration. Ceremony using fire plays a role in almost every religion; the Ennises acknowledged this in commissioning the bronze hood for the fireplace, which depicts Xiuheuctli, the ancient Mexican god of fire.

In April 1940 the Ennis house was purchased by John Nesbitt (1910–60), a motion-picture producer working for Metro-Goldwyn-Mayer. He was best known for a series of short features called *The Passing Parade*, which he both produced and narrated. Focusing on the commonplaces of everyday life, the features were designed to reach "the lowest common denominator of the mass public," while remaining both informative and entertaining. The series put Nesbitt "in the chips, but definitely."[68]

In his own judgment "cursed with perfect articulation," Nesbitt immediately sent a letter to Wright, pragmatically requesting a set of plans and suggestions for appropriate furnishings, but also confessing that it was "difficult to suppress the wish to communicate with an architect whose work communicates so much." He was concerned about the bulge in the south retaining wall, but added that "the house, after much neglect, is in superb condition. The heavy doors swing smoothly, the floors are perfectly true, the walls are clean and fresh." He concluded, "with apologies for editorial content in a stranger's request, but with the explanation that those who quote Walt Whitman in their technical teachings must put up with Walt Whitman's admirers."[69]

Wright responded that Nesbitt had a "remarkably fine, well built house. No need to worry about the slight bulge in retaining wall or anything else. . . . Unfortunately the house was turned over to ignorant clients before I had finished it and much is needed to be undone." He added that he "would love to see that dignified place come into its own, finally."[70]

Nesbitt began at once to make improvements under Lloyd Wright's supervision, adding a swimming pool to the north terrace and removing marble sills and some light fixtures, but concluded that the house "will always be a maimed thing."[71] In 1941, after he had owned the house for a year and after "disastrous" attempts to furnish it, Nesbitt again asked for

Wright's help; they agreed on a budget of $3,500 for renovations, which were to include "furnishings, a revised lighting system, some planting of the court and revamping of the pavement of the entrance and a general restoration of the original intention of the architect concerning the features of the house formerly neglected or aborted." [72]

Wright responded with three presentation drawings, dated September 14, 1941, that suggest changes and additions to the entry hall, living room, and dining room; they also reveal a new name, Sijistan, the "name of the palace of a famous Persian hero," for the house. The entry is unchanged, except for the addition of furniture: a chair, stool, and eight-foot-long table of simple design, based on the intersection of slabs of wood (Fig. 103). Alterations to the rooms upstairs are more dramatic and attempt to capture the spirit of the spaces as Wright had intended them to be in 1924. The greatest changes are to the ceilings. Several months earlier, Nesbitt had discussed dismantling the existing flat ceilings and selling them, so that Wright would have "a free hand with new materials while avoiding compromise with the old." [73] This was not done, however, and Wright worked with the existing structure, proposing to add new false ceilings to cover the flat surfaces. In the living room, he suggested mounting a pitched false ceiling of wood veneer, to begin at the cornice line of the long north and south walls and meet the flat ceiling at a point three block units, or four feet, into the room (Fig. 104). The dining room is treated similarly,

103. John Nesbitt alterations to Ennis house (project), entrance hall, 1941. FLLW FDN, 4017.063

104. John Nesbitt alterations to Ennis house (project), living room, 1941. FLLW FDN, 4017.062

105. John Nesbitt alterations to Ennis house (project), dining room, 1941. FLLW FDN, 4017.061

except that the pitched surface begins three block units lower, at the level of the cornice separating the room from the living room, and slopes in only eight inches, to a point where it meets a second pitched surface, which presumably rises to a peak at the center of the room (Fig. 105). The boards are sixteen inches wide, to correspond with the module of the building; in the living room they are to be separated by battens every fourth block unit, in the dining room, every third.

Wright's sketches furnish the living room sparsely, with high-backed, upholstered seating along the east and west walls, ottomans, and a cabinet to house Nesbitt's Capehart record player and large collection of phonograph records. He added abstract art that fits within the modular grid of the walls, and a row of three shelves overhead, between the piers separating the living room from the loggia, to increase the sense of separation. The dining room has a table seating twelve, whose length is perpendicular to the long axis of the room. He placed open cabinets along the low east wall that help block the view into the living room, and added more shelves to the openings between the dining room and loggia, to fill the void that was left when the Ennises did not build the proposed glass screen. The dining-room chairs are simple abstract constructions of three square or rectangular boards forming backs and arms whose edges do not touch; the only point of contact is with a fourth, horizontal board that forms the seat.

When he saw the drawings, Nesbitt responded that they produced "much mouth-watering delight," that one sat by them "as before a banquet." He observed that "the massive interior could become youthful and cheerful," but that "the sketches underline . . . the necessity of leaving furniture and fabrics as completely in your hands as the walls and ceiling." Still caught in his "gustatory eupheuisms [*sic*]," he added that it would be necessary for Wright to handle everything "from soup to nuts." [74]

Nesbitt also observed several inaccuracies in the drawings, mentioning "drapes in arches that don't exist, and certain heights that are a full block's width away from the actual construction." [75] In fact, the only major discrepancy is an enlargement of the alcove leading from the living room to Mabel Ennis's bedroom to accommodate the Capehart cabinet. Wright gained an extra block unit to the east, increasing the wall space from three units to four, by removing the pair of leaded-glass doors and substituting a portiere. The space to the west, however, increased in the drawing from three block units to at least six, is only wishful thinking, unrealizable, given the way the house was built.

The significance of these drawings is their imposition of Wright's 1941 style on a 1924 design and the opportunity they provide for analysis of the changes that had taken place in the intervening years. The evolution was from a reliance on complex interwoven geometric shapes, displayed in the two major works of the earlier period, the Imperial Hotel and the Barnsdall Olive Hill house, to a new interest in designing with flat sheets of wood. The concept can be traced to the furniture designed in 1931 for the Richard Lloyd Jones house, although the furniture for John Nesbitt, following in the same tradition, has more in common with 1938 designs for Fallingwater.

□ □ □

Though Wright's visions for concrete-block construction were more expansive, and other projects were on the horizon, the Millard, Storer, Freeman, and Ennis houses remain as our legacy of the textile block system. Certainly it is these buildings and not the more significant projects that have been accepted by critics as evidence of Wright's intentions. But they tell only part of the story. They are works in progress, leading to the fully integrated system of mono-material construction Wright envisioned in his autobiography.

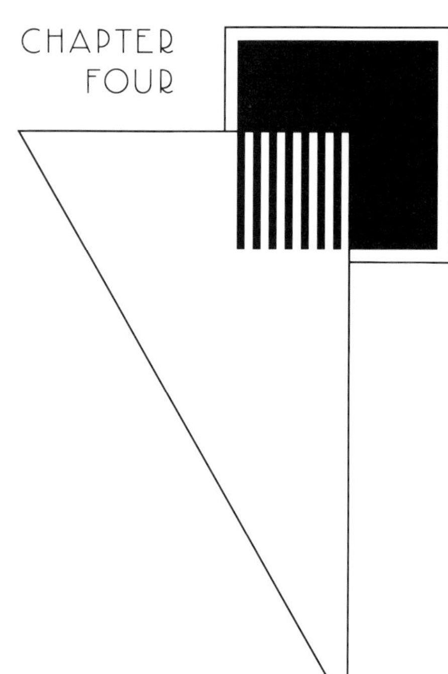

CHAPTER FOUR

LINGERING AND NEW PROSPECTS

The intensity of Wright's commitment to concrete block in his initial phase of exploration, and his eagerness to explore it in diverse locations, are confirmed by three more ambitious and little-known projects. One of these, a resort for Emerald Bay at Lake Tahoe, was undertaken early, in June 1923, during Wright's brief tenure in Los Angeles. The others, a residential compound in remote Death Valley and a new fraternity house for the University of Wisconsin, Madison, are slightly later; they were developed at Taliesin, while Richard Neutra was in residence.[1] None of the projects was built, and seemingly no working drawings were prepared; it can only be assumed that the structural system would have been the same as that used in the three Los Angeles houses.

Tahoe summer colony, Lake Tahoe, California

In a 1933 letter to Aline Barnsdall, Wright suggested that she buy property at Emerald Bay on Lake Tahoe, telling her, "There is nothing like it in the world for beauty."[2] He sent her drawings for a resort he had designed for the site ten years earlier, hoping perhaps to revive this exceptionally fine project. The site was two hundred acres rising steeply from the lake's edge; it was heavily forested and included a waterfall. There also was a small island in the center of the bay. Wright's recollection in his autobiography that he was called away to Tahoe while work was under way on the Millard house, together with one drawing signed "Los Angeles, June 29, 1923," establish an approximate beginning date for this project.[3]

Wright designed a series of cabins to be built on land and also on barges in the lake. The imagery of the group is altogether unlike the contemporary California work: the architect adapted tepee forms to harmonize with the tall trees in the area. Each building is an assured, festive statement; one senses that Wright's spirits were high. There are numerous variations, including at least four to be constructed of concrete block: the Wigwam, Fir Tree, Shore, and Lodge cabins. The simplest is the Wigwam, with a plan based on two squares, one rotated forty-five degrees within the other (Fig. 106). Only the perimeter retaining walls and chimney are concrete block; the superstructure is of wood (Fig. 107). The Fir Tree has an octagonal plan with two projecting wings; among the four cabins, it is perhaps of greatest interest because it features the innovation of diagonal blocks (Figs. 108, 109). The Shore cabin has concrete block continuing up from the base, forming walls in the superstructure; offset blocks form voids echoing the shape of the roof (Figs. 110, 111). Wright inscribed his intentions on the drawing: "White sand blocks, stained boards, copper hips and ridges." The Lodge is the largest of the group; its walls are built entirely of offset blocks, with a patterned block capping the base (Figs. 112, 113).

The client may have been Jessie Armstrong (1878 – 1978), whose father had purchased the property in 1892. Emerald Bay was by then an established destination for tourists, who arrived by steamer; facilities included a small hotel, rough frame cottages, and tents.[4] Late in life, Armstrong recalled Wright's visit. He would have taken the Southern Pacific to Truckee, California, and then transferred to a narrow-gauge train for the fourteen-mile trip to Tahoe City. From there the steamer *Tahoe* would have brought him across the lake to Emerald Bay. Wright came for lunch. According to Armstrong, "He was a delightful man; we enjoyed him very much. He would have given anything in the world to develop that property; he had never seen such a paradise on earth."[5]

Other evidence suggests that, like the Doheny Ranch scheme, the Tahoe project may have been entirely speculative; that real-estate promoters and not the Armstrongs were the catalysts for development. Armstrong stated that at the time of his visit Wright "had even begun to form his plans for how he would develop the property if this company took it over. We were rather hoping they wouldn't, and they didn't, because I think that even

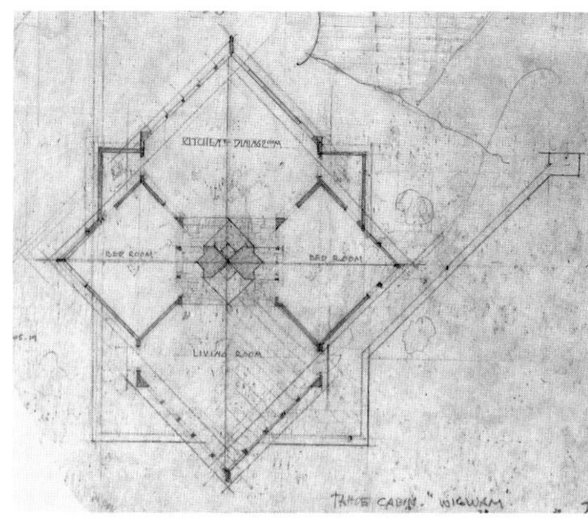

106. Tahoe Summer Colony, Wigwam Cabin (project), Lake Tahoe, California, plan, 1923. FLLW FDN, 2205.019

107. Tahoe Summer Colony, Wigwam Cabin (project), perspective, 1923. FLLW FDN, 2205.026

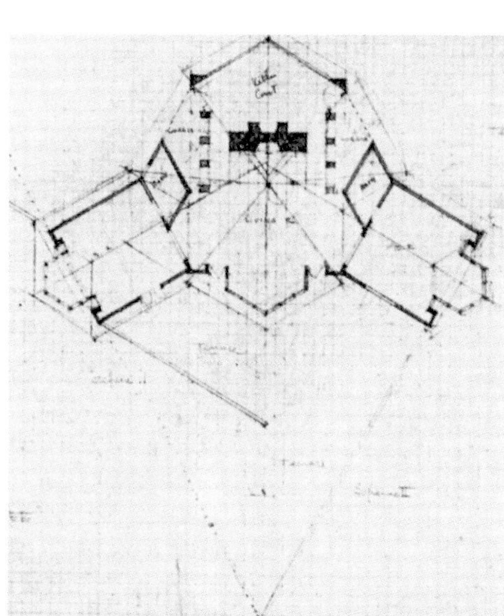

108. Tahoe Summer Colony, Fir Tree Cabin (project), plan, 1923. Reproduced from H. de Fries, ed., *Frank Lloyd Wright: Aus dem Lebenswerke eines Architekten* (Berlin: Verlag Ernst Pollak, 1926), p. 50

109. Tahoe Summer Colony, Fir Tree Cabin (project), perspective and partial plan, 1923. Reproduced from H. de Fries, ed., *Frank Lloyd Wright: Aus dem Lebenswerke eines Architekten* (Berlin: Verlag Ernst Pollak, 1926), p. 51

110. Tahoe Summer Colony, Shore Cabin (project), perspective and partial plan, 1923. FLLW FDN, 2205.003

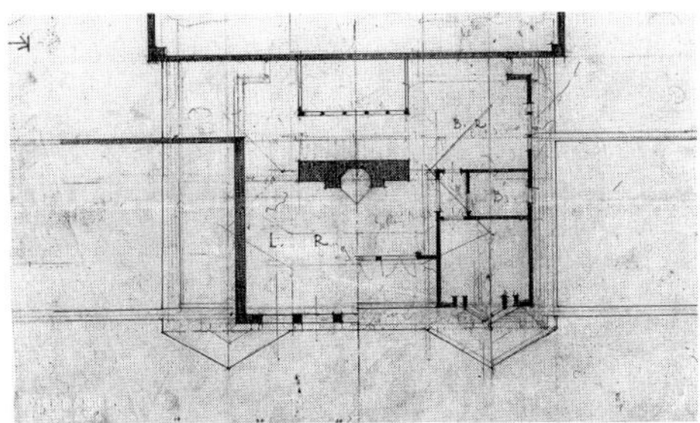

111. Tahoe Summer Colony, Shore Cabin (project), plan, 1923. FLLW FDN, 2205.018

though he had peculiar ideas of architecture, everyone didn't respond to them. He was going to build a bridge from the mainland to the island."[6]

Wright himself was interested in acquiring the property; correspondence between two attorneys, Frank P. Deering of San Francisco and E. E. Prussing of Los Angeles, provides tantalizing details. On December 5, 1923, Deering wrote to Prussing, stating that he would like to discuss "Mr. Wright's purchase of the Emerald Bay property. The owners will not sell for less than $150,000.00; $10,000.00 down; deed to be delivered upon payment of $75,000.00 with note and mortgage for the balance. These figures to be net, the buyer to pay Mr. Pizzotti's commission." Prussing replied two days later: "Wright has been away for two months and is

112. Tahoe Summer Colony, Lodge Cabin (project), perspective, 1923. FLLW FDN, 2205.001

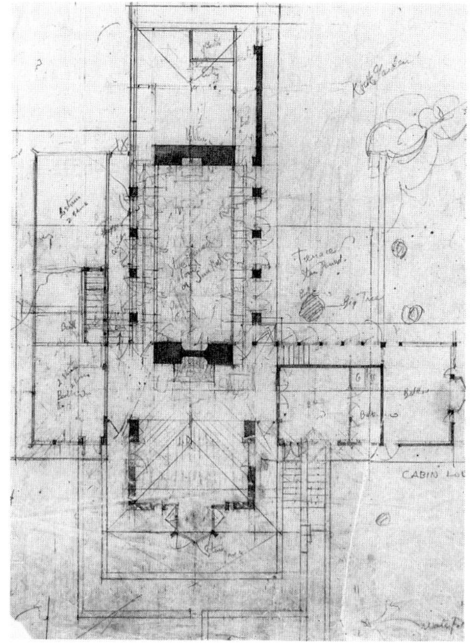

113. Tahoe Summer Colony, Lodge Cabin (project), plan, 1923. FLLW FDN, 2205.024

expected back on Sunday. There will be many matters to take up when he returns and the Emerald Bay property will be one to receive his first attention. . . . You do not say in your letter," he continued, "whether or not upon the payment of $10,000.00 down we are to receive a contract permitting us to pay $10,000.00 every 60 days until one-half is paid on the purchase price, and a deed is then to be given with a note and mortgage for the balance. Will that be agreeable?" [7]

One has to wonder what possible source Wright could have tapped to secure these sums of money. But the idea was still active the following May, when Wright telegraphed Lloyd that he was "Negotiating with Armstrongs owners Emeraldday [*sic*] If I go on with scheme they will cooperate Better go through me in dealing with them Letter from Jessie Armstrong yesterday suggesting cooperation." [8] Like the Doheny Ranch development, the Lake Tahoe project proved all too soon to be a phantom. Wright later told Aline Barnsdall, "I loved the whole thing and was broken hearted when I discovered th[e] realtors were merely exploiting my name to serve their own ends." [9]

Johnson compound, Death Valley, California

In late 1923 or early 1924 Wright began work on a large residential compound to be constructed of concrete block in Death Valley for A. M. Johnson. Johnson (1872 – 1948) was chairman of the National Life Insurance Company in Chicago, for whom Wright also designed an office building for a site near the present Water Tower Place, on north Michigan Avenue. The Death Valley project, however, was a direct outgrowth of Johnson's unorthodox relationship with Walter E. Scott, "Death Valley Scotty." Scotty (1872 – 1954) had toured with Buffalo Bill's Wild West Show between 1890 and 1902. Two years later he met Johnson in Chicago and received the first of many grubstakes for his nefarious gold-prospecting activities in the desert. Johnson's interest was further kindled the following year, when Scotty hired a special Santa Fe train and made a record-breaking run between Los Angeles and Chicago. In 1906 Johnson joined Scotty and his henchmen on a prospecting trip in Death Valley, on the pretext of learning the location of Scotty's mine. The climax of this escapade was a staged shoot-out, from which Johnson emerged unscathed. Scotty was a fraud, but Johnson found "his history, character, and his Death Valley experiences . . . more romantic than any romance." [10] He became Scotty's gold mine.

Drawn by the adventure and also by the beneficial effects of the climate on his fragile health, Johnson began purchasing property in 1915 on the extreme northern rim of Death Valley, at the base of the Funeral Mountains. Over the next twelve years, he accumulated approximately fifteen hundred acres that became known as Death Valley Ranch. The site was remote, difficult of access, and generally untouched by civilization; of course, these were the specific qualities that appealed. Johnson first set up camp in three tents: one for himself, another for his wife, and a third for cooking. Scotty had his own wooden shack.

With ever-increasing commitment to the site, Johnson initiated a building program in the fall of 1922. Beginning modestly, he erected a

114. Death Valley Ranch, Death Valley, California, ca. 1922. Courtesy of Scotty's Castle, Death Valley, California

two-story frame-and-stucco building ninety-six feet long and thirty-two feet wide, which may have provided firmness and commodity but could not possibly have delighted (Fig. 114). Upstairs were apartments for the Johnsons and their guests, with cooking and storage facilities and an apartment for Scotty below. Slightly later, a garage and smaller service building were added to the compound.

Soon after the buildings were completed, Johnson's visions became grander; he was an immensely rich client, capable of indulging his architectural fantasies. He approached Wright on the recommendation of their mutual friend, Alfred MacArthur.[11] Wright and Johnson visited the site in December 1923; Wright recalled in his autobiography that they "took a trip into Death Valley together where he and Death Valley Scotty had made a place in which to live. He drove his own car, a Dodge, I rode beside him and Nature staged a show for us all the way."[12]

Wright and Johnson passed through Deep Springs, California, on their way to Death Valley Ranch and spent the night at Deep Springs College. An account of their visit and the date were provided in 1987 by George Clark Lyon, a student at Deep Springs at the time. Lyon recalled "a two-car caravan of distinguished guests. . . . A. M. Johnson . . . drove a Dodge car with Frank Lloyd Wright as his passenger; Mrs. Jordan, driving a Jordan car manufactured by her husband, followed. Her passenger was Mrs. Perkins, whose father invented the arc light." All of the guests gave talks to the students; Wright described the survival of the Imperial Hotel after the recent earthquake; Johnson spoke on fundamentalism, saying that he believed every word of the Bible was literally true.[13]

Johnson had erected his first buildings at Death Valley Ranch in a small valley, chosen in part because of the availability of a natural water supply. Wright responded with a new scheme that incorporated the three existing buildings, as shown by a comparison of their locations and dimensions with his new drawings. He also added a new house with connected chapel for the Johnsons to the southwest, overlooking the rest of the compound from a low desert mound. Wright worked out the scheme on a photograph, orienting the house and chapel not with the existing buildings but according to the landscape, creating two intersecting orthogonal axes, one rotated sixty degrees (Figs. 115, 116). He used the chapel as a pivot and created a stepped waterfall on the sixty-degree angle, conforming to a natural dip in the terrain. Once he established the geometry of the compound, he wove the existing and proposed buildings together with his uniform system of construction: concrete-block walls link buildings and define space within the enclosure. Terraced lawns and a network of pools accentuate the tension between the oasis and the barren wasteland.

The concept was experimental. If the geometries of the compound do not collide, neither are they fully integrated; the northeast and southwest portions of the plan continue to read separately. However, this introduction of an oblique angle, untried earlier, lends the project significance it otherwise would have lacked. Though he never abandoned strictly rectangular planning, this precedent gave Wright new freedom of expression, which he explored with increasing confidence.

Although the general layout of the compound did not change as the project developed, the plan of the house and chapel and the elevations of all the buildings were reworked several times. The evolution of the house and chapel was from two separate buildings linked by a passageway to one integrated structure. In one of the preliminary versions, the house is a cubic volume articulated with faceted blocks forming concentric square patterns wrapping around the corners; the roof is a low, gently stepped pyramid (Fig. 117). The result has a strangely funereal appearance; one thinks of a mausoleum without classical apparatus and quadriga.

Another proposal has a similar wall treatment on the house, while the chapel and an entry building have telescoping block walls related to segments of the Ennis house. The house has a steep roof of blocks offset each course and in alternating rows of plain and patterned blocks; a spire over

115. Death Valley Ranch, with sketch of proposed new construction. FLLW FDN, 2306.022

the chapel is composed of blocks adjusted to a 30/60-degree angle (Fig. 118).

In the most carefully articulated and presumably final scheme, the chapel, though linked to the house at the second-story level, is given independent definition as an octagon; the squat spire of the earlier designs has been transformed into an attenuated cone apparently of some material other than concrete block (Fig. 119).[14] The house in elevation is a logical progression from the Ennis house: the telescoping forms have disappeared, and the walls are expressed as great battered planes, the final simplification Wright could make.

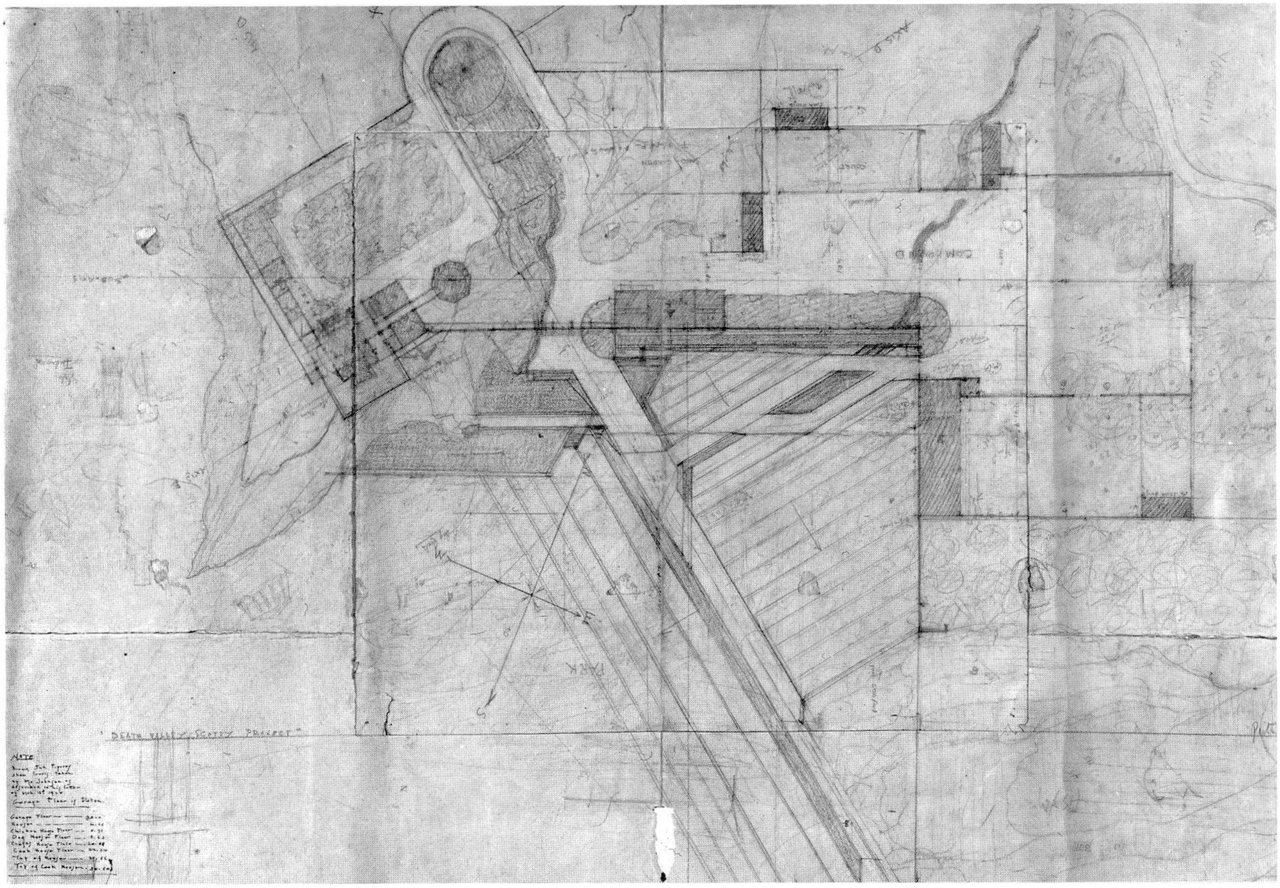

116. A. M. Johnson compound (project), Death Valley, California, plan, 1924. FLLW FDN, 2306.002

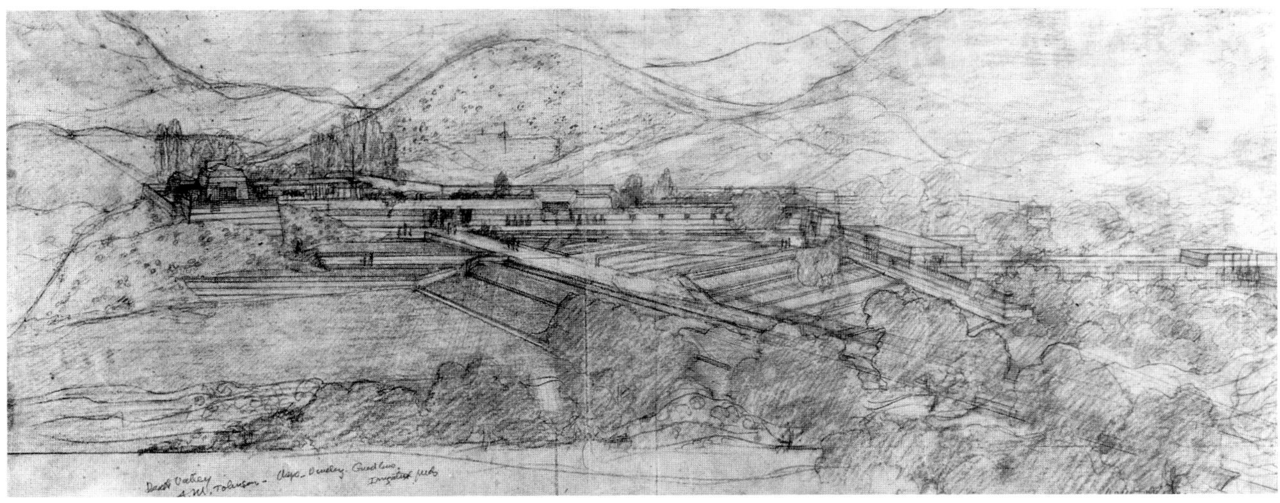

117. A. M. Johnson compound (project), perspective. FLLW FDN, 2306.001

118. A. M. Johnson compound (project), elevation. FLLW FDN, 2306.004

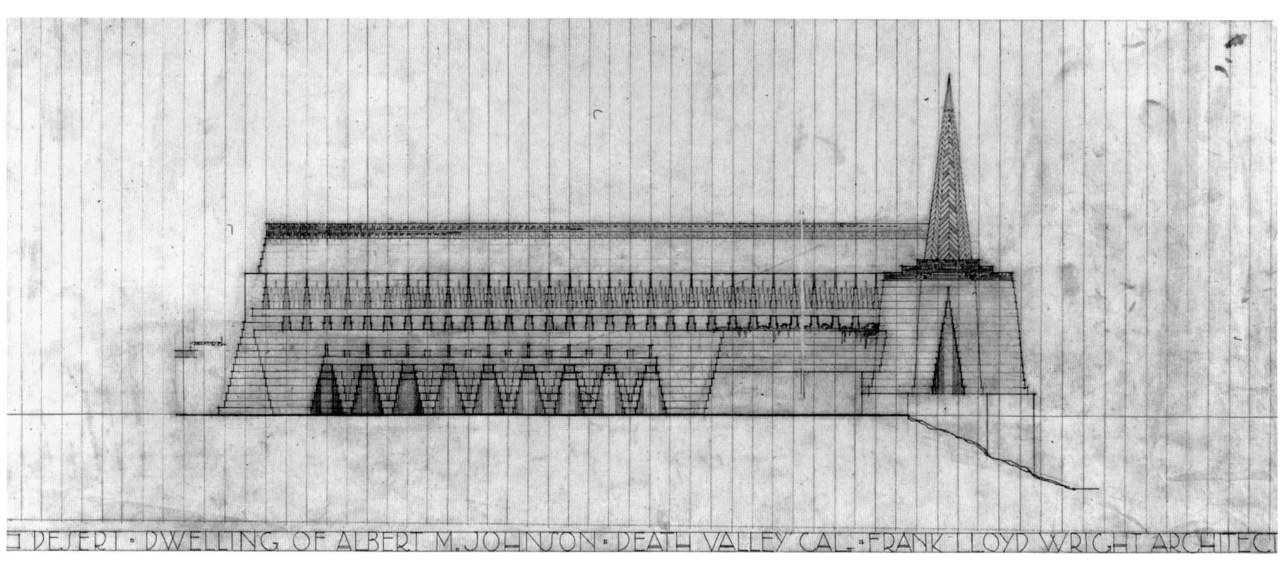

119. A. M. Johnson compound (project), elevation. FLLW FDN, 2306.021

This house offers spatial complexity possible only on a grand scale. The combined living and dining room extends ninety-six feet across the front of the building; the space is modulated into thirds by two bridges spanning the width of the room and allowing it to be seen from numerous perspectives (Fig. 120). The ceiling drops under the bridges; between them, it rises the full height of the building (Fig. 121). Axial extensions at the short ends

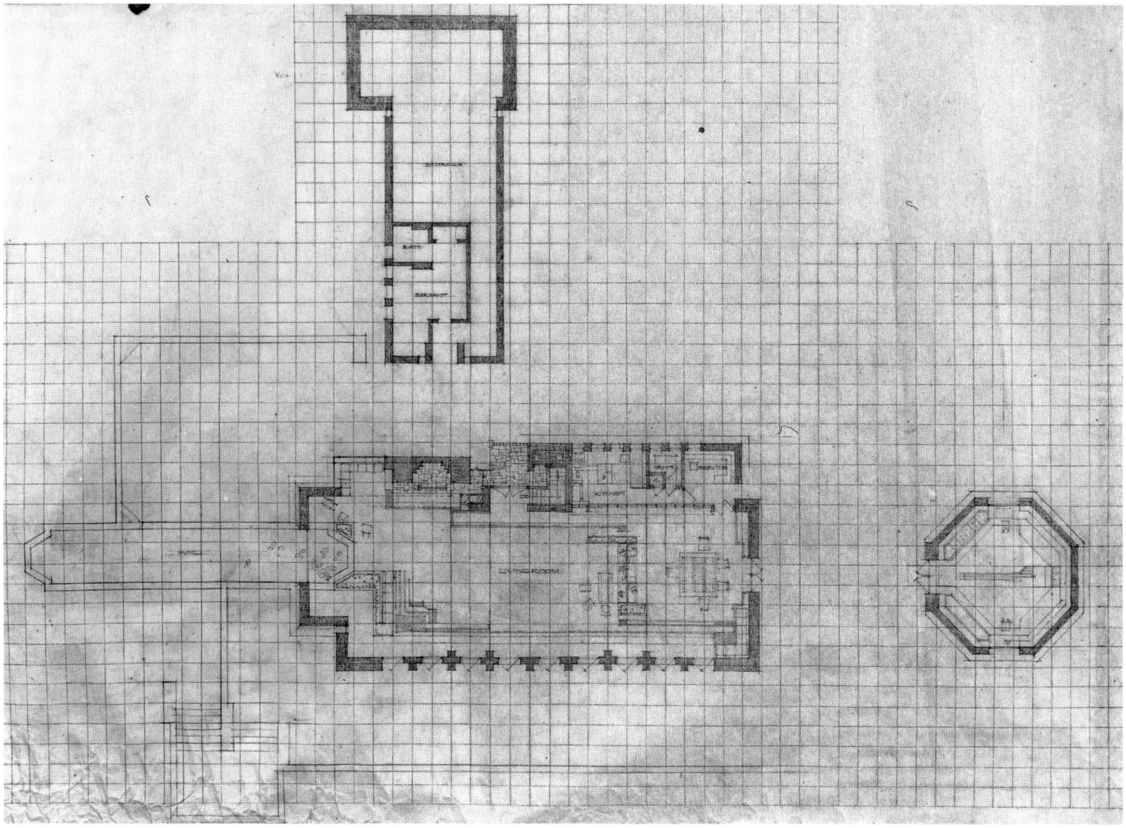

120. A. M. Johnson compound (project), plan. FLLW FDN, 2306.015

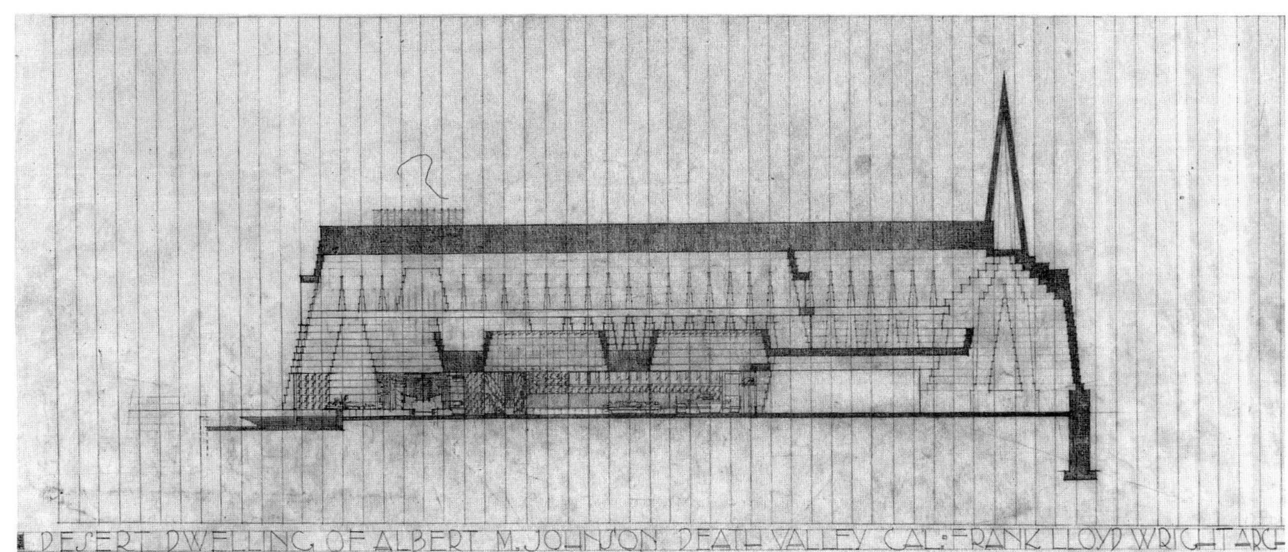

121. A. M. Johnson compound (project), section. FLLW FDN, 2306.017

of the room carry the space beyond the boundaries of the walls: a long, narrow pool projects into the desert to the southwest, and another overhead bridge penetrates the chapel.

The scheme was developed throughout 1924; the earliest date comes from a note on one drawing, referring to a letter of March 16 from Johnson. It was still on the boards in November; Richard Neutra, then in residence at Taliesin, commented in a letter to his mother-in-law that Wright wanted the house to look like a sprouting cactus.[15] The degree of interest Johnson had in carrying out the scheme became clear in early October, however, when he went to see the Los Angeles houses; Lloyd reported afterward to his father that Johnson was indifferent.[16] In any case, the project died a short time later, when Johnson approached Matt Roy Thompson, a construction engineer, to make improvements at the existing Death Valley Ranch.

Johnson's motivation was financial; he explained to Henry-Russell Hitchcock in 1941 that Wright's estimate "ran into several hundred thousand dollars and I did not feel like assuming that investment at the time although a little later I did put up a couple of buildings and the cost of these ultimately exceeded by many times Mr. Wright's estimate."[17]

PHI GAMMA DELTA FRATERNITY HOUSE, MADISON

Richard Neutra worked with Wright at Taliesin on one more concrete-block building, a fraternity house for Phi Gamma Delta at the University of Wisconsin, Madison. Wright obtained the commission through his cousin, Richard Lloyd Jones, an alumnus of the university and a member of the Fiji building committee. The committee voted in November 1924 to secure a site on Langdon Street for a new building.[18] The property overlooks Lake Mendota and slopes gently down to its shore.

Wright's scheme was well developed by January 1925; Neutra completed several of the drawings. The building was articulated in three masses, stepping down toward the lake and conforming to the natural grade of the site (Fig. 122). The uppermost unit, facing Langdon Street, is actually a separate, three-story building containing a reception hall and guest rooms (Fig. 123). The greatly elongated central section contains cubicles for forty-six students on its two upper floors and the dining room and kitchen on the two lower floors (Figs. 124, 125). A great hall, three stories high, terminates the structure at lake's edge (Fig. 126). While the building is convincingly resolved, its forms synthesize the past rather than anticipate the future. Elements are drawn from the Doheny Ranch project and from the Ennis house; there is none of the abstraction of the contemporary A. M. Johnson house. More progressive is the one important space in the building, the great hall. While the plan is not new—the Millard and Storer houses in southern California come quickly to mind—the ceiling is treated as a freely disposed, asymmetrical composition.

Wright presented his scheme to the committee at a meeting at Taliesin on April 4, 1925.[19] The response was that "the plans . . . were the best . . . that had ever been submitted to satisfy the requirements of a fraternity's program."[20] By October, however, the members had reconsidered and asked Wright to make some minor changes. The main request was that the sleeping quarters be separated from the study rooms to create a series of suites. The second floor of the Langdon Street building was to be modified similarly, with the rooms for alumni moved to the third floor, replacing an open dormitory.[21] Wright completed a new set of drawings as requested.

Because it was necessary for the fraternity to sell its existing building on Henry Street and to finance the purchase of the new lot, the project proceeded slowly. At another meeting of the committee in June 1926, attended by Wright and a contractor, the cost of the proposed building was discussed. The conclusion was that to construct Wright's building according to the original plans would cost close to $100,000, an unacceptable figure. Wright offered three options: that he retire from the project; that he find another contractor who could build it for the amount of money available; or that he redraw his plans to bring them within the committee's limit of $80,000. His third proposal was accepted; the scaled-down drawings were approved in September.[22]

Finally, on October 16, the committee decided that "under present conditions it would be impossible to proceed with plans of Frank Lloyd Wright." Estimates for the revised plans were now between $100,000 and $115,000.[23] Wright's modified plans were turned over to a local firm, Law, Law & Potter, who built the new fraternity house in a conventional collegiate-medieval style, though with a clear debt to Wright's floor plan. "Outside its 'inspiration,'" Wright commented, the building "is punk."[24]

122. Phi Gamma Delta fraternity house (project), University of Wisconsin, Madison, perspective, 1924. FLLW FDN, 2504.041

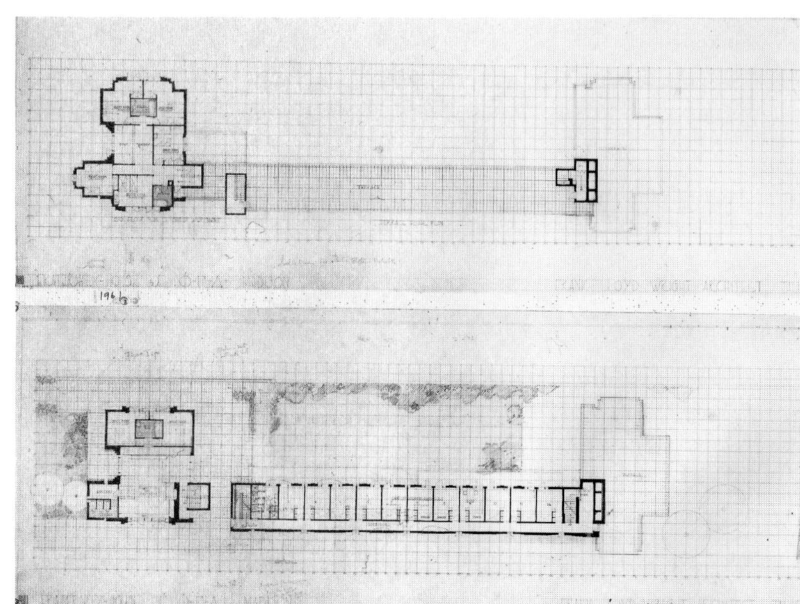

123. Phi Gamma Delta fraternity house (project), street-level plan, guest apartment, top-floor plan, center section (below); second-floor plan, guest apartment (above). FLLW FDN, 2504.013

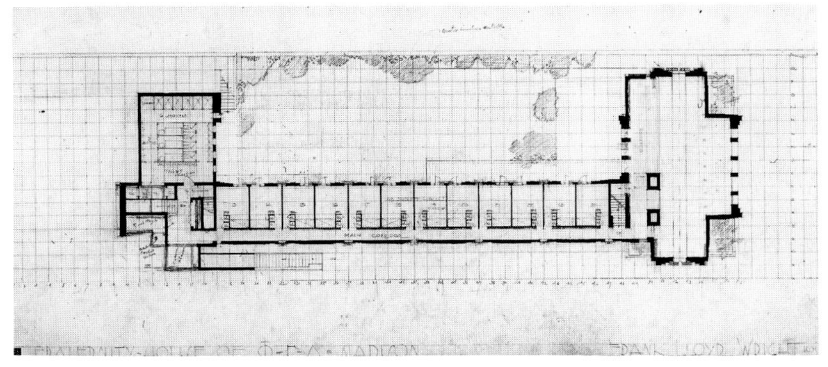

124. Phi Gamma Delta fraternity house (project), middle-level plan, center section. FLLW FDN, 2504.011

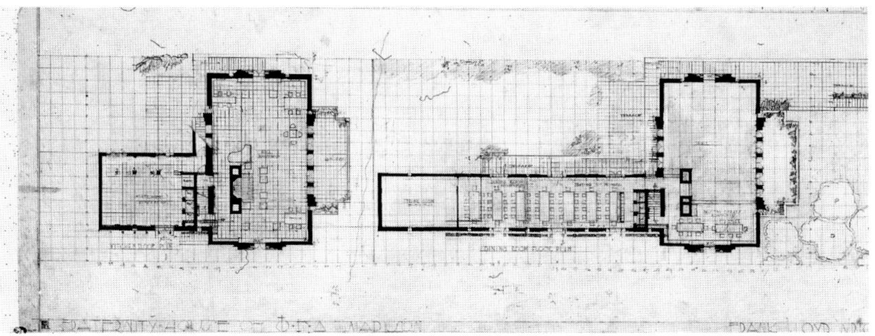

125. Phi Gamma Delta fraternity house (project), lower-level plan, center section (right); great hall plan (left). FLLW FDN, 2504.009

126. Phi Gamma Delta fraternity house (project), interior perspective. FLLW FDN, 2504.001

□ □ □

Wright had no new opportunities to build with concrete block in the mid-1920s, but he continued to be preoccupied with the concept; this was a period of reflection and ferment. In a brief article, published in German translation in 1926, he spoke of the clarity of the system and related it to the principle of standardization originating in the machine. In his view, the "whole technology of construction has been transferred to the architect's office and is a question of design—the blending of a uniform material into a uniform system. . . . Within the simple limits which the system itself sets, boundless multiplicity is possible."[25]

The following year, Wright summarized his Los Angeles experiences in a letter to A. N. Rebori, a Chicago architect who was preparing an article on the concrete-block houses for the *Architectural Record:*

> None of the advantages which the system was designed to have were had in the construction of these models. We had no organization—Prepared the moulds experimentally. . . .
>
> None of the accuracy which is essential to economy in manufacture nor any benefit of organization was achieved in these models. . . . The blocks were made of various combinations of the decayed granite and sand and gravel of the sites—The mixture was not rich—Nor was it possible to cure the blocks in sufficient moisture. The blocks might well have been of better quality.
>
> Some unnecessary trouble was experienced in making the buildings waterproof. All the difficulties met with were due to poor workmanship and not to the nature of the scheme.
>
> But it is seldom that buildings of a new type are built out-right as experimental models with less trouble than were these not withstanding our lack of organization and our concentration on invention.[26]

Wright followed up in an important series of articles published in the *Architectural Record* in 1927–28, restating the theories that had guided his work and giving additional insight into the intellectual underpinnings of the concrete-block experiments. He first underscored the thesis of an 1894 speech, "Architecture and the Machine," in asserting that "the Machine is the architect's tool—whether he likes it or not." It is, he continued, "an obedient, tireless fabricator of a non-sentient product." The result was standardization, which "as a principle is at work in all things with greater activity than ever before." He concluded that "standardization apprehended as a principle of order has the danger of monotony in application," but that properly understood, it "is no detriment to art or artist."[27]

In 1927 Wright described concrete as "still a mass material taking form from moulds, erroneously called 'forms,'" but demonstrated in textile block construction that "standardization enters as the *unit-system,*" which produces a "monolith *fabricated* instead of *poured.*" He contrasted the "primitive period in the development of concrete building when it was necessary . . . to build a rough building complete in wood as a 'mould' [as at Unity Temple, with] this easier more plastic method [in which] the making of the structural-unit and the process of fabrication become complete synchronized standardizations. . . . The process of elimination which *standardization* becomes has left only essentials. Here is a process that makes of the mechanics of concrete building a mono-material and mono-method affair."[28]

This was the first time that Wright discussed the textile block system in terms of mono-material construction. He projected "an outer shell and an inner shell separated by a complete air space. The inner walls, floors and ceilings which this inner shell becomes are the same as the outside walls, and, fabricated in the same way at the same time." He envisioned sheet-metal windows "standardized to work with the block slab units"; piping "cut to the standard unit-length in the shop and set into hollow spaces"; and no plastering, carpentry, masonry, formwork, or painting.[29]

After four years of exploration, and with scant building activity, the textile block system was theoretically mature. The experiment begun in 1923 essentially as a method of design based on repetition of standardized units was by 1927 a fully integrated system of modular design and construction. Only the technology of assembly remained to be resolved.

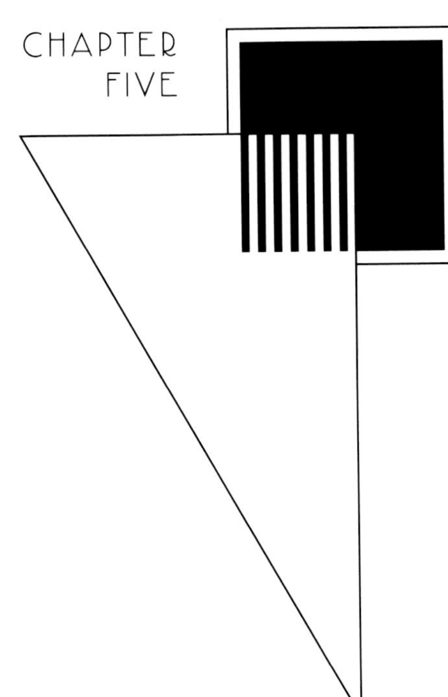

RENEWAL: THE ARIZONA DESERT

Wright's first opportunity to build after leaving Los Angeles came in 1928 at the invitation of Albert Chase McArthur, architect of the new Arizona Biltmore Hotel in Phoenix. McArthur was interested in using Wright's concrete-block construction system and approached the architect for permission. Wright agreed and traveled to Phoenix in January, working closely with McArthur for five months. While he was there, he received his own commission for another resort hotel, to be built of concrete block in the desert south of Phoenix. This new project was Wright's first major work since the Imperial Hotel; coming at a critical moment, it caused him to comment to his son John, "Phoenix seems to be the name for me too." He added, "It looks as tho I was well started now for the last lap of my life and work."[1]

Arizona Biltmore Hotel, Phoenix

Albert McArthur (1881–1951) had worked in Wright's Oak Park studio for two years, between 1907 and 1909; in 1918 he had spent six weeks with Wright at Taliesin.[2] This seemingly was his only architectural education. He had attended the Lawrence Scientific School at Harvard between 1901 and 1905, concentrating on mechanical engineering, and Harvard College in 1906–7, but had never received a degree.[3] McArthur's father,

Warren, is familiar as Wright's early patron. Two younger brothers, Charles H. and Warren, Jr., were pioneers in Phoenix, settling there in 1910 (two years before the territory of Arizona was admitted as a state) and 1913, respectively. In 1913 they established the McArthur Brothers Mercantile Company, whose most visible asset was a successful Dodge automobile dealership.[4] Much of their energy was directed toward building tourism in Arizona, and accordingly they promoted hotels in Tucson, Prescott, and Flagstaff. With considerable foresight, they envisioned the development of Phoenix as a major winter resort. In 1917 they suggested to Albert, who was visiting at the time, that he prepare sketches for a new hotel, which they would promote in cooperation with the Phoenix chamber of commerce. There were then two resort hotels in the area, the Ingleside Inn in Phoenix, opened in 1908, and the San Marcos Hotel, twenty-four miles south, in Chandler, opened in 1913. Only in 1925 did prospects for success seem certain; Albert then moved to Phoenix. Two more years passed before an alliance with the Los Angeles Biltmore Company was formed, leading to the creation of the Arizona Biltmore Corporation, which was to finance and own the new hotel. In 1927 the site was acquired, and preliminary designs were completed.[5]

The site was a 621-acre tract seven miles northeast of downtown Phoenix and just outside the city limits. Spurs of the Phoenix Mountains extended into the northernmost portion, and the Arizona Canal roughly bisected the property. Two hundred acres were reserved for the hotel; the remainder would be developed as a residential area.

The basic layout of the building was established in a preliminary scheme dated May 1927. Because of the acreage available to him, McArthur was under no constraint to design compactly. He proposed a structure with several wings extending in various directions from a central, three-story mass (Fig. 127). The irregular outline of the building is determined in part by the juxtaposition of rectangular to octagonal geometry. In front, two parallel wings form an entrance court reminiscent of that of the Imperial Hotel, which McArthur knew well from his 1918 visit to Taliesin. By adding a prominent asymmetrical wing to the east, however, he mitigated the formality of Wright's plan. In the rear, wings are placed at forty-five-degree angles, partially enclosing an octagonal patio. The effect is an undigested composition of dissimilar parts. The east wing is sadly out of scale and stylistically inconsistent with the more delicate main building. And the nonrectangular geometry, which Wright himself was only beginning to explore as a planning device, is not fully integrated into the design.

127. Arizona Biltmore Hotel, Phoenix, Arizona, preliminary perspective, 1927. Courtesy of Warren McArthur, Jr.

In another scheme, undated but obviously a step toward the finished design, the polygonal geometry is more convincing. The rear patio is shaped as a hexagon; its forms are repeated in a complex new wing projecting from the front of the building (Fig. 128). A fourth story has been added to the main unit, and freestanding cottages are indicated at the rear. A roadway separates the hotel from the Arizona Canal, shown in the foreground.

128. Arizona Biltmore Hotel, preliminary perspective, ca. 1927. Courtesy of Warren McArthur, Jr.

When he began working on the hotel, McArthur was not contemplating using the textile block system, and the early schemes were designed for some other, unspecified, method of construction. His interest in the system must have been prompted by an article describing Wright's experiments on the West Coast that appeared in the *Architectural Record* in December 1927.[6] Shortly after, McArthur wrote to his mentor in Spring Green, Wisconsin, asking for permission to use the system and for technical information. Wright telegraphed his answer:

> Dear Albert Congratulations Textile block ideal for your purpose Make plans and elevations sixteen inch unit in all directions Typical molds available in Los Angeles Pattern ideal for system if accurate size in block unit can be had Accurate size necessary to complete success Should come out to help you start perhaps Frank Lloyd Wright[7]

With some misgiving, McArthur consented, and Wright arrived in January 1928, undoubtedly contributing his stamp of genius to the project, but also engendering questions of attribution that remain controversial today.[8]

Wright remained in Phoenix through May, working with McArthur on the hotel. According to McArthur, on Wright's departure the "plans and some details were complete, as well as sketches for many other details. The detailed elevations, both exterior and interior, however, had not been begun, although some sketches, which were little more than indication of method had been attempted."[9]

There is substantial evidence to support McArthur's statements. The original plans, now in the possession of his nephew, Warren McArthur, Jr., are dated April 1928. Mr. McArthur also has blueprints for numerous details—perhaps most notably the splendid pierced-copper roof overhangs—which were completed virtually throughout the construction process; that is, in Wright's absence. These and other documents significantly clarify the roles of the two designers.

The general form of the hotel as it was constructed derives from McArthur's second, undated preliminary study and can therefore be safely attributed to him, though it is fair to assume that numerous refinements were made under Wright's supervision. The final elevation is revealed in a perspective drawing clearly showing concrete-block walls; it was therefore completed after Wright's arrival in Phoenix. The fussy and arbitrary geometry of the preceding scheme is replaced by a more ordered composition that would have resulted at least partially from the new construction system (Fig. 129). The building is more gently massed; the elevator tower is strengthened, giving welcome vertical contrast; and a hipped roof and festive spire have been added over the ballroom.

The main building extends approximately 342 feet in length and is four stories high. Public spaces—the main lobby, dining room, and sun room—and service areas occupy the first floor (Fig. 130). Guest rooms are above. Two single-story wings extend to the south, one perpendicular to the main building and containing shops, the other at a sixty-degree angle and containing a polygonal ballroom and lounge. The back of the main building and a pair of two-story wings to the east enclose four sides of a hexagonal patio. The other sides of the patio open to fifteen separate guest cottages, set on the grounds behind the hotel.

The building is not organized on the sixteen-inch module Wright recommended, but instead on blocks measuring eighteen inches by thirteen and one-half inches, six blocks forming one nine-foot unit. The innovation seems to have been wholly McArthur's, as he explained:

> In such a group of buildings, the functional factors call for no particular symbolic expression. Nevertheless I played with symbolism, both in the design of the ornament on the block unit and in the proportions throughout the

129. Arizona Biltmore Hotel, perspective, 1928. Courtesy of Edward Jacobson

> building, although I have never mentioned this to anyone . . . there is a continual repetition of 3, 5, & 7; and more complicated successions such as 3 + 1, 5 + 2, 7 + 3, 3 + ½, 5 + 1, 7 + ½; there are others, but all based on the same 3, 5, 7, with multiple increments. The block itself 18″ by 13½″, the height ¾ of the length keeps a definite rhythm throughout the design with harmonic proportions between horizontal and vertical lines. This, and the spacing of lengths of walls, and heights of openings, by no means a definite unit, in this case the length and height of the block (harmonic to one another) I call linear harmonics, and when properly applied can yield at least a well-ordered effect. In the hands of a master designer beauty will result.[10]

The dimensions of the blocks aside, the Arizona Biltmore structurally is a regression. It was the first concrete-block building designed after Wright's statements of theory in 1926–27, yet none of the innovations that had developed in the four-year gestation period since the California work were incorporated. Plans and specifications for the hotel and cottages call for textile block walls to be combined with various other building materials. Walls in the ground-floor public rooms are of double-block construction. In the corridors leading to guest rooms, they are single-thickness block, backed by plastered metal lath. Floors are concrete slabs;

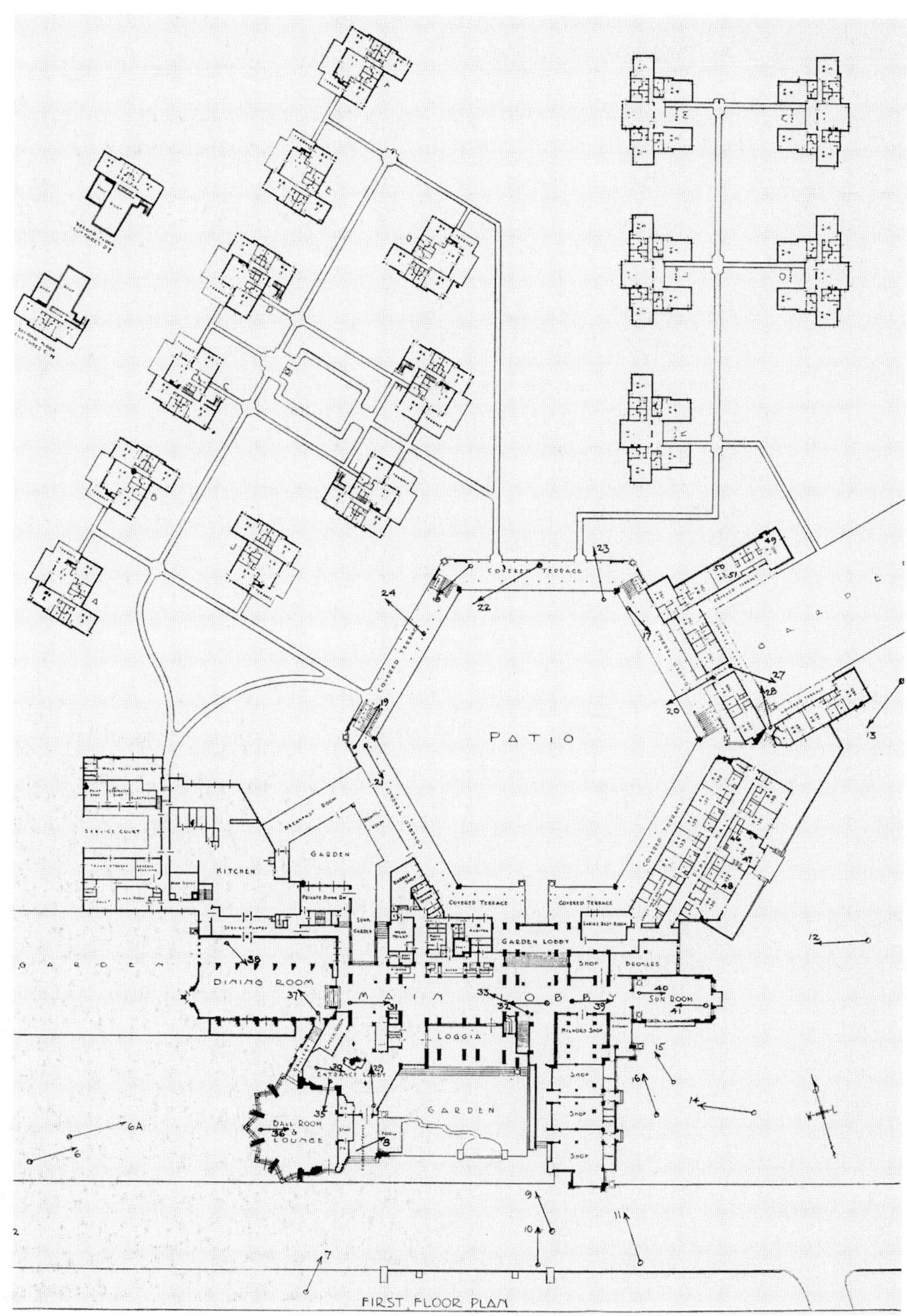

130. Arizona Biltmore Hotel, plans. Reproduced from *Architectural Forum*, December 1929, 20

partitions in guest rooms are wood frame and plaster; and balloon framing was specified for the pitched roofs (Fig. 131). "Columns"—the term used in the specifications—and beams were built by pouring concrete between the blocks. Wherever block shell walls required extra reinforcement, portions of the interior space were divided with boards inserted from above, and the space was filled with concrete to form a post.[11]

Plans were far enough along by mid-April to obtain bids; Wright told Lloyd, "The Arizona-Biltmore has reached the crucial stage when the contractor enters, costs must be met and the usual prejudices reckoned with and defeated."[12] The contractor was S. M. Benet of Los Angeles; before he took on the project, he requested one of the original "block machines," so that he could test the time it took to make a block. Wright suggested that Benet visit Lloyd, to "take a short cut to many conclusions you would otherwise arrive at, as we did at much time and expense." He also responded to Benet's idea that the blocks be made topside down, indicating that this had been tried, and that it created "certain difficulties."[13] A contract with Benet was signed in May. Soon after, Wright left Phoenix, although his involvement with the project was not over: he

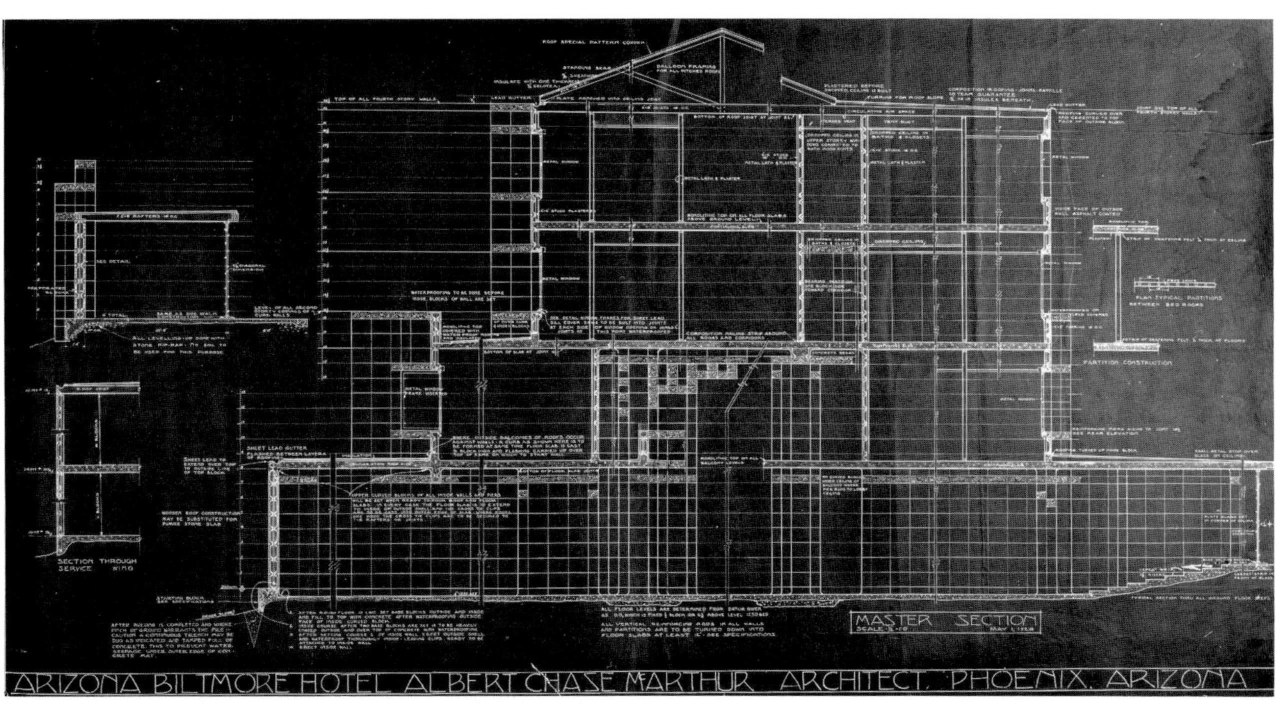

131. Arizona Biltmore Hotel, section. FLLW FDN, 2710.032

followed the building process closely and responded to McArthur's requests for assistance.

There was a special complication in getting the pattern molds made to cast the blocks for the Arizona Biltmore. McArthur recalled later that he had "tried in succession four sculptors and modellers, but all failed to interpret the drawings to [his] satisfaction."[14] "None of these sculptors," he complained, "could seem to sense the idea of the straight lines which were really subtle curves, and plane surfaces which only appeared to be planes. It took an architect to show them." He finally made his own model, which was adapted by Emry Kopta, a sculptor of local reputation. The molds were sent to Los Angeles, where aluminum forms for the twenty-nine block types were manufactured by Thornton Hamlin. The blocks were fabricated at the site, as before, and though the gravel was coarser than that used in Los Angeles, the basic procedure was the same as at the Ennis house.[15]

Construction was plagued with delays; work was to have begun June 5, but in fact did not start until mid-August. Wright passed through Phoenix briefly the next month and observed, "The wreck here at the Arizona-Biltmore is due directly to the lack of the architect's central and final authority in matters of construction."[16] Nonetheless, once under way, work proceeded quickly with ten-hour day and night shifts. By late October much of the concrete-and-wood skeleton was in place; later photographs show the concrete-block walls going up (Figs. 132, 133).

On November 28, McArthur sent a telegram to Wright at Taliesin, asking him to "kindly send finished renderings immediately," and requesting formulas for green copper and gold ceilings. The renderings were a group of six drawings Wright prepared in November and December—seemingly very late in the construction process—for the McArthur brothers, for which they agreed to pay him $1,000. Wright responded that two drawings, "smaller ones of less consequence," had been sent a few days earlier and that larger exterior and interior views would be ready soon.[17] Two of these drawings, an elevation and a view of the lobby, are known; they are based on sketches still in Wright's archive (Fig. 134, see Fig. 129). In addition, there are sketches for the entrance lobby, main lobby, dining room, and ballroom that depict the building essentially as it was completed.

In a letter written in December 1928, Wright commented that he was hearing regularly from the developers of the Arizona Biltmore: "They are expecting to have it open January 15 they say, and perhaps they will."[18] In

132. Arizona Biltmore Hotel, October 22, 1928. Courtesy of the Arizona Biltmore Hotel

133. Arizona Biltmore Hotel, with the dining room at left. Courtesy of the Arizona Biltmore Hotel

fact, the hotel opened on February 23, 1929, a bit behind schedule, but still after only six months' construction. Banner headlines in local papers praised the accomplishment of the McArthur brothers and the design of the building. Albert McArthur was given full credit as architect; Wright was mentioned as a consultant.[19]

Like many collective artistic efforts, the Arizona Biltmore both sings and is a compromised success. The front elevation has enormous presence. Its projecting wings, tower, and pierced roof overhangs do not prepare one

134. Arizona Biltmore Hotel, perspective. Courtesy of Edward Jacobson

for the banality of the rear (no less visible to guests approaching the building from outlying wings and cottages), with its utterly flat surfaces, relieved principally by engaged pilasters and casement windows (Figs. 135, 136). The windows themselves are poorly proportioned: although they fit within the modular grid of the building, they do not conform to the ratio of height to width of the individual blocks.[20] Also, they are feebly integrated into the design; Wright had demonstrated in California the expressive possibilities windows provide in concrete-block construction. The point is reinforced on comparison with the more articulate Phi Gamma Delta fraternity-house project, a not dissimilar design problem.

That McArthur's initial source was the Imperial Hotel seems irrefutable. In the two-year development period of the Biltmore, the significant changes that occurred were less to the elevations of the building than to the plan; the formal axiality of the Imperial gave way to calculated, if tentative, asymmetry. Entry is through a wing projecting from the building at a sixty-degree angle; however, the axis of the entry corresponds not with the oblique angle, but with the rectangular grid of the rest of the

135. Arizona Biltmore Hotel, front elevation. Courtesy of the Arizona Biltmore Hotel

136. Arizona Biltmore Hotel, rear elevation. Courtesy of the Arizona Biltmore Hotel

137. Arizona Biltmore Hotel, entrance lobby, looking north. Courtesy of the Arizona Biltmore Hotel

138. Arizona Biltmore Hotel, ballroom, looking east, toward the stage. Courtesy of the Arizona Biltmore Hotel

building (see Fig. 130). The entrance lobby itself is generous but amorphous and without clear focus, and there is no reinforcement of this angle in the other public spaces (Fig. 137). The reinforcement, in fact, is in the outlying wings and siting of the western cluster of guest cottages, a connection too subtle to be made by most observers.

The ballroom, or lounge, projects from the southwestern end of the entry wing; its polygonal shape can be traced to the undated second preliminary elevation. The form has been clarified somewhat: construction photographs reveal a regular, ten-sided skeleton of concrete posts and beams. One might challenge such a prominent use of a decagon in a building laid out as a partial octagon; in fact, the designers successfully obscured the shape of the structure by manipulating the enclosing walls. The basic device was to extend the space beyond the defining geometry of the skeletal frame, creating projecting right-angled bays between the posts. Ten great beams, rising like spokes, support the roof and provide a point of reference for the design (Fig. 138).

The angle of the entrance wing points to the main lobby, a great hall overlooked by second-story balconies and opening onto several other public spaces (Figs. 139, 140). The floor is finished concrete, stained green and scored to coincide with the block units; the ceiling is plaster with applied gold leaf. Block-faced concrete beams, resting on corbeled brackets, span the width of the room in pairs, establishing cadence and modulating the great length. Lighting is integral; translucent glass blocks in sheet-copper frames with reflectors behind them are set flush with the concrete blocks, a fine innovation. These lights terminate the corbels and are set into the piers; there also are freestanding columns built of the glass blocks on concrete-block bases.

This is an area to linger in; the rewards are many. The boundaries are defined less by walls than by piers, permitting the eye to travel and inviting exploration. There are no dead ends; a loggia opens to the right, a garden lobby up a short flight of stairs ahead to the left. This is a space unlike any in the California block houses, and there may be an object lesson here, that the textile block system is best suited to large-scale public buildings. Concrete block can be visually oppressive in a small space; its potency diminishes with a sense of amplitude.

The dining room, at the west end of the lobby, is the least animated public space in the hotel (Fig. 141). A row of concrete-block piers divides approximately one third of the room from the main space, a planning device Wright found satisfying; he repeated it a short time later in San

139. Arizona Biltmore Hotel, lobby, looking east. Courtesy of the Arizona Biltmore Hotel

Marcos in the Desert. Imposing wall hangings by Maynard Dixon and Edith Hamlin, specially commissioned by Albert McArthur, cover the blank wall between the dining room and kitchen. The hangings have a stylized Southwestern Indian theme and are a welcome and unexpected addition to a building that is generally unreceptive of art.

A men's smoking room is hidden away off a second floor corridor; this fine space is enhanced by surprise of encounter. It is virtually self-contained: walls are solid concrete block; the only windows are overhead, in an attic space. But there is no lack of richness. A great, animated fireplace of faceted blocks advances into the room; corner piers terminate in corbeled blocks; and elaborately framed flush lights fill the ceiling (Fig. 142).

The program of the Arizona Biltmore also included fifteen guest cottages behind the main building. The cottages are laid out in two clusters and are based on three floor plans, which are then also rotated 180 degrees

140. Arizona Biltmore Hotel, lobby, looking west, toward the dining room from the second floor. Courtesy of the Arizona Biltmore Hotel

141. Arizona Biltmore Hotel, dining room, looking northwest. Courtesy of the Arizona Biltmore Hotel

142. Arizona Biltmore Hotel, men's smoking room, looking south. Courtesy of the Arizona Biltmore Hotel

143. Arizona Biltmore Hotel, cottages, looking northwest. Courtesy of the Arizona Biltmore Hotel

and drawn as mirror images to create symmetrical compositions (see Fig. 130). The cottages in the larger group of ten are based on two plans: a one-story unit with four bedrooms; another with two stories and six bedrooms. The cottages in the smaller group are another one-story plan with four bedrooms. The cottages are very simple: their rectangular forms repeat none of the experimental geometry of the hotel itself and they are constructed primarily of plain blocks (Fig. 143). Wright was more satisfied with the structural system of the cottages than that of the main building; he recalled in his autobiography, "The details of the system itself were better followed with better results."[21]

Throughout the hotel and cottages, patterned and plain blocks are combined as in the California houses. Unlike the angular, nonrepresentational patterns Wright used, McArthur created an abstraction of subtle curves based on musical relationships and mathematics.[22] The patterned blocks appear in solid and perforated versions. The design is especially effective in multiples, and the blocks can be rotated 180 degrees to create a new, vertically oriented, interlocking pattern. There also are blocks that have less than a full face to accommodate special conditions; like Wright, McArthur made no provision for partial patterns. Because the design is based on vertical mirror images, it divides in half, convincingly, in this plane to create corner blocks. It works less well when divided horizontally; the design appears truncated.

If the design process for the Arizona Biltmore can be reconstructed in broad outline with some certainty, it remains more challenging to sort out the complexities of the relationship between Wright and McArthur. Wright's participation was, from the beginning, that of advisor, a role wholly unsuited to his temperament, and there are numerous reports that he overstepped his boundaries.[23] There are also indications that his assertiveness was welcomed, even needed, by McArthur. On June 27, 1928, three weeks after construction was expected to begin, Wright signed an agreement with McArthur and the Arizona Biltmore Corporation that stated, "Heretofore architect has performed certain services for the owner, and it is the purpose of the parties hereto that the architect shall hereafter perform additional services for the owner in connection with its hotel project." Six months after the hotel opened, McArthur warmly acknowledged Wright's contribution, writing, "Without you, whose loyalty stood behind me like a rock, I see clearly that I could not have done it."[24]

The most compelling evidence of Wright's contribution is the group of six conceptual sketches remaining in his archive, which were the prototypes for the renderings commissioned by the McArthurs in late 1928. Surely these are the sketches to which Albert McArthur was referring when he recalled that, on Wright's departure, "the detailed elevations, both exterior and interior . . . had not been begun, although some sketches, which were little more than indication of method had been attempted." Wright would have had little incentive to continue working on the design of the building after he left Phoenix—he had his own new commission for a concrete-block resort hotel to consume his creative energy—and if the sketches were McArthur's, it is improbable that Wright would have been asked to complete the renderings.

There also are unanswered questions about the structural timidity of the building. Wright offered only a partial explanation when he recalled that

> Albert encountered the usual opposition to the unusual in design and construction; he was unable to stem the co-lateral tide of suggested changes in technique which soon robbed the system of all economic value and left it standing as a novel and beautiful outside for an unintelligent engineers [*sic*] inside, whereas great technical economy was first and foremost a feature of the system had it been naturally allowed to work.[25]

Other reasons come to mind as well. When Wright agreed to serve as advisor on the project, he placed himself in the position of offering advice about a system with which he had had very little practical experience. The earlier work, of course, had been largely turned over to Lloyd, and Wright immediately wrote to his son for advice: "If you know of anything at all that can come out of the Los Angeles experiments latterly entrusted to you that will help me now—I should be glad to have it."[26] Wright also requested that one of the old molds be sent as an example for making the new ones.

Also, there were darker clouds on the horizon. Soon after Wright arrived in Phoenix he and the McArthur brothers signed an agreement that he would be paid ten thousand dollars "for his services in establishing suitable technique for use of the Textile and Blockslab Construction, invented and owned by him, in the plans for the Biltmore Hotel." During his last month in Phoenix, serious unanswered questions arose concerning ownership of the system; on June 27, Wright signed another agreement with Albert McArthur and the Arizona Biltmore Corporation, which specifically stated that he was owner of the patents.[27] Then the issue was put aside until 1930.

A greater affront to Albert McArthur than the patent controversy was his realization shortly after the hotel opened that his role as architect was being questioned. Although he had consistently been credited with the design, Wright's assistance was also noted. Aside from local coverage, the most significant publication of the Biltmore was an article that appeared in the *Architectural Record* in July 1929. It stated: "Throughout the effort of the architect has been to design in the spirit of Frank Lloyd Wright's concepts. . . . Mr. Wright came to Arizona and all the technical details for the use of the concrete-block type of construction were worked out under his direction."[28] Within months McArthur was combatting rumors that Wright was the architect, that his own name had been used without his having done the actual work. In April 1930, McArthur asked Wright for a written statement of their relationship.[29] Wright replied two months later:

> To Whom It May Concern;
>
> All I have done in connection with the building of the Arizona Biltmore near Phoenix I have done for Albert McArthur himself at his sole request and for him and none other.
>
> Albert McArthur is the architect of that building. All attempts to take the credit for that performance from him are gratuitous and beside the mark.
>
> But for him Phoenix would have nothing like the Biltmore and it is my hope that he may be enabled to give Phoenix many more beautiful buildings as I believe him entirely capable of doing so.
>
> Frank Lloyd Wright
> Taliesin
> June 2nd 1930[30]

McArthur published Wright's statement with remarks of his own in 1941. He was motivated by the appearance of two books in 1940 "which so misstate the facts, that it becomes my clear duty to make a public statement in vindication both of the truth, for the sake of the record, and of myself as the designer and architect of this project."[31]

Although they had kept in touch, McArthur was embittered. Rather than a beginning, the hotel was an end for the McArthurs in Phoenix. By August 1929, William Wrigley had taken over Charles and Warren's interest in the building and had foreclosed on land around it that had served as collateral for the loans secured for the project.[32] Albert moved to Los Angeles in 1930, and Wright saw him there five or six years later. After lunch at Wright's hotel in Hollywood, one of his apprentices, Blaine Drake, drove McArthur home. Drake recalls:

> He started to tell me his story of the Biltmore in Phoenix. He was quite bitter about FLLW, blaming him for the failure of the hotel project and ending his career as an architect. ACM said he had never invited FLLW to Arizona but had written asking for permission to use his block system. FLLW was not working at that time so he came out and took over the design of the hotel and control of his office and men. He said FLLW was responsible for the downfall of him and the McArthur family by recklessly increasing the cost of the hotel so that all of the family's capital was absorbed. He discredited and belittled ACM to everyone, especially the investors, persuading them ACM was not capable of handling the project.[33]

McArthur's statement contradicts the spirit of gratitude he expressed toward Wright soon after the hotel was finished, though we will probably never know if his mood had changed or if he was finally expressing latent sentiments. It is a commonplace to observe that McArthur never produced anything else on par with the Biltmore, though perhaps grossly unfair to suggest that he was incapable of doing so. The man's papers radiate musical and mathematical abilities closely akin to architectural creation; we are left with the dilemma of a tangled relationship with a genius who may have provided both seeds for inspiration and a path to defeat.

San Marcos in the Desert, Chandler

However troubled, Wright's association with the McArthur family and the Arizona Biltmore did have one consequence of singular importance in the history of the textile block system. While he was in Arizona, Wright met Dr. Alexander J. Chandler, founder of a new town twenty-four miles south of Phoenix (Fig. 144).[34] Chandler had followed work on the Biltmore closely and was inspired by the potential of the structural system. He had his own project for a new resort hotel in mind and discussed the idea with Wright. The result, called San Marcos in the Desert, is the project in which the textile block system came closest to technical and aesthetic resolution.

Alexander John Chandler (1859–1950) was born in Coaticook, Quebec, Canada. After graduation from the Montreal Veterinary College, he practiced as a veterinarian in Detroit for five years. In 1887 he was appointed veterinary surgeon for the Territory of Arizona and moved to Prescott, the territorial capital. Discouraged by a severe drought, he resigned one month later and went to Phoenix, en route to Los Angeles. While he was in Phoenix the drought ended—it reportedly rained for

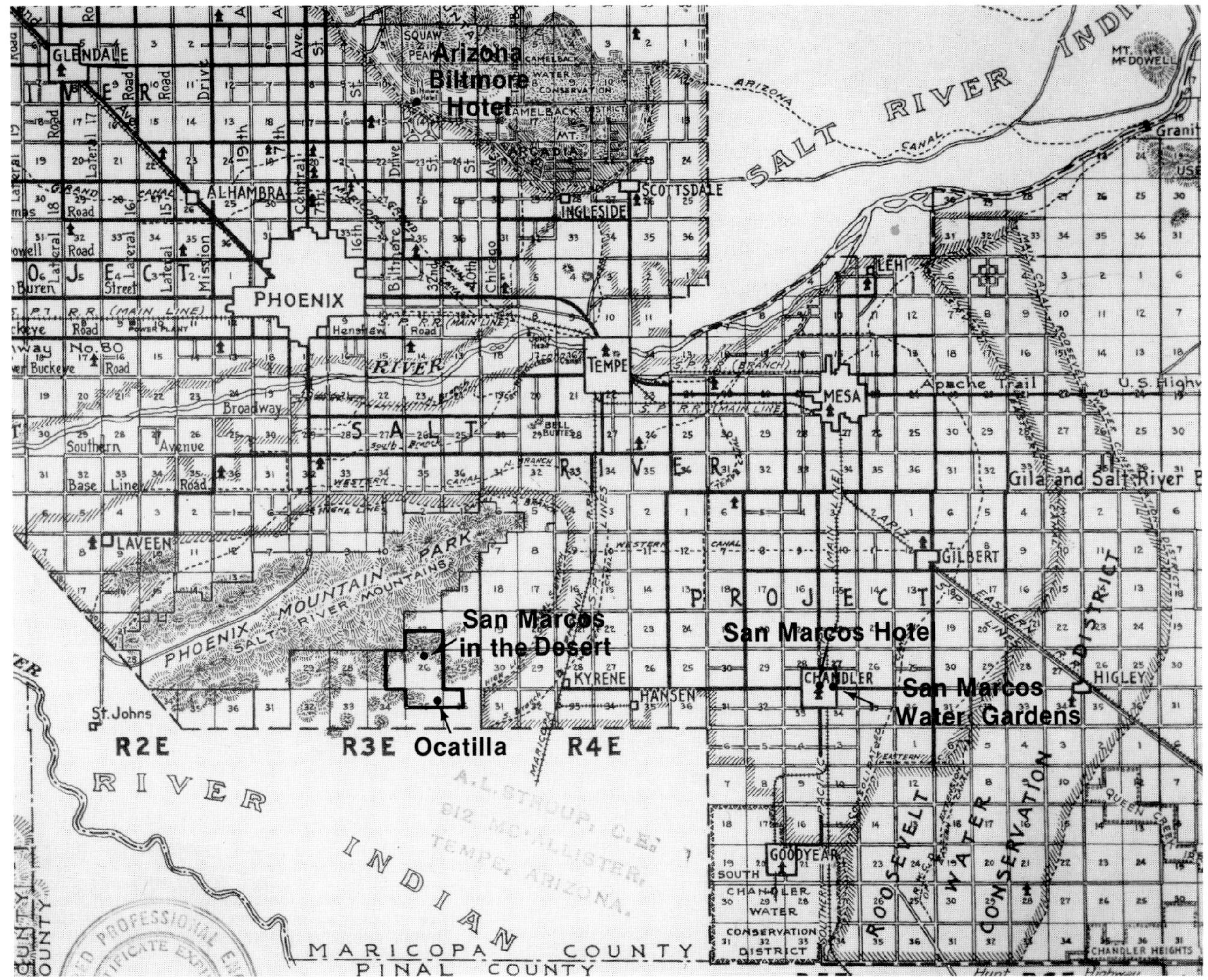

144. Map of the Salt River Valley and adjacent portion of Maricopa County, Arizona, compiled by the William H. Becker Engineering Co., Phoenix, Arizona, 1931. Department of Archives and Manuscripts, Hayden Library, Arizona State University, Tempe

three weeks—and Chandler realized the impact abundant water would have on the area. Frank Lloyd Wright later remarked, "God had need of you, Doctor, in His general plan, so sent the rain to prove to you what this desert could do with water."[35]

Although Chandler withdrew his resignation as veterinary surgeon, his interest clearly was refocused on irrigating and developing land in the Salt River Valley in south central Arizona. At the time, the area was irrigated by a network of canals, which was based on systems used in ancient Indian settlements. Chandler sought to enlarge and improve the system and in 1892 organized the Consolidated Canal Company. At the same time, he began accumulating land that became known as the Chandler Ranch.

Chandler's initiative was to some degree checked by government intervention. In 1902 the United States Reclamation Act was passed, providing for government construction of irrigation works; Chandler subsequently sold his canal system to the federal government. The dedication of Roosevelt Dam in 1911 brought further change: a new law limited the amount of water one landowner could receive. Chandler responded by subdividing his ranch and developing a new town with a luxury winter resort hotel as its focus. An ambitious plan based on the City Beautiful Movement was proposed, with a park occupying the central space and the hotel fronting on its western edge. The town of Chandler was founded on May 17, 1912, and though elements of the plan were carried out, in the end only the hotel approached the original vision. It was a Mission Revival style building, designed by Arthur Benton of Los Angeles, with inspiration from the California Building at the 1893 World's Columbian Exposition. It opened in November 1913, and quickly became an important economic and social asset, giving the community distinction it otherwise would never have achieved.

A group of eight bungalows designed by Reginald D. Johnson was built on the grounds west of the hotel in 1916–17; Paul Thiene landscaped the new addition. Then, in 1925, several more bungalows designed by Myron Hunt were constructed.[36] Other improvements followed, but none were more important to sustained growth than the inauguration of Southern Pacific railroad service in 1926 and the dedication of Chandler airport in 1928. Anticipating increased tourism, but certainly also with an eye to competing with the new Arizona Biltmore, Chandler decided to undertake a vast new hotel development on land he owned several miles west of town.

After their initial meeting in Phoenix, Wright spent two days at the San Marcos Hotel with Chandler, "looking ahead . . . into the future."[37] They visited the site, two great hills separated by a gorge at the foot of the Salt River Mountains (see Fig. 144). A ravine that carried rainwater from the mountains to the desert floor was lush with native shrubbery. The vista to the south stretched to the horizon and was dotted with saguaros. Wright later recalled, "There could be nothing more inspiring on earth than that spot in the pure desert of Arizona, I believe. Here was the time, the place and here was the man in Dr. Chandler. He looked like the man of independent power and judgment always necessary to characterize thoroughbred undertakings — in building or anything else."[38]

In his subsequent letter of appreciation, dated March 30, 1928, Wright expressed his eagerness to work with Chandler. At the same time, he clarified his own role as architect:

> I feel that my work is sufficiently established, and what I could do and wish to do now for you sufficiently outlined by our talks and visits to the grounds to enable you to make up your mind whether or not you would like to have me undertake that development with you if matters of compensation were adjusted to your satisfaction.
>
> Should preliminary studies of the specific hotel be further necessary to make up your mind on that point, — I should be disinclined to make them at any price. But, were you decided that you want me to do the work, I should be only too glad to make as many studies as to plan and as many beautiful drawings to illustrate the project as would enable you to finance the project. . . .
>
> But I could take no suitable interest in your project as a competitor for it on any basis of a submitted sketch. The spirit of that performance would seem as wrong to me now as it has always so seemed wrong to me in the past.[39]

One week later, on April 6, Chandler invited Wright to proceed with drawings. As before, Wright quickly drew Lloyd into the project, writing to his son on April 19, "The engineers are still working on the survey of the 'San Marcos in the Desert.' It will be some weeks before I can get anything ready for a rendering."[40] Then, on April 30, he told Chandler that he was "anxiously awaiting the plat and aeroplane views. They seem delayed." He continued that he had "the 'stills' cut and put together as they belong, making a good panorama. . . . The view is splendid and tempting." He was "all ready now to make drawings. The scheme has taken shape definitely."[41]

At the end of May Wright forwarded his layout to Lloyd with a letter explaining his intentions. San Marcos in the Desert was "an architectural theme based on the triangle"; the inspiration was the desert itself, "the mountains . . . rising behind,— triangles. The cross sections of the Suhuaro [*sic*] and all other desert plants,— triangles." The center section of the building, spanning the ravine and containing the public rooms, was to be "a forest of gigantic Suhuaro, triangles 5 - feet on each side, mingling with smaller ones,— all cut off abruptly at the top." An organ tower rose higher, continuing the "massed verticality." The guest rooms, projecting from the center section, were rows of terraces stacked up against the mountainside, "terraces eventuating into terraces."

Wright wanted Lloyd's rendering to "show the character of the site with desert-growth and the rock-masses as they are,—the building horizontally drifted between the rock ledges that terminate it,—belonging to all naturally." The planting of the building terraces was to be "gay in color, —flowering vines combined with tall spikes that harmonize, or brilliantly contrast with the desert garden." He added, "The color of the building will be that of the body of the desert, lit that is, (of course,) by atmospheric changes"[42] (Fig. 145).

Wright continued to work on the hotel project through the remainder of 1928. Leaving Phoenix in May, he moved to La Jolla; he reported to Darwin Martin in July that the sketches for San Marcos in the Desert were nearly ready. He added that he was working "by the ocean—with good effect—alone."[43] The preliminary studies were delivered in September; Chandler responded that they were "very interesting, and, in general, they meet with my approval." He instructed Wright to "go forward with the completion of these plans at once, in order that you can have prepared and submitted to me by January 1st, 1929, a set of plans and specifications complete in every detail."[44] Back at Taliesin in December, Wright told Chandler that he had a sanitary, heating, and electrical engineer working on the plans. He was "endeavoring to have all this branch of the work suited to the building,—extremely simple and effective." He was also

145. San Marcos in the Desert (project), Chandler, Arizona, aerial perspective, ca. 1928. FLLW FDN, 2704.048

having the structural engineering checked by Julius Floto, an engineer in Chicago who had worked on the Imperial Hotel.[45]

When Wright first undertook the design of San Marcos in the Desert, he proposed "camping down near the building site" to Chandler. He planned to undertake some experiments with the concrete blocks and wanted to "be right there with them for some little time at the beginning."[46] Presumably he had other reasons as well. When he confided to Chandler that he needed work more, he guessed, than he had ever needed it, he was referring to well-publicized legal and financial problems, including the foreclosure by the Bank of Wisconsin on a mortgage on Taliesin. This led him to tell Darwin Martin that in spite of renewed prospects he had "no place to work in."[47] Also the undeniable romance of the desert would have had strong appeal to Wright, who frequently sought new environments for creative rejuvenation.

The idea for the camp was renewed by Wright just before he returned to the desert in January. He was bringing with him an entourage of fourteen people, including his wife and two children; six draftsmen; Will Weston, a long-time carpenter and handyman at Taliesin, his wife, Anna, who would cook at the camp, and two of their children; and Mrs. Daigle, a governess for the Wright children.[48] Though Wright confessed in his autobiography that he had always wanted to camp in the region, his rationale for building was economic: it would cost no more than renting quarters for the group if Chandler provided the site and they did their own construction.

Chandler did provide the site: a low mound rising from the desert about a mile south of the Salt Range, where the new hotel was to be built (see Fig. 144). The mound was roughly triangular in shape and was defined by washes on the north and west sides.

The camp was designed in a day. Wright recalled that he "sat down in a cold, vacant office in the town to make the plans. The boys stood around shivering, watching, handing me the tools. We set up a drawing-board on boxes. And it was cold. They said in Chandler that it was the coldest season in thirty years. But the scheme was soon ready and next morning we started in to build." [49]

The camp took shape as a compound of small buildings arranged loosely around the perimeter of the mound and connected by a low wall (Fig. 146). The controlling geometry of the site plan was based on the 30/60 angles used in the hotel project, varied to avoid what Wright called "obvious symmetry." [50] The individual buildings clearly were inspired by the tent houses—structures with low wooden walls and canvas roofs—that

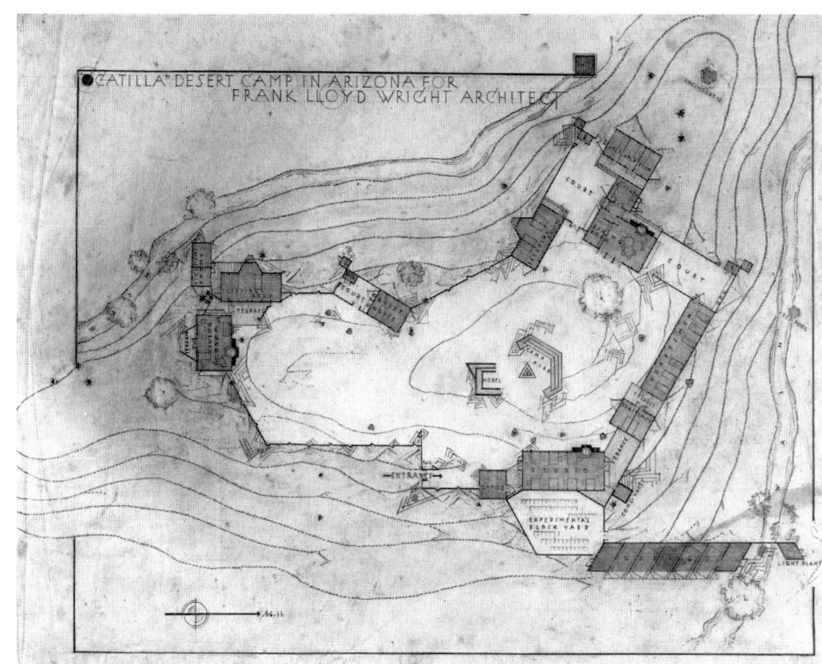

146. Ocatilla, Chandler, Arizona, plan, 1929. FLLW FDN, 2702.004

147. Ocatilla. FLLW FDN, 2702.009

dotted the region. Wright adapted the forms to the "one-two" triangle and constructed the cabins of horizontal boxboards and battens, painted a "dry rose" color to match the desert. Roofs were white canvas stretched on wooden frames. Openings also were canvas-covered wood frames, hinged with rubber belting (Fig. 147). In order not to disturb the desert, there was no excavation. The buildings were supported above the ground on posts, with horizontal siding carried down to ground level to establish visual connection with the earth.

Ocatilla — a name suggested later by Olgivanna Wright — was finished in a few days, put together by Wright and his draftsmen "with nails screws, hinges, . . . and ship cord."[51] Wright furnished the camp with canvas chairs, cots, and Navajo rugs purchased from a local hardware store, and, of course, a piano.[52] It was lighted at first by gas lanterns; then a Kohler plant was installed. Heat came from ten Air Tight brand stoves.

Ocatilla was ephemeral architecture, built to serve only during design and construction of San Marcos in the Desert. Wright likened the effect of the cabins, with their "wings" open, to "a group of gigantic butterflies [or] 'desert ships' . . . some kind of desert fleet," which would soon pass from sight. He contrasted his "impromptu effort," which hopefully would "drop a seed or two" with "the great sahuaro, standing there erect, six centuries old . . . whose blossom opens with the sunrise" and lasts but a day, but then bears fruit.[53]

Wright remained at Ocatilla through late May, developing plans for San Marcos in the Desert. Work was intense, and physical comfort was minimal — at first, all were very cold at night; then all were very hot during the day — but Wright was looking forward to his first major building since the Imperial Hotel, and he was once again a magnet: he received numerous guests at the camp. They included his son Lloyd, who prepared several renderings; Alice Millard, there to discuss new buildings to complement La Miniatura; Mrs. Richard Lloyd Jones, the wife of Wright's cousin, for whom he was designing a concrete-block house to be built in Tulsa; Paul Mueller, who had worked with him on the Imperial Hotel and was now overseeing San Marcos in the Desert; and Merle Armitage, a friend from Los Angeles.[54]

The quality of life in the camp, explaining the appeal of the region to a Midwesterner, is suggested in two letters Will Weston sent to the *Weekly Home News* in Spring Green. On March 1 he wrote:

> The days here are mostly warm and sunny but the nights are quite cold. . . .
>
> We have no frost here but some days we can see the snow on the mountains.
>
> We see the oranges hanging on the trees when we get out where the land is irrigated and suitable to grow them. . . .
>
> This desert is covered with "grease bush" and "mesquite" trees. The mesquite is our fire wood. . . . Just a little fire in the evenings is all that is required.

By mid-April, conditions were not quite so pleasant: "We are having real summer weather now with all the trimmings, including the flies and many other insects strange to us."[55]

In early May the energy of the group had nearly dissipated, as Wright indicated to Darwin Martin:

> We have been working here white heat now for some four months. . . .
> We have had hard sledding keeping everybody in line, and all have had to cooperate with almost no physical comfort, lately the weather becoming extremely hot and the light coming through the canvas tops almost blinding.
> I do not know how much longer we can hold out.
> The rattlesnakes keep us watching our step now. We have had seven as guests, to date,—two we put into captivity. Scorpions, centipede tarantula and various other damage dealing insects are appearing. You see we are in unbroken wilds—the flies are awful.[56]

Shortly before camp broke up for the summer, Wright constructed a plaster mock-up structure from the blocks intended for San Marcos in the Desert (Fig. 148). Remarkably, whole specimens of these blocks survived at the site into the 1960s and shards can still be found there today. Wright was hoping that the blocks for the actual hotel building might be manufactured with a "natural cement" from a deposit near Holbrook, a mining town in eastern central Arizona. Wright and Chandler visited the deposit and a block was made; tests conducted during the summer determined that the material was not usable in its raw state because it had no cohesive or lasting qualities, but that it might be of value if it were burned or calcined.[57]

Wright left Ocatilla on May 24, 1929, expecting to return in the fall.[58] Ten days later, on June 2, roughly one half of the camp was destroyed by fire. The next day, George Weldon, who had been left as overseer, wrote that the kitchen, dining room, cooks' dormitory, and Weston cottage had burned, and that the garage had caught fire, but was saved.[59]

Plans for San Marcos in the Desert were complete, however, and had been given to contractors for estimates. There was little change from the original concept that had been worked out by the end of May 1928; the working drawings, completed at Ocatilla one year later, simply resolved the way in which the various members would fit together. Details were worked out in twenty-six sheets of "complicated drawings" (the term is Wright's) and block schedules, window schedules and diagrams, and structural diagrams, all intended to "simplify the building operation," so that "our new scheme of construction may be used to great economic advantage."[60]

148. San Marcos in the Desert (project), concrete-block model, 1929. FLLW FDN, 2702.057

The hotel was laid out on two separate grids, square and diagonal, both based on a twenty-inch module. The diagonal system is used at the center and extreme ends of the building; the rest of the plan is based on square units (Fig. 149). The structure extends approximately nine hundred feet across the desert; because of this length, the plans are divided into three parts, for convenience of drafting and reproduction. The points of separation correspond to formal and functional divisions in the building itself: center section, east guest wing, and west guest wing.

The center section, which has a short wing in the shape of a partial

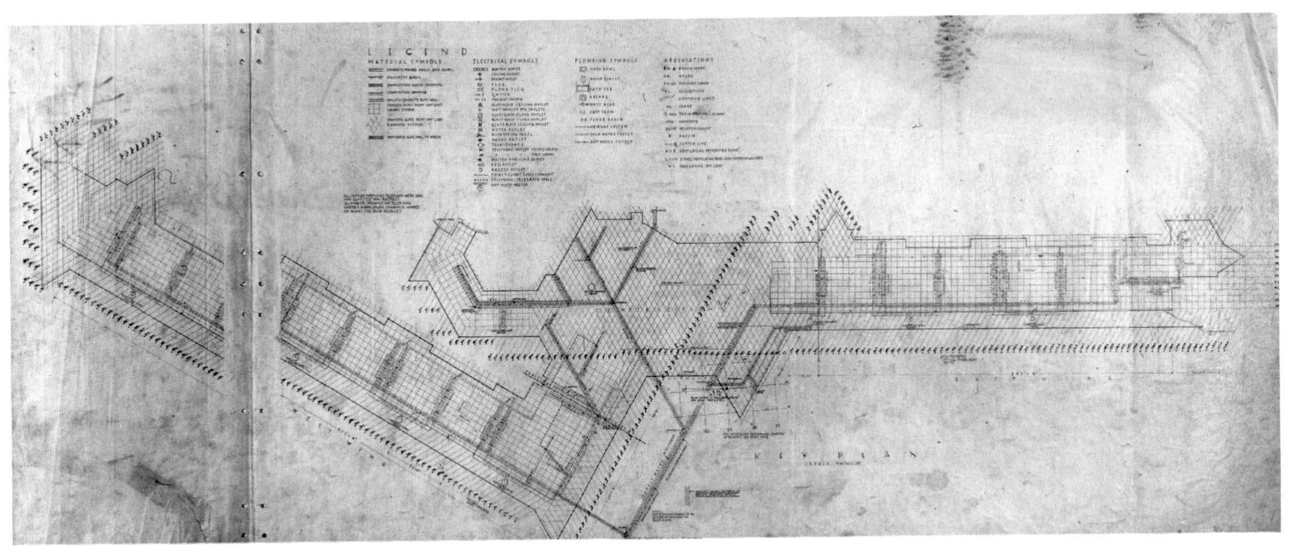

149. San Marcos in the Desert (project), key plan, 1929. FLLW FDN, 2704.090

150. San Marcos in the Desert (project), plan. FLLW FDN, 2704.092

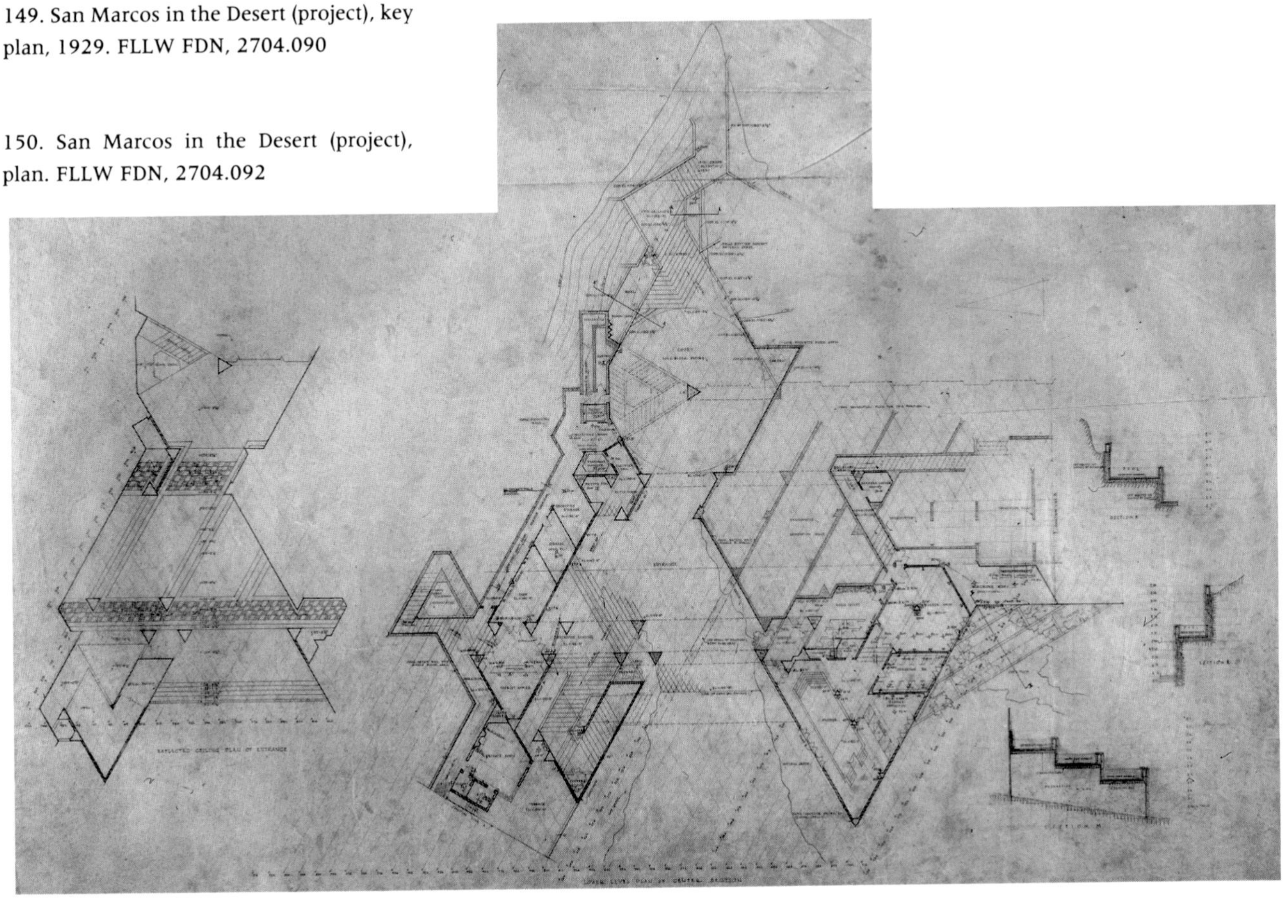

hexagon attached, includes the lobby ("living room"), dining room, kitchen, and guest apartments. The main entrance is below this section and is approached by automobile; a roadway following the course of the ravine leads to a sort of porte cochere, where guests and luggage are dropped off, then continues to a turnaround area (Fig. 150). At this level of the building, the plan is determined entirely by the diagonal grid, which produces a series of comparatively small, irregularly shaped triangular spaces. There is no provision here for parking cars; they are to be stored in a freestanding garage about twelve hundred feet away and out of sight from the main building.[61]

The living room and dining room are on the two floors above the entry and are reached by elevator or stairs adjacent to the tower on the north side of the building. The two rooms have much in common. Their plans are essentially the same: rhomboids whose boundaries are determined by parallel rows of triangular columns with glazing between on the north and south, running perpendicular to the grid, and by solid walls on the east and west, which are on the grid lines (Figs. 151, 152). Each room has a dependent space on the north, defined by a row of columns and a few steps. Highly sculptural concrete-block fireplaces dominate the west wall of each room; special blocks are combined to create convex and concave acute angles, recalling the thin vertical lines of the saguaro.

The experimental geometry notwithstanding, the living room is remarkably sober, lacking the complex spatial interweaving of similar areas in the Imperial Hotel and the Arizona Biltmore. In the earlier buildings, the main volumes open to smaller dependent spaces, are overlooked by balconies, and have frequent changes in ceiling height and floor level. Wright used these devices for animation in essentially closed, inward-focused rooms. By contrast, the living room at San Marcos in the Desert is externally focused, opening to and depending on the native beauty of the surrounding desert for effect (Fig. 153). Barriers between indoors and out are minimized, and the enclosed space is articulated principally by the triangular columns, Wright's "forest of gigantic Suhuaros." A network of continuous beams spanning the flat ceiling on the diagonal grid unifies the overall space.

The spatial climax is the dining room at the top of the center section, which is, in Wright's words, "treated, top-lighted and terraced as an arbor."[62] He achieved the effect with a ceiling of faceted copper and glass, worked out in a symphony of repeated geometric abstractions of the most wonderful exuberance (Fig. 154). Wright's love of ornament is here given

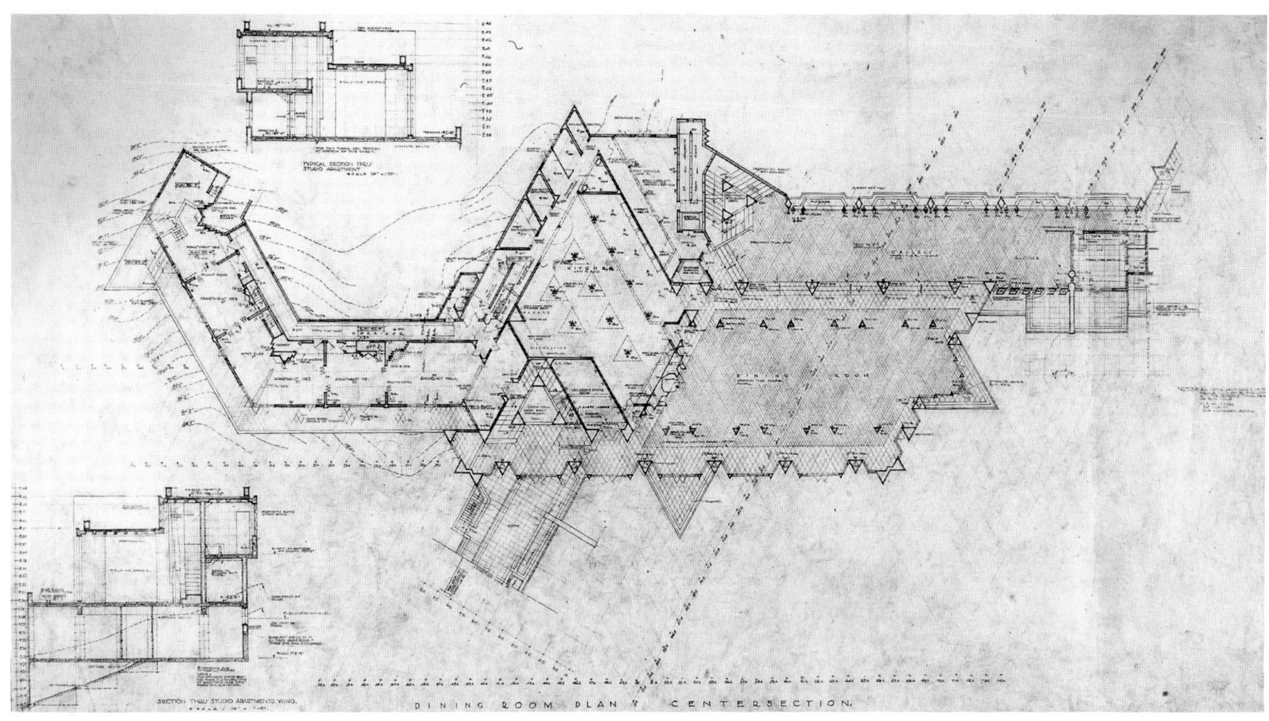

151. San Marcos in the Desert (project), top-level plan. FLLW FDN, 2704.095

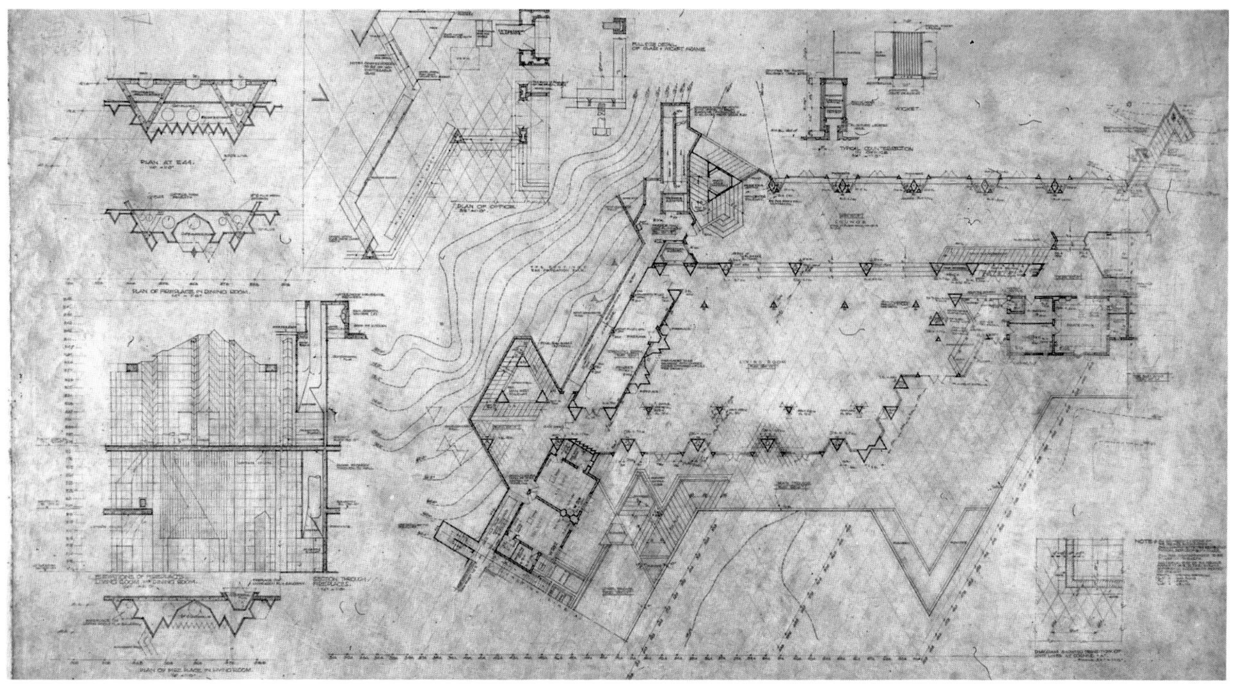

152. San Marcos in the Desert (project), middle-level plan. FLLW FDN, 2704.093

153. San Marcos in the Desert (project), interior perspective. FLLW FDN, 2704.051

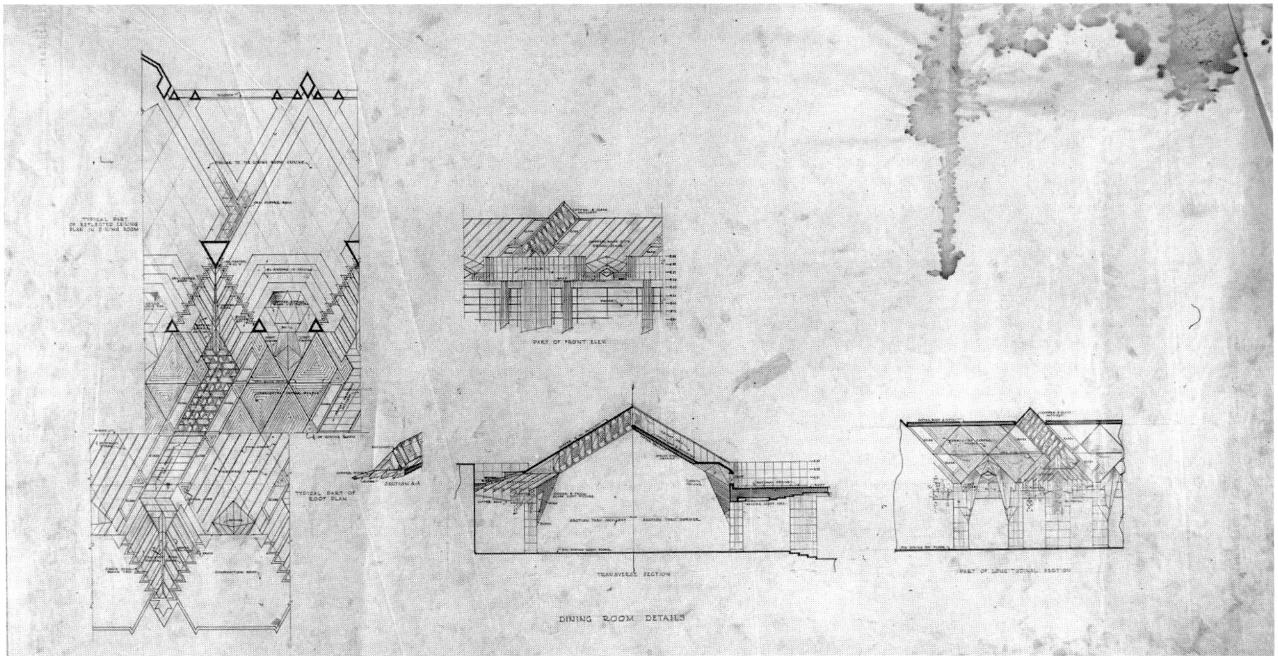

154. San Marcos in the Desert (project), dining-room details. FLLW FDN, 2704.113

one of its finest expressions, equaling any public space in the Imperial Hotel, but without the heaviness of that building. At the highest point, the ceiling approaches twenty feet, the intensity of the geometry diminishing toward the top. Three skylights cross the room on the diagonal grid (Fig. 155).

The hexagonal wing projecting at this level, separated from the dining room by the kitchen, comprises ten private suites, identified as supper rooms, each with a balcony, bedroom, and bathroom. The tower at the rear accents the verticality of the central mass and rises "as a natural

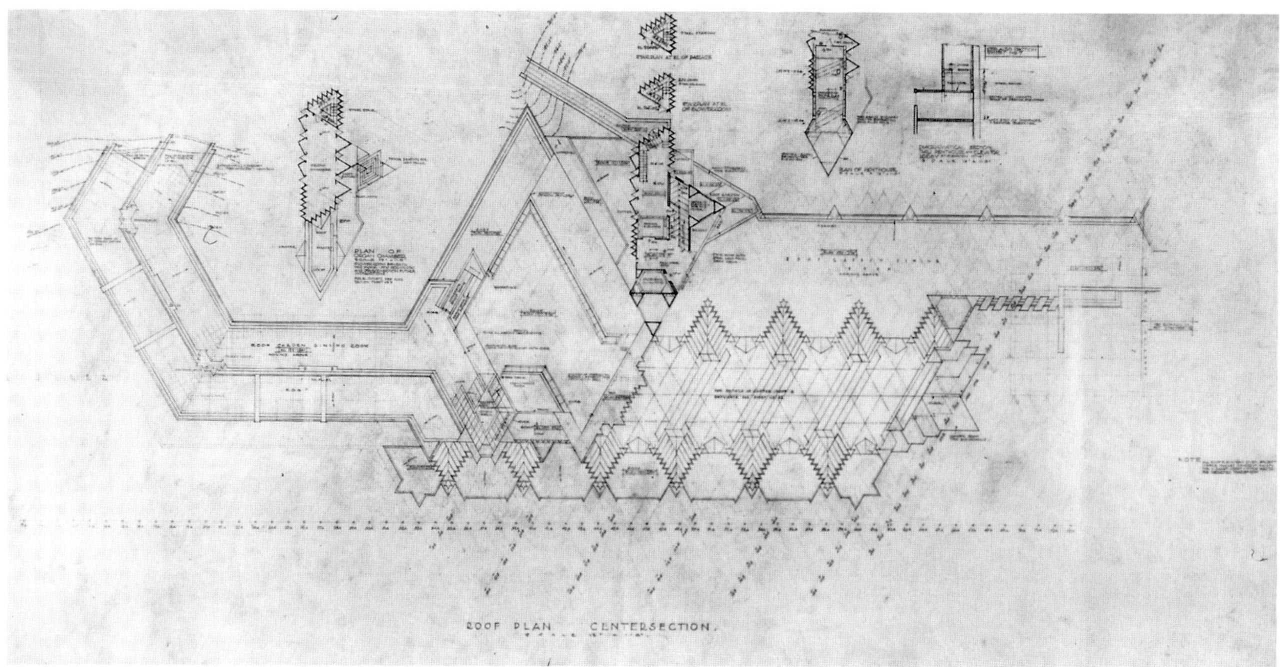

155. San Marcos in the Desert (project), roof and center-section plan. FLLW FDN, 2704.097

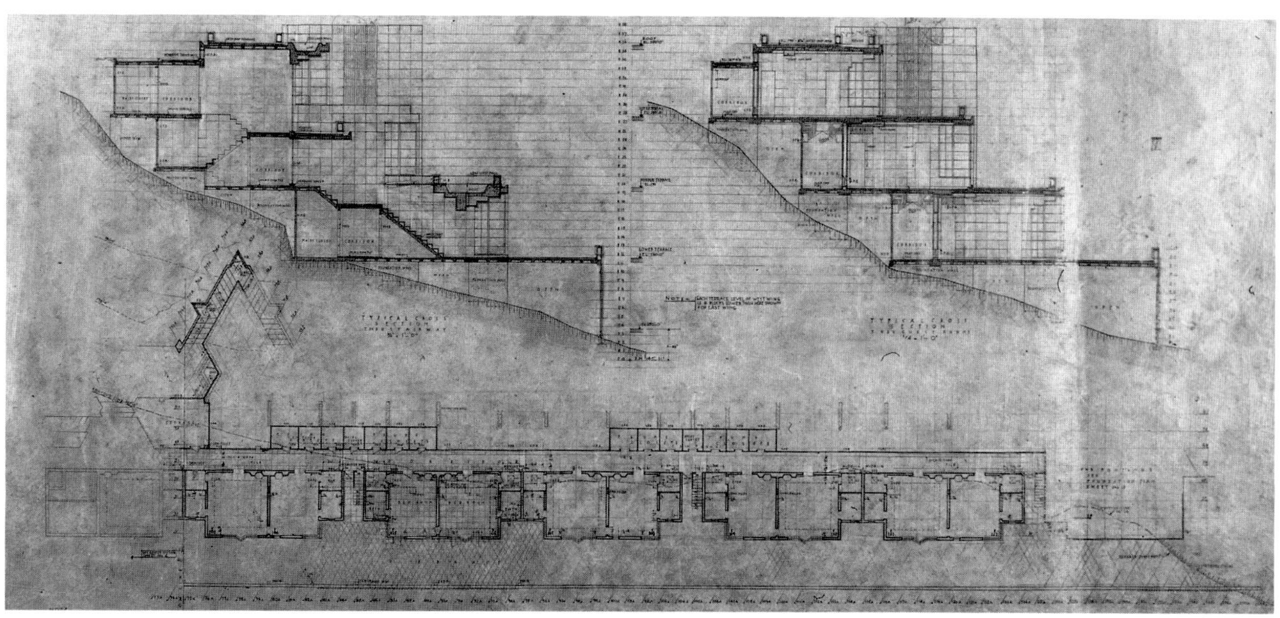

156. San Marcos in the Desert (project), first terrace of the east wing, plan. FLLW FDN, 2704.103

expression of the sahuaro-motive that also qualifies the other building forms." Pragmatically, it serves to carry the water reserve, and the upper portion is perforated to allow the sound from chimes and organ pipes to escape. Like the dining room, it is capped in copper. According to Wright, "The . . . tower and the lightning shaft beside it are the only efflorescence anywhere."[63]

The east and west bedroom wings are composed of repeated fifty-foot units, theoretically capable of infinite extension. Each unit contains two adjoining bedrooms, and the units are separated by a pair of bathrooms placed back to back (Fig. 156). The bedrooms in these units are of two kinds only, one larger than the other; the bathrooms are standardized and are all identical. Both wings are three stories high and are stepped back against the mountainside, the roof of each level serving as a garden terrace for the level above. All the rooms are masonry chambers—floors, walls, ceilings of concrete block—with the horizontal and vertical joints softened by special coved blocks. The bathroom floors have a top layer of cork tiling.

It was in San Marcos in the Desert that Wright came closest to achieving a building that was truly the result of his standardized-unit system of construction. The "ferro-block unit-slab system" was to be used to construct the hotel "so far as and wherever possible."[64] For the first time, floors, walls, and ceilings were to be built of blocks, and there was a specific block design to address every circumstance. There was to be "no woodwork of any kind in this structure,—nothing at all of what is ordinarily called trim."[65]

San Marcos in the Desert was designed to affect the surrounding landscape as little as possible. Excavation was minimal; the hotel would have been suspended above the sloping ground on cast-concrete piers and "dwarf walls," which in turn used the desert floor as a foundation.[66] Piers, used only in the center section of the building, are triangles five feet on a side; they are encased in concrete block and rest on solid rock. The east and west wings rest on segmental walls nine inches thick, unless otherwise marked, which were placed parallel with the prevailing grid, if not consistently on the grid lines. In all cases the layout of the foundation was to be gauged by the front terrace block walls, which were begun first.[67]

The hotel is designed for construction with five basic blocks and related half and quarter blocks, which are consistent in both the square and diagonal grids (Fig. 157). As in the earlier work, there are plain, patterned, and perforated blocks; and there are numerous variant block forms to

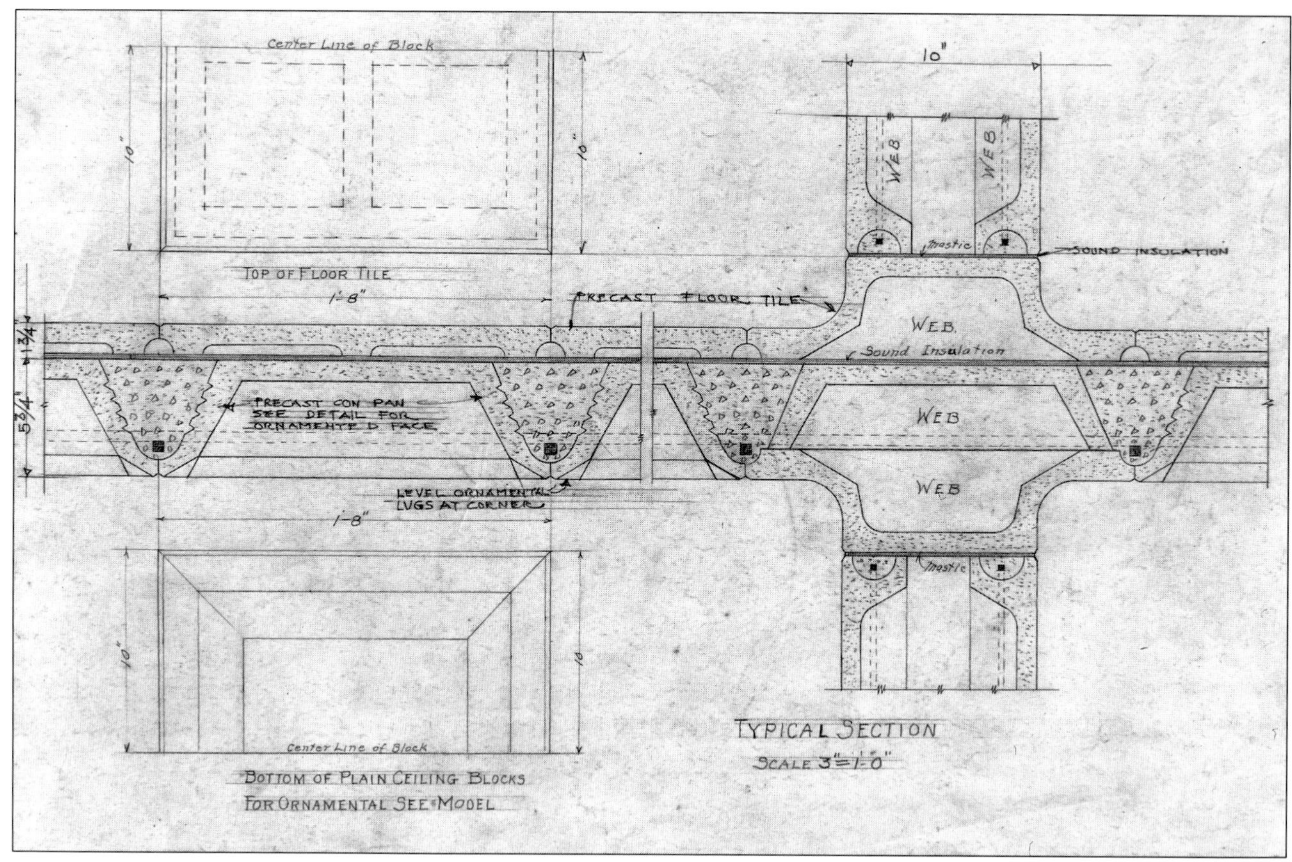

157. San Marcos in the Desert (project), block assembly diagram. FLLW FDN, 2704.165

accommodate every need. The block schedules remaining in Wright's archive call for a total of 116 different block forms, including left- and right-hand versions of the same block; however, five sheets of drawings are missing in the numbered sequence, indicating that the total number of block types was greater.[68]

The wall blocks closely resemble those of the California houses, though they are on a fifteen-by-twenty-inch module and are 3⅜ inches thick (Fig. 158). They are assembled with quarter-inch steel bars laid between the blocks vertically and horizontally and secured by "Toncan" steel clips. These clips—introduced for the first time—automatically space the blocks and hold the steel bars rigidly in place during the pouring of the grout between the blocks (Fig. 159). Each clip is to be double-dipped in heavy, hot, pure rock asphalt, as soundproofing protection.[69]

The most significant innovation, a technical improvement that should have made Wright's dream of mono-material construction a reality, is the combination of ceiling and floor blocks to permit their use in a horizontal span supported by a grid of concrete beams cast in forms made by the blocks themselves. The blocks are twenty inches square, with raised panels; instead of perpendicular sides with semicircular channels, they have sides projecting out from the top at a sixty-degree angle. The blocks are scored on the outside with a sawtooth pattern (Fig. 160). When they are assembled, continuous V-shaped channels, open at the top, result.

Ceiling slabs are formed by laying these blocks on standardized skeleton centering: two one-by-fours twenty inches on center one way, placed across four four-by-fours forty inches on center the other way, and supported on four-by-four uprights on center each way. The channels thus formed between the blocks are filled with half-inch deformed bars in both directions, and with grout. Finished floor tiles, also twenty inches on a side, are laid on top of the ceiling slab, separated from it by soundproofing mortar (Fig. 161). The transition between walls and floors or ceilings is accomplished with special coved blocks, and there also are separate floor blocks to be used under partitions (Figs. 162, 163).

Forms for special conditions include inside and outside corner blocks; window and door-jamb blocks, with recesses for frames; coping blocks; blocks for parapets; and fireplace and chimney blocks. Decorative blocks are formed with projecting 30/60-degree triangular shapes, which extend vertically in multiples of four along the face of the block (Fig. 164). Variants for parapets have the triangular shapes extending above and below the edges of the blocks (Fig. 165). Perforated blocks consist both of blocks cast with rectangular slits in their faces and those with a more intricate pattern of triangular-shaped openings (Figs. 166, 167).

In some cases, additional concrete reinforcement is required. This is accomplished in the walls by inserting vertical strips of concrete ⅞ by 3¼ by 15 inches (the width of the space between the blocks) against the Toncan clips as the walls rise and filling the resulting forms with concrete. Additional steel is added as required. Large diagonal floor beams in the center section are cast in the accustomed manner, with wooden forms (Fig. 168, detail).

The need for occasional nonconforming reinforcement aside, Wright envisioned San Marcos in the Desert as "a one-process, mono-material building . . . fabricated on a standard unit-system" that encompasses every detail.[70] Sanitary, heating, and electrical systems were to be incorporated into the walls or made part of the building and expressed accord-

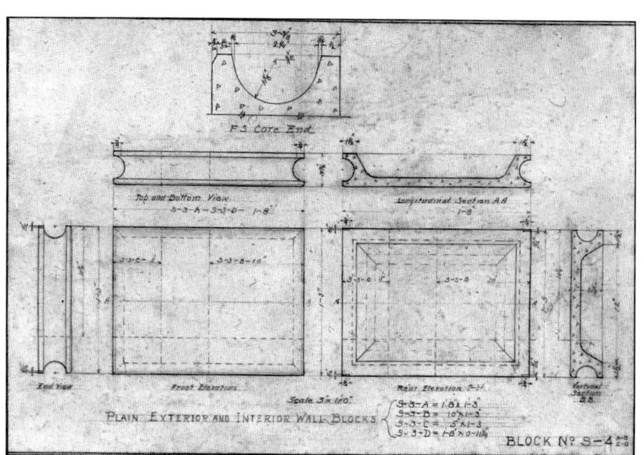

158. San Marcos in the Desert (project), wall block. FLLW FDN, 2704.124

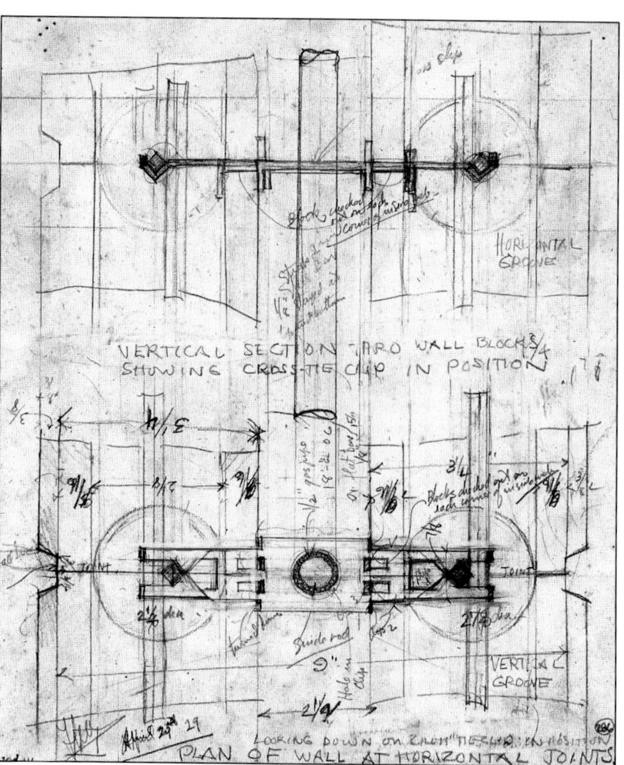

159. San Marcos in the Desert (project), Toncan clip. FLLW FDN, 2704.116

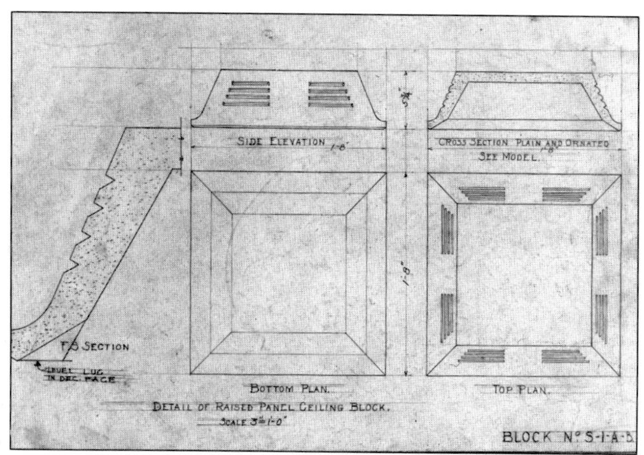

160. San Marcos in the Desert (project), ceiling block. FLLW FDN, 2704.118

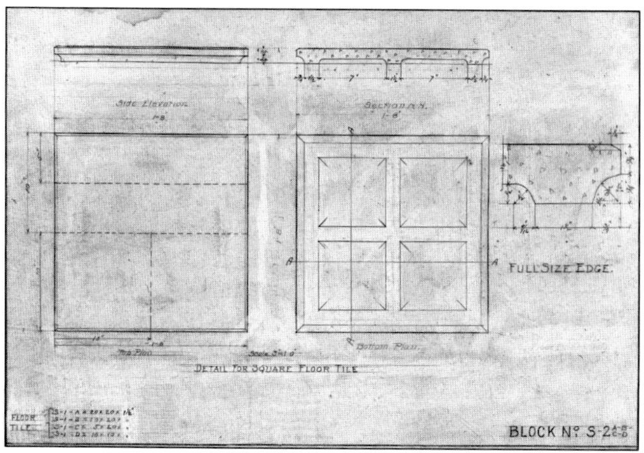

161. San Marcos in the Desert (project), floor tile. FLLW FDN, 2704.121

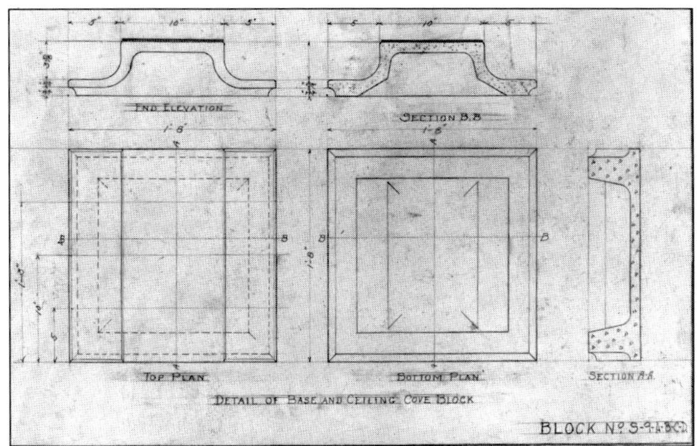

162. San Marcos in the Desert (project), base and ceiling cove block. FLLW FDN, 2704.130

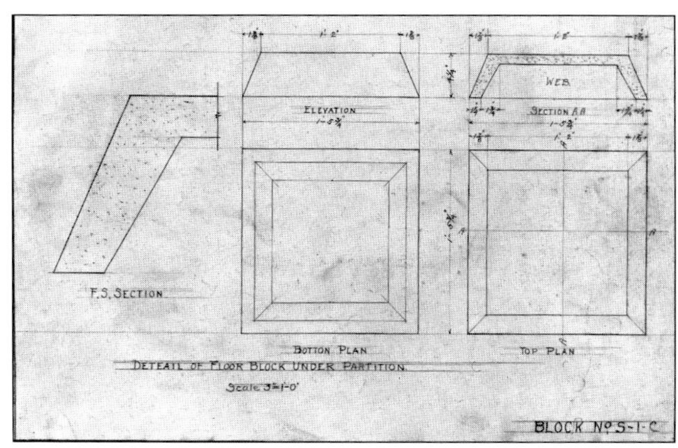

163. San Marcos in the Desert (project), partition block. FLLW FDN, 2704.119

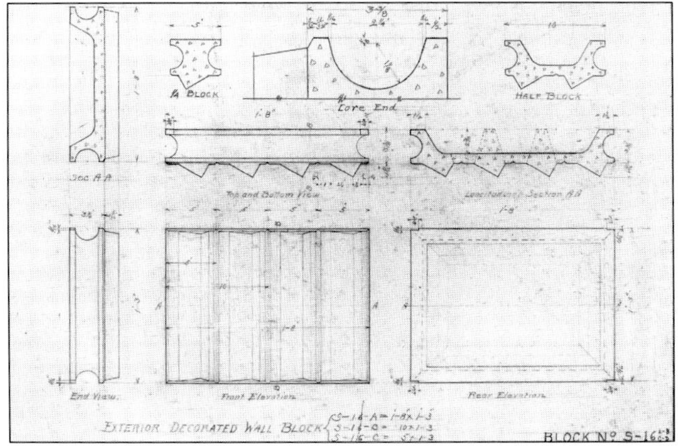

164. San Marcos in the Desert (project), decorated wall block. FLLW FDN, 2704.139

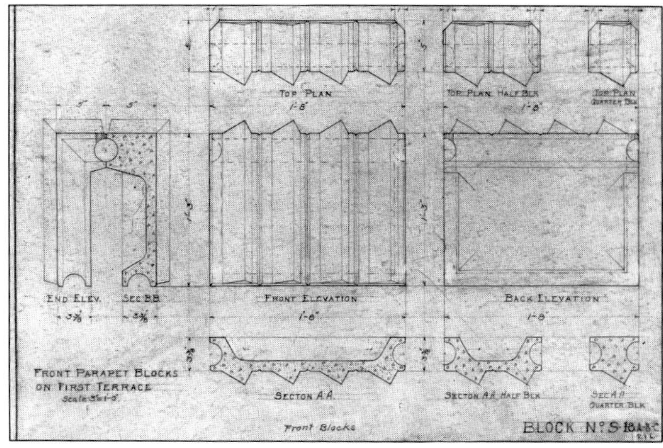

165. San Marcos in the Desert (project), parapet block. FLLW FDN, 2704.141

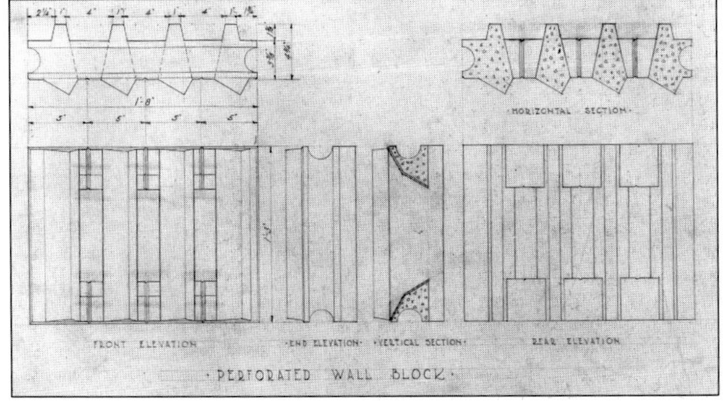

166. San Marcos in the Desert (project), perforated wall block. FLLW FDN, 2704.149

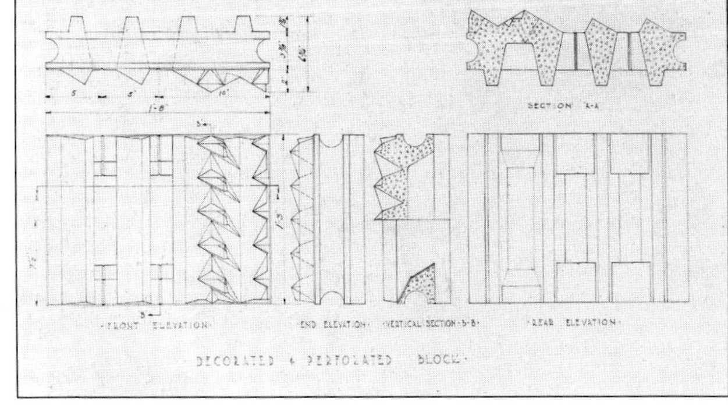

167. San Marcos in the Desert (project), decorated and perforated block. FLLW FDN, 2704.150

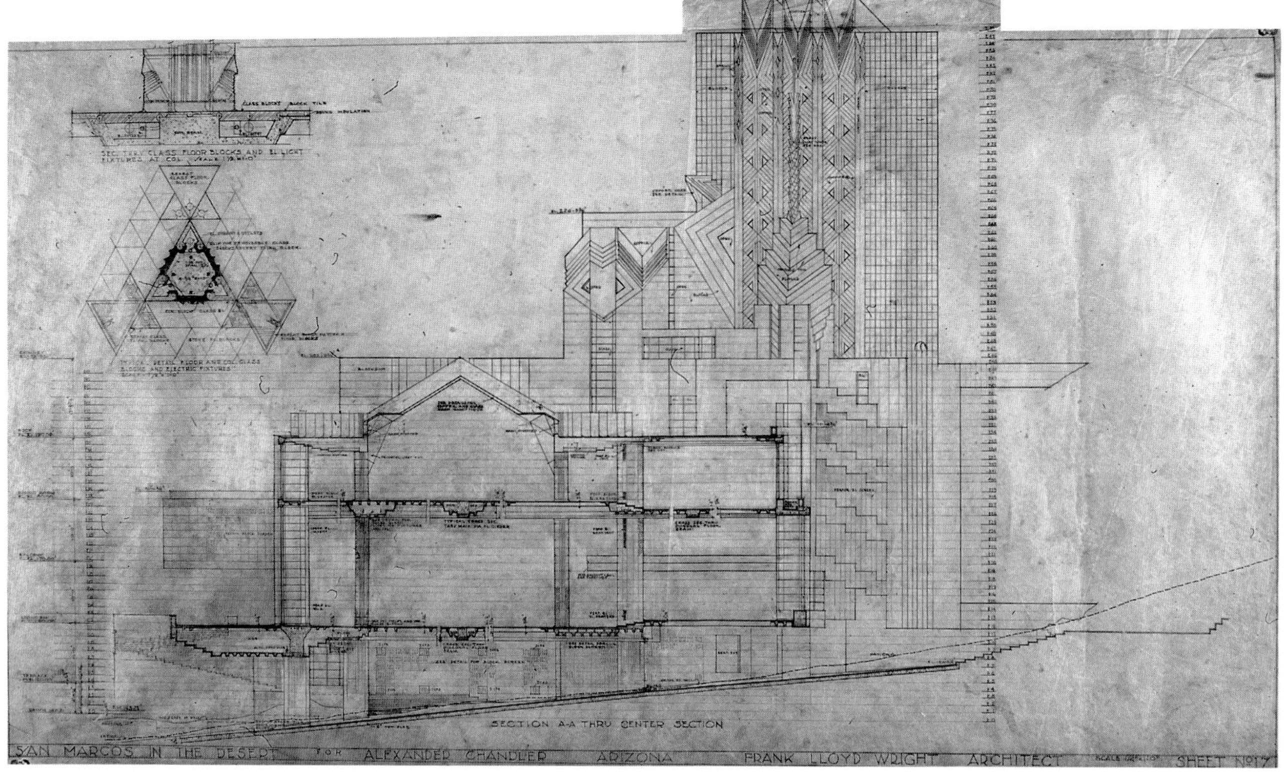

168. San Marcos in the Desert (project), section (center section). FLLW FDN, 2704.106

ingly; they were worked out by H. A. Durr, an engineer in Chicago.[71] Perforated blocks permitted natural ventilation, heating, and lighting without additional fixtures. Lighting also was to be accomplished using the system worked out for the Arizona Biltmore Hotel, in which concrete blocks in walls and the ends of corbeled beams were replaced with glass blocks and lighted from behind. Wright approached P. M. Cochius of the Leerdam Glasfabriek in Holland, explaining his intentions:

> In this building I want to substitute glass blocks for the concrete blocks as the lighting arrangements of the whole structure,—electric lights being placed in the empty space left behind the glass block. Doing this, there should be no metal edge around the block,—only a block of glass like the other blocks although they need not be so thick and have so deep an edge.

He was looking ahead as well, telling Cochius:

> I am very anxious to conduct the experiment either under your auspices in Holland or here in America, or both, of the glass building using the block

system, pouring the internal joints with cement and steel reinforcement. . . .

In other words, I would like to see developed in the glass industry a quality of glass suitable for building material. In some cases it would be necessary to have the glass clear so that it might be seen through, or at least let light through. In other cases, be opaque. In nearly every building both kinds would be required.[72]

Among the documents for San Marcos in the Desert in the Wright Archive is a furniture schedule that reveals Wright's intentions, although there is no record that he actually designed the pieces specified. The furniture was to be wicker throughout; the only clue to its appearance comes from the perspective drawing of the living room, which shows a couch and small table (see Fig. 153). Textiles were to be selected or specially designed by the architect. Each bedroom was to have a five-by-eight-foot wall tapestry, woven in a pattern to match the architecture. Table service was to be entirely of glass and produced by Leerdam Glasfabriek of Holland, the firm Wright had contacted to make the glass blocks for the lights.[73]

Alice Millard took a special interest in the furnishings for the hotel when she visited Wright at Ocatilla in April 1929. She wrote to the architect while en route to Europe the following June, offering suggestions. Wright responded that Chandler was likely to be "a pretty active shopper himself in connection with these items and furnishings . . . when the time comes." He added that she might collect fabric samples if anything turned up in Europe, and observed that the work of Paul Rodier was interesting.[74]

YOUNG AND CUDNEY HOUSES, CHANDLER

Chandler intended from the beginning to develop the land around San Marcos in the Desert with freestanding houses; Wright worked on preliminary sketches for at least two of these while he was at Ocatilla.[75] One of the houses was for Owen D. Young (1874–1962), a prominent industrialist and confidant of President Woodrow Wilson. The association was significant enough for Wright to mention it to Darwin Martin, and at one point there was hope that Young would help finance construction of the hotel. The other house was for the brothers Wellington and Ralph Cudney, about whom little is known, although they apparently were friends of the architect and his wife.[76]

The Young and Cudney houses can best be considered as a pair: each is a variation on a theme established in the hotel, and each contains seeds for future development. Both are designed for concrete-block construction; one is planned on the square grid of the wings, the other on the diagonal of the center section. The Young house has the more conventional layout: it is based on sixteen-inch-square units, arranged to produce a series of rectangular spaces (Figs. 169, 170). The two-story plan is dominated by a large solarium overlooking the desert; bed and service rooms are to the rear. The innovations in the Young house are in the elevation, which is

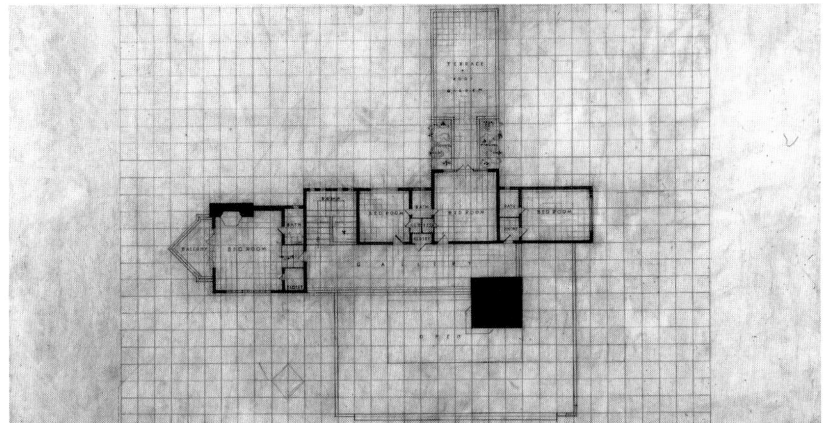

169. Owen D. Young house (project), Chandler, Arizona, second-floor plan, 1929. FLLW FDN, 2707.004

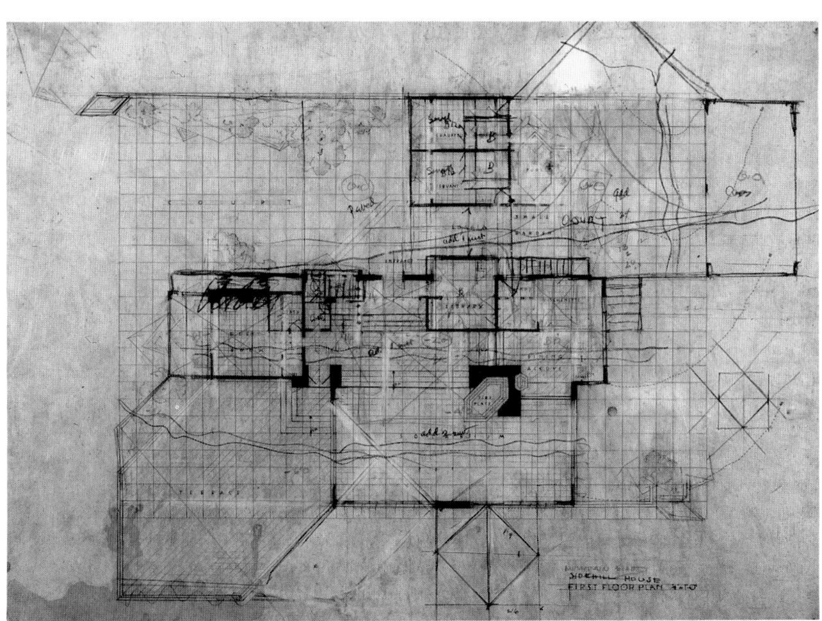

170. Young house (project), first-floor plan. FLLW FDN, 2707.003

171. Young house (project), perspective. FLLW FDN, 2707.001

conceived as a continuous fabric of sixteen-inch units of concrete block and glass, rotated on a diagonal axis (Fig. 171). The use of openable glass panes of the same dimensions as the blocks allowed Wright to dispense with conventional windows entirely, a development recalling the Luxfer Prism project of 1897 and anticipating the all-glass building Wright imagined in his letter to P. M. Cochius. If the plan of the house and the square blocks recall earlier work in California, as Hitchcock suggests, the diagonal skin creates an entirely new aesthetic — albeit with seeds in the Lake Tahoe project — and the introduction of units of glass of the same size as the blocks was an important step toward the architectural simplification and unity Wright was seeking.[77] The result, though, is not the happiest composition. The triangular forms are too assertive; geometry dominates rather than serves.

The Cudney house was lifted in spirit from the center section of San Marcos in the Desert; although on the same diagonal module, it does not mimic the form of the parent, but is roughly a V shape, the grid in smaller scale producing rooms as irregular hexagons (Figs. 172, 173). This also is a

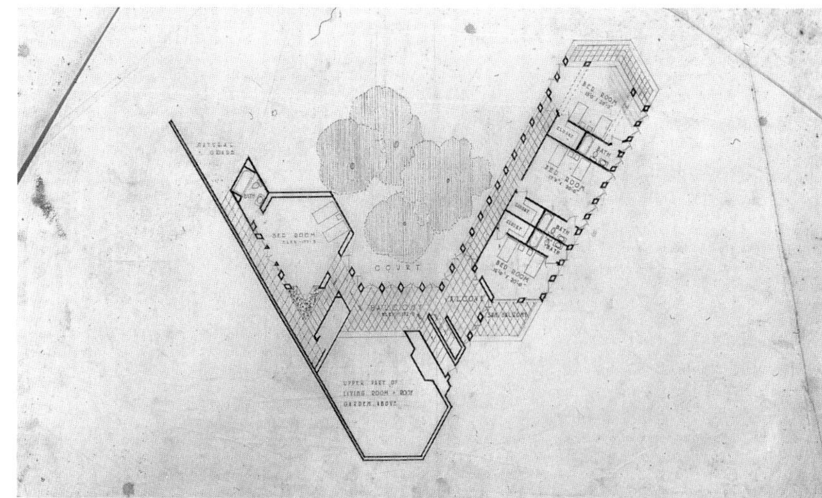

172. Wellington and Ralph Cudney house (project), Chandler, Arizona, second-floor plan, 1929. FLLW FDN, 2706.003

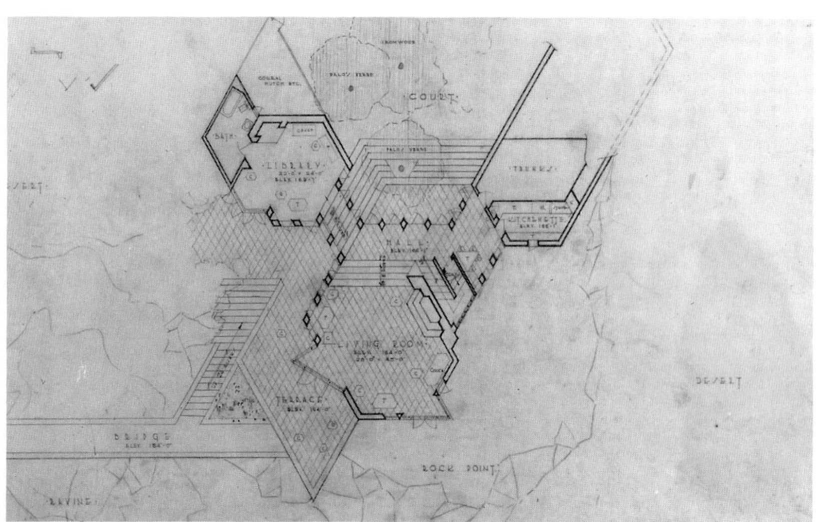

173. Cudney house (project), first-floor plan. FLLW FDN, 2706.004

two-story house, the lower floor containing the living rooms; the upper, the bedrooms. Perimeter walls are formed of diamond-shaped columns, alternating with glass. The house was to have been built of the same blocks proposed for the hotel; it has similar walls of glass that open to the desert (Fig. 174). The truly remarkable feature of the scheme is not the unorthodox geometry but the concept of building without conventional walls and windows; the implications are many. The alternating solids and voids of the walls suggest screens separating indoors from out. Light entering through the glass strips would be uniquely even throughout the house.

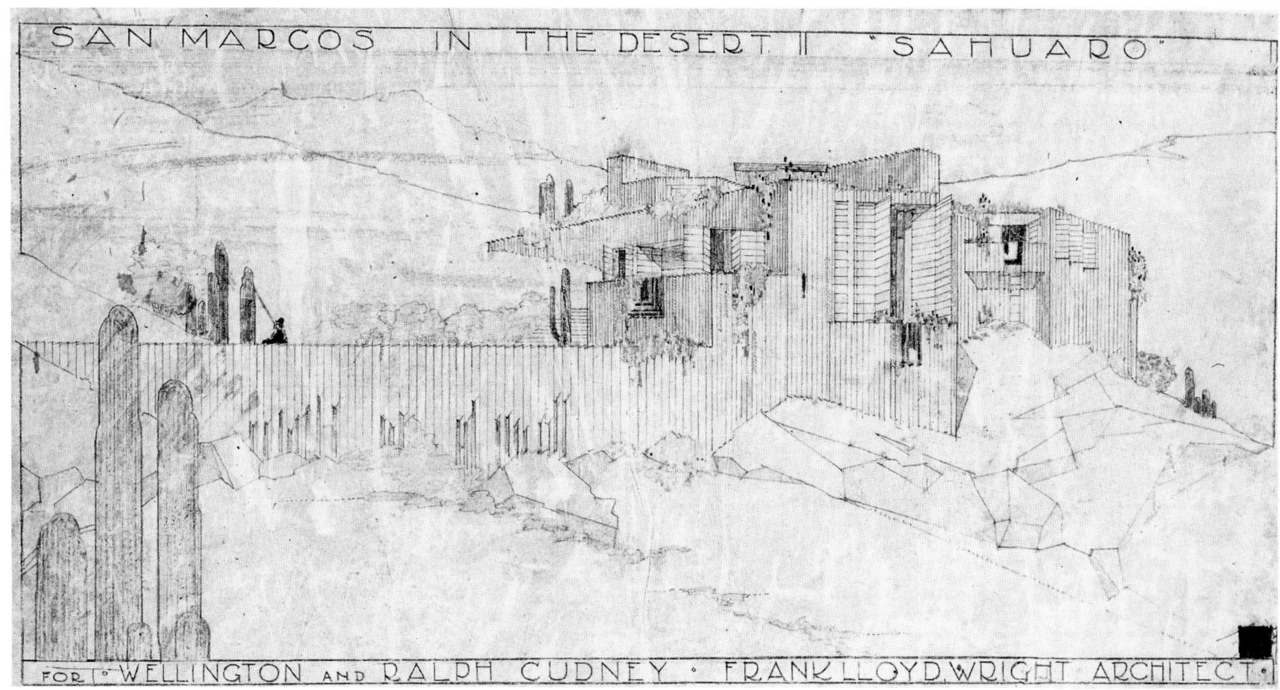

174. Cudney house (project), elevation. FLLW FDN, 2706.008

Directionality is established by the diagonal piers, animating both the plan and the individual spaces. Corners dissipate into glass voids.

San Marcos Water Gardens, Chandler

Yet another unbuilt project for Chandler was a tourist resort named San Marcos Water Gardens; Wright was working on the plans for this in July 1929.[78] Numerous cabins with concrete-block walls and roofs of wood and stretched canvas — recalling Ocatilla — were to be constructed in a compound and served by a larger building, containing a dining room, kitchen, and lounges (Fig. 175). The plan of the compound is no less remarkable than the individual buildings. It is based again on the 30/60 triangle, with cabins placed singly or in clusters along a minor system of canals that pay homage to Chandler's earlier efforts to irrigate the region (Fig. 176).

Chandler was not pleased by the prospect of canvas roofs. Wright had used canvas in another of their joint projects — a camp for laborers — and Chandler had found it very unsatisfactory.[79] Wright responded:

175. San Marcos Water Gardens (project), Chandler, Arizona, perspective, 1929. FLLW FDN, 2705.003

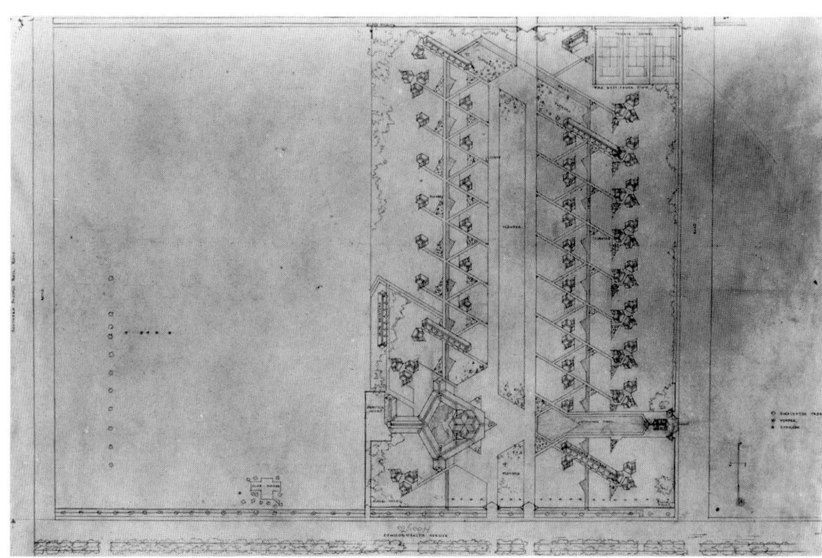

176. San Marcos Water Gardens (project), plan. FLLW FDN, 2705.004

> The fact is that only by the use of the canvas can we get that translucence inside that seems to belong to Arizona sunshine. My short sojourn in the region makes me feel that to be one of the most desirable features of life out there. That is to say, the beautiful diffusion of light within the buildings themselves. Glass could not give this even were the expense not considered. There is nothing that could give this effect but canvas or some similar fabric.

He continued:

> The structure of the buildings would, of course, be staunch and permanent, —concrete mat, for floors, concrete-block walls, substantial wooden-roof-framing,—and then this light element of fabrics filling certain spaces as openings. . . .

> The point I wish to stress is the advantage that comes to us from the use of this light material and the opportunity it offers us to create a new type of architecture, a type that it seems to me suits Arizona conditions perfectly.[80]

FINANCING SAN MARCOS IN THE DESERT

Chandler began advertising San Marcos in the Desert in several national magazines in 1928, laying groundwork for a campaign to raise funds to construct the building. The hotel was speculative not only financially but structurally; early on, Wright advised Chandler that he would "probably not be able to get very favorable figures as bonded estimates in connection with such a building as we propose unless Benet, who has had some experience with the construction, should be inclined to take hold." Wright continued, however, that he found Benet to be "somewhat of a grouch, a good deal of a gossip, and no very experienced builder himself."[81] By May 1929, Paul Mueller had taken over the project.

Before Chandler approached potential backers, he asked an engineer, Edward L. Mayberry, and a landscape architect, Aurele Vermeulen, both based in Los Angeles, to review the plans. According to Lloyd, Mayberry reported that the plans were at best well-advanced sketch studies, without dimensions; that footings were entirely unsatisfactory and had no steel in them; and that all beams, girders, and slabs were under-figured from 50 to 100 percent and in some cases were beyond the elastic limit of the steel called for. Wright responded to Chandler, "You are up against,—primarily I think,—the usual inability to grasp the block-system. . . . The plans are very complete. Everything in the structure to the smallest block has been diagrammed and counted and properly listed. . . . The steel has been figured by the best engineers in Chicago. The fact that Mayberry criticizes the plans as having no figures on them ought to let Mayberry out of court. The plans need no figures if the unit system is understood." Writing again, two days later, the architect explained, "Our ground is fine foundation in itself . . . and all the tall parts of the building stand on solid rock, which I know and Maybury [*sic*] apparently does not."[82]

Vermeulen's larger role was to plat the acreage surrounding San Marcos in the Desert for development. He also suggested modifying the entrance to the hotel, adding a post in the center and making a heavy cut in the bank to the right. Wright responded, "In general . . . the scheme is feasible and desirable—all except the architectural means taken by Vermeulen to accomplish it. The post . . . is decidedly objectionable—fatal, in fact. But, we will manage this in our own way and no doubt work out something desirable."[83]

Although, apparently, he still felt the need for additional information, Chandler began approaching backers in the summer of 1929. By August he was expressing confidence that he would get the money in the East and could begin construction in late November. At the same time, however, Albert McArthur told Wright that he had "heard disquieting rumors about the Chandler project"; by October, Wright himself was expressing concern, commenting to Chandler, "There seems to be a 'big silence' out in the West." [84]

Possibly to reassure Chandler and potential backers, Wright decided to obtain scientific validation of his block system. The idea had come up before: in April 1928, before construction of the Arizona Biltmore had begun, he had told S. M. Benet that "block tests etc. from official sources" were available; he probably was referring to the tests conducted for Charles Ennis.[85] By December, in anticipation of building San Marcos in the Desert, he had decided to have additional tests made by the United States Bureau of Weights and Measures in Washington, D.C. He wrote to Albert McArthur from Taliesin, requesting several molds, so that he could cast some blocks, which could then be sent for tests. He anticipated that the tests would include ceilings and floor construction.[86]

Wright seems not to have pursued the tests seriously until 1929, when he apparently visited the Bureau of Standards in Washington on October 16. A few days later he received a follow-up letter that outlined the procedure and the cost for the tests he had requested. Eighteen "wall specimens" and one floor panel were to be submitted for compressive tests, transverse tests, and bend tests. Work was to be performed by a research associate, who would construct the specimens and assist in testing; the bureau would provide general supervision and would prepare the report. Wright would be obligated to employ the research associate at approximately $3,000 per year, and to pay the cost of constructing the specimens. It was established that one year would be required for the testing procedure and preparation of the first draft of a report on the investigation.[87]

Seemingly, the tests were never carried out, and the probable reason can easily be surmised: the fate of the hotel was sealed on October 29.[88] At the time, Chandler indicated to Wright that he believed "the big slump in the stock market is going to be of great advantage to us." He also reminded Wright that he had never received a complete statement of costs.[89] Wright sent the requested estimates in late November; the total was $743,969.71, or $5,945.90 per room. He contrasted these figures with money spent on the Arizona Biltmore, which had cost $1,480,000 for two hundred rooms, or $7,400 per room, and with the Santa Barbara Biltmore, at $9,000 per room.[90]

Chandler was still cautiously optimistic in February, writing to his architect, "I have been doing my very best to make some progress," but noting, "What we will be able to do . . . is problematical on account of the stressed financial conditions which certainly are affecting the whole country." He continued that the weather had been quite warm and that he had "studied every situation" at the Biltmore "comparing same with the possibilities with which we will have to contend." Chandler noted that on entering, "with the natural cement sidewalks and the cement entrance the glare was quite severe; and the sunroom in spite of the hangings looked glary." Wright reassuringly explained that "there is no fair comparison to be made between the Biltmore and our lizard out in the desert. Our walls are all fluted so that there is no sun defiance anywhere. Sunlight will filter into the surfaces of our walls so that no glare will be possible. The floors are made of tiles — the joint lines breaking the surface with hollow spaces beneath them."

He continued, "Our rooms are cool masonry caverns, when you want them to be. The double walls and the deep reveals give us a great advantage either in heat or cold. The Biltmore walls of course are flat. . . . By glancing at the drawing we are sending to you you will see to what extent all the surfaces of the building are relieved by masses of green and flowers. Even water-pools tucked away on the flower beds of the terraces."[91]

Chandler reported in July 1930 that "some things look quite encouraging," but continued, "in the East everyone I saw was talking hard times and the possibility of starting something new at this time is out of the question."[92] Finally, in June 1931 he observed, "instead of getting better, it seems to be continually on the downgrade — at least so far as I know, there has never been a period of harder times than we are having right now, and, of course, we are unable to proceed under present conditions." Although he still expressed optimism in 1934, Chandler's own empire was unraveling. He lost control of the San Marcos Hotel a short time later, and the visions that he and Wright had shared simply slipped away.[93]

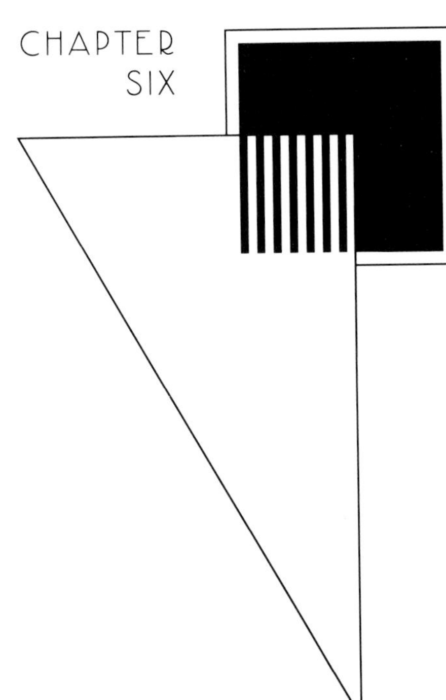

CHAPTER SIX

PROTECTING AND ADDING TO LA MINIATURA

In April 1928, while Wright was in Phoenix, working on the Arizona Biltmore Hotel, Alice Millard again renewed their professional relationship. A remarkably energetic woman, undaunted by past experience, she now initiated the first of several schemes for developing the property around La Miniatura. Her goals were aesthetic, to protect La Miniatura; pragmatic, to liquidate her antique business; economic, to provide income for a lifestyle beyond her present means; and, finally, public-spirited, to create a permanent museum and gallery for her own and other collections. Like her architect's, however, her visions exceeded her ability to pay for them.

ALICE MILLARD HOUSE II, PASADENA

At the time, she was dreaming of purchasing and building on the two lots north of La Miniatura, while they were still vacant (Fig. 177, Lots 11 and 12).[1] A realtor with whom she discussed the project advised strongly against it, but he also saw "all the arguments—both aesthetic and practical—for protecting 'La Miniatura,'" and thought "that if it could be done simply without a loss, it might be worth while." He gave her a detailed list of requirements, proposing two two-story houses with three or four bedrooms each, but assured Millard that "most buyers want the wholly commonplace."[2]

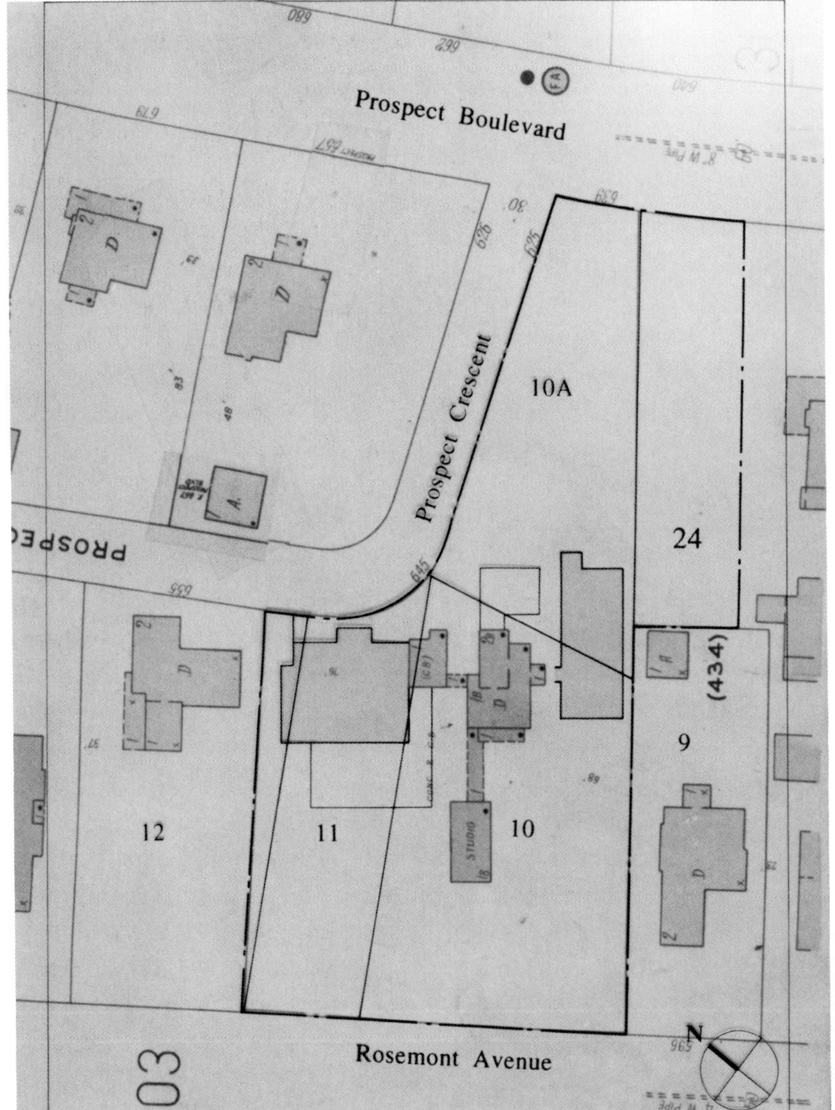

177. Map of the Alice Millard site, Pasadena, California, 1929. Insurance maps of Pasadena, California, Vol. 3 (New York: Sanborn Map Company, 1931), map 347. Courtesy of Urban Conservation Section, Planning Division, City of Pasadena. Overlay courtesy of Eulogio Guzman

Millard sought Wright's services against the advice of her financial counselor as well; he considered La Miniatura "a very bad investment . . . very badly built of very poor material. . . . Its plan is not adapted to the home life of an average family [and] the unfortunate notoriety of the leaking roof would greatly prejudice any possible buyer." In his judgment she would be unlikely ever to recover her investment if the house were offered for sale. Millard insisted, however, that she "could not work wholeheartedly with the design of any [other] architect." Any negative image would be "neutralized by [their] working together again, wisely." She added that "a larger garage is imperative in order to make this property either salable or rentable."[3]

By February 1929, only Lot 11, immediately to the north of La Miniatura, was still available (see Fig. 177, Lot 11). The owners of Lot 12 had built a house designed by Roland Coate; Millard telegraphed her architect with her innate sense of urgency that "La Miniatura must be protected before worst happens but only with your plan." She followed up with a letter two weeks later, describing the neighboring building as an "early California house [that] glistens like freshly fallen snow, and has grass green blinds." She also reiterated her feeling that anything built on the remaining parcel "would detract from the beauty and value of La Miniatura,— unless it were of your design. Therefore I am standing like a rock on this point." Her financial advisor agreed, " 'provided that Mrs. Millard and Mr. Wright will be practical!' "[4]

In the same letter, Millard related the intricacies of her business and personal affairs to Wright, making clear that her underlying goal in building was financial salvation. She had invested heavily in antique furniture, for which she had not found a ready market. The furniture was stored in a warehouse where, she observed, very few people had sufficient imagination to see its beauty. She added that her architect friends frequently brought their clients to the warehouse — unsuccessfully — and they were urging her to find space for proper display. After the furniture was gone, she would sell the house, unless her work "should develop in such a way as to justify its continued use."

Millard repeated the list of requirements that she had sent to Wright ten months earlier; she also added some special requests to accommodate her antiques. She wanted the dining room to be "a continuation of the Living Room — possibly two steps higher." She had "a very fine old walnut Altar 'Balustrado' with a gate, — which would make a fine partition between the two rooms — then hangings could be drawn across when one wanted privacy. . . . Perhaps the Living Room could be two stories, to give me walls for showing tapestries? And there could be a Minstrel Gallery over the Dining Room end of it." Finally, on a more pragmatic note, she reminded Wright of the need to enlarge her existing garage, suggesting "that by bringing the addition out towards the Crescent, it would house two small cars — tandem."[5]

The plans Wright sent to Millard in March 1929 answered all of her requests admirably. The drawings call for a fifty-two-foot-square, two-story building attached to La Miniatura by an addition to the existing garage (Fig. 178). An entrance hall leads to a two-story living room with a dining room, up three steps, at the far north end. The second floor contains three bedrooms and a balcony overlooking the living room (Fig. 179). No elevation drawings have been found. From the plans, however, it appears that the east or entry façade is the only disappointing feature of the house. Flanking garages dominate the building, and the entrance is through paired gates facing Prospect Crescent. In order not to obstruct the view to the north and west from La Miniatura — another of Millard's requests —

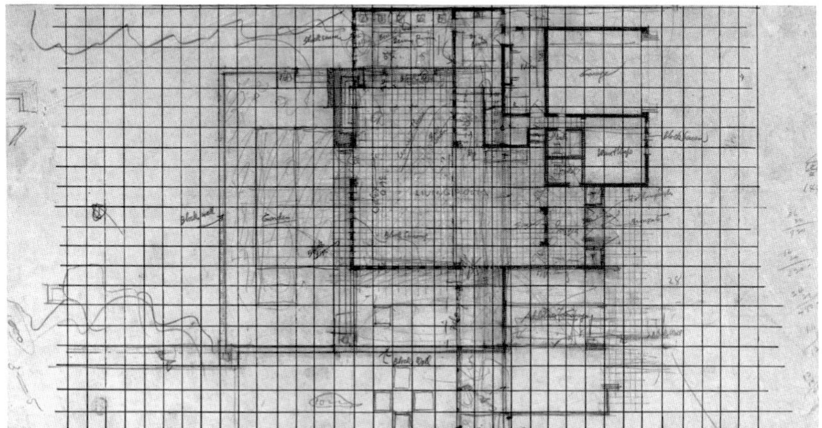

178. Alice Millard house II (project), Pasadena, California, first-floor plan, 1929. FLLW FDN, 2907.003

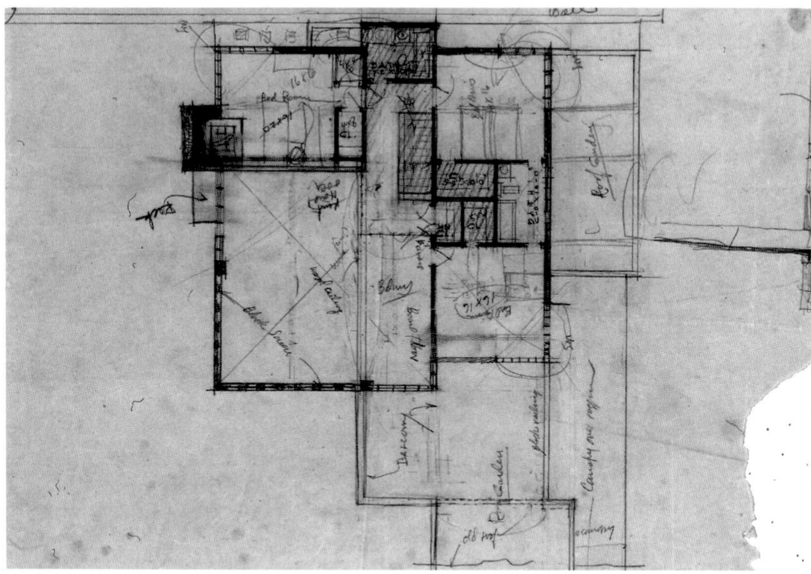

179. Millard house II (project), second-floor plan. FLLW FDN, 2907.001

the house is placed close to the street, with the result that none of the ceremony of arrival at which Wright was so skillful is achieved.

At the time the plans were prepared, Millard did not own the necessary property on which to build. Several months later, she told Wright, "A friend has lovingly purchased the 87 feet adjoining — to protect me for the time being — hoping that it may be mine later. So our lovely house will be built there ultimately — but it may be years."[6]

Although Mrs. Millard acquired the lot north of La Miniatura in 1929, the idea of developing it lay dormant until 1934, when she explained to Wright that she was no longer able to keep the land. She was still hoping, however, that if she could control it, "something might be built there which would really be an asset to this property." She turned to Wright this time not to follow through on the house they had originally contemplated, but instead for "a tentative design for a garage and possibly a connecting wall, just what would be visible as one drove about Prospect Crescent."[7] She suggested that perhaps the young couple who were interested in buying the lot might let Wright design a little house for them later. Wright did not respond at the time, and the couple purchased a lot elsewhere.

Six months after Millard's request, Wright sent designs for five houses for the lot adjoining La Miniatura. He had not taken on the project himself, but had turned it over to a group of apprentices at the new Taliesin Fellowship. Three of these projects remain in Wright's archive; they are simple designs based on Wright's 1929 plan for the site. They are for single block-shell construction, plastered inside.

Millard was "keenly disappointed" with the designs, which looked to her like "workmen's cottages. . . . The one signed by John Howe has certain possibilities but the others are quite out of the question." Wright responded that she was "quite wrong about the sketches," that if his " 'students' . . . could do little houses like these, left to themselves, they would have little need to come here to work."[8] Nevertheless, nothing came of any of these proposals.

MILLARD GALLERY EXTENSION, PASADENA

Much of Millard's energy was focused on her annual exhibitions of rare and fine books, to which the public was invited. For a time these shows were held at the Biltmore Hotel in Los Angeles; in 1925 she approached Wright about building a gallery on her property in Pasadena. When she received no response for three months, she gave the commission to Lloyd, with the condition that the plan be submitted to Wright for approval.[9] Lloyd designed a simple rectangular building of stuccoed wood-frame construction. It was placed in the garden, overlooking the pool, and was attached to La Miniatura by a bridge extending from the living-room balcony. Work was completed in 1926.[10]

Given the moniker "Doll's House," the work pleased neither client nor elder Wright, although Wright approved the plan before construction, with the comment, "Lloyd seems to have done very well." In 1930 Millard asked Wright if she might "take the curse off the Dolls House as a temporary improvement by putting a pilaster of 2-½ blocks on either side of the door toward the pool and on either side of the end window, on the exterior? This . . . will give a sense of depth to those openings and make the building look less high and thin." Later she wrote that she had "an idea that the whole 'Doll's House' may go when a really fine development takes place later," to which Wright responded that "the Dolls house, of course, must go and the sooner the better." [11]

Although most sources state that Wright did design a gallery in 1925, no record of it has been found.[12] Millard revived the idea in 1929, when she was discussing a new house for the property to the north — hoping this time to build on the thirty-two feet remaining on her lot to the south of La Miniatura. She also was trying to acquire additional footage in the ravine to the east, so that there would be space for an entrance terrace, linking the gallery directly with the street.[13]

Wright had preliminary sketches ready by April, when Millard went to Ocatilla to get them; they were lost a few months later, but can be partially described from surviving correspondence. They called for a two-story building fifty feet long — the length of the space between the existing southeast property line and the western elevation of the house — and twenty-five feet wide, with a bedroom and bath over the gallery, and a bridge approach from the street. Millard took the plans with her to Europe, writing on board ship in June to her architect that the cost of the second story would be prohibitive, and that the entrance bridge, as designed, would sacrifice an important tree. She also suggested that the new addition should be "about the height of the present Garage — not much, if any, higher."[14] Wright responded in July that he would carefully take all the points she raised into account, but that he had no plans — she had all the plans there were. After some procrastination, Millard confessed that during her "hectic wanderings," the "sketch" had gotten away from her.[15]

Wright had expressed concern earlier about the "uncertainty" of the additional property that might be available in the ravine to the east; Millard originally had been offered twenty feet, but she later asked for twenty-two or twenty-five. In October she learned that her neighbor would concede twenty-two feet.[16] The plans Wright sent to her in February 1930 are based on the new property line; they call for a rectangular building seventy-two feet long and twenty-eight feet wide. The new gallery is designed as a suitably muted addition to a strong building: the side walls are virtually unrelieved, save for their patterned concrete-block surface on the upper story; the shorter end elevations have tall windows, recalling the parent house (Fig. 180).

This is a building offering greater spatial complexity than its exterior forms suggest. The gallery has an eighteen-foot ceiling and a lower "cloister," separated from the main space by a row of five piers along one side; Wright explained that windows above the cloister would throw light on the north wall, where Millard could put a "panel" (Fig. 181).[17] The western end of the building is divided into two levels by a balcony, with a bedroom and bath above and a "storage" room with desk and fireplace below (Fig. 182). The building is attached to La Miniatura by an umbilical-cord bridge at the balcony level, corresponding with the balcony overlooking the living room, and also can be entered on the main level from a terrace.

The terrace is in the ravine, reached from the street by stairs; it could be argued that its presence is an intrusion, that the impact of the house rising directly from the ground is compromised. In fact, Wright uses the terrace to frame nature and his buildings; the path of circulation provides an opportunity for more intimate association with the ravine and ultimately leads to it. The lowest point, from which the house rises, is untouched.

In March Lloyd obtained a bid of $15,000 to construct the new gallery, but two months later Millard told Wright that she was "without a halfpenny in sight."[18] By September she had another bid of $11,000, from a contractor who was to build a house nearby, designed by David Adler; she was hoping to obtain financing in New York. She was not successful in this and by the end of the year was reconciled to the necessity of abandoning the project temporarily.[19]

Millard's enthusiasm was rekindled a little more than a year later, when she was asked about the "wisest final destination of a priceless collection of books" she had built up for a client, and which was ultimately to be left to an institution. Her friend, the architect Gordon Kaufmann, suggested

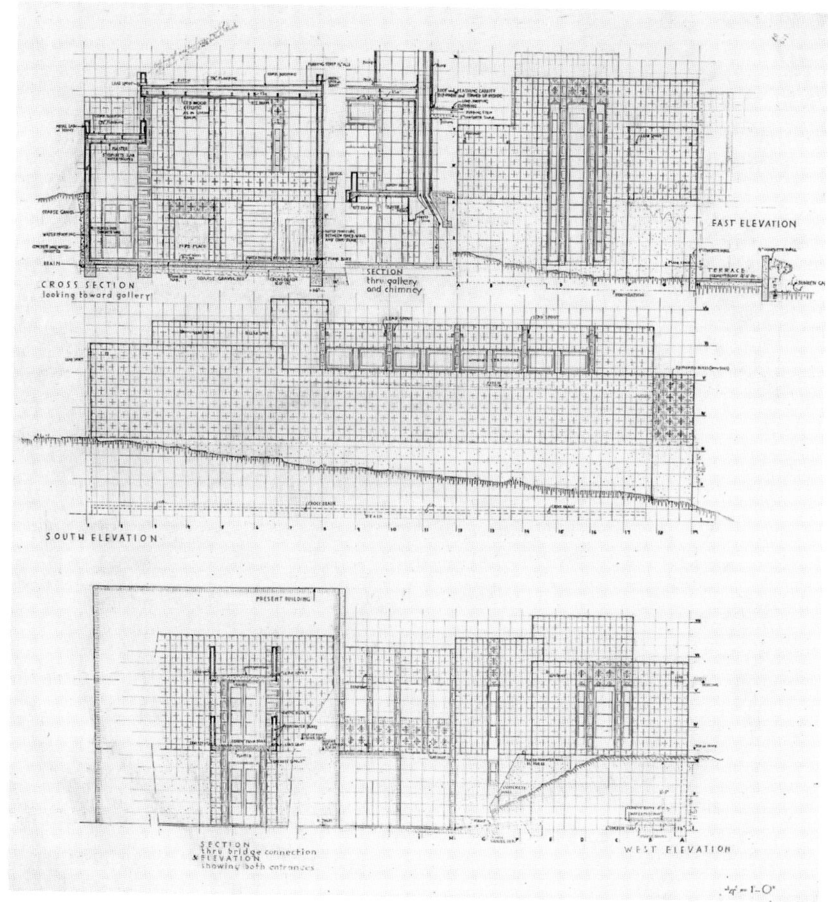

180. Alice Millard gallery (project), Pasadena, California, elevation, 1929. FLLW FDN, 2503.004

that "the only possible correct destination for such a collection was in an enlarged La Miniatura" and that the property should be developed according to Wright's plans, in cooperation with the California Institute of Technology. The entire development, including La Miniatura, ultimately would become a permanent museum and "would confer great distinction upon the Institute." As Millard explained to Wright, "all went swimmingly until the question of financing arose and then, nobody could find any money."[20]

Gordon Kaufmann's suggestion was entirely in the spirit of the times. In the first three decades of the twentieth century, assembling private collections of rare books and manuscripts was a favored pastime of the rich, just as investing in contemporary art has cachet today. Then, as now, provision was often made for the collections to be kept intact and available to

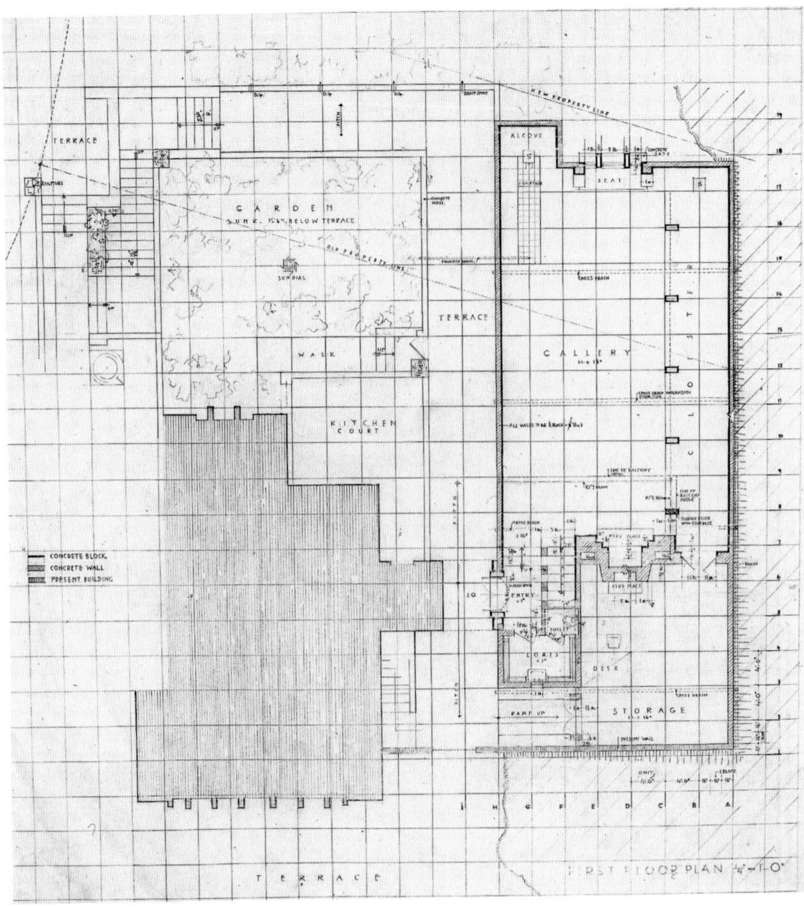

181. Millard gallery (project), plan. FLLW FDN, 2503.002

the public. Millard counted among her clients Henry E. Huntington, William Andrews Clark and, beginning in 1932, Carrie Estelle Doheny; all of whom eventually provided buildings and endowments to maintain their collections for public benefit.

Alice Millard lived in this world of immense wealth only peripherally, yet she shared a vision with her patrons in wanting to establish a permanent collection at La Miniatura. With her husband, she had assembled a collection illustrating the "Evolution of the Book" which was to be the focus of her museum; other collections were to be added. She was interested in reaching as wide an audience as possible, including the "Youth of California,—who comprise the book-lovers and collectors of the future."[21]

When it was clear that funds were not available from the California

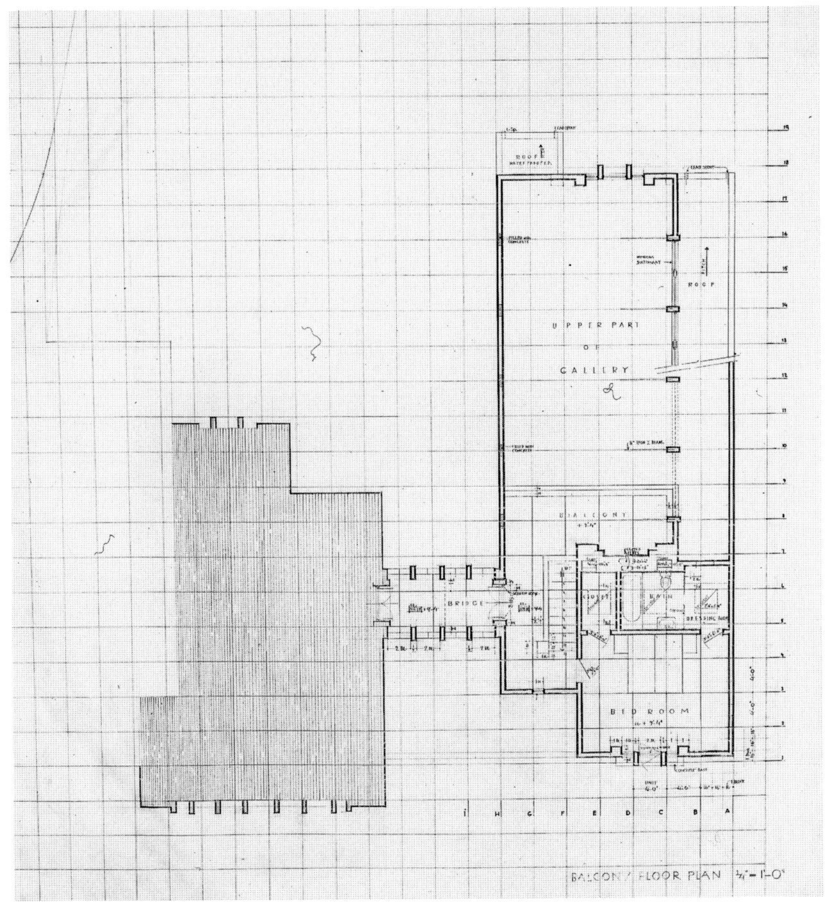

182. Millard gallery (project), balcony plan. FLLW FDN, 2503.003

Institute of Technology, she attempted to undertake the project on her own. In November 1931, she wrote to Carrie Estelle Doheny, "In order to quickly realize the sum necessary for enlarging my Little Museum and building an Art Gallery, I have suddenly decided to offer my entire stock at absurd prices."[22] The gallery, of course, was only a dream; in anticipation of building, however, and with Gordon Kaufmann's encouragement, she acted quickly to obtain the remainder of the ravine and three-fourths of the adjoining lot (Lots 10A, 24).[23] There is a sketch in Wright's archive for development of this property; he suggested a network of pools and bridges, linking La Miniatura and the gallery with a new house at the eastern, or Prospect Boulevard, extremity of the site. This is simply an extension of the earlier bridge scheme, and no more disturbing to the site.

In the end, additions to her garage and to the Doll's House were the only new construction Millard was able to undertake at La Miniatura. She had first mentioned the need to enlarge the garage to Wright in 1928; work was delayed until she assembled the necessary property and capital.[24] Construction was carried out in 1931, under Lloyd's supervision. His plan was to repeat the present garage, offsetting it to the west two and one-half block courses; provision was also made at the rear for storage.[25] Wright saw and approved the plan, specifying that he wanted the blocks "to be set in the same way as the original House to produce a precisely similar effect." Apparently referring to bureaucratic interference, he continued: "Whatever is necessary to satisfy the department we will do — It ought not to be much — or else they ought to tear the present house down.[26]

The addition to the Doll's House was first contemplated in late 1931; Millard had in mind an eight-by-twelve-foot alcove to the west. As always, she solicited Wright's approval, explaining that she had "studied the problem from Lester Avenue and this little bay would fit right into the bank and really not be noticeable at all." He responded that he had no objection, if she were "so foolish as to indulge in more makeshifts." Work was completed in 1933, the size of the addition being increased to ten by thirty-eight feet; Lloyd served nominally as architect.[27]

□ □ □

Toward the end of her life, Alice Millard came to the sad realization that La Miniatura probably could not be developed or preserved as she had envisioned. She requested that her books be deposited at the Huntington Library in San Marino, if they were removed from the house. She died at La Miniatura in 1938; part of the collection was purchased by a group of her friends and given to the library the following year.[28]

CHAPTER SEVEN

CODA: ANSWERING THE INTERNATIONAL STYLE

He has nothing to say today to the International Group.
—Philip Johnson[1]

The concrete-block experiments of the 1920s drew to a close with a house for Wright's cousin, Richard Lloyd Jones, in Tulsa, Oklahoma. This was followed in 1931 by a house designed especially for the "Modern Architecture" exhibition at the Museum of Modern Art in New York. These buildings, seemingly so very different from the California works, in fact synthesize the previous decade of exploration both structurally and formally, and represent a narrowing of the gap—aesthetically, if not theoretically—between Wright and the International Style.

JONES HOUSE, TULSA

Richard Lloyd Jones (1873–1963) was publisher of the Tulsa *Tribune*. Before moving to Tulsa, he had owned the Madison, Wisconsin, *State Journal* and was among those coming to Wright's aid after the murders and fire at Taliesin in August 1914. He also had served on the Fiji building committee when the fraternity was planning construction of a new house at the University of Wisconsin. He and the architect had a combustible friendship. Their written exchanges are peppered with vitriolic, though often humorous, retorts. At one point, Jones castigated his cousin's "autocratic mind" and concluded that in his "own statement there are only two classes of architects in America, Frank Lloyd Wright and all the rest. And all the rest are to be despised."[2]

Jones's four-acre site sloped down gently to the north and overlooked the hills of the Arkansas River valley for forty miles; Turkey Mountain could be seen to the southwest.[3] He wanted to build a house there to accommodate his family of five and in which he could entertain large groups. He detailed his program in a November 1928 letter to Wright:

> It must have on the ground floor. 1 living room, 1 dining room that will accommodate a party of twenty, 1 study, which shall be sizeable not less than 16 × 24 (that is a work shop, I don't want any dinky little den, it is not a place to read, it is a place to work. I dictate all my stuff, I like to walk around when I am dictating, go from bookcase to table and all that sort of thing). I want a pool room which shall not be less than 22 × 16. All this makes a pretty sizeable first floor arrangement, when you add kitchen, pantries, and perhaps something in the way of a vestibule or a receiving hall. For bedrooms we want 5. One of fairly good proportion which shall be the bedroom with twin beds which shall be used by George [Mrs. Jones] and myself, That will have its own bath and I would like a combination tub and shower. We want a comfortable bedroom for Florence with the same type bathroom, and a comfortable bedroom for guests, and we want two bedrooms with a joint bath, this bathroom may be smaller and will only have a shower. This will be for the two boys. This will make five bedrooms for sleeping arrangement. The best exposure for bedrooms is south, so get as many bedrooms for the south bedrooms as can work in for our cool breeze in the warm weather is always from the south.
>
> If it is possible I would like to have a roof of part of the first floor flat so that it could be used as a summer terrace and this should be a roof that would give us a view to the south, west and north. The least desirable outlook is toward the east.
>
> Separate from the house we should provide a garage space for four cars. I would like to drive through a gate into a court yard so that in inclement weather we could merely stall our cars, without closing the doors, but instead close the gate of the driveway, which would lock the cars in the court. Over the garage we should have about three servants rooms and they could have a balcony which would face the east, therefore giving us the protection of facing the street.[4]

Wright responded on December 14 that he "had already spent some days making drawings. . . . I feel that I have already struck 'pay dirt' in the way of scheme." He wanted to use his new system of concrete-block construction, which "has gone beyond the experimental stage," and noted that he was training several men to use the system.[5]

In fact, it is not clear that concrete-block construction was contemplated initially. Jones's son Jenkin recalled in 1979 that the first design was for a "rambling home of wood and stucco, with a low-pitched roof and surrounding a courtyard."[6] He may have been referring to Wright's preliminary sketches, which reveal a plan based on 30/60-degree angles, with a steeply pitched roof over the second-story section, but give no information about the method of construction (Figs. 183, 184).

After a delay of several months, Wright prepared a set of finished drawings at Ocatilla in 1929. In spite of numerous suggestions from his cousin, the layout adheres closely to the original sketch.[7] The plan is determined by a diagonal grid; perimeter walls are composed of rows of diamond-shaped concrete-block piers, alternating with vertical rows of glass of the same width (Figs. 185, 186). In several rooms the points of the hexagons are enclosed entirely in glass, an inspired resolution of a pragmatic request. Jones had explained that his daughter Bisser [Florence] was "an enthusiastic amateur botanist" and needed a "flower room, green house, whatever you want to call a plant room." Jones called it a "Bissorum"; since there are several of these glass prows, we may then call them "Bissora."[8]

The plan surpasses the Cudney house, to which it is closely related, in the complete integration of structural system and plan; every element is subordinate to the grid. Still, the plans and structural systems of the Cudney and Jones projects have much in common. Their elevations, however, are very different. The Cudney site is on a mountain slope; arms of the house reach back into the mountain and meet the desert below on several levels, producing an elevation of great liveliness. The Jones site was nearly flat. Wright's response was to design a building of unprecedented horizontality; it is as if he had slipped the living-room level of San Marcos in the Desert out of its original context and planted it directly on the ground (Fig. 187).

Unfortunately, Jones seems not to have understood the subtleties of this plan. He wrote to his architect on June 4:

> The more I study this diagonal block, the more I see a definite charm in it as a picture, but I do not think it would live well. It limits your view just exactly as blinders on a horse's bridle will limit the view of a horse. . . . I will sacrifice art gladly for the joy of seeing out of doors. . . .
>
> We hesitate a little bit about being the first to experiment with the diagonal blocks, particularly, as I have illustrated it limits the outlook of every room. . . .
>
> You said you would give us a layout that would take the square block and

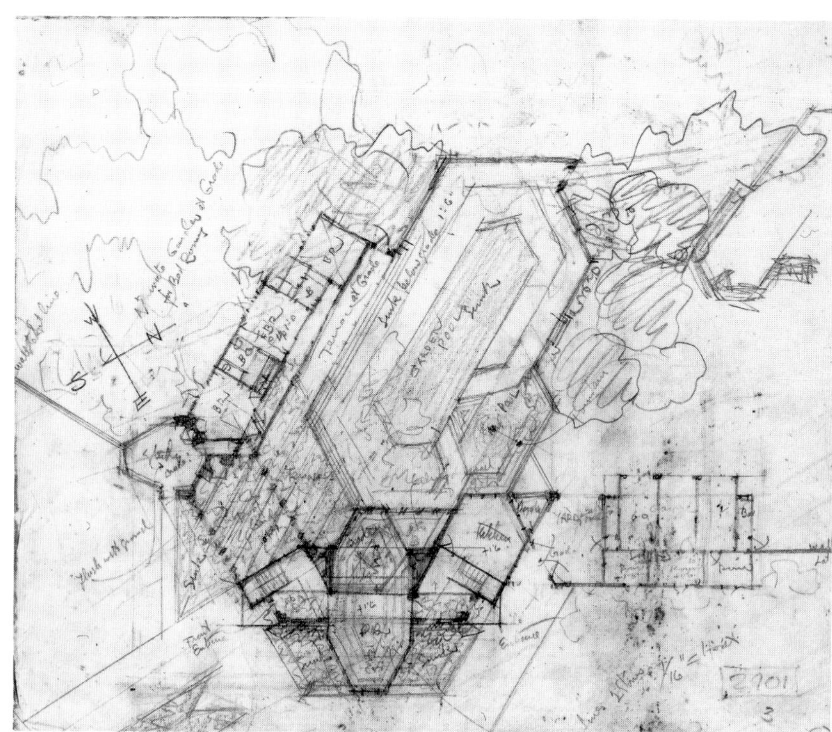

183. Richard Lloyd Jones house (project), Tulsa, Oklahoma, plan, 1929. FLLW FDN, 2901.001

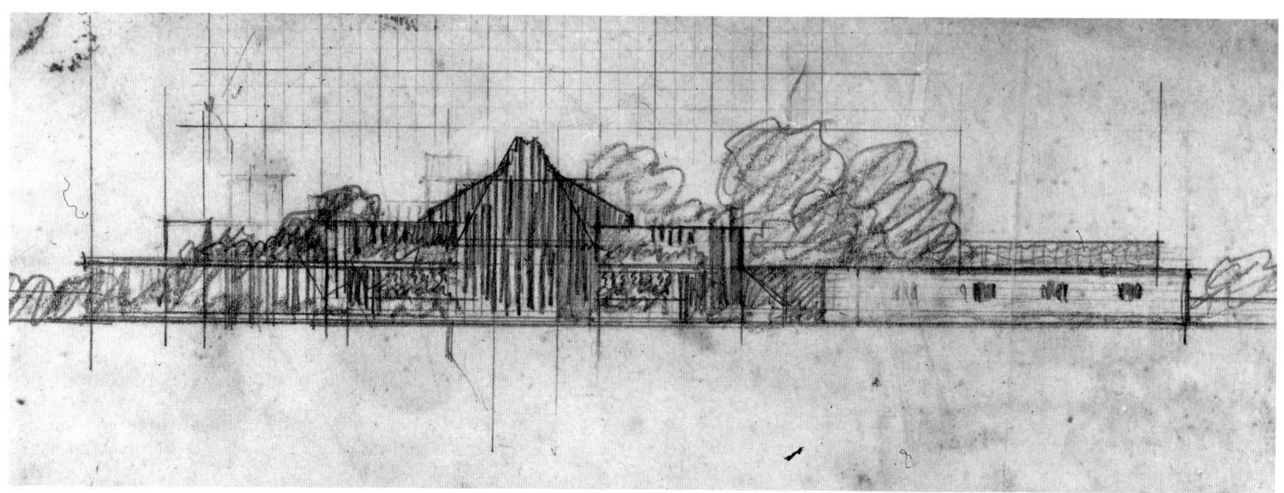

184. Jones house (project), perspective. FLLW FDN, 2901.003

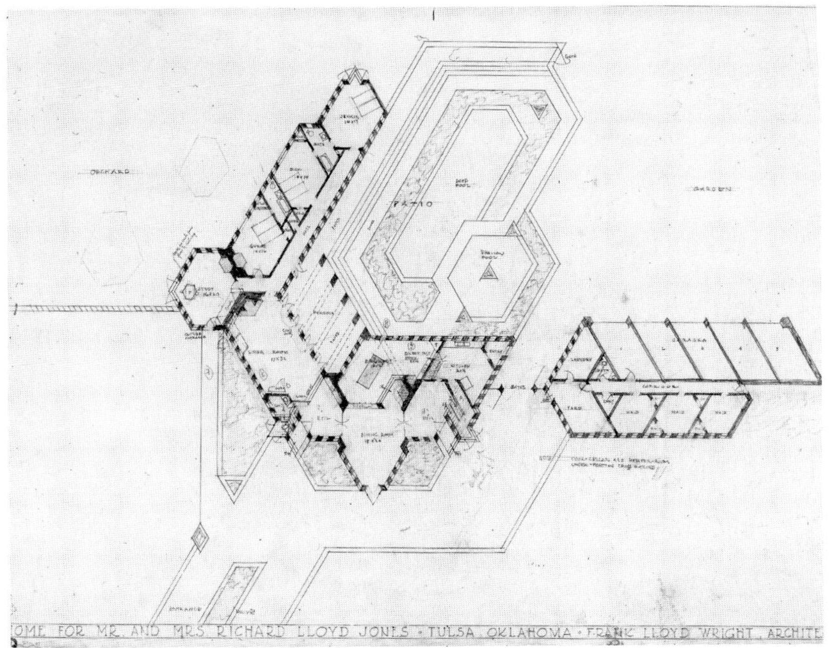

185. Jones house (project), first-floor plan. FLLW FDN, 2901.007

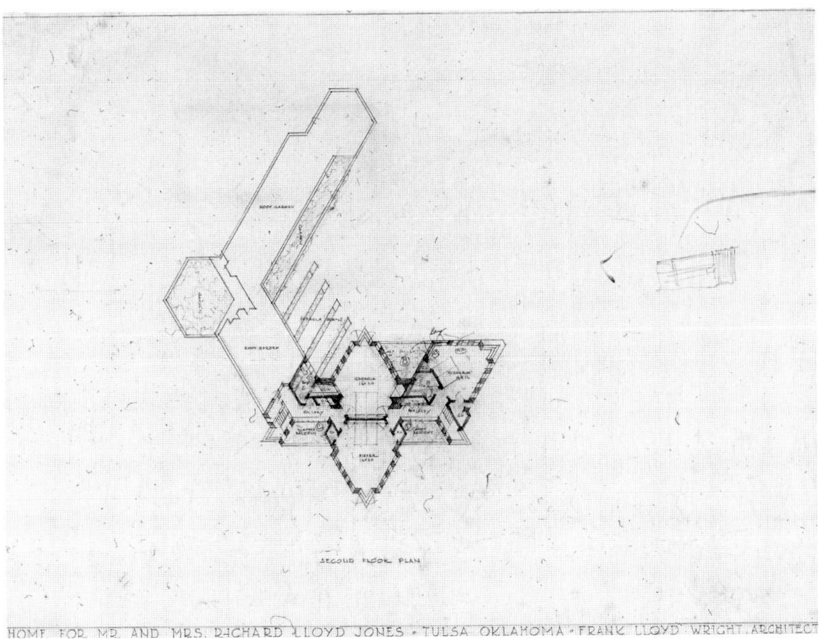

186. Jones house (project), second-floor plan. FLLW FDN, 2901.010

187. Jones house (project), aerial perspective. FLLW FDN, 2901.002

188. Jones house, isometric view. FLLW FDN, 2902.019

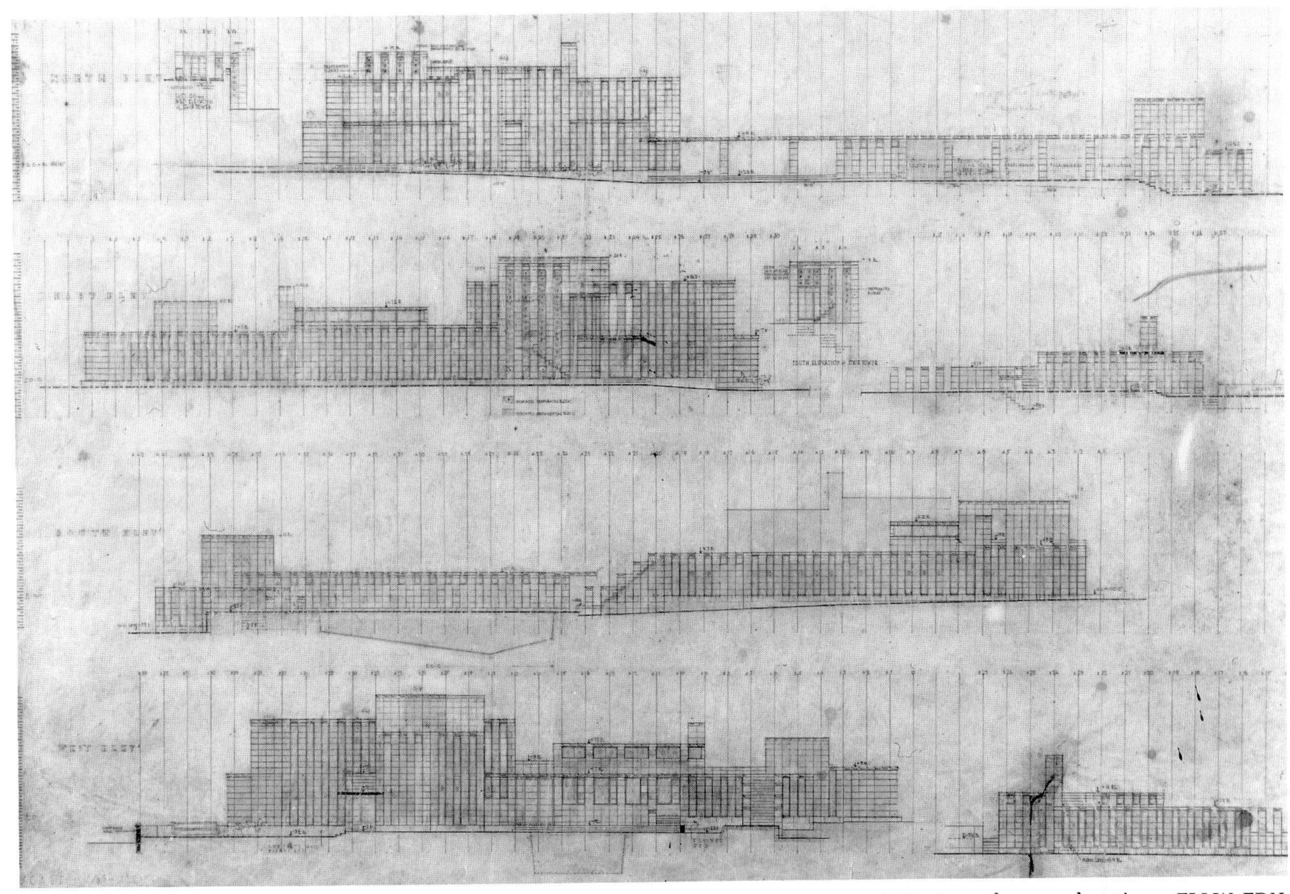

189. Jones house, elevations. FLLW FDN, 2902.015

which would give us windows out of which we could get panoramic pictures.[9]

In the summer of 1929, as requested, Wright prepared a new scheme, based on the square grid. The basic layout of the house was unchanged; Wright simply modified the geometry (Fig. 188). Jones liked the plan, but he still questioned the "alternate vertical strips of wall and glass"; he explained that he could not stand in the center of the living room and see Turkey Mountain, to the southwest. In short, he "would infinitely rather have your old style of architectural exterior, with the long horizontal windows."[10]

"As usual," Wright responded, "you misinterpret a good many of the points on the plan." He explained that the house was oriented to the most important view, down the length of the court. On the question of "vertical articulation," he suggested that from the proper viewpoint, the "whole living room wall becomes a window with vertical mullions. All the walls become such (Fig. 189). And you have outlook in every direction more than you could possible [*sic*] have by building a wall and cutting a whole [*sic*] to look out of." If, he concluded, what is wanted is "a lot of broad windows we will have to abandon this scheme entirely and give you another kind of a house."[11]

Threaded through this exchange is Jones's notion that the plan should be developed independently of the elevation and structural system; he repeatedly asked for a plan "sketch" that he could analyze and respond to. The suggestion was antithetical to Wright's design process; at one point he chidingly asked his cousin if he couldn't "by concentrating firmly on the point in hand, grasp the idea that it is as impossible for me to make you a mere sketch as for a camel to enter through the eye of a needle into heaven."[12] Nevertheless, Jones persisted; he and his wife were "first essentially interested in floor layout. [We have] tried it your way, won't you please try it our way and send us some sketch of your room arrangement, showing approximately the ground that you cover."[13]

While Wright acknowledged to his cousin that "things looked pretty dark, between us, for this scheme, for awhile," one senses that they both enjoyed the repartee.[14] And Wright prevailed; his second scheme was built, though the plan was rearranged somewhat before construction began. The most important — and unfortunate — change was the transposition of the dining and billiard rooms. This was done at Jones's request; he saw the billiard room as "a sort of alcove or enlargement of the central hall with the billiard table as the decorative center."[15] Sociologists might offer one interpretation of this request; architects would be more likely to conclude that the expected hierarchy of spaces is reversed (see Fig. 188).

Although the system for using blocks overhead that was developed for San Marcos in the Desert is indicated in the Jones house drawings, the latter was intended to be a comparative study in technical simplicity. Only six basic block forms are specified for construction; these are combined with reinforced-concrete slabs (Fig. 190). The perimeter-wall screens are built of twenty-inch-square hollow piers, alternating with twenty-inch-wide glazed strips. The piers are formed with twenty-by-ten-inch blocks, assembled in pairs, with channels at the joints for vertical metal reinforcement (Fig. 191). Metal frames for fixed or movable sash fit into vertical channels at the point of intersection of the blocks (Fig. 192). Solid walls are built of ten-by-twenty-inch plain blocks (Fig. 193). Ceilings are formed of twenty-inch-square coffered blocks; square tiles are laid on top (Figs.

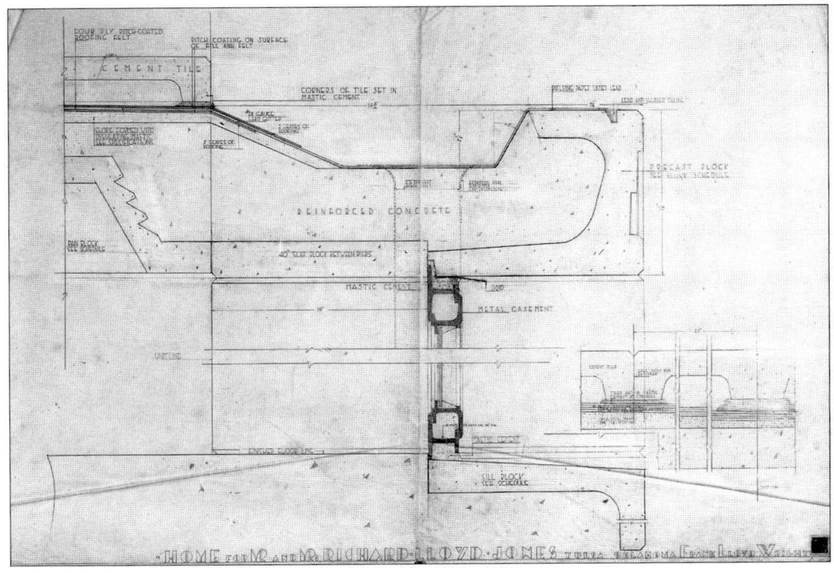

190. Jones house, block assembly diagram. FLLW FDN, 2902.039

194, 195). The projecting edge is finished with patterned fascia blocks (Fig. 196). The ground floor is of poured concrete; sill blocks twenty inches wide and ten inches deep fill the voids between the piers (Fig. 197). Patterned perforated blocks are used to conceal heat vents and for integral wall lighting (Fig. 198).

Wright wanted Paul Mueller to build the house and first recommended him to Jones in October 1929. He followed up early the next year in a letter to Mueller: "My cousin's house is to be ready to start April 1st and he would like you to build it all things being proper as to price." Wright and Mueller then spent several months working on estimates, Jones in the interim telling Wright that he was "willing to build now and start now if I can be assured from you and your contractor that my building bill shall not exceed $75,000 maximum"; and Wright telling Alexander Chandler that he was "starting a $100,000 block house for my cousin in Tulsa." Finally, in the summer of 1930, Mueller and Jones signed a contract, stating that work would start immediately and would be substantially completed by December 1, for the sum of $72,500.[16]

Mueller moved to Tulsa in July—for what became a much longer stay than either he or Jones anticipated—and began working with molds and test blocks.[17] The primary concern was to produce blocks that would be waterproof. This was an old problem that Wright had mentioned in his 1927 letter to A. N. Rebori, but he had there blamed the difficulty on poor

191. Jones house, pier block. FLLW FDN, 2902.043

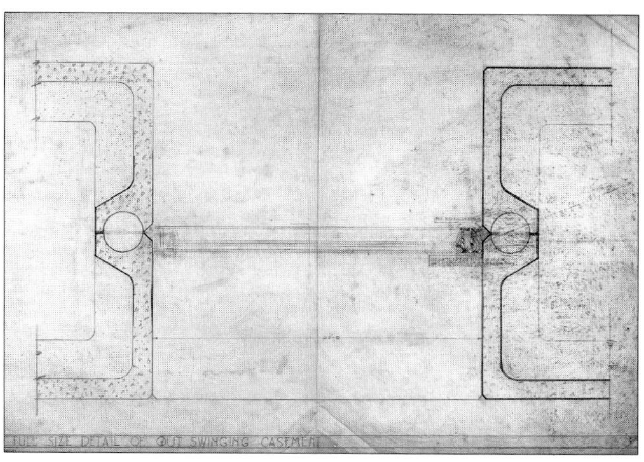

192. Jones house, sash detail. FLLW FDN, 2902.035

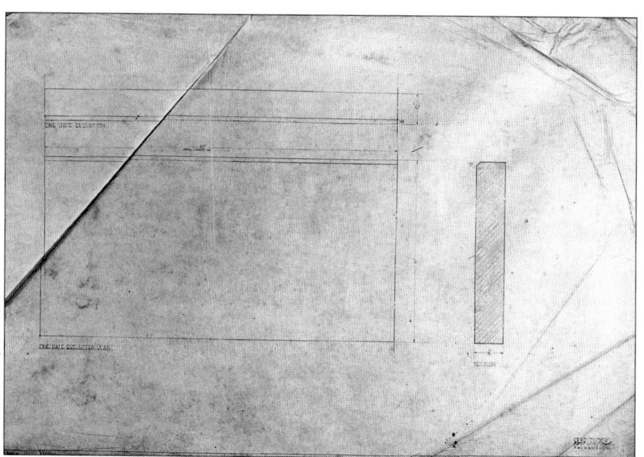

193. Jones house, wall block. FLLW FDN, 2902.032

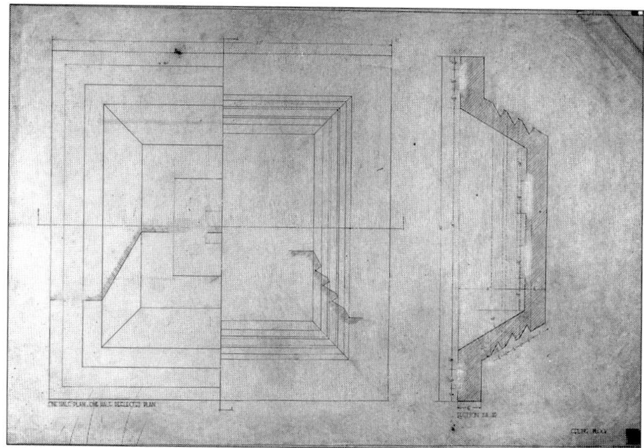

194. Jones house, ceiling block. FLLW FDN, 2902.023

workmanship, not on inherent defects in the system. Of course there was an inherent defect: blocks produced with the dry-pack method Wright had used in southern California cannot be made waterproof. Only in 1930 did Wright acknowledge this inadequacy; he wrote to Jones that Mueller was experimenting with a "wet block" and that if it were a success they would "prefer it because of its water-proof qualities." In fact, the blocks were not waterproof; Jones told Wright that "they soak up water like a sponge." Wright intended to coat the insides of the blocks with asphalt paint, but Jones insisted on the addition of a surface sealer as well.[18]

Pigment was also added to the concrete mixture for the first time. The

195. Jones house, ceiling tile. FLLW FDN, 2902.037

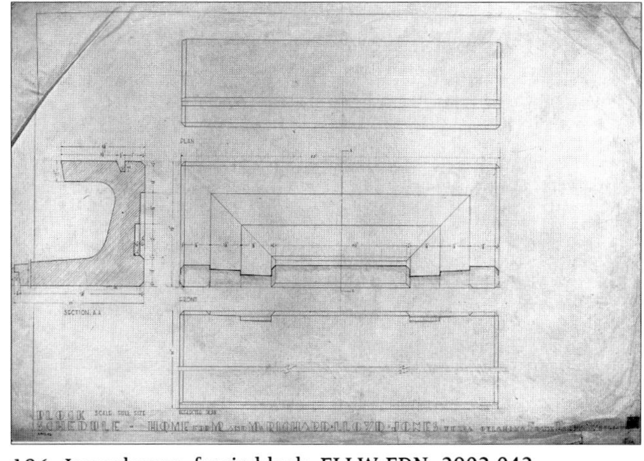
196. Jones house, fascia block. FLLW FDN, 2902.042

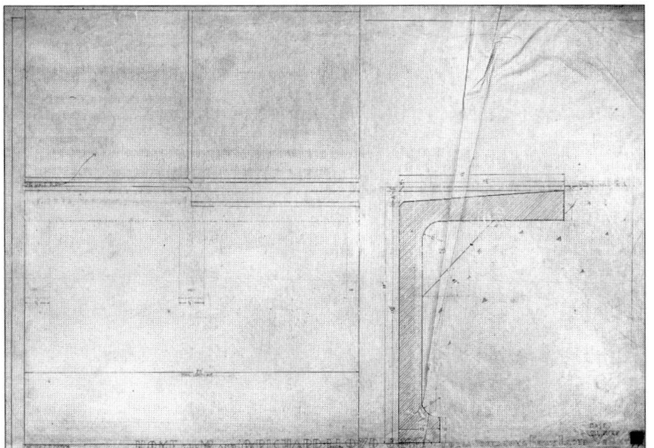
197. Jones house, sill block. FLLW FDN, 2902.041

198. Jones house, patterned block. FLLW FDN 2902.029

idea was not entirely new; Wright had indicated color on drawings for Doheny Ranch and had suggested to Lloyd that color would help the Storer house. In those cases, however, color was used in certain blocks, as an accent, while all the blocks of the Jones house were "sort of a cool 'old rose.'" Wright was concerned about the effect, cautioning Mueller that "there will be so many deep reveals that the house will naturally look quite dark," and advising him to "make all your mistakes on the light side."[19]

Molds still at the house in 1993 indicate that at least three general types were used. The basic pier blocks were fabricated in elaborate hinged-metal containers, whose weight and size could only have made them cumbersome to use. Wooden molds were used for the patterned fascia blocks, plaster forms for the patterned perforated blocks.

Correspondence during construction demonstrates that, in spite of great theoretical advances, the textile block system remained difficult to manage in application. Young Bruce Goff, who assisted Paul Mueller for a time, claimed that many special block sizes were needed to complete the house.[20] Also, there was an unexplained modification of the block system itself. Blueprints remaining at the house and partial investigation of the structure reveal that blocks having returns on two sides only, forming parallel rows of beams two feet on center, were substituted in many areas for the square ceiling blocks, which formed a grid of beams. And, as always, there were delays. On January 24, 1931, when the house was nearly two months behind schedule, Mueller told Wright that the "Second Story walls are partly up to roof." By July, Jones's mood recalled that of the California clients when he told his architect, "This house will be one year in building and I am beginning to lose interest in it."[21]

The house was essentially complete by August 1931: the kitchen cabinets were being installed, bathroom fixtures were in place, and the grounds were sodded. The question of furniture had come up earlier; in June 1930 Wright had told Jones that he was working on furniture drawings and a curtain list. The following March, Wright's secretary, Karl Jensen, wrote Jones that he was sending the "'Bauhaus' book containing 22 different rug patterns,—the work of the students in that School." The implication that Wright had indeed discovered modernism is reinforced by his interest in using a new material, Met-L-Wood, for the furniture and doors. Met-L-Wood was a sandwich of wood overlaid with thin sheets of aluminum; it would have produced a decidedly slick, industrial effect. Jones was unenthusiastic, however; he told Wright that the metal "tarnishes at the touch and will be a constant source of expense and annoyance." Ultimately it was not the impractical material but cost overruns that precluded furnishing the house to Wright's specifications; Jones was indignant when he wrote, "I will not have one dollar for a rug or a curtain to say nothing about a screen or a stick of furniture."[22]

However, a few pieces of furniture were completed to Wright's designs, including bookcases, a cabinet placed between the dining and billiard rooms, and a desk and chair for Jones's study. The furniture was designed for construction with one-quarter-inch-thick Met-L-Wood; when it was subsequently translated into plywood, Wright attempted to maintain the exceptionally thin appearance he had first envisioned. He specified quarter-inch plywood; wood seven-sixteenths-inch thick was used, but it still quickly proved to be unsatisfactory. The bookcases sagged badly with only slight pressure; the doors on the desk warped; and Jones said that the chair was "about as strong as a cigar box." Wright responded that because of a trip to South America he had not seen the drawings for the desk and chair before they were sent to Tulsa, but that "thin slab furniture is all right if made right." He noted that steel angle plates were to have been added, and that maybe there were not enough of them.[23]

□ □ □

Near the end of construction, Wright commented to Lloyd, "Richard's house has won the town. It is a house without walls. The effect is strange and delightful. The house volatilizes. After you have been in it and come away there seems no enclosure. Yet it is very strong and private, almost a fortress."[24] His observations are difficult to evaluate: certainly the chiaroscuro image conveyed in early black-and-white photographs is misleading, and there is a flow of space between indoors and out that is unparalleled in the California houses, but otherwise time and a succession of owners have modified the original effect. The lines of the building are softened today by mature landscape; and the rose-tinted concrete has been painted, diluting what must have been rather surrealistic juxtapositions of light and shadow (Plates 8, 9).

Still, the basic forms remain; the Jones house is Wright's severest statement in concrete block. Formal variety is minimal; ornament almost nonexistent. The insistence of the rows of identical piers is mitigated by variations in massing and by the crystalline greenhouses—the "Bissora"—modernist follies pointing toward nature and creating intimacy with the parklike setting. But one can only conclude that the square module is less successful in every way than the original diagonal grid. There is a distinct loss of animation in the translation (Fig. 199).

It is easy to observe in this building, both as first designed and as later constructed, a new direction in Wright's work, though the change is less abrupt and less subject to external influence than the finished house might suggest; only with caution can we interpret the development as anything but a logical evolution in his practice. The transition from building to building—from the center section of San Marcos in the Desert to the Cudney house to the first Jones concrete-block scheme—is altogether too clear. Still, the correspondence with contemporary developments in Europe, and Wright's awareness of them, need to be acknowledged. He was

199. Jones house, air view. Courtesy of Florence Lloyd Jones Barnett

at no loss when Alice Millard inquired in 1929 about modern French architects, responding that "Andre Lurcat, Corbusier, Mallet Stevens, and quite a number of others . . . are all doing interesting creative work. . . . The Studium Louvre is executing some interesting work. Paul Poret also is extravagantly engaged in the new movement. Prima-Verd also executes interesting work. The work of Venice Vexteta is good and probably on exhibition in Paris."[25]

It is probably an accident of fate, however, that in adhering to his cousin's wishes and redesigning the Jones house on the square grid, Wright created a building with an unmistakable visual kinship (if no common theoretical basis) with a much earlier project by another modernist architect, working not in France but in Germany. In 1910 Ludwig Mies van der Rohe had entered a competition for a monument to the memory of Otto von Bismarck; his recent biographer might have been discussing the Jones house when he described Mies's design as "an abstract colonnade with piers the same width as the spaces between them" (Fig. 200).[26] The project was rooted in the Neoclassical theories of distillation and reinterpretation of Karl Friedrich Schinkel; Wright displayed the same spirit of reduction to an essence in the Jones house.

Surely it was this quality that appealed to Henry-Russell Hitchcock and Philip Johnson, prompting them to include photographs of the house in their famous "Modern Architecture" exhibition at the Museum of Modern Art in 1932. Hitchcock observed, in his catalogue essay: "Unwilling

200. Mies van der Rohe, Bismarck Monument (project), Bingen am Rhine, Germany, elevation, 1910. Mies van der Rohe Archive, the Museum of Modern Art, New York. Gift of the Architect

like certain of his European contemporaries to accept a discipline established by his juniors, [Wright] has nevertheless advanced parallel with them. But the distance between him and even Le Corbusier, whose influence he particularly distrusts, grows ever less."[27] A similar analogy was made by Bruce Goff: in his estimation, the house was "CLEAN without the barren, mathematical, inhuman qualities in the work of Le Corbusier and his group."[28]

HOUSE ON THE MESA, DENVER

By early 1931 the Richard Lloyd Jones house was well under way; the future of the projects for Alexander Chandler and Alice Millard was not optimistic, and little else was on the horizon. It had been nearly a decade since Wright had begun exploring the technical and aesthetic possibilities of concrete-block construction; he had prepared numerous schemes, yet he had built little. It was surely Wright's need to assert his unsuppressed vitality — and the need to stay in the competition — that prompted him to respond to an invitation to design a house specifically for the exhibition at the Museum of Modern Art; any sense of winding down is dispelled in this project. Called House on the Mesa, it represents the sort of pure design possible in a climate free of pragmatic constraints.

Wright outlined the program for House on the Mesa in a manuscript dated April 25, 1932, two months after the project was first exhibited. It was designed for a "moderately wealthy American family of considerable culture, — master, mistress and four children, cook and two maids, chauffeur and gardener." The house was to be a demonstration of "machine-age luxury, that would compare favorably in character and integrity with the luxury of the Greeks or Goths," but had "what might truthfully be called twentieth-century style."[29]

According to Wright, the inspiration for the design arose from a visit to the house of George Cranmer, who lived "on the mesa" in Denver—hence the identification with that city.[30] George Cranmer (1884–1975) had made money in the stock market; he had retired in 1928 at age forty-four and, in his words, "traveled and loafed for a few years." Between 1935 and 1947 he served somewhat controversially as manager of improvements and parks for the city of Denver. He and his wife, Jean (1886–1974), were strongly committed to cultural improvement in the city; their large Italian Renaissance house, designed by Jules Jacques Benois Benedict and completed in 1917, was a mecca for artists passing through.[31] Cranmer invited Wright to be their guest when the architect was in town, in December 1930, to speak at the Denver Art Museum; this apparently was their first meeting. Wright explained later that he had "used" the Cranmers' "family and situation merely as an ideal American family . . . as an example to the country," when designing House on the Mesa; their "'set up' seemed . . . worth interpreting." He added that he "had no idea" whether they "would at all like the interpretation."[32]

House on the Mesa was designed for a site with a panoramic view of the Rocky Mountains. Wright described several acres that were nearly flat and opened to a small lake, grass plains, and surrounding woods (Fig. 201). He may have had a small but inspiring and readily accessible park in front of the Cranmers' house in mind; it overlooks the Front Range and Pikes Peak. Visiting Mountain View (now Cranmer) Park sixty years later, one can easily imagine House on the Mesa there. However, Wright also indicated that the site extended along a "motor highway"; as depicted, this could only have been the street separating the Cranmers' house from the park; this street was vacated in 1923.[33] Also, the elevation drawings indicate a cardinal orientation that would have been impossible on this site and, curiously, suggest that the house as oriented to the view could not have been built in Denver at all.

Wright wanted the house to reflect "the sweep of the Mesa." He accomplished this by designing an extraordinarily long building—it extends approximately 360 feet; the Ennis house, by comparison, is 248 feet long—whose composition accentuates rather than fragments the horizontal line. The elevation close to the street is essentially a solid wall with little

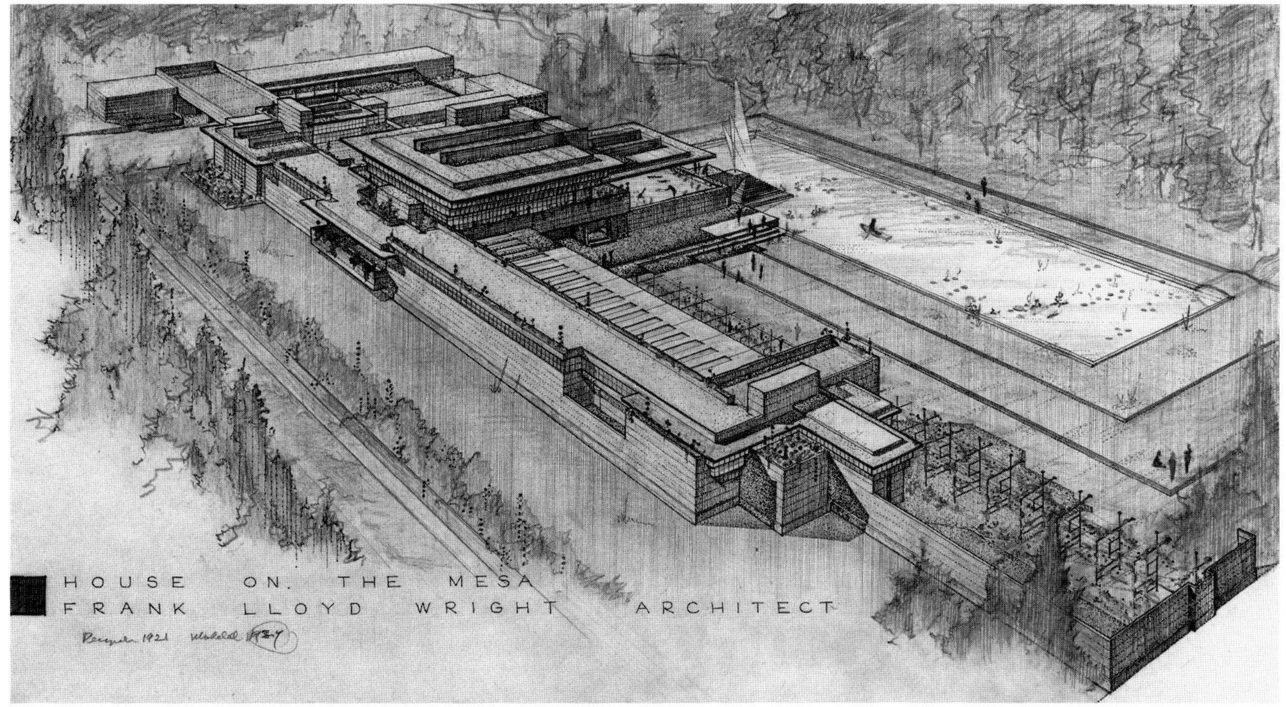

201. House on the Mesa (project), Denver, Colorado, perspective, 1931. FLLW FDN, 3102.021

articulation. Several projecting wings make the opposite side, which opens to the view, more three-dimensional, but again, the great length of the building is accentuated with a rhythm of repeated forms.

A loggia spans the length of the building and links the various spaces. A large entrance court with four-car garage at the northeast end of the plan is connected to the house by a second-story bridge on axis with the loggia, and serves, in Wright's words, to acknowledge "the motor car" as "the feature of American life it is fast becoming."[34] Service wings, framing the motor court, extend to the southeast. Entry to the house is under the bridge, a few steps up from the garage court, and leads directly into the loggia. On the ground floor the loggia gives access to the dining room, two guest bedrooms and three children's bedrooms on the right, and the master suite at the far end. A cross axis is formed at midpoint in the loggia by a stairwell leading to the second floor, and by the extension of the billiard room and swimming pool to the southeast (Fig. 202). The living room on the second story, above the billiard room, is expressed as the focus of the house in plan and elevation (Fig. 203).

House on the Mesa was to be built with concrete-block shell walls; floors

202. House on the Mesa (project), first-floor plan. FLLW FDN, 3102.006

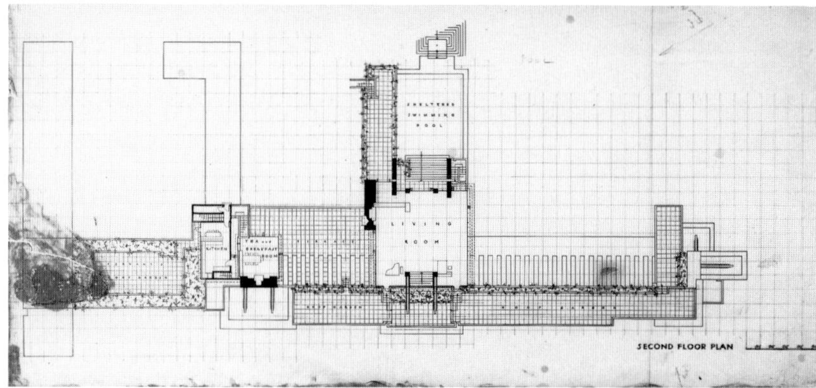

203. House on the Mesa (project), second-floor plan. FLLW FDN, 3102.009

and ceilings are reinforced-concrete slabs, hung from above by cantilevered beams projecting from the masonry chimney masses. Wright described this as "a modern scheme of construction," an "individualized and integrated" design "characteristic of our new resources — steel in tension, glass, and concrete."[35] This is a departure from the notion of mono-material concrete-block construction Wright had worked so hard to perfect; in fact, concrete block seems almost incidental to the scheme. Having brought the concept to its logical conclusion in San Marcos in the Desert, Wright retreated to the earlier practice of using blocks only for wall construction, though without the formal contrivances of the earlier buildings. There are no offset blocks and pattern is all but abandoned; there is occasional use of a cruciform design, recalling the blocks of the Millard house.

Wright gave up not only the reality of mono-material concrete-block construction but also the appearance; he could have attached blocks to the undersides of the concrete slabs, as he had done earlier (though by 1931 this idea probably was untenable). The accomplishment of San Marcos in the Desert was not publicized at the time; in the absence of technical and cost constraints and client demands, one questions why Wright skipped so highly visible an opportunity to validate a concept that had been a major preoccupation throughout the preceding decade.

The answer, suggested earlier, may well lie in a gradual shift in Wright's aesthetic responses, provoked—if not forced—by his awareness of modernism as it had developed in Europe. Perhaps he recognized that the concrete-block buildings he had designed earlier offered the notion but not the iconography of machine-age construction. Although disinclined to abandon concrete block entirely, Wright was willing to modify its application to meet the situation.

House on the Mesa is not an International Style building, but it is a calculated response to the work of the European modernists and to their visual ideals—lightness of construction; use of industrial materials; and smooth, planar surfaces. Wright was still designing with mass materials, but in this house he dematerialized conventional structure. Horizontal and vertical planes almost never touch. Cantilevered roof slabs float over walls; glass screens suspended from the slabs fill the voids. The point is made most dramatically in the living room: entire walls of glass, stepping inward from the top, are hung from above (Fig. 204). The windows themselves are steel-framed and formed as series of cantilevered steps, each horizontal plane opening for ventilation. The concrete-block walls do not rest directly on the floor slabs but are offset for ventilation (Fig. 205).

Discussing House on the Mesa in the exhibition catalogue, Hitchcock

204. House on the Mesa (project), interior perspective. FLLW FDN, 3102.020

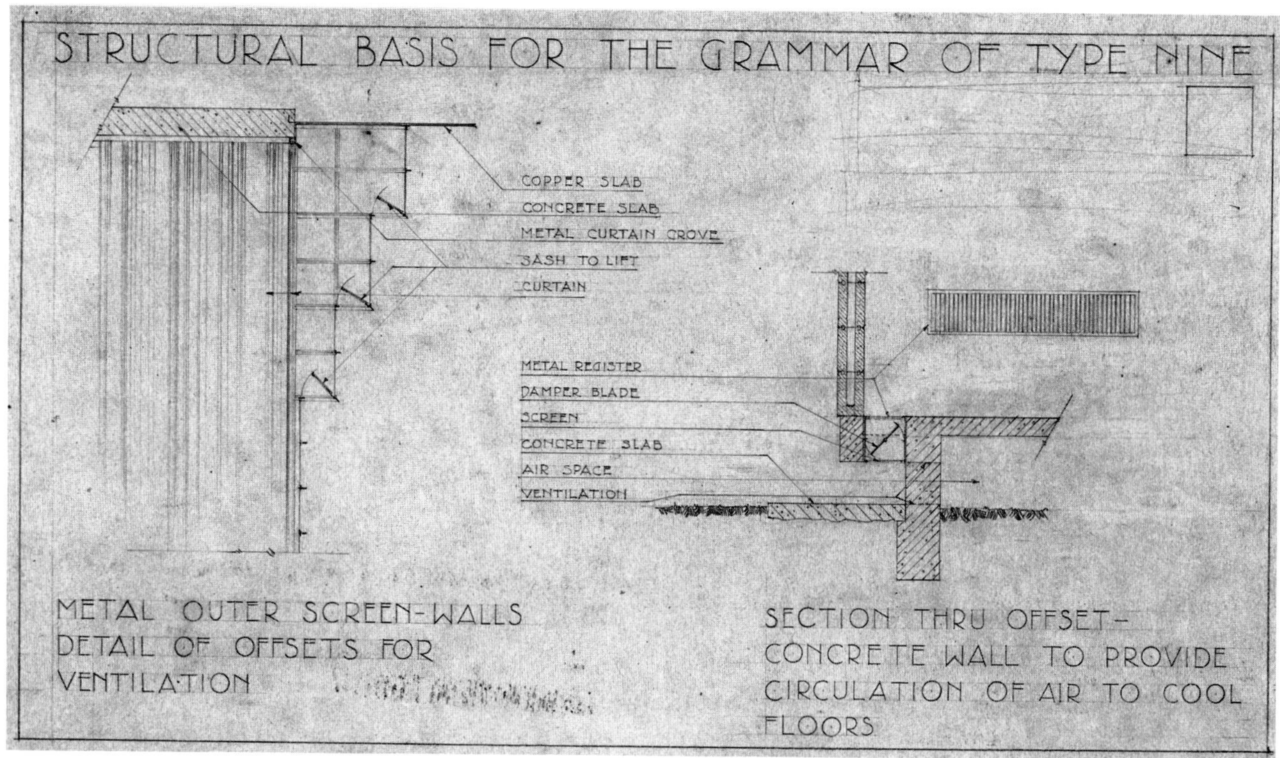

205. House on the Mesa (project), details.
FLLW FDN, 3102.036

commented sympathetically, "Beside the classical formalism of the houses of Oud, Le Corbusier and Mies van der Rohe, this latest house of Wright's is a striking aesthetic statement of romantic expansiveness."[36]

The Conventional House

Wright also prepared a design for a "Conventional House" that might be built in multiples near House on the Mesa. It was intended to solve the housing problem of the well-to-do American family at a cost between $12,500—one-tenth the budget for House on the Mesa—and $15,000. He suggested "an average town lot one hundred feet wide of the usual depth and regulation of building line . . . the lawn toward the street is managed so as not to destroy the general effect characteristic of the American town."[37]

The plan of the Conventional House is a direct adaptation of the Chandler block-house project, designed for Arizona. It is intended to accommodate a family with several children, one servant, and "a Ford or two." The

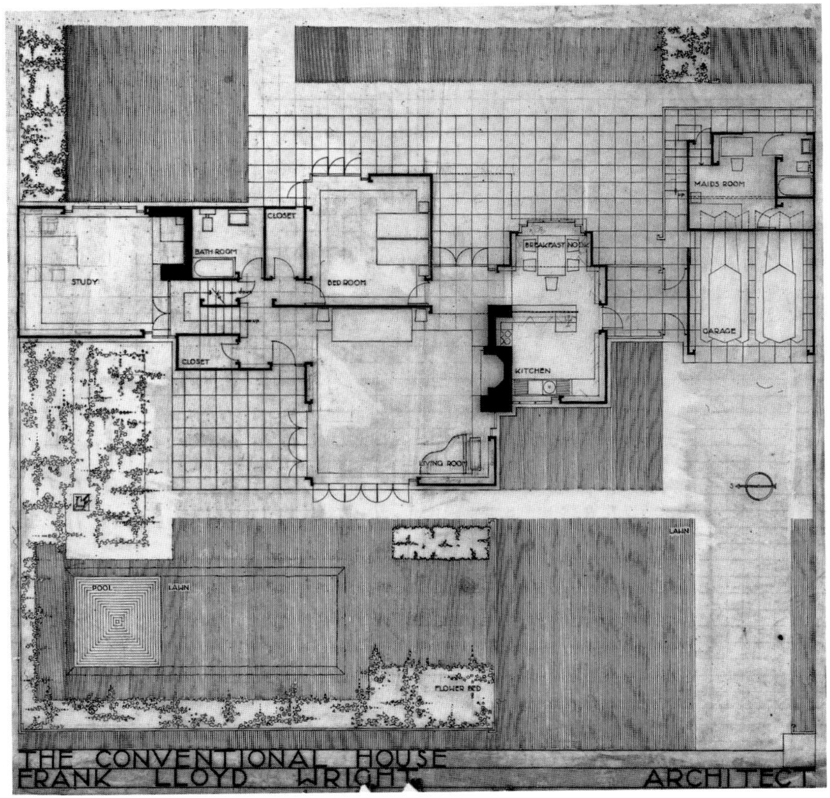

206. Conventional House (project), plan, 1931. FLLW FDN, 3201.002

living room, study, one bedroom, and kitchen are on the ground floor; a second studio-bedroom is upstairs (Fig. 206). A landing at midpoint in the stairwell overlooks the study, and the studio-bedroom overlooks the living room (Fig. 207). The semidetached garage includes a room for the maid to the rear. Not so modest as it first appears, the plan extends the full one-hundred-foot width of the lot. All of the ground-floor rooms open onto paved terraces; this feature and the crisp lines of the elevations invite comparison with the Arizona Biltmore cottages (Fig. 208).

The Conventional House was to be of single-shell block construction—an idea tested first in 1923 in Alice Millard's garage and proposed in 1929 to Alexander Chandler—using reinforced concrete blocks twelve inches tall and twenty-four inches wide.[38] The standard blocks have plain faces; decorated blocks are used sparingly, in horizontal bands, as trim. The roof and floor are reinforced-concrete slabs. Windows are floor-to-ceiling metal sash, opening in series.

□ □ □

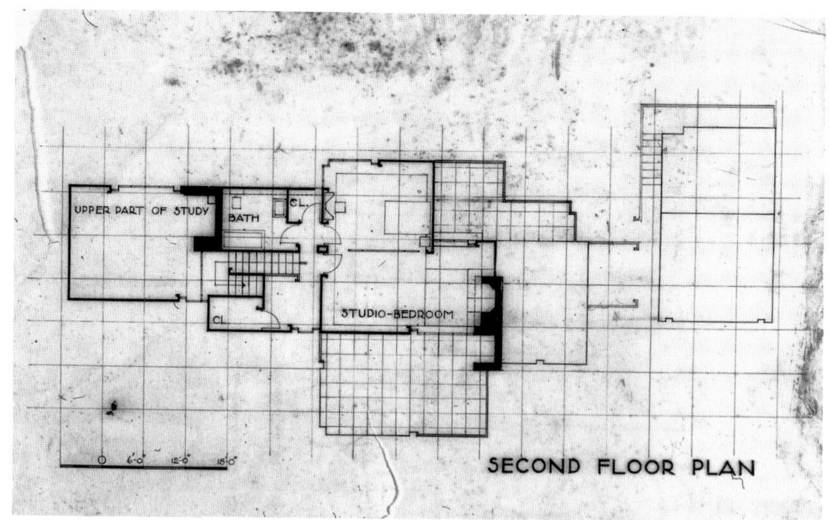

207. Conventional House (project), plan, 1931. FLLW FDN, 3201.005

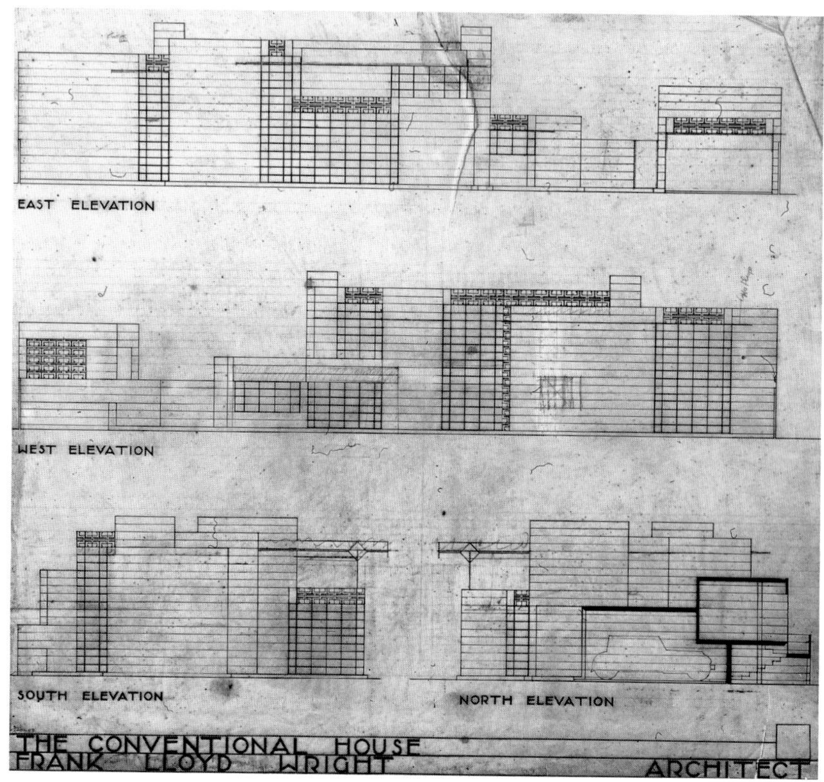

208. Conventional House (project), elevations, 1931. FLLW FDN, 3201.003

The decision to include Wright in the "Modern Architecture" exhibition was made in December 1930; Lewis Mumford apparently first broached the idea to him in March of the following year. The architect's participation was from the outset charged politically by the curators' sentiment that he could not conveniently be excluded and by his own conviction that he was being exploited. Shortly after the show closed in New York, Philip Johnson told J. J. P. Oud, another participant, "Wright was included only from courtesy and in recognition of his past contributions." Wright, on the other hand, felt that he had "been used merely to give authority to the exploitation."[39]

Wright had expected to be among his peers: Corbusier, whom he respected; Mies van der Rohe, whom he admired. He was peeved when he learned that Richard Neutra and Raymond Hood had been invited to participate. He described Neutra as "a type I have learned to dislike by cumulative experience and to suffer from." Neutra was "the eclectic 'up to date', copying the living." Hood was "the eclectic copying the dead." On January 18, three weeks before the show was to open, Wright wired Johnson:

> Dear Philip
> My way has been too long and too lonely to make a belated bow to my people as a modern architect in company with a self advertising amateur and a high powered salesman No bitterness and sorry but kindly and finally drop me out of your promotion
> Frank Lloyd Wright

Mumford again interceded on the museum's behalf, wiring Wright that his "absence from Modern Museum architectural show would be calamity." Wright responded, "All right Lewis your sincere friendship trusted I will stay in the New York show The two exceptions I made were chiefly important because showing up the show as the usual politics and propaganda."[40]

When Lloyd questioned his father's participation in the exhibition, Wright responded, "Much of the 'International' is . . . our own sterilized." He had, he said, "remained with the show," yielding "to the friends who thought it better to stay in if the propagandists would make my position theirs. I hope you will see that they do when the show arrives in L.A."[41]

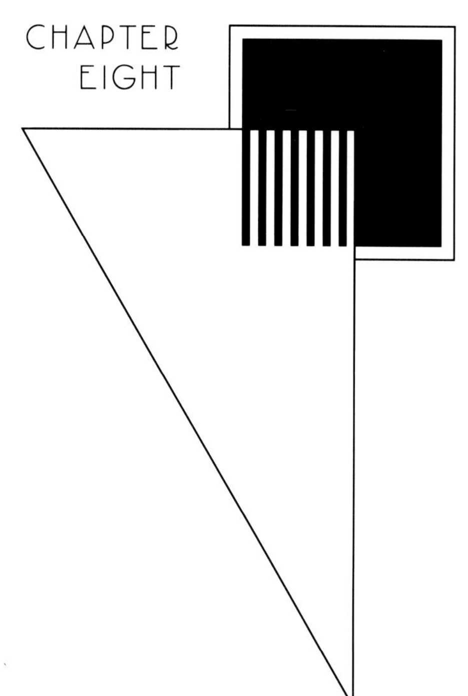

SOURCES

Never, throughout a decade of exploration in which he pursued the notion of building with concrete block and brought it to a logical conclusion, did Frank Lloyd Wright reveal the catalyst for his sudden inspiration in early 1923. He said only — and with hindsight — that the idea had been forming gradually in his mind since he came back from Japan, after work on the Imperial Hotel; and he referred obliquely to his son Lloyd, though the clear implication was that Lloyd's role was peripheral to the impulse of creativity. Nor as Wright's system became increasingly sophisticated did he acknowledge awareness of parallel developments.

There was, by 1923, a well-established concrete-block industry; in fact, Wright's newfound enthusiasm developed rather more at the end than at the beginning of an explosion of technology firmly established in the nineteenth century. At the same time, there was growing interest in developing an architecture in which the method or unit of construction was clearly expressed, in implication if not always in fact. Nevertheless, though clearly he was working in the shadow of a fading Zeitgeist, Wright's experiments were very much a logical synthesis and continuation of his own earlier work and theory.

Giving and Taking Credit

Certainly the most frequently offered explanation is that Lloyd Wright's earlier use of concrete block provided the impetus for his father, and that

Wright developed an idea he had observed in a house designed by his son, as Lloyd explained: "I had already done the Bollman house (1922) . . . in cast block similar to the Millard house, and in looking for some way to get it to hold together and coordinated I worked up this core system." The blocks were cored, the steel run through vertically and horizontally, and the core filled with concrete. The Millard house was overlapping block, without reinforcing steel. "Father saw it and saw that this concept could be worked into a total system, so he put me in charge of his first total-system block house, the Dr. Storer house." [1]

Lloyd's statement, published forty-four years after the fact, was a benign gesture entirely in line with Wright's own acknowledgment in his autobiography that he had drawn his son into the effort in the beginning. There is some evidence to support Lloyd's claim. The drawings for his Bollman house are dated December 1, 1922, and the building permit was issued on December 22, which indicates that construction coincided with the design of the Millard house.[2] Also, the design was modified during construction by the addition of a cantilevered balcony on the front elevation, similar to the one at the Millard house, further substantiating the overlapping chronologies of these buildings.

In the end, however, Lloyd's role as a catalyst for the textile block system remains unconfirmed. Wright's initial exploration does not suggest intimate familiarity with existing technology, and while it is entirely possible that his imagination was triggered by something he saw at the Bollman house, the surviving evidence is inconclusive. Lloyd's description of his "core system" suggests circular channels either cast or drilled through the blocks, not semicircular cavities on the perimeter, but there are no drawings to clarify the form or the method of assembly.[3]

Lloyd does seem to have pursued the concept vigorously on his own. In 1928 he wrote to his father that he had built eleven buildings with the blocks and offered advice based on his experience. He recommended using only metal for the molds, though pattern forms could be of wood or plaster. He suggested that the blocks be four or, preferably, six inches thick, which would allow them to be erected faster without rocking, eliminating the need for bracing and wedging, and which would allow for a larger core for the steel and grout. In Lloyd's opinion, the amount of concrete [*sic:* cement?] used in the early blocks had made them heavier and stronger than necessary; he suggested using as little concrete as possible. Finally, he addressed the issue of waterproofing, stating that no material put on or in the blocks would make them impervious to moisture. He

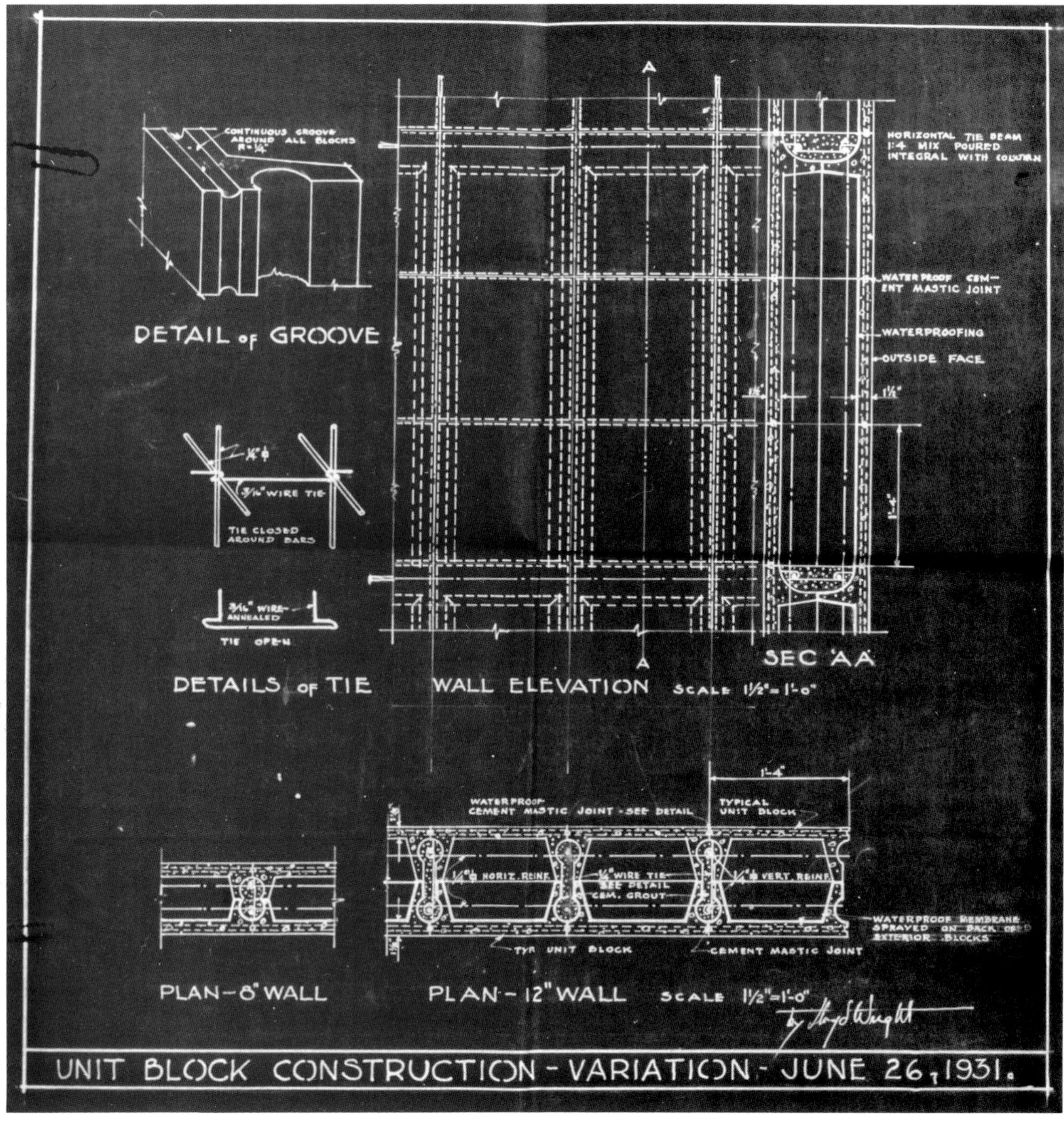

209. Lloyd Wright, block revision, 1931. FLLW FDN, Fiche W 282

concluded that only a waterproof membrane or complete separation of the shell walls was effective.[4]

Then, in 1931, Lloyd sent his father a proposal for a "Unit Block Construction Variation." It was based again on blocks reinforced with metal rods placed in internal joints, but the blocks were assembled with mastic between them (Fig. 209). Lloyd argued that the new system would produce a lighter wall, requiring half the steel, satisfying all building-department regulations, and still producing the essential hollow-wall slabs.[5]

Wright answered him: "The unit block revision has some good points. However, when the block has to be buttered all around with mastic—the original aim is lost." He objected to the horizontal contact that occurred at every third course and that would facilitate the transfer of heat, moisture, and sound. He concluded:

> To make a success of the idea as I have seen it, and see it still, all plastering, pointing, buttering or anything else in connection with the wall must go. Extreme accuracy in block-making is the only solution. And molds should have study put on them to that end.[6]

Another reinforced-concrete block system, predating the textile block system and frequently compared with it, was devised by Wright's former employee Walter Burley Griffin, in 1916–17. Called Knitlock, the concept relied on two basic components, or segments: "vertebral" segments, which locked together to make the framework or skeleton; and "tesseral" segments, used as infill for curtain walls. The vertebral segments were shaped on a ninety-degree radius; assembled in single or double pairs they formed a T or cross shape as required, providing strength and the ability to turn corners. The tesseral segments were square and thin, like tile; they also were assembled in pairs to create two-ply curtain walls, attaching to and stretching between the vertebral columns (Fig. 210). All of the segments were based on a six-inch unit and were ribbed to interlock on their inside faces. The construction was reinforced with metal rods, placed vertically in the voids between the ribs, and these voids were filled with grout. A layer of bitumen was added as insulation between the segments. When assembled, a wall only two and one-half inches thick resulted. Griffin also designed a compatible roof tile for his "Segmental Architecture"; interlocking twelve-inch-square tiles of clay or cement were intended to be laid diagonally.

210. Walter Burley Griffin, Knitlock Construction. Reproduced from Richard J. Neutra, *Wie Baut Amerika?* (Stuttgart: Julius Hoffmann, 1927), p. 58

Walter Burley Griffin is best remembered neither as the inventor of

Knitlock Construction, nor as one who passed through Wright's office, but as winner in 1912 of a competition to design a new capital city for Australia. He had worked for Wright between 1901 and 1905, then left under fire and practiced independently, with notable success. In 1914 he moved to Australia; it was there that he worked out his unit system of reinforced-concrete construction. According to his biographer, Donald Leslie Johnson, he was drawn to the task while developing designs for "typical workmen's cottage plans." [7] He collaborated with a local builder, David Charles Jenkins; together, they received patents for the wall system in New Zealand in 1918, and for the roofing tiles in Australia in 1919.[8]

The extent to which Wright drew on—or was aware of—the inventions of Griffin and his partner is unclear. However, Griffin showed a reciprocal awareness in a statement published in 1927:

> In Southern California, Mr. Frank Lloyd Wright has recently carried out houses on a scheme having tesseral elements of the same facial size and similar appearance, though quite different in structural significance, since they form cavity walls in the ordinary sense, stable because of their mass rather than through specialized columnar or concentrated supports, and there are no vertebral segments.[9]

Griffin may have been hostile to Wright, but, as Johnson observes, he carefully avoided any suggestion of plagiarism. In contrast, Griffin's wife, Marion Mahoney Griffin, who also had worked for Wright, had decidedly insidious intentions when she wrote in her unpublished autobiography that Wright had stolen the idea from Griffin. She claimed that George Taylor, editor of the Australian architectural magazine *Building,* had described the system to Wright during a visit to the United States and that Wright "listened to the knitlock story and shortly after built this structure [the Freeman house] in California. He was always quick on the uptake." [10]

The primary similarity between Griffin's "segmental architecture" and the textile block system is more philosophical than structural: the simplification and economy of building with standardized modular units, while maintaining plasticity of expression. Wright's enclosing walls were load-bearing; Griffin's were skeletal, with nonstructural infill. Griffin pointed out that his method of construction "spans openings without lintel members," and that "the uniform supporting power of interior and exterior walls invites the introduction of courts or the breaking up of the mass of even the smallest house." [11]

□ □ □

Most to the point is the work of William E. Nelson, an inventor who had designed and patented a mortarless reinforced concrete block construction system bearing strong formal resemblance to the textile block system but predating it by several years. Nelson's system was based on standardized concrete blocks twelve inches square, but whose thickness could be varied as required. The blocks had smooth faces on both sides. They were cast with semicircular channels around their edges (Fig. 211), and were assembled edge to edge in a single vertical layer—unlike Wright's cavity walls—creating circular channels between the blocks. They were reinforced vertically and horizontally through the channels with metal rods and a rich mixture of grout (Figs. 212, 213). Nelson's system went beyond Wright's in providing blocks for curved walls, columns, and floor beams, but it did not address other conditions requiring special blocks (Fig. 214). Corners were poured in place, using two-inch planks, after the walls were erected.

Nelson also designed a special flatbed car, on which the blocks were cast and then moved to a steam room, where they were cured. Redwood forms were arranged in rows six units long and four deep on the surface of the car and filled. The cars had slightly deformed wheels to create vibration as they rolled along a track (Fig. 215). The vibration caused the concrete to pack solidly, producing a dense block.[12]

Nelson received five patents for his system and apparatus for making blocks between 1920 and 1925. However, there were lapses of time of from ten months to four and one-half years between dates of application and receipt of patent. It is obvious that at the time of his first two applications, in May 1919, for the building system and block mold, Nelson had the concept clearly in mind.[13]

Little biographical information is available on William E. Nelson. In a 1919 newspaper article he is described as an architect who had recently moved from San Antonio to Fort Worth, Texas, to construct a new hotel in nearby Arlington.[14] In 1920 in San Antonio he established the Nel-Stone Company of Texas, the first plant to produce his blocks. Additional plants, established as franchises, were opened in Washington, D.C.; Omaha; San Bernardino, California; and Los Angeles. Licensees had the exclusive right to manufacture, sell, and use Nel-Stones and to erect concrete structures within a defined territory. Numerous buildings using the system were erected across the country.[15]

The Nel-Stone system was publicized nationally and locally. Detailed drawings and descriptions of Nelson's inventions were published in the

211. William E. Nelson, Nel-Stone Concrete Block. Collection of the author, gift of Robert T. Gelber, Gibson, Dunn & Crutcher

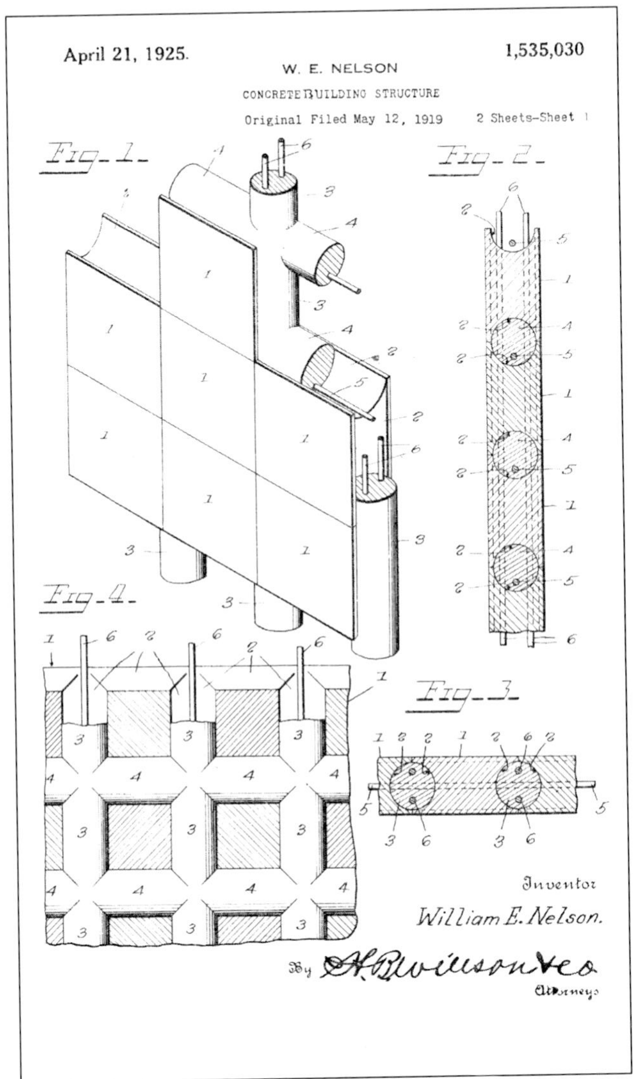

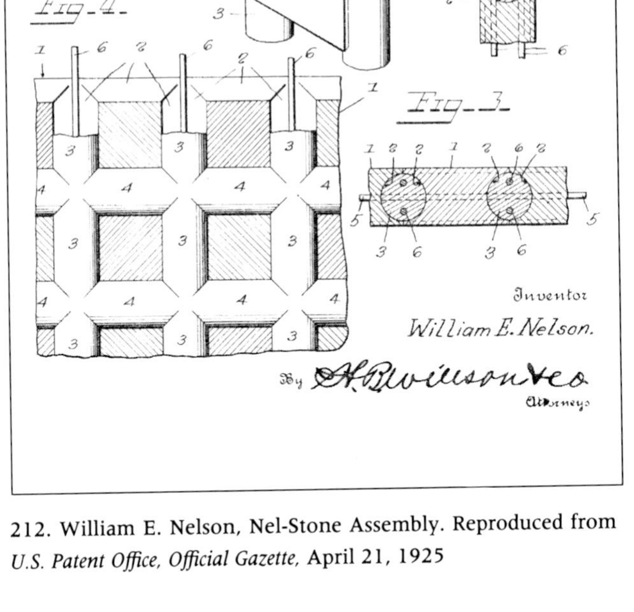

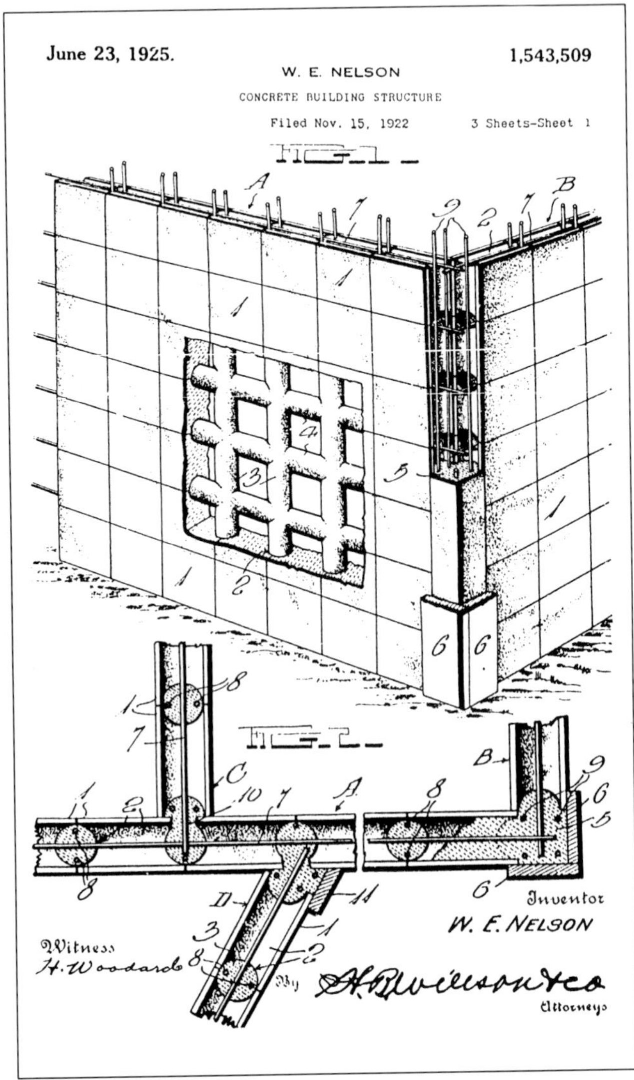

212. William E. Nelson, Nel-Stone Assembly. Reproduced from *U.S. Patent Office, Official Gazette,* April 21, 1925

213. William E. Nelson, Nel-Stone Wall Construction. Reproduced from *U.S. Patent Office, Official Gazette,* June 23, 1925

Official Gazette of the U.S. Patent Office as they were patented. Specifically, two designs for molding apparatus appeared in the March 30, 1920, and October 31, 1922, issues. A third design for molding apparatus appeared on March 10, 1925. Designs for the building system appeared on April 21 and June 23, 1925. Two articles on the system appeared in the trade publication *Concrete Products,* published in Chicago, in September 1923,

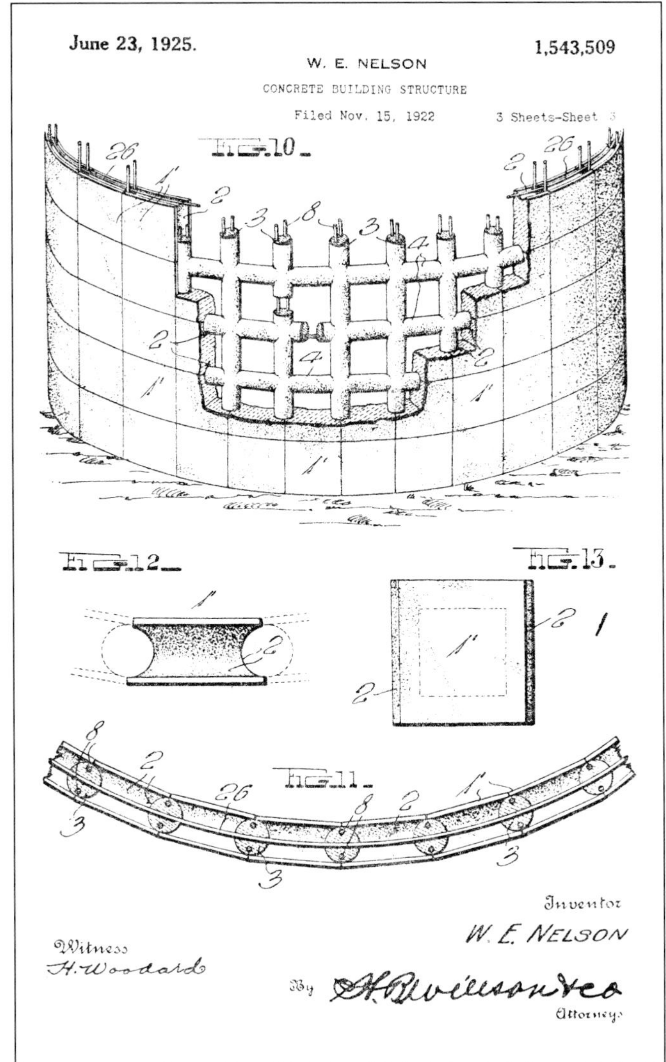

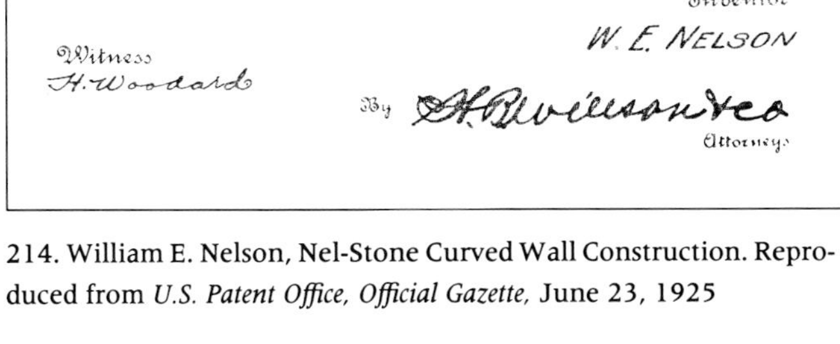

214. William E. Nelson, Nel-Stone Curved Wall Construction. Reproduced from *U.S. Patent Office, Official Gazette,* June 23, 1925

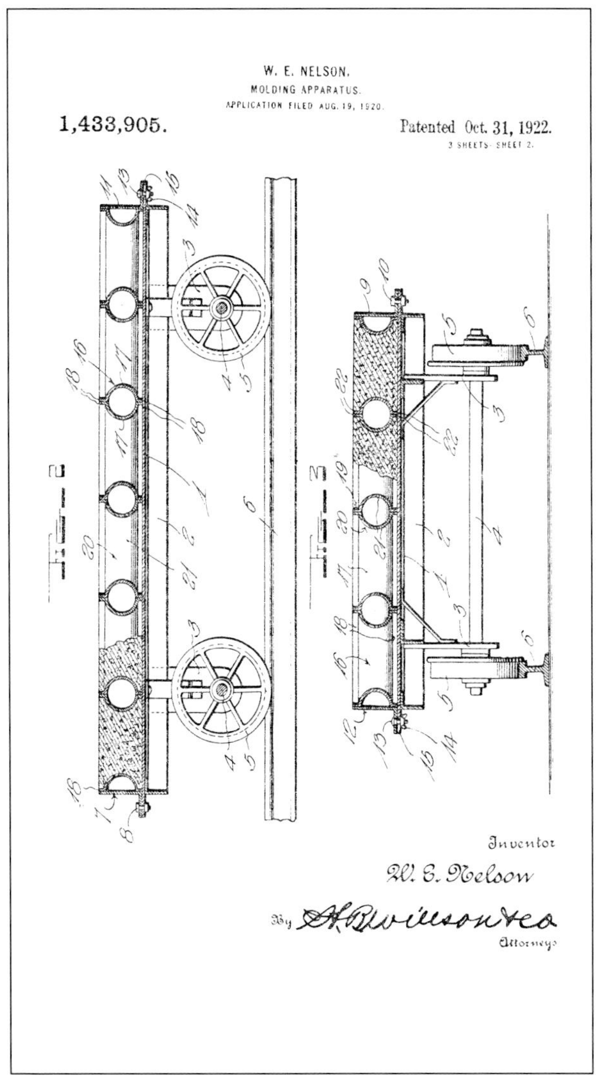

215. William E. Nelson, Nel-Stone Molding Apparatus. Reproduced from *U.S. Patent Office, Official Gazette,* October 31, 1922

and March 1924.[16] In addition, the regional Nel-Stone outlets distributed circulars and advertised in local newspapers; the strength of the blocks was a major selling point (Fig. 216).

It may never be known when and how Wright first learned of the Nel-Stone system, though he knew of it by February 1930.[17] The suggestion is that he was not aware of it in the early months of 1923, when he

216. Nel-Stone blocks loaded with sixty tons of sand. Courtesy of Attilio Gerodetti, Jr.

proposed a very different construction system for the Millard house. In the unlikely event that he did see the obscure patent-office publications, the 1925 date is too late for him to be accused of infringement. The 1923 article in *Concrete Products* appeared at least one month after drawings for the Community Playhouse and Storer house, the first buildings in which Wright proposed the concept of internal joints filled with metal reinforcing rods and grout.

Still, Wright had friends in Chicago who seem likely to have kept abreast of such developments and could easily have told the architect about Nelson's work. The most obvious, though unconfirmed, sources of wisdom are the engineers Paul Mueller and Julius Floto. Mueller was Wright's master builder, as O. W. Norcross had been H. H. Richardson's, yet, unlike Norcross, he remains an elusive figure. Mueller and Wright both passed through J. Lyman Silsbee's office in the 1880s, but they apparently first met when they were working for the firm of Adler and Sullivan.[18] Mueller subsequently built all of Wright's significant early public works: the Larkin Building, Unity Temple, Midway Gardens, and the Imperial Hotel. He later served as consultant for San Marcos in the Desert and constructed the Jones house.

Julius Floto had a distinguished career in Chicago as an architect and engineer; his daughter, Katharine Loverud, recalled in 1988 that structural engineering was his love.[19] He too worked with Wright on the Imperial Hotel. Wright and Floto subsequently had a falling out over the structure of the Imperial; Floto nonetheless praised the building for its resiliency in earthquakes in an article published in 1924.[20]

If Nelson's and Wright's systems were formal twins, they parted company theoretically. The Nel-Stone system was envisioned and marketed principally as a cost-efficient system of construction. Its chief claims were pragmatic: the elimination of form work in monolithic construction and consequent saving of the cost of lumber and skilled labor. There was no provision for ornament in Nelson's system; in fact, beauty is mentioned only in passing. The utilitarian buildings for which it was intended, barns, silos, culverts, and water tanks, were left blank and exposed. Houses and commercial buildings were plastered inside, permitting painting and papering, and stuccoed on the outside. Photographs of completed buildings show that a variety of period effects was achieved (Figs. 217–219).

Though Nelson would later confront Wright with claims of patent infringement, and Wright's response was circumspect at best, the larger issue remains Wright's creative use of the idea. He was foremost an artist, but he also carried the technology of assembly well beyond anything Nelson accomplished.

Nelson apparently learned of Wright's experiments from the article

217. House constructed with Nel-Stone blocks, ca. 1923, Alamo Heights, Texas. Courtesy of Attilio Gerodetti, Jr.

218. House constructed with Nel-Stone blocks. Courtesy of Attilio Gerodetti, Jr.

219. Theater constructed with Nel-Stone blocks, Kansas City, Missouri, September 25, 1925. Courtesy of Attilio Gerodetti, Jr.

published in the *Architectural Record* in December 1927. Entitled "Frank Lloyd Wright's Textile-Block Slab Construction," the text was accompanied by illustrations of the Freeman house and a schematic drawing of the wall construction. In July 1929, the *Record* followed up with coverage of the Arizona Biltmore Hotel.

Nelson's formal response came from two attorneys in Los Angeles: Ford W. Harris, and Herbert F. Sturdy of Gibson, Dunn and Crutcher. Harris wrote two letters in January 1930, to the hotel and to the building contractor, S. M. Benet & Co., claiming infringement of two of Nelson's patents and seeking damages. In July and August similar letters were sent to Mabel Ennis and Alice Millard by Herbert Sturdy, who by then was representing Nelson.[21]

With the interesting exception of Alice Millard, the letters to the alleged infringers do not seem to have provoked much of a response, nor were they aggressively pursued. There is no record of reply to Harris's letters concerning the hotel.[22] Mabel Ennis's lawyer, Donald Barker, wrote that she was unfamiliar with the patents and that until specifications were reviewed, he could not advise her concerning liability.[23] After a lapse of nearly two years, Barker informed Sturdy that there was a "serious question as to the validity" of Nelson's patents, and that if valid, they would "not have been infringed by the form of construction" used on the Ennis house.[24] Millard replied that the patents could not possibly apply to her house, as the blocks had been cast in molds made by a carpenter, and that the house had been finished in March 1924, thirteen months before the second patent in question was issued. She added that an acquaintance knew Nelson and had volunteered to explain to him the difference between her construction — as it actually was — and what Nelson thought it to be.[25]

Forced to explain the controversy, Wright acknowledged that he held no patent on the textile block system. He had never submitted an application. Wright offered several inconclusive and vaguely contradictory reasons for this lapse. Writing to Albert McArthur in February 1930, he explained that Nelson's patent (which he dated to 1912) had interfered with the completion of his own application. His corporation, Frank Lloyd Wright, Inc., had hoped to secure and renew this patent, which was about to expire.[26] His response to Henderson Stockton, a Phoenix lawyer representing the Biltmore who had written threatening suit for patent infringement, is more revealing. He mentioned the problem of the conflicting patent, but stated that it had already expired. His lawyer initially had had no doubt that a patent would be granted. He had been advised to mark all his plans and details "patent applied for" and to proceed as though he held it.[27] This probably explains his action in selling McArthur a license to use the textile block system that stated specifically that he owned the patent. For his own protection, he had allowed all concerned to believe that the patent was standing, until the system could be properly protected.

Writing with greater candor to Lloyd, referring to his earlier attempts to obtain a patent, Wright explained, "As for Litzenberg I didn't have enough money to go on. That's simple isn't it?"[28]

ZEITGEIST

Whatever their importance in the formation of the textile block system, Lloyd Wright, Walter Burley Griffin, and William E. Nelson—three designers who conveniently emerged to take credit—were but bit players in a much larger and very sophisticated theater of concrete-block technology that, at least indirectly, was the seedbed of Wright's experiments. The history of concrete itself as a building material is well known: after its use by the Romans, it was abandoned until the late eighteenth century, when it was reintroduced in Europe, first in France, then in England.[29] By about 1840 its popularity had spread to the United States, where it was rapidly assimilated in the construction of utilitarian buildings.

Concrete block was introduced at roughly the same time, as a low-cost alternative to brick. The degree of interest can be traced with some thoroughness in the *Official Gazette* of the U.S. Patent Office. In spite of an early introduction, real momentum was not generated until the first decade of the twentieth century: between 1904 and 1910, an average of thirty-four patents for concrete blocks and apparatus for producing them were issued each year. The phenomenon was not confined to inventors: this was an age of consumer enlightenment, and advertisements for concrete-block houses appeared regularly in homemaker magazines. Nor was Wright immune to the spirit of the times. He responded in 1906 with a design for a concrete-block house, his earliest essay in the material (Fig. 220). In the years 1910–25, the average number of patents issued dwindled to thirteen, although this decline was offset by burgeoning interest in concrete construction in general.[30]

Many of the patents issued were very similar; sorting them out is a process of deciphering the accompanying descriptions, which are written to the specifications of the patent office and readily intelligible only to the initiate. However, the basic block forms and their application in wall construction were worked out early and were conveniently summarized in a book published in 1906; the authors define four phases of development.[31] The earliest blocks were solid, like brick, and were very plain. Their usefulness was limited: the only variations were half and quarter

220. Harry E. Brown house (project), Geneva, Illinois, perspective, 1906. FLLW FDN, 0623.001

blocks; and surface texture was restricted to patterns that could be produced with a simple change of face plate. These blocks also had inherent technical deficiencies. Because concrete is porous, they were difficult, if not impossible, to waterproof; and insulation was a problem.

In an attempt to remedy these shortcomings, a new system of double-wall construction was introduced: two layers of block were separated by an air space and tied together with metal strips. Water could penetrate the outer surface but since it could not pass through the air space, the interior remained dry. Buildings proved to be warmer in winter and more comfortable in summer; however, the metal ties were subject to rust and corrosion.

The disadvantage of metal strips was addressed by a new hollow-block form: inner and outer surfaces were separated by a cavity; when the blocks were assembled, a continuous air space resulted. The first American patent for a hollow block was issued in 1866. The claim was that the air space would absorb moisture from the outside and would prevent water from penetrating to the inside surface, rendering a waterproof face; the blocks also were to receive a waterproof coating on the exterior surface.[32] Numerous other patents based on this concept were issued late in the nineteenth century. Experience proved, however, that even in designs with multiple rows of air cavities and in which there were no webs passing directly through the wall, it was impossible to prevent the passage of moisture by capillary action.

The fourth step in the evolution of concrete-block wall construction was the development of various forms of angle blocks, which interlocked in double layers. No single block had both an inner and an outer face, and there was no continuous contact between the two walls. Block shapes were based on modifications of the E, L, T, or U; Wright used versions of these as a starting point in 1923.

Most of these early systems depended on a standard mortar bed for assembly; there was, however, another line of development, with special significance in light of Wright's later experiments. Seemingly from the beginning there was interest in eliminating the mortar bed; a British patent issued in 1850 described hollow blocks that were to be filled with concrete, the wall becoming "one mass of artificial stone, so there will be no necessity to put mortar between the blocks to bed them."[33] Another patent for an "Improved Mould for Building-Blocks," issued in America in 1868, featured hollow blocks that had dovetail grooves formed in their ends; when they were joined together in forming a wall, a continuous internal joint resulted.[34] After the blocks were assembled, the joints were to be filled with cement.

By 1923 the block-fabrication process was conventionalized. The character of the blocks—their appearance and strength—would depend largely on the ratio of aggregate to cement, the amount of water added, the method of compacting the mixture in the mold, and the nature of the mold itself. All of these variables also affected the degree to which the blocks would be waterproof, a problem that plagued Wright and builders long before, and has done so since.

A mixture of one part cement to three or four parts aggregate was standard, although many other formulas were possible. Richer mixtures, with a higher percentage of cement, produced stronger, denser blocks that were heavier but were also more waterproof. Cement is a bonding agent; water causes it to solidify with aggregate and become concrete. The amount of water could be varied as required; mixtures were commonly classified as dry, to which a bare minimum of water was added, medium, or wet. Likewise, there were three methods of compacting the mixtures in the molds: tamping, pressing, and pouring. Dry and medium mixtures were tamped or pressed; wet mixtures were shaken or vibrated. The molds themselves were generally metal, although wood could be used.

Wright's interest in producing many blocks rapidly and inexpensively led him to the dry-pack method of manufacture. The blocks could be removed from the molds as soon as they were tamped, and cured nearby, reducing the number of molds needed. In deciding to use this method, however, he ignored a reality of physics: the porosity of concrete diminishes in reverse proportion to the quantity of water added, and no amount of tamping will produce density in a mixture lacking sufficient moisture.

□ □ □

It would be short-sighted, if not misleading, to present the textile block system only as an outgrowth of the general technological exploration of concrete block. Wright's experiments also coincided with a larger interest in developing an architecture based on standardized components that had been gaining momentum since the nineteenth century. In 1922 Ernest Flagg—whom Wright seems to have respected—published a book, *Small Houses: Their Economic Design and Construction,* offering a philosophy remarkably in accord with Wright's. Flagg described the virtues of standardization, stating that "the use of the module, in construction, induces a degree of accuracy and precision almost unknown in this class of work. . . . Where the processes and apparatus are used, over and over again, great economy should result." Like Wright, he took pride in working drawings laid out on grid paper, without dimensions: "All dimensions, horizontal or vertical, may be ascertained by counting the squares." [35]

Richard Neutra summarized the situation as it had developed commercially by the mid 1920s in his first book, *Wie Baut Amerika?,* published in Stuttgart in 1927 but written while he was sharing Schindler's Kings Road house in West Hollywood. Neutra observed the "immense, well organized building material market," in which "the influence of the architect, who entered the stage fairly late, did not become decisive." The architect "rarely has the opportunity to invent . . . building materials himself, manufacture them on a trial basis and . . . project them on such a basis. The building material manufacturers find the apparatus, the time and the financiers for such trials. The opportunity to do this on the building site is often lacking." [36]

The forces of modular design and construction were pervasive; the usefulness of concrete block was realized early on. Isolated claims of artistic value aside, however, it was most commonly perceived as a utilitarian building material, often to be camouflaged with stucco or plaster. One early critic noted that "although working with a plastic material capable of almost limitless variations in form and texture the block maker succeeded only in producing one of the most rigidly regular and monotonously uniform building units ever put on the market." He criticized architects as well for their failure to adapt designs to standard blocks produced by the machine then in use.[37]

Still, there were architects seeking appropriate expressions for concrete block. Some experimented with surface texture, others combined the blocks with classical details molded in concrete. The shapes and proportions of the blocks could be modified within certain limits, and patterns could be cast on the surface; the effort was to create a richness that was otherwise lacking.[38]

The lingering question that emerges from this body of information is why Wright seems to have taken so little advantage of it. Why such a focus on invention, as he described in his 1927 letter to A. N. Rebori? The answer, and a key to many of the great technical flaws of the textile block system, may be Wright's own self-assurance. He was an enormously creative and experienced designer who preferred to develop his work in its own context, not in light of the accomplishments of others.

In context

The case for internal development of the textile block system is strong indeed. The formal and structural simplification displayed throughout Wright's exploration of concrete-block construction was entirely consistent with his earlier practice; he correctly identified the process as an outgrowth of a goal constantly pursued. Wright addressed the notion of simplification and stated a principle that guided his work in his earliest published speech, "Architecture and the Machine," of 1894. He interpreted simplicity as "something with graceful sense of beauty in its utility from which discord and all that is meaningless has been eliminated," and advised that "there is no one part of your building that may not be made a thing of beauty in itself as related to the whole."[39] The concepts Wright established in this speech were restated and refined over the next few years. In 1896 he substituted the word honesty for simplicity, stating, "To be honest commonly means to be undisguised, frankly showing purpose, free from deceit and hypocrisy"; and, writing in 1900 on the Japanese print: "It has preached the gospel of simplification as no other means has ever preached it and taught that organic integrity within the work of art itself is fundamentally a law of beauty."[40]

Wright continued the theme in his 1901 Hull House speech, "The Art and Craft of the Machine," pleading for an understanding of the "significance to art of that word—SIMPLICITY—for it is vital to the Art of the Machine." Simplicity is "not merely a neutral or a negative quality," but "a synthetic, positive quality in which we may see evidence of mind, breadth of scheme, wealth of detail, and withal a sense of completeness found in a tree or a flower." He concluded that "a thing to be simple needs only to be true to itself in an organic sense."[41]

Wright's concept of simplicity by no means precluded ornament; he commented in his 1894 speech that "decoration . . . is of no use to you unless you do understand and appreciate it."[42] He amplified his theory of ornament in an article published in the *Architectural Record* in 1908. Reviewing his past work, he stated that "in the matter of decoration the tendency has been to indulge it less and less. . . . What architectural decoration the buildings carry is not only conventionalized to the point where it is quiet and stays as a sure foil for the nature forms from which it is derived . . . but it is always *of* the surface, never *on* it." He explained that "in the main the ornamentation is wrought in the warp and woof of the structure." This element ". . . is the most fascinating phase of the work, involving the true poetry of conception."[43]

Wright inserted a note of moralism the next year, in a speech to the Nineteenth Century Club in Oak Park: "The matter of ornament is primarily a spiritual matter, a proof of culture, an expression of the quality of the soul in us. . . . It behooves us . . . to find out what ornament means, and . . . to do away with most of it; to . . . feel safer and more comfortable with plain things. Simple things are not necessarily plain, but plain things are all that most of us are really entitled to, in any spiritual reckoning, at present."[44]

Speaking again of ornament in the introduction to *Ausgeführte Bauten und Entwürfe,* dated June 1910, Wright continued his earlier theme of internal development: "In a structure conceived in the organic sense, the ornamentation is conceived in the very ground plan, and is of the very constitution of the structure."[45] The concept of organic growth expressed here precedes by four years Wright's published definition of organic architecture. In 1914 he wrote, "By organic architecture I mean an architecture that *develops* from within outward in harmony with the conditions of its being as distinguished from one that is *applied* from without."[46]

Wright's goals were explored more or less simultaneously in theory and practice. His notion of simplicity led quickly, if not always visibly, to an architecture based on the concept of modular organization, to a controlling unit as the definer of space in plan and elevation. He explained that the modules were established "to simplify technical difficulties of execution," and varied from building to building according to the construction system and the architect's own sense of proportion.[47] Perhaps the earliest example of this notion was an office building he designed for the Luxfer Prism Company in Chicago. Luxfer Prisms were four-inch-square glass tiles intended to replace ordinary glazing; they were molded with a sawtoothed relief on one side that refracted light, causing it to travel farther into a room. Wright was not responsible for the concept of Luxfer Prisms, but in 1897 he was asked to design an office building for the company using its product. He responded with a façade organized into a grid of forty-eight squares composed entirely of the prism lights (Fig. 221). Each of the squares was subdivided into a grid of sixteen units, which were reduced again to the essential four-inch module on which the design was based.

Luxfer Prisms were not structural in the sense that concrete blocks were; however, other parallels exist. Both systems dictated designing and building with standardized modular components of machine precision, with the inherent grid lines clearly expressed. And in each case a decorative pattern could be cast on the surface of the individual units at the time of fabrication.

Wright received forty-one design patents for the decorative patterns molded onto the surface of Luxfer Prisms in 1897; he explained in his specifications that some patterns were based on "series of concentrically-arranged ornamental lines which interlace or overlap each other, so as to produce a grid-like appearance"; while others were "series of groups, each group composed of a series of lesser designs or figures, the whole appearing, when seen, both as a series of groups and as series of lesser designs within the groups" (Figs. 222, 223).[48] In all cases, when the individual patterned units were assembled edge to edge, new interrelated designs resulted. Finally, it seems fair to draw an analogy between the prism lights with which Wright proposed to create walls in the 1890s and the interest he expressed in 1929 in a modular, all-glass building system, an intriguing idea he did not develop.[49]

Wright early demonstrated his control of modular organization, in the 1904 Martin house in Buffalo. Here brick was the basic unit; using it in multiples, he established modules of seven feet, nine inches and three feet, nine inches in rhythmical patterns. For the wood-and-plaster Coonley house of 1907, he used a four-foot module with sixteen-inch centers, based on standard lumber lengths and economical spacing of studs. He later cited both buildings as examples in which the construction method shaped the plan.[50]

There were parallel developments in concrete as well. Wright's 1901 Hull House speech significantly referred to "this plastic covering material, cement" as "another simplifier, enabling the artist to clothe the structural frame with a simple, modestly beautiful robe where before he dragged in . . . five different kinds of material to compose one little cottage."[51] The Concrete Monolithic Bank project, published that same year, seems to

221. Luxfer Prism Building (project), Chicago, Illinois, ca. 1897. Reproduced from *Inland Architect and News Record* 30 (January, 1898): n.p.

222. Luxfer Prism Patterns. Reproduced from *U.S. Patent Office, Official Gazette*, December 7, 1897

223. Luxfer Prism Patterns. Reproduced from *U.S. Patent Office, Official Gazette*, December 7, 1897

have been Wright's earliest exercise with the material. He intended the building to be cast as a monolith in concrete, the mold being constructed of wood, with waterproof-paper linings. Ornament was to be cast integrally at the time of construction, with plaster molds.[52] Describing the project, he referred to "this ingrained human love of ornament," and concluded that "we may be thankful that we still possess it, for back of it are probably the only instincts that make life bearable or desirable."[53]

Unity Temple, built of concrete in 1906–8, was Wright's first monomaterial structure, although he did not use the term at the time, and the interior walls were covered with plaster. It was also a significant formal and theoretical advance over the Concrete Monolithic Bank project. The bank was a monolith both structurally and formally; Unity Temple was a "jointed monolith"—a term Wright used to describe the Imperial Hotel. That is, the building was a composition of separate, repetitive units. In the few years separating the two buildings, Wright had developed the machinelike notion of building with repeated forms and actions; the same molds were used where possible on all sides of Unity Temple. The molds themselves were wood, as before, and were based on sixteen-inch units, suited to timber construction.[54] The ornament, a repeated motif, was cast in relief integrally with the columns.

As we trace the antecedents of Wright's concrete-block experiments, four projects of the teens also deserve special attention: Midway Gardens, 1913; the American System of House Building, 1916; Hardy Monolith Homes, 1919; and the Imperial Hotel, begun 1914. When challenged in 1930 to establish the genesis of the textile block system, Wright responded, "The first wall of this character that I know about, cast in moulds somewhat similar to those used in the [Arizona] Biltmore were the walls of

224. Midway Gardens, Chicago, 1913. Cast-concrete frieze. Collection of the author, gift of Mrs. Richard Neutra

the Midway Gardens, erected in Chicago in 1914."[55] Midway Gardens was essentially a brick building; Wright was referring to the upper walls, which were formed of concrete panels with identical geometric patterns cast in relief on their surfaces (Fig. 224). These panels were praised at the time as an early and significant use of concrete for ornamentation.[56] They also represent a significant simplification of the process used to create the Coonley house frieze, where colored tiles were set into inscribed plaster. In Midway Gardens, ornament and material were unified in a single fabrication and construction process.

Between 1911 and 1917 Wright explored the possibilities of a prefabricated "system of construction and design" in which standardized members could be assembled in many ways for a variety of effects.[57] He was working with conventional materials—wood, stucco, and plaster—toward a simplification of the building process. The concept was introduced in 1916 as the American System of House Building in Milwaukee; Wright stated in 1929 that it led to the development of the textile block system. He added, "We have had all the timber construction that the country ought to have. This light concrete block construction might be standardized and managed as a more flexible, economical and desirable construction than any ready cut house now on the market."[58]

Hardy Monolith Homes were undertaken while Schindler was working in Wright's Oak Park studio; many of the surviving drawings for the project are by Schindler, leaving open questions of attribution. The houses were designed for construction with simple concrete-slab walls and roofs; theoretically and formally, they are extensions of the designs for Unity Temple and a 1906 project for a concrete Fireproof House for Richard W. Bock. All anticipate Wright's interest in mono-material concrete-block structures.

Wright's major work of the teens was, of course, the Imperial Hotel. So little reliable information on the structure of this building is available that analogy with the textile block system is risky. Still, one longs to find influence on the concrete-block experiments in Tokyo, following as they did Wright's work on the hotel. The influence may be seen in Wright's sustained fascination with ornament, as expressed in the early block buildings; it does seem to be an extension of a similar preoccupation in the hotel. The architect had become almost intoxicated as he watched his designs being carved into soft oya stone, with more and more ornament added in the process. Concrete block offered even greater plasticity, and the decorative patterns could be cast mechanically, rather than carved by hand. This argument is strengthened with the realization that the Storer piers and the checkerboard pattern of projecting and receding blocks on the south elevation of the Freeman house are transcribed directly from the hotel.

One other connection with the Japanese experience should be made. Wright devoted several pages of his autobiography to a discussion of the native Japanese house, stating that he found it "a perfect example of the modern standardizing I had myself been working with." It was a "supreme study in elimination . . . of the insignificant" that he had earlier identified with the Japanese print, a spiritual cleanliness, "the sense that abhors waste as matter out of place." "The truth is the Japanese dwelling owing to the Shinto ideal 'be clean' is in every bone and fiber of its structure honest."[59] There is a link here with the textile block system and the concept of mono-material construction, but it is based more firmly in theory than form and needs to be interpreted less as a direct outgrowth of the Japanese experience of the teens and early twenties than as the ongoing pursuit of the concept of simplification Wright established before the turn of the century.

CHAPTER NINE

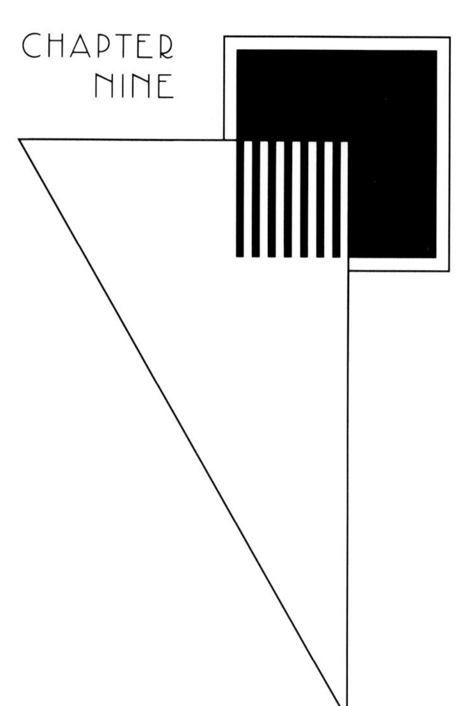

WITH HINDSIGHT

In 1928 Frank Lloyd Wright told Darwin Martin privately that the textile block system was all he had to offer.[1] This statement, written in a moment of personal and professional despair, invites dissection. Was it a confession of bankruptcy? Or was it an insight into future salvation? More than any of Wright's public comments, it provides a window on the importance he assigned the block system, and it suggests critical analysis of the system itself. What precisely did Wright have in the textile block system by the late 1920s? Was it, as he said in his autobiography, a sensible, feasible system of building construction? Was it permanent, noble, beautiful? Was it fit for a phase of modern architecture? Predictably, the answers are not simple.

A SENSIBLE, FEASIBLE SYSTEM

As an avenue of redemption, the textile block system held greatest promise as an idealized philosophical concept and as an instrument for personal architectural development. In Wright's hands, it became far more than a method of building with concrete block. It emerged intuitively, seemingly without strong theoretical convictions, and concluded as a fully integrated mono-material system of design and construction, a synthesis of structure and form that Wright brought to a climax in the Solomon R.

Guggenheim Museum in New York. Certainly the buildings he created with the system are beautiful, and for a variety of reasons. In the process of exploration, he successfully rethought earlier formal and spatial theories; refined his concept of modular organization; investigated new structural technologies that permitted previously untried uses of concrete block; developed nonrectangular planning for the first time; reconsidered the use of ornament; and even flirted with the idea of replacing concrete block with glass block to create an all-glass building. Throughout the decade he displayed a limbering up of approach that comes not from diminished intensity but from maturity. There is no earlier precedent for the freedom of the Doheny Ranch layout; nor would the resolution of San Marcos in the Desert have been possible in 1923. And to contrast House on the Mesa with the earlier, big concrete-block houses—Barnsdall, Ennis, Johnson—is to see that Wright indeed achieved an "architecture, as free, compared with post and lintel, as a winged bird compared to a tortoise."[2]

But if the system was a philosophical success, pragmatically, it cannot be remembered as the feasible system of building construction Wright optimistically described. The houses were difficult to build, consistently over budget, and demanded constant upkeep. Alice Millard, for example, reported that "eternal vigilance" was required to maintain the "cement pointing" that filled the voids between the block walls and the wooden window and door openings.[3] While the problems with the houses in California may be overlooked in the spirit of invention, those in the Jones house confirm the technical inadequacies of the system. Only with trepidation does one speculate on the construction process for San Marcos in the Desert. Wright was never able to make any of the buildings watertight. Stories of leaks are legend: in 1933 Millard told Wright that during a recent storm "water came through the side walls, until the house was a discouraging sight." She concluded, "I know you are sincere in your contention that the water comes only through the parapet, but we have definitely proven that this is not the case." Two years later, Richard Lloyd Jones reinforced his earlier statement about the blocks: "The walls are made of a tamped cement. I have had it waterproofed three times and it still absorbs water like a sponge." Then, in 1941, John Nesbitt, discussing renovations on the Ennis house, reported, "the walls d---p and the roof l---ks."[4]

Even the notion of prefabrication implicit in the block system was challenged a few years after the buildings were finished. In 1936 Wright's responses to an inquiry about the system were published in *The Evolving*

House, by Albert Bemis; the Ennis blocks were used for illustration. The author began with the observation that "Frank Lloyd Wright is perhaps the greatest of contemporary American architects—certainly that is his reputation outside his own land." Although he found "Textile-Block slab construction" to be "of unquestioned organic quality and beauty in effect," he continued that "this system does not seem to go very far toward pre-fabrication."[5]

On the question of permanence, all of the houses and the Arizona Biltmore Hotel have endured the vicissitudes of time and ownership; they stand today in varying states of repair. A flood caused by a clogged city drain filled the basement and rose to the ground floor of the Millard house in late 1932, causing the foundations to settle and cracks to appear.[6] A general problem in the Los Angeles houses is that if the walls are broken, either by nature or human agency, and water is allowed in, the reinforcing rods rust, causing the concrete to spall and ultimately to collapse. Of the group, the Storer house has been the most thoroughly reconditioned. The Jones house has remained structurally sound, though some insensitive modifications were made by the second owner, an architect. Finally, the Arizona Biltmore was severely damaged by fire in June 1973; the fourth floor of the main building was consumed, and the roof collapsed. The damage was repaired under the direction of Wright's successor firm, Taliesin Associated Architects, and the hotel reopened three months later.

As David De Long has observed, the houses now seem to be attracting a special class of owners, who are taking steps to secure their future. The Freeman house is owned by the University of Southern California School of Architecture, which plans to use the building to house visiting distinguished faculty and for seminars, research, and public tours. Restoration to date has involved technical research into the properties of the concrete block and methods for consolidation and repair of the material and the system. Test conservation projects are in progress under the direction of Jeffrey Mark Chusid. The Ennis house is managed by a private nonprofit trust; a large section of the south retaining wall has been reconstructed, though much more remedial work is necessary. This house also is open for tours, validating Wright's prophesy in 1924 that "pilgrimages will be made to it by lovers of the beautiful—from everywhere."

A phase of modern architecture

Was the textile block system fit for a phase of modern architecture, as Wright suggested? According to several prominent contemporary critics, it was indeed. The California houses were published soon after they were completed, the earliest response coming from Europe, where images appeared in Dutch and Swiss periodicals in 1925 and 1926, though without editorial comment. These were followed by a similar presentation in France in 1927.[7]

The finest presentation appeared in a monograph on Wright published in Berlin in 1926, which contained color reproductions of drawings for the California projects and construction photographs of the houses that were built. Richard Neutra assisted with the publication of this book; he also contributed a particularly cogent analysis of Wright's experiment and the famous schematic drawing of the system, signed RN (Fig. 225). Neutra concluded that a consistent unity of material, of scale, of structural system, and a homogeneity of exterior and interior had been attained.[8] He also anticipated further development of the system in which ceilings would be made from the blocks with the same two-way reinforcement. And he

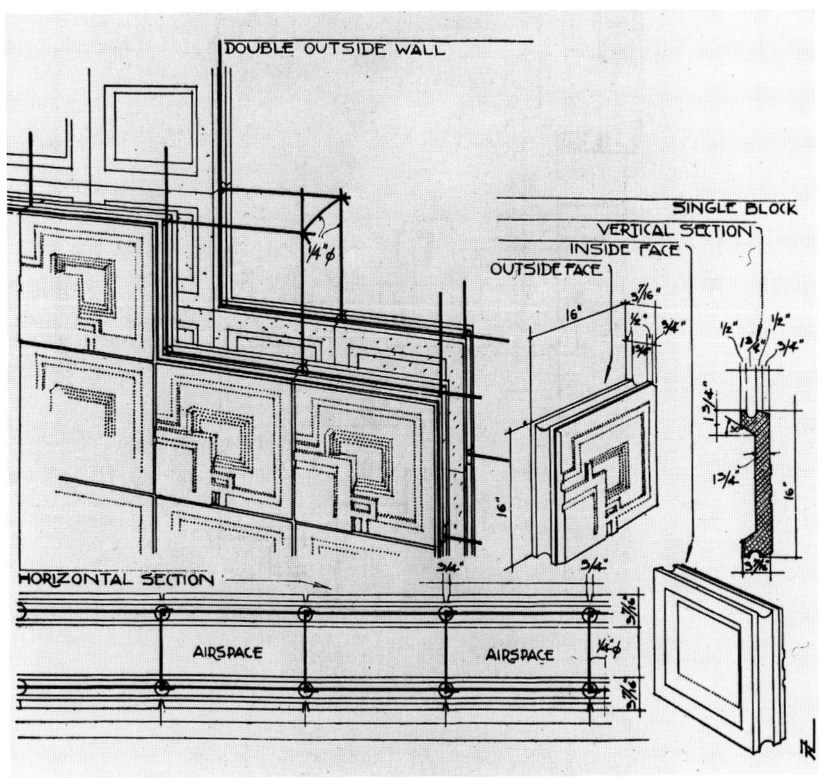

225. Richard Neutra, concrete-block assembly. FLLW FDN, 2111.001

called attention to Wright's innovative method of drawing plans on grid paper, each grid unit corresponding to three block units, or four feet.

The first American critic to comment was A. N. Rebori, a Chicago architect whose article appeared in the *Architectural Record* in December 1927. Written with Wright's cooperation, it correctly praised the system as the outgrowth of "a fixed ideal constantly being developed."[9] The author observed that "Wright has succeeded in breaking the old traditions by making use of mechanical methods, modern structural forms and their application by the shaping of monolithic masses and finally by devising a method of building construction calling for the use of ornamented reinforced concrete blocks."

An early observation that especially pleased Wright came from Arthur Millier, art critic for the *Los Angeles Times*. Discussing the years between 1893—with reference to the World's Columbian Exposition—and 1930, he was speaking the architect's language when he wrote of "the battle for supremacy between man and the machine." He continued that "the basic idea underlying the planning of Wright's . . . California hill houses was simple, natural and sound. With the machine as servant . . . he sought to create houses which should . . . grow out of the region."[10]

Henry-Russell Hitchcock discussed the block system twice in the 1920s, first in a thin monograph published in France in 1928 and therefore before Wright's renewed activity at the end of the decade. Hitchcock concluded that "since 1923, the technical aspect of his work in California has been of the utmost importance." He was equivocal about the ornament, however, observing in one paragraph that the "wealth of his clients allowed him to indulge his excessive taste for ornamentation," and in the next that "since the unity of the surfaces which delimited the studied masses with brilliant art had to be shattered by the joints, the casting of designs into the blocks themselves should probably not give rise to regret." Hitchcock spoke with guarded approbation. "Although this formula is far from the 'pure ornamentation' suitable for the Age of the machine, it is more discrete and of a healthier originality than badly understood cubism or the exoticism of the immediately preceding decorative works."[11]

Hitchcock pursued this line of thought two years later, in his first major book, *Modern Architecture: Romanticism and Reintegration*, speaking misguidedly about steel reinforcement in the walls of the Millard house and contradicting his earlier statements about Wright's use of ornament in the block system. He now saw a "new method of construction which permitted [Wright's] love of ornament its finest expression . . . especially as those patterns, occasionally cut through to form grilles, are simple and admirably suited to the process of manufacture. . . . His ornament is subordinated to the whole scheme as it had never been before."[12]

Sheldon Cheney, in his book *The New World Architecture*, published in 1930, praised Wright for having "done more than any other individual to demonstrate that new methods and new philosophies of building have already displaced the old, wherever man has come to spiritual honesty and creative inspiration; and . . . in California he has recently built houses that answer boldly and stirringly the challenge of the new age."[13] Cheney assigned to the concrete-block houses a new, well-defined style that "grew out of Wright's own invented method of building with pre-cast concrete slabs," but was derived from the Barnsdall house, whose forms were "heavier in aspect . . . but at the same time lightened by a very distinctive, and at times almost jewel-like ornament." The new designs were "frankly and obviously compositions built up with articulated slabs: the structural feature is emphasized and the ornament is integral to the slab-casting. All-over pattern becomes a matter of such ease . . . that these latest buildings are more richly dressed than the designer's earlier works. Again Wright has created an expression that is unmistakable, distinctive, outstanding."[14]

Cheney's thoughtful book was followed two years later by the catalogue accompanying the "Modern Architecture" exhibition at the Museum of Modern Art. In it Hitchcock, the most prolific of twentieth-century architectural historians, first discussed the Barnsdall house in Hollywood. "More successful in every way," he wrote, "were the houses built in the next few years in California in which the concrete block shell with reinforced joints was introduced. The Millard House . . . was the first and the best of these. Wright, planner par excellence before the War, now became preeminently an innovator in construction."[15]

Hitchcock contrasted Wright's experiments with those of contemporary, though younger, European architects. "The methods," he noted, "were very different and so were the results." On the specific question of form, however, he found "important similarities." He observed that "both in California and in Europe, the roof terrace replaced the sloping roof and the projecting cornice disappeared. Wall planes were emphasized and the conventional features of domestic architecture were all modified beyond recognition."[16]

He focused primarily on the Millard house when discussing the textile block system in his seminal 1942 study, *In the Nature of Materials.* In his estimation it "compares in quality with the finest of Wright's Prairie houses. And if it seems to differ from them entirely, those differences derive from the most fundamental of Wright's principles. It is, indeed, these recurrent differences, the apparently inexhaustible variety of his individual solutions, which make Wright's architecture universal."[17]

The most provocative and commonly reiterated thesis is that Wright turned to pre-Columbian sources for inspiration for his concrete-block designs. The source of this conclusion is an article written by Dimitri Tselos and published in *Magazine of Art* in 1953, although the subject had come up much earlier, in 1928, when Wright commented to Darwin Martin, "Architecture is essentially human. . . . In that respect we are no nearer Maya than Egyptian or any other primitive race."[18]

Tselos cites specific Mesoamerican buildings of which Wright would have had knowledge from full-size casts displayed at the 1893 World's Columbian Exposition, and whose influence first appeared in his work in the 1890s. Although he found Mayan influence in the Barnsdall house—which he mistakenly thought to have been constructed of poured concrete—and in the related theater project, he felt that "the opportunity for more effective utilization of the Central American sources was to come upon [Wright's] invention of the pre-cast concrete block," in which he "may have used massive forms and decorative features inspired by Pre-Columbian architecture."[19]

In a second article, published sixteen years later, Tselos concluded that "the over-all relief or 'mosaic' effects produced by the ancient Americans by deep carving, studding, or inserting cut stones into the walls of their palaces and temples in the form of broad or high friezes over a virtually bare lower zone have been adapted by Wright, first to some extent at the Midway Gardens and more extensively at most of his California houses built of pre-cast or 'textile' blocks."[20]

Wright responded obliquely to Tselos's first article in 1953: "Had I not loved and comprehended pre-Columbian architecture as the primitive basis of world-architecture, I could not now build as I build with understanding of all architecture."[21] Yet Tselos was careful to distinguish between historic revivalism in Wright's work and fresh new forms that were created from an awareness of past styles.

There is threaded throughout the observations of Millier, Hitchcock, Cheney, and Tselos the notion that Wright's concrete-block system, and hence the forms of the buildings, were worked out as a specific response to southern California. Certainly Wright's concrete-block houses of the 1920s do come to mind most readily as a manifestation of the area. The small concentration of work built here; the architect's own statements and, to some extent, those of his apologists; and the fact that so little attention has been paid to the later work, all combine to create a myth of regionalism that is less a result of duplicity than of circumstance.

Wright's revived interest in concrete-block construction and his decision to explore the idea in California occurred at the same time, from the same stimulus—the need for renewal—but they seem otherwise unrelated. Still, when he began the experiments in February 1923, he attempted to establish a line of continuity with the preceding work on Olive Hill, which he identified as "a new type in California, a land of romance, —a land that, as yet, has no characteristic building material and no type of building except one carried there by Spanish missionaries in early days, a version of the Italian church and convent." He was thus "still engaged in this effort to produce an integral Architecture suited to the climatic needs of California."[22]

The concept of regionalism was easily established and enormously appealing; looking back three years later, Wright commented that the concrete-block houses were "literally created out of the ground on which they stand, for the soil in California is for the most part nothing but sand, shingle or gravel." In reference to the Doheny Ranch project, he suggested that by designing some of the houses for canyons, he was doing "justice to the hilly terrain" and not building on the hilltops or crests so as not to spoil the skyline.[23]

Wright continued this theme in his autobiography:

> So, when called upon by Aline Barnsdall—her metier the theatre—to build a house for her in Hollywood, why not make architecture stand up and show itself on her new ground, known as Olive Hill, as Romance? . . . Hollyhock house was to be a natural house, naturally built; native to the region of California as the house in the Middle West had been native to the Middle West. . . . Any house should be beautiful in California in the way that California herself is beautiful. . . . A house free in form that takes what is harmonious in the nature of the doing and the purpose and with honest

> sentiment (not false sentimentality) brings all *significantly* out into some enchanting visible "form."

He concluded a few pages later with the comment that the Millard house was "nothing more or less than a distinctly genuine expression of California in terms of modern industry and American life—that was all."[24]

What do these comments mean? Only that Wright wanted to think of his work as regionally responsive. Significantly, however, he never suggested that concrete block was uniquely suited to southern California. He continued to propose his unit system of construction over and over for a remarkably diverse series of projects in equally diverse locations throughout the decade of the 1920s. In 1927 he suggested that Darwin Martin build a block house in Buffalo, "and if Darwin don't want it. Sell it!" Writing again to Martin in 1928, he said that concrete block would be ideal for the Rosenwald School in Hampton, Virginia, but acknowledged "It's too much trouble to try and sell it from this distance." A few months later, he asked Victor Patrosso, manager of the El Tovar Hotel at the Grand Canyon, to "run down to Phoenix and try to imagine what the block construction you see there might be like were it broadly and quietly handles [*sic*] as low-lying masses somewhere on the rim of the Canyon." In December 1928, Wright told Alexander Chandler, "We are getting ready to build a block of thirty textile block concrete houses on a lake subdivision at Milwaukee." The following year, discussing an apartment house he would be designing for Elizabeth Noble, Wright proposed "a little block building, construction that is similar to that of the Arizona Biltmore, only adapted to her needs."[25]

No drawings for these projects are known, and the building forms can only be surmised in view of the gradual shift occurring at the same time in Wright's other work. But their mention does demonstrate his eagerness to build with concrete block wherever he found opportunity. There is even evidence that Wright was interested in marketing the blocks commercially. Ralph Fletcher Seymour, publisher of several small books for Wright, wrote to Schindler in March 1924, inquiring if it were possible to buy the "cement tiles . . . which Mr. Wright told me were to be made and sold under his supervision." Wright was still thinking of commercial exploitation in 1927 when he wrote to Darwin Martin that "the National cement organizations are after the textile block Construction—I am on the verge of a negotiation with them." He was wary, however, commenting at the same time to A. N. Rebori, "I am pretty sure to be robbed of the benefit of my work as usual unless I can get some action started right away."[26]

□ □ □

Frank Lloyd Wright never abandoned the concept of concrete-block construction, though the period of invention essentially ended in 1929. Portions of Florida Southern College, begun in 1939 and continued in stages through the 1940s, were designed for elongated concrete block assembled in the same manner as the earlier buildings. In the 1950s Wright developed his Usonian Automatic houses, which again were built on the textile block principle; single layers of blocks were used in horizontal overhead spans, their coffers exposed; hollow blocks with glass inserts replace conventional windows. The Adelman house in Phoenix is the first example; several others followed. Most satisfying is the Tonkens house in Cincinnati, supervised during construction by Wright's grandson, Eric.

Wright was ready to build anywhere. Forms, materials, and sites were interchangeable. Two of his earliest concrete-block designs for southern

226. Nezam Amery house (project), Teheran, Iran, perspective, 1957. FLLW FDN, 5801.006

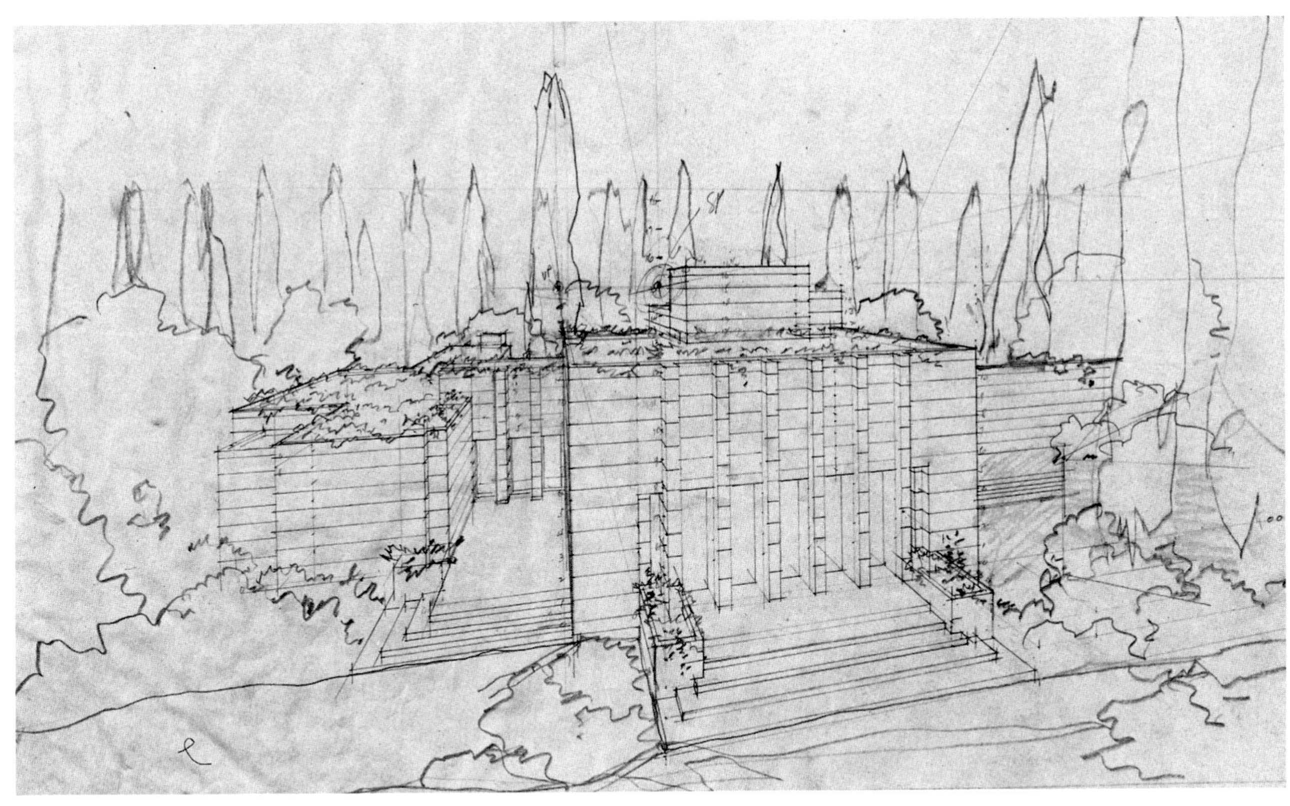

California, the Millard house and the Community Playhouse for Aline Barnsdall, surfaced again later in his career without apology. In 1944 Wright suggested building the Community Playhouse on the campus of Florida Southern College and in 1957 he was asked to create a grand version of the Millard house for a site in Teheran. This was a completely new project — as the design for Florida Southern was not — worked out on a metric scale, but the source is unmistakable (Fig. 226). Wright's heirs, Taliesin Associated Architects, have adopted a similarly pragmatic approach: the clubhouse designed for San Marcos Water Gardens was built of stucco in 1984;[27] and renewed interest has been expressed in constructing San Marcos in the Desert.

San Marcos in the Desert could not be built today as it was designed, however, and perhaps instead of creating more textile block buildings, we need to focus on preserving the examples we have. They are the major evidence of the period in Wright's career that bridged his return from Japan and his development of the Usonian houses in the 1930s — a period of unsurpassed creativity, in which he built so little.

1. Millard house, Pasadena, 1923.

2. Millard house, Pasadena, 1923. Annie Kelly, interior design. Tim Street-Porter

3. Storer house, Los Angeles, 1923. Oberto Gili, courtesy *HG*

4. Storer house, Los Angeles, 1923. Oberto Gili, courtesy *HG*

5. Freeman house, Los Angeles, 1924. Tim Street-Porter

6. Freeman house, Los Angeles, 1924. Tim Street-Porter

7. Ennis house, Los Angeles, 1924. Tim Street-Porter

book—with the exception of Wright's clients, whose dates appear in the text—will be found in the index.

8. Louis Christian Mullgardt, "A Building that Is Wrong," *Architect and Engineer* 71 (November 1922): 81–89. *Architect and Engineer* followed up with additional reinforcement for Mullgardt's comments. One article, reprinted from the *Washington State Architect,* concluded: "The pictures of the building bear out in the fullest degree the scathing criticism which the writer of this article applies to the structure. The building, while it was erected by an American architect, is the greatest hodge-podge of architecture that it has ever been our privilege to see illustrated." In "More Anent the New Imperial Hotel at Tokio, Japan," *Architect and Engineer* 72 (February 1923): 83–84. F. W. Fitzpatrick, a Chicago architect, concurred: "it was a flagrant offence and calculated to harm all things American in the eyes of our distant neighbors." In "Approves Mr. Mullgardt's Criticism," *Architect and Engineer,* Vol. 71 (December 1922): 107.
9. See *Louis Christian Mullgardt, 1866–1942: An Exhibition Marking the Centennial Year of the Architect's Birth,* ex. cat., Art Gallery, University of California, Santa Barbara, April 5–May 8, 1966; M. H. de Young Memorial Museum, San Francisco, June 27–August 7, 1966.
10. Thomas S. Hines, Jr., review of *Frank Lloyd Wright: His Life, His Work, His Words,* by Olgivanna Lloyd Wright, *Prairie School Review* 4, no. 2 (Second Quarter 1967): 29.
11. Frank Lloyd Wright, "In the Cause of Architecture: 'He Who Gets Slapped,'" ms., January 7, 1923. John Lloyd Wright Collection [xxix/3], no. 107, Avery Library, Columbia University, New York. Wright possibly knew of Andreyev's play from the first English translation, which appeared in *The Dial* 70 (March 1921): 250–300. See Alexander Kaun, *Leonid Andreyev* (New York: B. W. Huebsch, 1924), 315, 330.
12. Howard Van Doren Shaw to Wright, January 11, 1923.
13. Frank Lloyd Wright, "The New Imperial Hotel," *Japan Advertiser* (Tokyo), February 7, 1923.
14. Wright to Sullivan, February 5, 1923.
15. "Noted Architect Locates Here," *Holly Leaves* (Hollywood, Calif.), April 20, 1923.
16. Wright to Sullivan, n.d., but late February or early March 1923. The work to which he referred was a new house for Aline Barnsdall in Beverly Hills, the Millard house in Pasadena, and the rebuilding of the 1895 Nathan G. Moore house in Oak Park, Illinois, after a 1922 fire. Wright noted with satisfaction that these clients were "repeaters," three who "came back."
17. The Harper Avenue house recently became a minor preservation issue when a new owner applied for a demolition permit. In the end, it was not possible to save the house and it was torn down in November 1987, though it was documented in drawings and photographs beforehand. Copies of the documentation were given to the author, to the City of West Hollywood, and to the

Frank Lloyd Wright Foundation, Scottsdale, Arizona. Author to City of West Hollywood, October 10, 1986; November 28, 1986.

18. Frank Lloyd Wright, "In the Cause of Architecture: The Third Dimension," unpublished ms., Los Angeles, February 9, 1923. John Lloyd Wright Collection [III/2], no. 8, Avery Library, Columbia University, New York.
19. Ibid.
20. Bruce Brooks Pfeiffer, *Frank Lloyd Wright Monograph, 1914–1923,* ed., with photographs by Yukio Futagawa (Tokyo: A. D. A. Edita, 1985), 204.
21. Wright, *Autobiography* (1943), 235.
22. Wright to Sullivan, n.d., but late March 1923. The Doheny family can offer no assistance. Timothy Doheny to author, September 24 and 26, 1985. It may be useful to note that Wright's project coincided with efforts to annex portions of the Doheny Ranch tract to the City of Los Angeles in early 1923. Doheny successfully blocked the move. See "Laurel Canyon Annexation Open Letter to E. L. Doheny," *Hollywood Daily Citizen,* February 24, 1923; "Dough-heny Wins Laurel Canyon Fight," *Holly Leaves,* March 2, 1923; "Sherman Annexation Is Subject of Attack," *Hollywood Daily Citizen,* March 8, 1923.
23. William T. Evjue, "Wright Now Being Acclaimed as World Leader," *Capital Times* (Madison), October 18, 1923.
24. Charles Lockwood and Peter V. Persic, *Greystone Historical Report* (submitted to the city council, City of Beverly Hills, August 30, 1984), appendix 5. Greystone was the house designed for Edward Laurence Doheny, Jr., by Gordon B. Kaufmann, and constructed between 1926 and 1928 on a site immediately adjacent to the Doheny Ranch.
25. Lucille V. Miller, "Edward and Estelle Doheny," *Ventura County Historical Society Quarterly* 6, no. 1 (November 1960): 6. Miller was librarian and personal secretary to Carrie Estelle Doheny between 1931 and 1958.
26. Lloyd Wright to Wright, ca. 1940, ELW.

CHAPTER TWO

1. Kathryn Smith, "Frank Lloyd Wright, Hollyhock House, and Olive Hill, 1914–1924," *Journal of the Society of Architectural Historians* 38, no. 1 (March 1979): 29.
2. Wright to Sullivan, early March, 1923.
3. "Noted Architect Locates Here," *Holly Leaves,* April 20, 1923.
4. "Will Build in Beverly Hills," *Holly Leaves,* May 18, 1923. Barnsdall's decision to leave Hollywood sparked external predatory interest in Olive Hill. It had, for one observer, "the same dominant, crowning position in all this city of Hollywood and Los Angeles, that the Acropolis held to the City of Athens," and would be "of inestimable value in the not distant future for some great

public building." "'Save Olive Hill!' Is Plea, Ford Urges Immediate Purchase," *Hollywood Daily Citizen*, February 22, 1923.

5. Kathryn Smith, *Frank Lloyd Wright: Hollyhock House and Olive Hill, Buildings and Projects for Aline Barnsdall* (New York: Rizzoli, 1992), 221–22, n. 22.
6. Masami Tanigawa, *Measured Drawing: Frank Lloyd Wright in Japan* (Tokyo: Gurafikkusha, 1980), 32; Tanigawa, "Frank Lloyd Wright: Yamamura House," *GA Houses 27* (Tokyo: A. D. A. Edita, 1989), 7.
7. This information comes from a note penciled on one drawing by Henry-Russell Hitchcock during preparation of his monograph on Wright, *In the Nature of Materials* (New York: Duell, Sloan and Pearce, 1942).
8. Alice Millard to Wright, April 4, 1928; Wright to Millard, April 6, 1928; Millard to Wright, May 3, 1928.
9. Sydney Ford, "New Nook for His Hobbies," *Los Angeles Times*, February 22, 1914.
10. "Noted Book Lover Passes," *Los Angeles Times*, November 8, 1918.
11. Wright, *Autobiography* (1932), 244.
12. Diary of Olive Percival, February 27, 1923. Collection 119, box 28, p. 674, Department of Special Collections, University of California, Los Angeles. Percival's diaries contain numerous references to George and Alice Millard between 1915 and 1930. The late Robert Rosenthal, curator of special collections, University of Chicago Library, made me aware of this material.
13. Wright, *Autobiography* (1943), 242.
14. Millard to Wright, February 24, 1929.
15. A. C. Parlee v. Alice Millard, C145047, June 4, 1924, *Memoranda on Behalf of Defendant*, 3, Los Angeles County Archives, Superior Court Records. Schindler also had a role: his handwritten time sheets, preserved in his archive, indicate that he worked on the Millard project between March 12 and April 4, 1923, for a total of 109½ hours. Architectural Drawing Collection, University of California, Santa Barbara.
16. Parlee v. Millard, *Amended Answer and Counter Claim of Alice Millard, Exhibit "A", Agreement*, March 15, 1923.
17. *Application for the Erection of Building*, Permit no. 1493C, March 12, 1923 [grading]; *Application for the Erection of Frame Building*, Permit no. 2655C, July 10, 1923 [building], Urban Conservation Section, Planning Division, City of Pasadena.
18. Wright, *Autobiography* (1932), 245.
19. Millard to Wright, May 3, 1928. Dates for the photographs were provided by Kameki and Nobu Tsuchiura. Atsuko Tanaka to author, December 23, 1989.
20. Wright, *Autobiography* (1932), 244.
21. Millard to Herbert F. Sturdy, August 11, 1930, GDC.
22. Wright, *Autobiography* (1932), 246.
23. A. C. Parlee v. Frank Lloyd Wright, *Complaint (For Money)*, C135722, January 16, 1924, paragraphs 1, 2, 4, Los Angeles County Archives, Superior Court Records.

24. Parlee v. Millard, *Stipulation for Reference,* 2; *Amended Answer and Counter Claim of Alice Millard,* paragraph 7.
25. Parlee v. Millard, *Amended Answer and Counter Claim of Alice Millard,* paragraphs 7, 8.
26. Parlee v. Millard, *Complaint (Foreclose Claim of Lien),* paragraph 7.
27. Telegram, Hahn to Wright, April 17, 1925; Wright to Hahn, April 17, 1925.
28. Parlee v. Millard, *Memoranda on Behalf of Defendant,* 4. The actual blocks were cast 15½ rather than 16 inches square to allow space for the mortar.
29. Ibid., 3.
30. Telegram, Wright to Hahn, April 15, 1925.
31. Parlee v. Millard, *Memoranda on Behalf of Defendant,* 2; Parlee v. Millard, *Stipulation,* March 10, 1926.
32. Wright, *Autobiography* (1932), 247.
33. Ibid., 241.
34. Lucille V. Miller, "Remembering Alice Parsons Millard, (1870?–1938)," April 1984, 4–5. Carrie Estelle Doheny Collection of the Edward Laurence Doheny Memorial Library, St. John's Seminary, Camarillo, Calif. I thank Rita S. Faulders for bringing this manuscript to my attention.
35. Wright, *Autobiography* (1943), 242.
36. Alexander Inglis, *Among Quiet Friends* (San Francisco: Printed for Mrs. George M. Millard, 1926), 2. From the Pasadena *Star News,* n.d.
37. Arthur Millier, "Great Art Could Grow from Modest Center," *Los Angeles Times,* n.d. Carrie Estelle Doheny Collection of the Edward Laurence Doheny Memorial Library, St. John's Seminary, Camarillo, Calif., courtesy of Rita Faulders.

CHAPTER THREE

1. Wright, *Autobiography* (1932), 250.
2. "Creative Education," n.d., copy from Kathryn Smith.
3. Wright, *Autobiography* (1932), 250.
4. Hitchcock, *In the Nature of Materials,* 124.
5. *Application for Erection of Buildings,* Permit no. 53782, November 7, 1923, Department of Building and Safety, City of Los Angeles. Special thanks to Tom Owen of the Los Angeles Public Library for locating this permit.
6. A. C. Parlee v. Aline Barnsdall, C143096, *Complaint on Contract,* May 7, 1924, paragraphs 1, 2; *Answer; Stipulation of settlement,* July 9, 1925, Los Angeles County Archives, Superior Court Records.
7. "Olive Hill for Park," *Holly Leaves,* December 7, 1923; "Changes in Park Situation," *Holly Leaves,* April 4, 1924.
8. Wright, *Autobiography* (1932), 250. Though the general layout clearly is indebted to Wright's plan for the integrated Community Playhouse and Theodore Barnsdall Memorial, Schindler's precise role in the new design and the dates of construction remain unclear. One drawing by Schindler, titled

"Sketch of a Fountain" and dated April 1924, shows the various elements as they were completed. Architectural Drawing Collection, University of California, Santa Barbara. See also, Archiplan and Martin Eli Weil (restoration architect), *Theodore Barnsdall Memorial Historic Structures Report,* Barnsdall Art Park, 1992. Weil has speculated that the blocks cast by A. C. Parlee for the Community Playhouse were used to build the new design. Weil to author, November 19, 1992. Certainly, the quantity would have been adequate: 7,500 blocks were indicated in the lawsuit; approximately 3,500 are visible today. However, none of the blocks have patterned faces, suggesting that if they were indeed intended for the Community Playhouse, the building would have been completed with none of the sophisticated articulation Wright envisioned.

9. Notes of Harriette Von Breton, gathered in an interview with Lloyd Wright, September 1970. David Gebhard and Harriette Von Breton, *Lloyd Wright, Architect: Twentieth Century Architecture in an Organic Exhibition* (Santa Barbara: University of California, 1971), 27–28. Lloyd's mention of the Chandlers and General Sherman provides some clue to the level of Wright's contacts. Harry Chandler was publisher of the *Los Angeles Times* between 1917 and 1944. "General" Moses Hazeltine Sherman was a pioneer developer of the electric railway in Los Angeles and was a major land holder; he and Wright toured portions of the San Fernando Valley together.
10. Wright to Sullivan, April 2, 1923.
11. "Eyewitness Gives Details of Holocaust," *Los Angeles Examiner,* September 3, 1923; "Imperial Hotel in Path of Fire," *Los Angeles Times,* September 4, 1923.
12. Merle Armitage, "Frank Lloyd Wright: An American Original," *Texas Quarterly* 5 (Spring 1962): 85–86. Wright's concern was noted sympathetically at the time: "Probably no resident of Hollywood is more deeply affected by the Japanese catastrophe than is Frank Lloyd Wright," in "Local Folk in Quake," *Holly Leaves,* September 7, 1923. The survival of the hotel was reported in the same newspaper two weeks later: "Imperial Hotel Stands," *Holly Leaves,* September 21, 1923. Although the building was badly damaged during World War II, it was repaired, but ultimately succumbed to economic pressure. The hotel was demolished in 1968, though the center section was reconstructed in Meji Mura Village, near Nagoya, Japan, in 1976.
13. Wright, *Autobiography* (1932), 222. Chandler's assistance was noted by Wright in a telegram to Sullivan, September 8, 1923.
14. Wright to Sullivan, n.d.; ibid., September 26, 1923.
15. The original typescript is in Wright's archives in Arizona. *Experimenting with Human Lives* was published in Chicago by Ralph Fletcher Seymour in 1923.
16. *Holly Leaves,* October 12, 1923; "Says Angeleno Shuns Crowds," *Los Angeles Times,* October 15, 1923.
17. William T. Evjue, "Wright Now Being Acclaimed as World Leader," *Capital Times* (Madison), October 18, 1923.
18. Wright, *Autobiography* (1932), 234–35.
19. *Application for the Erection of Buildings,* Permit no. 53788, November 7, 1923, Department of Building and Safety, City of Los Angeles. I thank Rod Grant for

finding this permit. Research published in 1979 reveals that Louise and Walter Conrad Arensberg, collectors of early twentieth-century avant-garde art, were living in Residence A at the time. See Kathryn Smith, "Frank Lloyd Wright, Hollyhock House, and Olive Hill, 1914–1924," *Journal of the Society of Architectural Historians* 38, no. 1 (March 1979): 31. The widows of Storer's two sons can offer no additional information. Mrs. Horace P. Storer and Mrs. John Storer, Jr., to author, March 14, 1983; July 11, 1984.

20. Records of the American Medical Association, Chicago. Fred Hunter, Research Assistant, American Medical Association, to author, June 23, 1986. The California licensing agency, the Board of Medical Quality Assurance, has no listing for Dr. Storer. Board of Medical Quality Assurance to author, February 22, 1982.
21. Articles of Incorporation of Superior Building Company, August 27, 1921, California Secretary of State, Sacramento. The directors and subscribers were John Storer and two lawyers, Henry G. Bodkin and Mortimer A. Kline. The corporation was suspended by order of the Franchise Tax Board on May 1, 1931, for not complying with statutory requirements. Bodkin's son recently recalled hearing his father mention Storer, but indicated that he had no records. Henry G. Bodkin, Jr., to author, March 18, 1987.
22. The date of the translation into concrete block is unknown. Schindler's time sheets include several references to the Lowes project in May and June, but they do not identify the scheme. Thus, it is unclear if he was still working for Wright or had already taken over the commission. Schindler's fully developed drawings for the house as it was finally built are dated September 1923, and are in the Architectural Drawing Collection, University of California, Santa Barbara.
23. "Cielo Vista Terrace," *Holly Leaves,* October 12, 1923. The article includes John Storer among those who had purchased building sites.
24. "Residence Built for the Superior Building Company. Inc. Cielo Vista Terrace . . . Hollywood Boulevard . . . Los Angeles California . . . Frank Lloyd Wright . . . Architect . . . 1600 Edgemont Hollywood," ELW.
25. John Storer v. A. C. Parlee, *Complaint—Claim and Delivery,* 133959, paragraph 1, December 15, 1923, Los Angeles County Archives, Superior Court Records.
26. Telegram, Wright to Lloyd, April 19, 1924, ELW; Lloyd to Wright, n.d.; Wright to Lloyd, September 15, 1924, ELW; telegram, Wright to Lloyd, October 10, 1924, ELW.
27. Wright to Lloyd, September 15, 1924, ELW.
28. Lloyd to Wright, October 25, 1924, ELW.
29. Completion Notice no. 1298, October 27, 1924, Los Angeles County Department of Registrar—Recorder/County Court Clerk.
30. Los Angeles County Archives. Storer is first listed at 8061 Hollywood Boulevard (incorrectly; the correct address is 8161) in the March 1925 Los Angeles telephone book; the final listing at that address appears in September 1926. He is so listed in the Los Angeles city directory only once, in 1927. Byron

Vandegrift, who as a young man worked as a laborer and draftsman on several projects for Lloyd Wright in the 1920s, and whose mother knew Aline Barnsdall socially, recalled in 1983 that he went to the Storer house soon after it was occupied to fix some leaks. He described Storer as "older, short and heavy set," and stated that the house wasn't "decorated elegantly at all." Byron Vandegrift, interview with author and Charles Calvo, March 29, 1983.

31. Pauline G. Schindler to Mrs. [Olgivanna] Wright, March 1, 1931. Mrs. Schindler had earlier justified moving into the house to her father, who was supporting her: she was there as a caretaker, paying a nominal sum each month; the house was to serve as a "background" for the work she was "planning to do,—which involves an active association with four or five modern architects here, and which has the purpose of selling their design services to the rest of the world." Her intention was "to influence the culture of the coast, but from a business end." Her statements that "r.m.s. is going to look it over with me this afternoon, to design furniture," and that "there is a great deal of equipping to do," validate Vandegrift's recollections of the interiors. Pauline G. Schindler to her father, n.d., but early 1930, courtesy of Mark Schindler. R. M. Schindler prepared one tentative drawing, including plans of the living and dining rooms and suggestions for furniture placement. Architectural Drawing Collection, University of California, Santa Barbara.
32. Hitchcock, *In the Nature of Materials,* 77.
33. Wright to Lloyd, n.d., ELW.
34. Richard Wallace and Mary Wallace v. Charles H. Druffel and Helen K. Druffel, C399918, *Complaint: Abatement of Nuisance* and *Specific Performance,* June 7, 1935, paragraph 6, Los Angeles County Archives, Superior Court Records. The complaint was settled in the Druffels' favor, *Findings of Fact* and *Conclusions of Law,* 5. I thank the Druffels' daughter, Jean Duggan, for making me aware of this litigation.
35. Druffel to Wright, June 10, 1935.
36. Quoted in Diane Kanner, "Freeman House Deeded to USC," *Los Angeles Times,* March 25, 1984.
37. Jeffrey Mark Chusid (architect), *Historic Structure Report: Samuel and Harriet Freeman House, Hollywood, California, Frank Lloyd Wright, 1924.* Prepared for the School of Architecture, University of Southern California, July 1989.
38. *Architect's Contract . . . In Re: Freeman House, Los Angeles . . . January 26th, 1924,* courtesy of the University of Southern California.
39. *[Agreement, January 29, 1924, between H. J. D. Wolff and Samuel and Harriet Freeman],* courtesy of the University of Southern California. Information on Wolff's role at Olive Hill comes from Frank Lloyd Wright v. Aline Barnsdall, *Notice to Produce Certain Documents and Writings,* February 28, 1924, C138515, paragraph 4, Los Angeles County Archives, Superior Court Records.
40. *Memorandum of Agreement between Mr. & Mrs. Samuel Freeman and Frank Lloyd Wright,* February 26, 1924, courtesy of the University of Southern California.
41. *Application for the Erection of Frame Buildings,* no. 17362, April 8, 1924, Department of Building and Safety, City of Los Angeles.

42. Byron Vandegrift, interview with author and Charles Calvo, March 29, 1983.
43. Wright to Lloyd, September 15, 1924; telegram, Wright to Lloyd, October 10, 1924; telegram, Lloyd to Wright, November 19, 1924; telegram, Lloyd to Wright, January 9, 1925, all ELW.
44. Los Angeles County Department of Registrar—Recorder/County Court Clerk.
45. Telegram, Wright to Lloyd, January 8, 1925, ELW.
46. *Notice of Completion,* no. 1125, March 23, 1925. Los Angeles County Department of Registrar—Recorder/County Court Clerk; ELW.
47. Charles M. Calvo, "De betonblok-ontwerpen van Frank Lloyd Wright [The Concrete-block Designs of Frank Lloyd Wright]," *Forum* (Amsterdam) 30, no. 4 (1986): 172.
48. Chusid, *Historic Structure Report: Samuel and Harriet Freeman House.*
49. Wright to Mr. and Mrs. Ennis, September 4, 1924, ELW.
50. In 1913 Charles Ennis's income was assessed at $14,000. *Southern California Blue Book of Money: Taxpayers Assessed on $5,000 and Upwards In Los Angeles, Pasadena, South Pasadena, Long Beach, Pomona, Monrovia, Arcadia, Santa Monica, Venice, etc., Also San Diego* (Los Angeles: James Edward Condon, 1913), 33.
51. "Chas. W. Ennis, L.A. Merchant, Is Mourned," *Los Angeles Evening Herald,* December 18, 1928. "Last Rites Tomorrow for Charles W. Ennis," *Hollywood Daily Citizen,* December 19, 1928. In 1933 Mabel Ennis's lawyer, Donald Barker, asked Wright if he could help find a buyer for the house, explaining that Mrs. Ennis lived in it alone, in a difficult financial position, and that the house could be purchased at a figure very much below its original cost; Barker to Wright, January 28, 1933. Also in 1933, a Warner Brothers motion picture, *Female,* starring Ruth Chatterton, George Brent, and Johnny Mack Brown, was filmed at the house. A mock-up of the courtyard was constructed; an illustration appears in Donald Albrecht, *Designing Dreams: Modern Architecture in the Movies* (New York: Harper and Row, in collaboration with the Museum of Modern Art, 1986), 127. Michel Choban brought this reference to my attention. Since then the house has been the backdrop for numerous films, television programs, commercials, and print advertisements.
52. *Memorandum of Agreement between . . . Mr. & Mrs. Charles W. Ennis . . . Owners . . . and Lloyd Wright Builder,* February 25, 1924; labor vouchers, week ending March 8, 1924; J. R. Buchanan, Aluminum Castings Company, to Lloyd Wright, April 22, 1924, ELW.
53. *Application for the Erection of Frame Buildings,* Permit no. 20648, May 1, 1924 [house]; Permit no. 20649, May 1, 1924 [garage], Department of Building and Safety, City of Los Angeles.
54. Smith-Emery Company to Lloyd Wright, July 23, 1924, ELW.
55. Telegram, Lloyd to Wright, August 19, 1924, ELW.
56. Wright to Mr. and Mrs. Ennis, September 4, 1924, ELW.
57. Telegram, Lloyd to Wright, September 15, 1924; telegram, Wright to Lloyd, September 26, 1924, both ELW.
58. Telegram, Lloyd to Wright, October 8, 1924; [agreement], Los Angeles, December 10, 1924, both ELW.

59. Lloyd to Wright, February 4, 1925, ELW; Wright to Mrs. Chas. W. Ennis, February 5, 1925.
60. Lloyd to Mr. Charles W. Ennis, February 25, 1925, ELW.
61. Lloyd to Mrs. [Laura] Belknap, March 13, 1937, ELW.
62. Dietzmann featured his work for the Ennis house in an advertisement that appeared in *The Lintel* (Los Angeles) 1, no. 11 (December 1929): 22. Biographical information is in *Who's Who in Los Angeles* 1926–27, (Los Angeles: Chas. J. Lang, 1927), 48.
63. Judson Studios ledger, n.d., 159. According to Judson family tradition, all of the tiles and windows for the Ennis house were done by the Judson Studios. The designs were worked out by Charlie Grolle with Walter H. Judson and submitted to Wright for approval. Walter L. Judson, Jr., to author, May 16, 1983.
64. The garage was completed December 13, 1924; the house, August 14, 1925. City of Los Angeles, Department of Building and Safety, permit record; C. A. Edwards v. Mrs. C. W. Ennis, W. A. Clark, et al., *Complaint to Foreclose Mechanic's Lien,* C219961, March 22, 1927, paragraphs 4–7, Los Angeles County Archives, Superior Court Records.
65. "Art of the Architect," *Los Angeles Times,* Rotogravure Section, November 28, 1926.
66. Hitchcock, *In the Nature of Materials,* caption to ill. 257, n.p.
67. Frank Lloyd Wright, "On Building Permits: The Millard House," [December 12, 1954], in *Frank Lloyd Wright: His Living Voice, Selected and with Commentary by Bruce Brooks Pfeiffer* (Fresno: Press at California State University, 1987), 42.
68. *International Motion Picture Annual,* 1960; Theodore Strauss, "A Peddler's Progress," *New York Times,* June 7, 1942.
69. Strauss, ibid.; John B. Nesbitt to Wright, April 15, 1940.
70. Wright to Nesbitt, April 24, 1940.
71. Nesbitt to Wright, August 7, 1940; September 20, 1940. No building permit for the pool has been found. Confirmation of Lloyd's role is in correspondence from Wright to Lloyd, May 28, 1940: "Pool is in the right place," ELW. Lloyd seems to have sought his father's approval on all the work; on June 6, 1940, Eugene Masselink wrote to Lloyd, "The Ennis drawings are on their way to you today—Mr. Wright needed the time to go through them," ELW.
72. Nesbitt to Wright, November 4, 1940; April 7, 1941; Wright to Nesbitt, n.d.; Nesbitt to Wright, April 14, 1941.
73. Nesbitt to Wright, May 21, 1941.
74. Ibid., September 22, 1941.
75. Ibid.

CHAPTER FOUR

1. Research published in 1990 indicates that Wright initially proposed using concrete block for yet another project at the end of 1923, the Nakoma Country Club in Madison. This conclusion is based on one drawing in the Wisconsin

State Historical Society: concrete block was to be used for the entire structure below the roof; the blocks were offset to create a battered effect. Mary Jane Hamilton, "The Nakoma Country Club," in Paul E. Sprague, ed., *Frank Lloyd Wright and Madison: Eight Decades of Artistic and Social Interaction* (Madison: Elvehjem Museum of Art, University of Wisconsin, Madison, 1990), 79, 81.

2. Wright to Barnsdall, December 15, 1933.
3. Wright, *Autobiography* (1932), 249. Wright also mentioned the project in an interview published on his return to the Midwest in October 1923, in William T. Evjue, "Wright Now Being Acclaimed as World Leader," *Capital Times* (Madison), October 18, 1923.
4. Edward B. Scott, *The Saga of Lake Tahoe: A Complete Documentation of Lake Tahoe's Development over the Last One Hundred Years* (Crystal Bay, Lake Tahoe, Nev.: Sierra-Tahoe Publishing, 1957), 127, 129, 131.
5. Mrs. Walter Bush, interview with Jessie Armstrong, ms., 70/130 C, Bancroft Library, University of California, Berkeley. Kathryn Smith located this document in August 1991, and kindly passed it on to me.
6. Ibid.
7. Deering to Prussing, December 5, 1923; Prussing to Deering, December 7, 1923. Copies from Kathryn Smith.
8. Telegram, Wright to Lloyd, May 6, 1924, ELW.
9. Wright to Barnsdall, December 15, 1933.
10. A. M. Johnson to Mother and Cliffe [his sister], [October, 1905], Scotty's Castle, Death Valley.
11. MacArthur had worked for Johnson at the National Life Insurance Company since 1907. How he met Wright is unknown, but between approximately 1911 and 1918 he and his family lived in the architect's Oak Park house. In the 1920s he was closely involved in Wright's legal and financial difficulties. Levering Cartwright, "A Sacrifice to Death Valley," *Best's Life News* (August 1966): 25. I thank Richard Joncas for bringing this article to my attention. Donald Kalec confirmed that MacArthur lived in Wright's house, but could not give firm dates.
12. Wright, *Autobiography* (1932), 253.
13. George C. Lyon, "A. M. Johnson Visits Deep Springs and the Visit is Returned." James E. O'Barr, curator of Scotty's Castle, made this rewarding manuscript available to me on my second visit to the site, March 22, 1989. When pressed for a more specific date, Lyon stated that the visit had probably been in December 1923. This information coincides with Wright's known travels; he was in Los Angeles between September 1 and October 14, when he returned to the Midwest. He went back to the West Coast in December. The intense heat in Death Valley would seem to preclude a visit earlier in the year. George C. Lyon to author, April 14, 1989. There is no record of the visit in the archives of Deep Springs College. Matt Pierson, Librarian, to author, March 29, 1989. A slightly different version of this trip was offered by Johnson in 1941: he recalled that "[Wright] went in my car along with a Mr. Harold

McCourtney and my chauffeur." A. M. Johnson to Henry-Russell Hitchcock, June 18, 1941, Scotty's Castle, Death Valley.

14. The drawing is one of a group for Wright's project that has remained at the castle. Neil Levine made me aware of the drawings; Susan Buchel showed them to me on April 3, 1985.
15. Richard Neutra to Muetterli [his mother-in-law, Lilly Mueller Niedermann], November 1924, in Dione Neutra, *Richard Neutra: Promise and Fulfillment, 1919–1932, Selections from the Letters and Diaries of Richard and Dione Neutra* (Carbondale and Edwardsville: Southern Illinois University Press, 1986), 129–30.
16. Telegram, Lloyd to Wright, October 9, 1924, ELW.
17. Johnson to Hitchcock, June 18, 1941, Scotty's Castle, Death Valley.
18. Minutes of Fiji Building Association annual meeting, November 14, 1924. John Kiehnau generously provided all of the minutes cited from his fraternity's archive in Lexington, Ky. Jones's role is traced in Mary Jane Hamilton, "The Phi Gamma Delta Fraternity House," in Sprague, ed., *Frank Lloyd Wright and Madison,* 69–76.
19. Records of Phi Gamma Delta directors' meeting, April 4, 1925, Lexington, Ky.
20. Ibid.
21. Ibid., October 17, 1925.
22. Ibid., June 12, 1926, and September 25, 1926.
23. Ibid., October 16, 1926.
24. Wright to Jones, October 10, 1929.
25. Frank Lloyd Wright, "Anmerkungen des Architekten Frank Lloyd Wright zu Seinen Zementblockhäusern," in H. de Fries, ed., *Frank Lloyd Wright: Aus dem Lebenswerke eines Architekten,* trans. Janice Murray (Berlin: Verlag Ernst Pollak, 1926), 65.
26. Wright to Rebori, September 15, 1927.
27. Frank Lloyd Wright, "In the Cause of Architecture, I: The Architect and the Machine," *Architectural Record* 61 (May 1927): 394; Wright, "In the Cause of Architecture, IV. Fabrication and Imagination," *Architectural Record* 62 (October 1927): 318; Wright, "In the Cause of Architecture, II: Standardization, the Soul of the Machine," *Architectural Record* 61 (June 1927): 478, 479.
28. Frank Lloyd Wright, "In the Cause of Architecture, IV: Fabrication and Imagination," *Architectural Record* 62 (October 1927): 319, 320.
29. Ibid., 320.

CHAPTER FIVE

1. Wright to John, n.d., but April 1928, John Lloyd Wright Collection [XIII/7], no. 90, Avery Library, Columbia University, New York. The date can be established by the reference to the commission for San Marcos in the Desert and by the address on the letter, 129 Country Club Drive. Wright moved to less expensive quarters at the end of April.

2. Warren McArthur, Jr., "The Arizona Biltmore, the McArthur Brothers, and Frank Lloyd Wright," in *Triglyph,* no. 6 (Summer 1988): 37. The author quotes from his uncle's autobiographical notes: "Made arrangements at Wright's office October 18, 1907, 4:00 P.M. Began work October 19, 1907, 8:30 A.M. Left Wright's employ October 19, 1909, 4:00 P.M." I thank Jim Johnson for bringing this article to my attention. Information on McArthur's 1918 stay at Taliesin comes from his handwritten autobiographical notes, ca. 1940, now in the possession of his nephew, Warren McArthur, Jr. He incorrectly states that he was at Taliesin in 1919. He had left by March 13, 1918, when he wrote to Schindler from Chicago, asking that some items he had left behind be sent. A copy of McArthur's letter (written in German) was provided by Barbara Giella.
3. Robin M. Carlaw, Curatorial Associate, Harvard University Archives, to author, January 29, 1987. In an autobiographical statement published in 1930, McArthur indicated that he had prepared at Armour Institute of Technology; however, that institution has no record of him. "Albert Chase McArthur," in Harvard College, *Class of 1905, 25th Anniversary Report* (Cambridge, Mass., 1930), 390. Guy Price, Director, Alumni Relations, Illinois Institute of Technology, to author, October 31, 1988.
4. *History of Arizona, Biographical,* vol. 4 (Phoenix: Record Publishing Co., 1930), *s.v.* Charles Henry McArthur, Warren McArthur, Jr., 225–26.
5. McArthur Papers; Warren McArthur, Jr., to author, August 11, 1983. Sylvia Lee Bender-Lamb, "Chandler, Arizona: Landscape as a Product of Land Speculation" (Master's thesis, Arizona State University, 1983).
6. A. N. Rebori, "Frank Lloyd Wright's Textile-Block Slab Construction," *Architectural Record* 62 (December 1927): 448–56.
7. Cited in Finis Farr, *Frank Lloyd Wright: A Biography* (New York: Scribner's, 1961), 208.
8. McArthur Papers.
9. Ibid.
10. Ibid., possibly written for the *Architectural Record* in 1929.
11. Cited in "*Specifications for the Arizona Biltmore Hotel, Phoenix,* Albert Chase McArthur, architect, Phoenix, Arizona, May 1928," courtesy of the Arizona Biltmore Hotel.
12. Wright to Lloyd, April 19, 1928, ELW.
13. Wright to S. M. Benet, April 25, 1928, ELW.
14. McArthur Papers.
15. Lloyd to Wright, n.d., but approximately 1930. Specifications call for a mixture of clean-washed sand and fine gravel, combined with Riverside Cement in a ratio of 1 : 2 : 4. The gravel had to pass through a three-eighths-inch sieve, rather than the quarter-inch mesh used in Los Angeles.
16. Wright to Dr. Alexander J. Chandler, September 27, 1928.
17. Telegram, McArthur to Wright, November 28, 1928; Wright to Ben E. Paige [*sic*], November 16, 1928; Wright to McArthur, December 5, 1928.
18. Wright to Chandler, December 18, 1928.

19. See, for example, "Phoenix Heralded around World as Biltmore Opens Today," *Arizona Republican* (February 23, 1929); several articles follow under the banner headline.
20. The standard windows are four block units (54 inches) high and five block units (90 inches) long [4 × 13.5 = 54, 5 × 18 = 90; .75 × 90 = 67.5]. The openings would have had to be increased one block unit in height [5 × 13.5 = 67.5; 67.5 = .75 × 90] or reduced one block unit in length [4 × 18 = 72; 54 = .75 × 72] to maintain the proscribed ratio of height three quarters to length.
21. Wright, *Autobiography* (1932), 301.
22. McArthur explained the relationships in handwritten notes on his drawings: "G-Maj; E-Min; B♭ Maj; G Min." The wife of Emry Kopta contended late in life that the design "is simply an improvisation of a palm tree leaf and trunk," worked out by her husband. "Biltmore Memories Told by Mrs. Kopta," news clipping, source unknown, courtesy Arizona Biltmore Hotel.
23. Charles H. McArthur to *Arizona Highway[s] Magazine,* March 5, 1956, McArthur Papers.
24. *Contract,* June 27, 1928, McArthur Papers; McArthur to Wright, August 6, 1929.
25. Wright, *Autobiography* (1932), 301.
26. Wright to Lloyd, February 1, 1928, ELW.
27. *Memorandum of Agreement,* January 25, 1928, Darwin D. Martin Papers, Department of Special Collections, M355, box 4, folder 6, item 10, Stanford University Libraries, California; *License,* June 27, 1928, McArthur Papers.
28. "The Arizona-Biltmore Hotel, Phoenix, Arizona: Albert Chase McArthur, Architect," *Architectural Record* 66 (July 1929): 19. A photo essay was published in *Architectural Forum* 51, no. 6 (December 1929): 655–59. Another article, published earlier, includes construction photographs: Guy Rowell, "Arizona's New and Distinctive Hotel," *Progressive Arizona and the Great Southwest* 7, no. 5 (November 1928): 21, 22. It may be useful to note that the swimming pool, bath house, cabanas, and stables were undertaken after William Wrigley took control of the hotel; they were designed by Robert T. Evans and completed by the Evans Construction Company in 1931. Some effort was made to approximate the style of the hotel in the bath house and cabanas, though they were constructed of native adobe, plastered to look like concrete. The stables were intended to simulate the appearance of a Pueblo village. "The Arizona Biltmore's New Swimming Pool," and "The Arizona Biltmore's New Pueblo Stables," *Adobe: A Magazine of Arizona Architecture* (7th Issue, 1931): 6–11, courtesy of Arizona Biltmore Hotel.
29. McArthur to Wright, April 2, 1930.
30. Wright to McArthur, June 2, 1930.
31. McArthur Papers; "Behind the Record," *Architectural Record* 89 (June 1941): 7. The books are: Erna Fergusson, *Our Southwest* (New York: Knopf, 1940); and *Arizona: A State Guide* (New York: Hastings House, 1940).

32. Wright to McArthur, August 10, 1929. Albert McArthur had no financial interest in the hotel. See Paul M. Angle, *Philip K. Wrigley: A Memoir of a Modest Man* (Chicago: Rand McNally, 1975), 47–48.
33. Blaine Drake, "F.LL.W.: My Years with Frank Lloyd Wright," unpublished ms., n.d., ms. in possession of author. McArthur also recalled supervising the construction of the Robie house, in Chicago, while Wright was in Italy. He was concerned about the design of the structural steel, especially in the long roof projections. He believed that if he had not redesigned the structure the house would not still have been standing. Fred Koeper first brought this manuscript to my attention; Bernard Michael Boyle kindly secured Drake's permission to publish this excerpt.
34. Mrs. W. P. Willson to Richard Joncas, April 6, 1987. Mrs. Willson is the widow of Alexander Chandler; she stated that the meeting took place at the McArthur's home. Courtesy of Richard Joncas.
35. Quoted in Robert Conway Stevens, *A History of Chandler, Arizona, 1912–1953* (Tucson: University of Arizona Press, 1954), 16. Much of the background information on Chandler, Arizona, is drawn from this publication. Also useful are: Bender-Lamb, "Chandler, Arizona"; and *A Valley Reborn* (Phoenix: Salt River Project, n.d.).
36. Myron Hunt (architect), Los Angeles, Calif., *Final Report: San Marcos Expansion, Chandler, Az.*, February 6, 1923, Hoak Collection, Huntington Library, San Marino, California. The late Alson Clark made me aware of this recondite item.
37. Wright to Chandler, March 30, 1928.
38. Wright, *Autobiography* (1932), 302.
39. Wright to Chandler, March 30, 1928.
40. Wright to Lloyd, April 19, 1928, ELW.
41. Wright to Chandler, April 30, 1928.
42. Wright to Lloyd, June 1, 1928, ELW.
43. Wright to Martin, July [1–10], 1928, Darwin D. Martin Papers, Department of Special Collections, M355, box 3, folder 15, item 2, Stanford University Libraries, California.
44. Chandler to Wright, September 25, 1928, Darwin D. Martin Papers, Department of Special Collections, M355, box 4, folder 10, item 27, Stanford University Libraries, California.
45. Wright to Chandler, December 18, 1928.
46. Ibid., April 30, 1928.
47. Ibid., March 30, 1928; Wright to Martin, June 1, 1928.
48. Telegram, Wright to McArthur, January 11, 1929; "Wright Goes to Arizona," *Baraboo Weekly News,* January 17, 1929; "Taliesin Household to Arizona," *Weekly Home News,* January 24, 1929; "New Resort Hotel to Rise on Desert West of City," *Chandler Arizonan,* January 31, 1929. Wright identified his draftsmen as Heinrich [Klumb]; Donald [D. Walker]; Vladimir [Karfick]; Cy [Jahnke]; and "brave" George Kastner. Wright, *Autobiography* (1932), 306. Also there, briefly, were "Cueball" Kelly and Francis C. Sullivan, who died of

tuberculosis at Eucalyptus Sanatorium in Phoenix on April 4. Sullivan had known Wright at least since 1911 and probably collaborated with him on several Canadian projects in the early teens. See H. Allen Brooks, *The Prairie School: Frank Lloyd Wright and His Midwest Contemporaries* (Toronto: University of Toronto Press, 1972), 272–73. The events surrounding Sullivan's death are mentioned by Brooks, 278–79, and are discussed in greater detail in correspondence between Wright and Sullivan's sister, Mabel Whalen, between April 3 and July 27, 1929.

49. Wright, *Autobiography* (1932), 303.
50. Ibid.
51. Frank Lloyd Wright, "In the Cause of Architecture: Arizona," unpublished ms., FLW Foundation, 2401.063; id., *Autobiography* (1932), 306.
52. *Reliable Hardware Company v. Frank Lloyd Wright, Complaint,* 31404, *Execution and Order of Sale,* January 2, 1930, Clerk's Office, Superior Court of Maricopa County, State of Arizona.
53. Wright, *Autobiography* (1932), 305, 306.
54. Merle Armitage, "Frank Lloyd Wright: An American Original," *Texas Quarterly* 5 (Spring 1962): 85–90.
55. Will Weston, "From People You Know," *Weekly Home News,* March 7, 1929; April 18, 1929.
56. Wright to Martin, May 9, 1929.
57. Wright to Mueller, July 16, 1929; E. H. Ward & Company Chemical Laboratories to Mueller, July 27, 1929.
58. "Architect Leaves for Home in Wisconsin," *Chandler Arizonan,* May 30, 1929.
59. Weldon to Wright, June 3, 1929.
60. Wright to Martin, May 9, 1929.
61. "Cost Summary for San Marcos in the Desert," January 1, 1930, 2, FLW Foundation, 1082.028.
62. "San Marcos in the Desert for Alexander Chandler, Chandler, Arizona: Frank Lloyd Wright, Architect," 2, FLW Foundation, 1082.028.
63. Ibid., 1.
64. Ibid., 2.
65. Wright to Chandler [January 14, 1929?].
66. "San Marcos in the Desert for Alexander Chandler, Chandler, Arizona, Frank Lloyd Wright, Architect: Ferro-Block Unit-Slab Construction, Skeleton Specifications," 2, FLW Foundation, 1082.028.
67. Ibid., "Foundation Specifications," FLW Foundation, 1082.028.
68. Ibid., Block Schedules, FLW Foundation, 1082.042.
69. Ibid., "Skeleton Specifications," 3, FLW Foundation, 1082.028.
70. "San Marcos in the Desert for Alexander Chandler, Chandler, Arizona: Frank Lloyd Wright, Architect," FLW Foundation, 2401.250.
71. "San Marcos in the Desert for Alexander Chandler, Chandler, Arizona, Frank Lloyd Wright, Architect," 2, FLW Foundation, 1082.028; Wright to Chandler, December 18, 1928; Wright to H. A. Durr, July 24, 1929.
72. Wright to P. M. Cochius, March 5, 1929.

73. "Furniture Schedule for San Marcos in the Desert for Alexander Chandler, Chandler, Arizona, Frank Lloyd Wright, Architect," 1–3, FLW Foundation, 1082.028.
74. Millard to Wright, June 24, 1929; Wright to Millard, July 10, 1929.
75. Chandler told Wright that he was "planning various other developments in and about Chandler, and it may be that I shall request your services in connection with these projects." He continued, "It is agreed that the textile block system designed and owned by you, or by your corporation, shall be at my disposal for use . . . in connection with any other work which I may undertake in and about Chandler," Chandler to Wright, September 25, 1928. Darwin D. Martin Papers, Department of Special Collections, M355, box 4, folder 10, item 27, Stanford University Libraries, California.
76. Wright to Martin, May 9, 1929; Wright to Ferdinand Schevill, April 12, 1930; "Owen D. Young, 87, Industrialist, Dies," *New York Times,* July 12, 1962. Young's papers are in the Owen D. Young Library, St. Lawrence University, Canton, N.Y.; a search of the index revealed mention neither of Wright nor of the proposed house in Arizona. Lynn Ekfelt, University Archivist, to author, March 29, 1988. The Wrights' association with the Cudneys is mentioned in Wright to Chandler, July 10, 1929.
77. Hitchcock, *In the Nature of Materials,* caption to ill. 285–86, n.p.
78. Wright to Chandler, July 10, 1929.
79. Telegram, Chandler to Wright, September 9, 1929.
80. Wright to Chandler, September 14, 1929.
81. Ibid., n.d., but January 14, 1929(?).
82. Lloyd to Wright, n.d., but July 1929; Wright to Chandler, July 22, 1929; ibid., July 24, 1929.
83. Wright to Chandler, November 9, 1929; February 17, 1930.
84. McArthur to Wright, August 6, 1929; Wright to Chandler, October 24, 1929.
85. Wright to Benet, April 25, 1928, ELW.
86. Wright to McArthur, December 5, 1928.
87. L. J. Briggs, Acting Director, United States Department of Commerce, Washington, D.C., to Wright, October 17, 1929.
88. Robert W. Coren, Assistant Chief, Civil Reference Branch, National Archives, to author, January 3, 1989.
89. Chandler to Wright, November 2, 1929.
90. Wright to Chandler, November 20, 1929.
91. Chandler to Wright, February 12, 1930; Wright to Chandler, February 18, 1930.
92. Chandler to Wright, July 21, 1930.
93. Ibid., June 5, 1931; April 28, 1934. Chandler continued living in his cottage at the hotel until his death: "Chandler Founder Succumbs," *Arizona Republic,* May 9, 1950.

1. Alice Millard to Wright, April 4; April 6; May 3, 1928.
2. Ibid., April 6, 1928.
3. Ibid., May 3, 1928.
4. Telegram, Millard to Wright, February 10, 1929; Millard to Wright, February 24, 1929.
5. Ibid., February 24, 1929.
6. Ibid., June 24, 1929.
7. Ibid., July 2, 1934; July 11, 1934.
8. Ibid.; Wright to Millard, July 13, 1934.
9. Millard to Wright, July 17, 1934.
10. *Application for the Erection of Frame Building,* Permit no. 2143D, April 23, 1926, Building Division, City of Pasadena.
11. Millard to Wright, July 17, 1934; September 1, 1930; November 26, 1931; Wright to Millard, December 9, 1931.
12. The first list of Wright's work published after 1925 appeared in 1932, in the catalogue of the "Modern Architecture" exhibition at the Museum of Modern Art, New York. It places the gallery in 1930 and includes a note that the list was provided by Wright, together with the recorded dates. The project is not mentioned again until 1942, when it appears in the list prepared by Hitchcock and published in *In the Nature of Materials;* it is there assigned a date of 1925. All subsequent lists have accepted this date.
13. Telegram, Millard to Wright, April 26, 1929; Millard to Wright, May 1, 1929.
14. Ibid., June 24, 1929.
15. Wright to Millard, July 10, 1929; Millard to Wright, September 21, 1929.
16. Telegram, Millard to Wright, April 26; Millard to Wright, June 24; September 21; telegram, Millard to Wright, October 22, 1929; Wright to Millard, July 10, 1929.
17. Wright to Millard, February 17, 1930.
18. Lloyd to Wright, March 7, 1930; Millard to Wright, May 12, 1930.
19. Millard to Wright, September 1; December 27, 1930. The house by David Adler was designed for the Rev. and Mrs. C. Pardee Erdman; plans were completed, but the structure was never built. Richard Pratt, *David Adler* (New York: M. Evans, 1970), 200.
20. Millard to Wright, November 26, 1931.
21. Millard to Carrie Estelle Doheny, May 11, 1931, Carrie Estelle Doheny Collection of the Edward Laurence Doheny Memorial Library, St. John's Seminary, Camarillo, California.
22. Ibid., November 30, 1931, Carrie Estelle Doheny Collection of the Edward Laurence Doheny Memorial Library, St. John's Seminary, Camarillo, California. "Collector's Art Gallery Plans Told; Mrs. G. M. Millard Will Finance Project by Sale of Books," *Pasadena Star News,* November 30, 1931.

23. Telegram, Millard to Wright, September 11, 1931; Millard to Wright, November 26, 1931.
24. Ibid., May 3, 1928.
25. Telegram, Millard to Wright, June 24, 1931; *Building Alteration,* Permit no. 8626E, September 12, 1931, Building Division, City of Pasadena.
26. Wright to Lloyd, July 7, 1931, ELW.
27. Millard to Wright, November 26, 1931; Wright to Millard, December 9, 1931; *Building Alteration,* Permit no. 3459H, June 5, 1933, Building Division, City of Pasadena.
28. *The Alice and George Millard Collection Illustrating the Evolution of the Book,* acquired for the Huntington Library by a group of their friends. San Marino, California, Huntington Library, 1939.

Chapter Seven

1. Philip Johnson to Lewis Mumford, January 3, 1931, quoted in Terence Riley, *The International Style: Exhibition 15 and the Museum of Modern Art* (New York: Columbia University Graduate School of Architecture, Planning and Preservation, 1992), 26.
2. "Richard L. Jones Sr., Tulsa Publisher, 90," *New York Times,* December 5, 1963. Jones to Wright, November 12, 1929.
3. Jones to Wright, June 4; November 12, 1929.
4. Ibid., November 26, 1928.
5. Wright to Jones, December 14, 1928.
6. Jenkin Lloyd Jones, "A House for a Cousin: The Richard Lloyd Jones House," *Frank Lloyd Wright Newsletter* 2, no. 4 (Fourth Quarter 1979): 1.
7. Jones to Wright, December 28, 1928; April 15, 1929; April 19, 1929.
8. Ibid., April 15, 1929. Jones's daughter, now Mrs. Howard G. Barnett, told the author emphatically on December 8, 1991, that she does not have a "green thumb" and did not have special interest in plants when the house was being designed. She stated that the glass structures were to be filled with birds.
9. Ibid., June 4, 1929.
10. Ibid., November 12, 1929.
11. Wright to Jones, November 18, 1929.
12. Ibid.
13. Jones to Wright, December 19, 1929.
14. Wright to Jones, March 30, 1930.
15. Jones to Wright, November 12, 1929.
16. Wright to Jones, October 10, 1929; Wright to Paul F. P. Mueller, n.d.; Jones to Wright, April 12, 1930; Wright to A. J. Chandler, April 12, 1930; "Standard Form of Agreement between Contractor and Owner for Construction of Buildings," Tulsa, June 15, 1930. The contract was not signed until later; Wright to Jones, June 26, 1930; Jones to Wright, July 8, 1930.
17. Jones to Wright, July 8, 1930; Wright to Jones, July 30, 1930.

18. Wright to Rebori, September 15, 1927; Wright to Jones, July 30, 1930; Jones to Wright, September 10, 1930; Mueller to Wright, September 13, 1930; Jones to Wright, September 10, 1930.
19. Wright to Jones, July 30, 1930; Wright to Mueller, n.d., but September 1930.
20. Information from David G. De Long.
21. Mueller to Wright, January 24, 1931; Jones to Wright, July 7, 1931.
22. John McCurry to Wright, August 18, 1931; Wright to Jones, June 26, 1930; K. E. Jensen to Jones, March 10, 1931; Mueller to Met-L-Wood Corporation, April 11; April 30, 1931; Jones to Wright, April 17; May 13, 1931. According to Tulsa city directories, John D. McCurry was a draftsman for Rush Endacott & Rush, the same firm for which Bruce Goff worked.
23. John McCurry to Wright, August 1, 1931; McCurry to Karl Jensen, October 14, 1931; Jones to Wright, November 19, 1931; Wright to Jones, November 21, 1931. Wright went to Rio de Janeiro, as a guest of the Pan American Union, to be the North American judge in a competition for a lighthouse to memorialize Christopher Columbus. Wright left for Brazil on September 19, sailing on the Munson-Liner *American Legion;* he returned to New York on October 27.
24. Wright to Lloyd, July 7, 1931.
25. Millard to Wright, June 24, 1929; Wright to Millard, July 10, 1929.
26. Franz Schulze, *Mies van der Rohe: A Critical Biography* (Chicago: University of Chicago Press, 1985), 49–50.
27. Henry-Russell Hitchcock, Jr., "Frank Lloyd Wright," in *Modern Architecture: International Exhibition,* ex. cat. (New York: Museum of Modern Art, 1932), 36.
28. David G. De Long, *Bruce Goff: Toward Absolute Architecture* (New York and Cambridge, Mass.: Architectural History Foundation and MIT Press, 1988), 46. Quoted from Bruce Goff, "Frank Lloyd Wright, Architect, 1931: The Richard Lloyd Jones House, Tulsa," *Tulsart* (August 1, 1931): 7.
29. Frank Lloyd Wright, "The House on the Mesa," April 25, 1932, ms. 120, FLW Foundation.
30. Wright to Jean and George Cranmer, February 8, 1932.
31. "Biographical Data Requested by the State Historical Society of Colorado," August 26, 1942, Colorado Historical Society, B-Cranmer, George, vertical file; Thomas J. Noel and Barbara S. Norgren, *Denver: The City Beautiful and Its Architects, 1893–1941* (Denver: Historic Denver, Inc., 1987), 188–89; Arlynn Nellhaus, "Mrs. Cranmer Remembers," *Sunday Denver Post,* May 7, 1972.
32. Cyril Kay Scott, Director, Denver Art Museum, to Wright, November 22, 1930; Wright to George and Jean Cranmer, February 20, 1932.
33. Dick Henry, "George Cranmer Is Silent When Asked If He Intends to Quit Post in Land Grab," *Rocky Mountain News,* May 9, 1937. The author recalls, "Mr. Cranmer's ability to obtain 'gifts' from city officials extends back 14 years, 12 years before he became a city official. . . . On May 28, 1923, City Council passed an ordinance vacating Cherry st. from E. First to E. Third aves.," i.e., the portion of the street passing directly in front of Cranmer's house.
34. Wright, "House on the Mesa."

35. Ibid.
36. Hitchcock, *Modern Architecture,* 38.
37. Frank Lloyd Wright, "The Conventional House," filed with ms. 120, "House on the Mesa," FLW Foundation.
38. Ibid.
39. "Preliminary Proposal for an Architectural Exhibition at the Museum of Modern Art by Philip Johnson," in Riley, *International Style,* appendix 1, 213–14; Mumford to Wright, March 29, 1931; Johnson to Oud, April 16, 1932, quoted in Riley, *International Style,* 41; Wright to Mumford, February 1, 1932.
40. Wright to Johnson, n.d.; Wright to Mumford, January 19, 1932; telegram, Wright to Johnson, January 18, 1932; telegram, Mumford to Wright, January 21, 1932; telegram, Wright to Mumford, January 21, 1932.
41. Lloyd to Wright, n.d.; Wright to Lloyd, n.d., ELW.

Chapter Eight

1. Esther McCoy, "Lloyd Wright," *Arts and Architecture* 83, no. 9 (October 1966): 23–24.
2. Permit no. 46598, December 22, 1922. Department of Building and Safety, City of Los Angeles.
3. Greg Sipe, in an article published in New Zealand in 1979, accepts Lloyd's claim, concluding, "Some of the studies by the two men are so similar as to make one wonder who was following whom." "From Prairie House to Usonia: Wright's Wilderness Years, Part 1, Los Angeles and the Birth of a Building System," *New Zealand Architect,* no. 4 (1979): 24–25. The discussion continued in 1983: John Beech stated, "The ornamental-block system, for which the elder Wright has always received credit, seems to have been conceived by Lloyd, whose first block buildings predate his father's." "Lloyd Wright's Sowden House," *Fine Homebuilding,* no. 14 (April–May 1983): 70. A reader responded: "Not so. Frank Lloyd Wright's first textile block house, La Miniatura, was under construction in 1922 [*sic*]; Lloyd Wright's Bollman house . . . was still in a preliminary design stage in December, 1922. Frank saw this house under construction and subsequently redesigned his block system." Rod Grant to editor, no. 16 (August–September 1983): 4.
4. Lloyd to Wright, February 8, 1928, ELW.
5. Ibid., n.d. [June 1931]; Lloyd Wright, "Revision of Block," June 26, 1931.
6. Wright to Lloyd, July 7, 1931, ELW.
7. Donald Leslie Johnson, "Notes on W. B. Griffin's 'Knitlock' and His Architectural Projects for Canberra," *Journal of the Society of Architectural Historians* 29, no. 2 (May 1970): 189.
8. "Structural Component," patent no. 38914, *Patent Office Journal* (Government Printing Office, Wellington, New Zealand) 7 (August 22, 1918): 349; also in *N.Z. Building Progress* 14 (September 1918): 315. Donald Leslie Johnson provided this information.

9. Marion Mahoney Griffin, *The Magic of America*, ms., New-York Historical Society, n.p.
10. Ibid. Griffin does not reveal the date of Taylor's visit, making it impossible to evaluate her accusation.
11. Ibid.
12. "Molding Apparatus." United States Patent Office, *Official Gazette* 303 (October 31, 1922): 936, patent no. 1,433,905.
13. The patents were published in the U.S. Patent Office, *Official Gazette*, as follows: "Molding Apparatus," 272 (March 30, 1920): 799, patent no. 1,335,254; "Molding Apparatus," 303 (October 31, 1922): 936, patent no. 1,433,905; "Apparatus for Molding Concrete Building Units," 332 (March 10, 1925): 374, patent no. 1,529,079; "Concrete Building Structure," 333 (April 21, 1925): 792, patent no. 1,535,030; "Concrete Building Structure," 335 (June 23, 1925): 1046, patent no. 1,543,509.
14. *Fort Worth Star Telegram*, August 17, 1919. Nelson was listed in the San Antonio city directory only in 1931–32. The first Nel-Stone Company listing appeared in 1926, the last in 1937. J. Myler, Librarian, San Antonio Public Library, to author, September 9, 1986.
15. William B. Eastwood, "Nel-Stone Construction: A Precast Monolithic System," *Concrete Products* 25, no. 3 (September 1923): 26. The franchise for the Nel-Stone Company of Texas was acquired around 1925 by Hannibal Pianta, James Kapp, and Attilio Gerodetti. I met with Gerodetti's son and son-in-law in San Antonio on August 13 and 14, 1992; they stated that the basic block and modifications of it were in production in San Antonio into the 1950s, when labor costs made their use in construction prohibitive, Attilio Gerodetti, Jr., and Robert Streckfus to author.
16. Eastwood, "Nel-Stone," 25–28; "More about the Nel-Stone Precast Monolithic System," *Concrete Products* 26, no. 3 (March 1924): 45–46, 55. Advertisements for the Nel-Stone System appeared in both these issues.
17. Wright to Henderson Stockton, ca. 1930.
18. Mueller worked for Dankmar Adler and Louis Sullivan briefly in 1883. He then worked for Silsbee as an engineer for three years. He returned to Adler and Sullivan in 1886, the year before Wright is believed to have joined the firm. Hugh Morrison, *Louis Sullivan: Prophet of Modern Architecture* (New York: Museum of Modern Art and W. W. Norton, 1935), 84–85.
19. Katharine Floto Loverud to author, September 26, 1988.
20. Julius Floto, "Imperial Hotel, Tokyo, Japan," *Architectural Record* 55 (February 1924): 119–23.
21. Ford W. Harris to Biltmore Hotel, January 8, 1930; Harris to S. M. Bennett [*sic*] & Co., January 8, 1930; Herbert F. Sturdy to Mabel Ennis, July 25, 1930; Sturdy to Mrs. George Madison Millard, August 1, 1930, GDC.
22. Charles McArthur suggested much later that William Wrigley had settled with Nelson. Charles H. McArthur to *Arizona Highway[s] Magazine*, March 5, 1956, McArthur Papers.
23. Donald Barker to Gibson, Dunn & Crutcher, July 29, 1930, GDC.

24. Donald Barker to Mr. Sturdy, June 30, 1932, GDC.
25. Alice Millard to Herbert F. Sturdy, August 11, 1930, GDC.
26. Wright to Albert McArthur, February 17, 1930.
27. Wright to Harrison Stockton, n.d.
28. Wright to Lloyd, n.d. [August? 1930].
29. Francis S. Onderdonk, Jr. *The Ferro-concrete Style* (New York: Architectural Book Publishing Co., 1928). Peter Collins, *Concrete* (New York: Horizon, 1959).
30. United States Patent Office, *Official Gazette,* 1885–1925.
31. H. H. Rice and William M. Torrance, *The Manufacture of Concrete Blocks and Their Use in Building Construction* (New York: Engineering News Publishing Company, 1906), 70.
32. No. 53004. Clark S. Hutchinson, Burlington, N.J., "Improved Building-Block" (March 6, 1866), *Annual Report of the Commissioner of Patents for the Year 1866,* vol. 1 (Washington: Government Printing Office, 1867), 485, mentioned in Rice and Torrance, *Manufacture,* 33.
33. British patent no. 13,071 to Joseph Gibbs, November 17, 1850, mentioned in Rice and Torrance, *Manufacture,* 32–33.
34. No. 80358. Thomas J. Lowry, Conneautville, Pa., "Mould for Building-Blocks" (July 28, 1868). *Annual Report of the Commissioner of Patents for the Year 1868,* vol. 2 (Washington: Government Printing Office, 1870), 278, mentioned in Rice and Torrance, *Manufacture,* 33.
35. Ernest Flagg, *Small Houses: Their Economic Design and Construction* (New York: Scribner's, 1922), 3.
36. Richard J. Neutra, *Wie Baut Amerika?* (Stuttgart: Julius Hoffmann, 1927), 47. Translated by Neutra's sister-in-law, the late Regula Fybel. This book also includes Neutra's essay on Wright's concrete-block designs, first published in 1926 (see chapter 9, n. 8).
37. Rice and Torrance, *Manufacture,* 8.
38. Maurice M. Sloan, "Concrete Block Houses." In *The Concrete House and Its Construction* (Philadelphia: Association of American Portland Cement Manufacturers, 1912), chapter 8, 205–13. Edgar Kaufmann, jr., brought this book to my attention.
39. *Frank Lloyd Wright on Architecture: Selected Writings, 1894–1940,* ed., with an introduction, by Frederick Gutheim (New York: Duell, Sloan and Pearce, 1941), 3.
40. Ibid., 5, 21.
41. *Frank Lloyd Wright: Writings and Buildings,* ed. Edgar Kaufmann and Ben Raeburn (New York: Horizon Press, 1960), 64–65.
42. Gutheim, *Wright on Architecture,* 4.
43. Frank Lloyd Wright, "In the Cause of Architecture," *Architectural Record* 23 (March 1908): 161.
44. Frank Lloyd Wright, "Ethics of Ornament," *Prairie School Review* 4, no. 1 (First Quarter, 1967): 16–17. From *Oak Leaves* (Oak Park, Illinois), January 16, 1909, where it appeared under the heading "On Ornamentation."

45. Frank Lloyd Wright, *Ausgeführte Bauten und Entwürfe von Frank Lloyd Wright* (Berlin: Ernst Wasmuth, 1910), n.p.
46. Frank Lloyd Wright, "In the Cause of Architecture: Second Paper," *Architectural Record* 35 (May 1914): 406.
47. Wright, "In the Cause of American Architecture," (March, 1908): 160.
48. Frank Lloyd Wright, "Design for a Prism-Light," specification forming part of Design no. 27,977, United States Patent Office, *Official Gazette* 81 (December 7, 1897); Frank Lloyd Wright, "Design for a Prism-Light," specification forming part of Design no. 27,978, United States Patent Office, *Official Gazette* 81 (December 7, 1897).
49. Wright to P. M. Cochius, March 5, 1929.
50. Frank Lloyd Wright, "In the Cause of Architecture, 1: The Logic of the Plan," *Architectural Record* 63 (January 1928): 51.
51. Kaufmann and Raeburn, *Writings and Buildings,* 67.
52. Frank Lloyd Wright, "The Village Bank Series" (1901): rept. in Bruce Brooks Pfeiffer, ed., *Frank Lloyd Wright: Collected Writings,* vol. 1, 1894–1930 (New York: Rizzoli, in association with the Frank Lloyd Wright Foundation, 1992), 70.
53. Frank Lloyd Wright, "The 'Village Bank' Series, V," *Brickbuilder* 10 (August 1901): 160.
54. Wright, *Ausgeführte Bauten und Entwürfe,* n.p.; Wright, "In the Cause of Architecture, I," 51.
55. Wright to Henderson Stockton, ca. 1930.
56. "Decorative Features of Midway Garden," *Rock Products and Building Materials* 15, no. 5 (January 7, 1915): 26–27. There is no information about the nature of these panels for Midway Gardens in the drawings preserved in Wright's archive. However, analysis of a photograph taken during demolition of the building and investigation of one surviving panel now on display at the Art Institute of Chicago seem to refute Wright's claim. The photograph suggests that the panels were in no way structural, that they were simply applied decoratively with mortar to a brick wall. Paul Kruty to author, November 11, 12, 1992. The panel at the Art Institute has smooth, flat edges at right angles to the face; i.e., there is no provision for weaving the blocks together with internal joints around the perimeter, and on one side there are remains of mortar that seems to have oozed from the back. Pauline Saliga, Department of Architecture, Art Institute of Chicago, to author, November 17, 18, 1992. Tim Samuelson, Historical and Architectural Landmarks Commission, Chicago, to author, November 17, 1992.
57. FLLW FND, 1506.892.
58. Wright to Louise M. Webb, *East Bay Builder,* August 8, 1929, ELW.
59. Wright, *Autobiography* (1932), 196, 200.

Chapter Nine

1. Wright to Darwin Martin, July 25, 1928, Darwin D. Martin Papers, Department of Special Collections, M355, box 4, folder 9, item 14, Stanford University Libraries, California.
2. Frank Lloyd Wright, "In the Cause of Architecture, The Third Dimension." Los Angeles, February 9, 1923. John Lloyd Wright Collection [III/2] no. 8, Avery Library, Columbia University, New York.
3. Millard to Wright, July 17, 1934.
4. Ibid., January 7, 1933; Jones to Barrett Company, April 8, 1935; Nesbitt to Wright, September 22, 1941.
5. Albert Farwell Bemis, *The Evolving House,* Vol. III (Cambridge, Massachusetts: Massachusetts Institute of Technology, 1933), 584–86.
6. Millard to Wright, January 7, 1933; Lloyd Wright to Donald Daniels, February 29, 1940. Lloyd mistakenly indicated that the flood occurred "about 1928," ELW.
7. W. Moser, "Frank Lloyd Wright und amerikanische Architektur," *Werk* 5 (May 1925): 129–57 (Freeman, Millard houses); "Frank Lloyd Wright," *Wendingen* 7 (1926): 95 (Millard); *L'Architecture vivante* (Winter 1927), pl. 31 (Millard).
8. Richard Neutra, "Eine Bauweise in bewehrtem Beton an Neubauten von Frank Lloyd Wright, in H. de Fries, *Frank Lloyd Wright: Aus dem Lebenswerke eines Architekten* (Berlin: Verlag Ernst Pollak, 1926), 64.
9. A. N. Rebori, "Frank Lloyd Wright's Textile-Block Slab Construction," *Architectural Record* 62 (December 1927): 449, 452.
10. "Of Form in Architecture," *Los Angeles Times,* July 1, 1928.
11. Hitchcock, *Frank Lloyd Wright,* n.p.
12. Henry-Russell Hitchcock, *Modern Architecture: Romanticism and Reintegration* (New York: Payson and Clark, 1929), 116.
13. Sheldon Cheney, *The New World Architecture* (London: Longmans, Green, 1930), 22.
14. Ibid., 205–6.
15. Hitchcock, "Frank Lloyd Wright," in *Modern Architecture,* ex. cat. (New York: Museum of Modern Art, 1932), 35.
16. Ibid.
17. Hitchcock, *In the Nature of Materials,* 75–76.
18. Wright to Darwin Martin, n.d. [July 1–10,] 1928. Darwin D. Martin Papers, Department of Special Collections, M355, box 3, folder 15, item 2, Stanford University Libraries, California.
19. Dimitri Tselos, "Exotic Influences in the Architecture of Frank Lloyd Wright," *Magazine of Art* 46 (April 1953): 163–64, 166.
20. Dimitri Tselos, "Frank Lloyd Wright and World Architecture," *Journal of the Society of Architectural Historians* 28, no. 1 (March 1969): 66.

21. Wright to Robert J. Goldwater, ed., *Magazine of Art,* n.d., but 1953. The statement is unsigned. A transcription appears ibid., 72.
22. Wright, "In the Cause of Architecture: The Third Dimension," 12.
23. Frank Lloyd Wright, "Anmerkungen des Architekten Frank Lloyd Wright Zu seinen Zementblockhäusern," in de Fries, *Frank Lloyd Wright: Aus dem Lebenswerke,* 65.
24. Wright, *Autobiography* (1932), 226–27, 241.
25. Wright to Martin, September 13, 1927; ibid., July [1–10], 1928, Darwin D. Martin Papers, Department of Special Collections, M355, box 3, folder 15, item 2, Stanford University Libraries, California; Wright to Patrosso, November 17, 1928; Wright to Dr. A. J. Chandler, December 18, 1928; Wright to Harold McCormick, October 24, 1929. Information on the location for the Rosenwald School project, that it was designed for the campus of the Hampton Normal and Agricultural Institute in Hampton, Virginia—not for a site in La Jolla, California—comes from correspondence in the Martin-Wright Papers at Stanford University. This location is confirmed by records in the archives of the Hampton Institute. Wright's project was one of many school buildings for the education of Negro children supported by the Julius Rosenwald Fund. Fritz J. Malval, D.A.A., Director of the University Archives, Hampton University, to author, October 2, 1991.
26. Seymour to Schindler, March 14, 1924, Architectural Drawing Collection, University of California, Santa Barbara; Wright to Martin, September 13, 1927; Wright to Rebori, September 13, 1927.
27. The clubhouse was built at Paradise Peak West; it was based on Wright's design for Leesburg Floating Gardens (also identified as Floating Gardens Resort, FLW Foundation, 5216), which was in turn a reworking of San Marcos Water Gardens. John Rattenbury, Taliesin Architects, to author, December 1992.

INDEX

Figure references appear in italics following page references.

D

E

F

G

H

I

O

P

R

S

T

U

V